Dear John,

I'm impressed [illegible] daughter Clare in every aspect of the work, besides you are a treasure for trying to make

iVillager

My Lifetime Journey from Kokoland to America

a difference in my country - Sudan. Enjoy.

LACI - Los Angeles - 03/07/2019

ABBA GONY MUSTAFA

First Edition

PAGE PUBLISHING, INC.
New York, NY

First originally published by Page Publishing, Inc. 2018

ISBN 978-1-64298-265-7 (Paperback)
ISBN 978-1-64298-266-4 (Digital)

Printed in the United States of America

Kokoland:

- Western education was considered haram and, for that reason, forbidden.
- It was believed that the Antichrist was the one who cracked the sky into two halves, one Friday, in 1956.
- Elvis Presley was mistaken for Yuri Gagarin.
- The Earth was thought to be flat and has edges with sharp cliffs.
- It was believed that humans have never landed on the moon; it was a big lie.
- It was believed that evaporation is not the cause of rain.
- Flogging was used for curing and ridding sick bodies of evil spirits.
- It was believed that the nuclear bomb is the size of a grain of millet.
- Bullying was redefined and new meanings were given to the words hunger and deprivation.
- Donkeys were central to everyday life.
- Speedy donkeys were a sign of wealth and a visa to marrying beautiful brides.
- Buying a life insurance policy amounted to faithlessness and blasphemy.
- Dead and dry chameleons and bats could bring love into a man's heart.
- Living in the wild was better than attending school.
- Doctors die, too.
- American Football was a Kokoland invention, I am convinced.
- It was believed that God created some tribes after he had done creating flies; a sign of those tribes' insignificance.
- Conversations were held inside straw huts about the best hunting grounds for juicy squirrels and fat jack rabbits, and at the same time listening to a lecture on *the Magna Carta* and English law principles of *ratio decidendi and obiter dicta,* all while sipping local alcohol drink from perfectly round red clay pots.

Acknowledgments

Kokolanders (people who live in the village of Kokoland) are decent and respectful people, and I am proud to be one of them. Anything negative in this book is not a reflection or representation of who they are. In the grand scheme of things, my bad experiences are a drop in an ocean, if compared with the good ones. They aren't the norm and don't reflect on the millions of beautiful and well-charactered people of Sudan.

I thank my mother for telling me, "Take care of yourself, your brother, and your sister." These were her last words for me before passing away. She taught me the meanings of self-reliance and self-denial, so I grew up appreciating the idea of depending on myself and admiring those who are unselfish, kind, and go out of their way to help others.

I thank my father for teaching me the meaning of kindness and sharing, standing up for what is right, and the importance of fighting injustice. I also thank him for showing me the value of education. He told me that people who were educated could make such things as the planes that occasionally flew over our village. I knew nothing about their origins or destinations, but I was determined to find out, and time did tell.

I thank my wife, Sophia, for standing by my side for the past thirty years and tolerating me despite my far-from-perfect personality. She has been a good wife to me and a model mother for my boys. She is a blessing to our family. She was the one who encouraged me to embark on writing my memoirs, and, for that, I give her all credit.

I thank my son Rumzee for making me a proud father. He was right when he told me he was a source of motivation for my hard work. I also thank him for constantly pushing me to better myself. I learned a great deal from him.

I thank my two younger sons, Ameenov and Moon, aged seven and nine, for showing extreme interest in this book. They urged me to complete writing it so they could read it. I am grateful to them for their help in editing it.

I thank my extended family members for their unwavering and continuous support. They may find some of the stories, ideas, events, and incidents embarrassing, but I kindly request that they look at my memoirs in a positive way and forgive me if they thought I had revealed family secrets I should not have.

I thank and appreciate the help I received from my high school math, English, and art teachers, Omer Abdullah Adam, Bellay Gessesse, and Dr. El Nour Hamad, respectively, for giving me directions, paving the way for my future, and drawing my attention to the existence of worlds beyond the borders of Kokoland. They were visionaries and a crystallization for everything to do with forward thinking. I tremendously benefited from their foresight and prudence.

I am grateful to the help and encouragement that I received from the many people I met during my journey to America. Above all, I must also thank those who made my life so miserable that they forced me to turn around and look for alternatives. They might have pushed me over the edge to hit rock bottom, but that rock bottom turned out to be a platform from which I was able to spring to a much better place.

Contents

Introduction

I am in my fifties. This is a story of my life from the 1960s to the present time. It is an attempt to give some idea of everyday life about my place of origin. Told through the eyes of a villager, from the country of Sudan in Africa, who happened to travel the world before settling in the United States, my story is both comical and tragic. I grew up in a dusty village in Western Sudan, which I name Kokoland for reasons I will explain later. It was a great place for living, as long as you were unaware that the rest of the world existed. As amazing as this may sound, many of my people did not know that the earth is round. They believed it to be flat and have edges beyond which one could fall off into a bottomless abyss. Throughout my early childhood, I too thought that my village was the center of the universe, and so did many of my childhood friends, and that the rest of the world revolved around it. We couldn't have been more wrong.

I hope my story helps to explain the disparity in living conditions between Kokoland and the rest of the world. For example, there is an irreconcilable difference between my background and my son's experience growing up here in the United States. Whereas I had opportunities that were few and far between, my son became a California high school gold medalist track and field champion, which afforded him the National Collegiate Athletic Association (NCAA) scholarship at Texas A&M University College of Architecture. His team went on to win a pair of NCAA championships, which garnered them an invitation from President Barack Obama and First Lady Michelle Obama to the White House, where he later served as an intern. Considering my background, this is something beyond my wildest dreams and that there is no way I could have planned for it. In many ways, my story crystalizes the multitudes of individual experiences that symbolize America, the land of opportunity, especially for immigrants like us. We are blessed.

I had difficulties fitting into my local societal norm for reasons I will explain later. So I always wanted to venture away and look for a place with opportunities and prospect for success. I did not arrive in America until I was in my thirties, so it is understandable that I don't completely belong in here either. However, when I went back to Kokoland after being gone for thirty years, I found myself a complete stranger. Nothing made sense to me anymore. That was the time I decided I should write a book, hoping to introduce Kokoland and the world to one another. I thought, in the process, I might be able to bridge some of the gaps that exist between the two worlds. My predicament is typical of Africans living in the diaspora. They return to their respective countries hoping to bring about change, only to find themselves overwhelmed by the situation there. Many of them end up facing array of problems far beyond their means and abilities for handling.

Few of my people knew much about what was going on around the world. Once, I told my niece that it took me thirteen hours of continuous flight from America, just to reach half of my destination. She was one of the enlightened girls in the village, so people listened to her wisdom. I heard her relay the information to another woman. She said to her, in a matter-of-fact manner, "My uncle lives near the end of the border." You would wonder what border she was talking about.

I haven't used the real names of individuals for two reasons. First, not every story in the book is positive. Whereas some people were praised, others were heavily criticized. Second, even though the contents are factual, I wanted to freely express my views and worry less about the consequences of misinterpretation by others.

Part of this book attempts to refute a general misconception that people with backgrounds similar to mine are destined to live in places like Kokoland for their entire lives. My hope is that those who aspire to improve the living conditions for themselves and, perhaps, for others could see in my experience a tangible example to follow.

I worked very hard at school to improve my situation. I went to colleges in Sudan, Britain, and America. I worked in the Middle East for some time, but finally moved to America. Once I got here, I realized that I had brought along my own baggage, which I could not easily discard so I could learn new rules for social engagements. I was a minority in my own village, Kokoland, an alien in Britain, an expatriate in the Middle East, and a man with a foreign accent here in America. The moment I spoke, people were quick to ask me, "Where are you from?" I was invariably dumbfounded for I never had a ready answer to give.

I crossed vast lands, dealt with many different cultures, and it took me a long time to get from Kokoland to America. Nevertheless, in many respects I am still a villager inside. People might consider some of what I have written as gross, naive, simple, wrong, tragic, unbelievable, or politically incorrect. However, this is exactly the point I am trying to get across. I hope to bring awareness to people that different points of views do exist, however strange, weird, and abnormal they may be.

Every migrant has a story to tell, and this is mine in its crudest form, to say the least. Nothing in this book is conventional because it is a chart for my routes in life, and mine alone. Therefore, readers should consider the events described in this book within the context of geography, culture, living standards, and, above all, time. I have shared my thoughts at different ages, times, and locations that reveal the variations in my understanding of the issues. It is my hope to encourage people who find themselves in similar unfavorable situations not to surrender. They can break away from these situations and transform their lives, if they desire. It is simply a matter of believing in oneself. I have lived through many experiences that took me in different directions. However, I always found myself in a favorable situation, even though I could not always find a logical explanation for that. My life has been truly blessed.

Sadly, some sections in this book describe incidents that are cruel to both humans and animals and that could be hard to read.

Also, they might not reflect positively on some of the places I have written about, and that might not be appreciated by some of you. By all standards, these incidents remain unacceptable, abusive, gross, and not funny, and I am advocating none of that. It is not my intention whatsoever to undermine or offend any individual, group of people, or place. It is rather a statement of facts about personal experiences during my long journey. For this reason, I, again, request that you view the contents of this book within the contexts of different times, places, and cultures.

When I told one of my friends that I'm writing a book, he got intrigued by the idea and excitedly asked me, "What type of book?" I responded, "My memoirs." His jaws dropped and looked somewhat puzzled. After a few seconds, he gathered his thoughts and, with some fury, said to me, "But you aren't famous, are you?" I said, "No, I'm not, and that is why I'm writing it." I am indulging myself in such an act usually reserved for famous people. Who knows, if I'm able to make a breakthrough, I may encourage others to write about their own stories. Together, we may make a difference in the world.

My ultimate goal is to use the proceeds of this book's sale to help finance the creation of a health and a vocational center in Kokoland. This is a long overdue opportunity to give back and help the community. To that end, I have included an appendix with architectural designs for the project.

Lastly, I am not a writer. I am simply telling you my story, so pardon my unconventional and limited English writing skills. English is my third language. I wanted you to hear the voice of Kokoland and learn about its existence, so I decided to tell you about it despite my linguistic shortcomings. Please bear with me.

Warning: There are sections in this book containing graphic description of cruelty to humans and animals, so readers' discretion is advised.

CHAPTER 1

Dusty Kokoland

To Google Earth's satellite cameras, my village, Kokoland, is a remote and dusty piece of land with few fabricated structures consisting mostly of mud-and-straw houses. It is a land "beyond the sea of darkness" as people of the Dark Ages might have called it. To me, it was the center of the universe because I knew little of the world beyond the ten-kilometer radius from the village center.

Kokoland is not the real name of my village. I chose this name to use in the book for three reasons. The first reason is that the word "Cuckooland," which I modified it to "Kokoland," was used in reference to a faraway and mysterious land that no one knows much about, and my village is exactly that. Second, the real name of my village is so indecent that I decided not to mention it here. I really don't know who gave it that name or why. All I know is that it had it for at least one hundred years. A few of us school-goers did our best to rename it, but the "commoners" accused us of "elitism."

In the 1970s, a group of us (mostly middle and high school students) called the people in the village for a meeting to give the village a new name, Tiboon, which means water ponds, because there were many ponds around it, then. We argued that the village's name was indecent, uncivilized, and embarrassing to all of us, but especially to the village girls. We told them that the sign at the elementary school gate reading "—— Elementary School for Girls" was especially bad. We also argued that the sign on the local bus reading "—— Travels" was also embarrassing because the bus travelled to the city and provided ample opportunity for city dwellers to mock us. The bus was a source of entertainment for people whenever it passed by. Unfortunately, our efforts were to no avail. Many people rejected our idea of renaming the village. Jabir and Hammad were particularly vocal in their opposition to the new name, arguing that their ancestors had named the village, so it should not be changed. They exclaimed, "Do you children know better than our ancestors?" Unfortunately, we lost the renaming bid, so the old name is still in use today. My uncle, a truck driver, used to say, "I am driving to the village with the embarrassing name." Sometimes, members of my family here in America jokingly ask me, "Where did you say you come from?" I even hid the village's true name from my friends until one of them, who happened to be a lawyer, found out when he was going through some documents I had given him for certification.

The third reason I chose to call the village Kokoland is to honor a man named Koko, who happened to be mentally incapacitated. He lived and died in the village. He bothered no one except when he was "djinn-ridden," a term Kokolanders used to describe Koko when he was in a rage. Sometimes, he would hold a thick stick horizontally at eye level and start shouting in a language no one could understand. He would then storm out of his shack screaming and head toward the outskirts of the village. We believed that he was screaming at the evil spirits, which annoyed him so much, forcing him to get up and chase them out of town. He would be gone for an hour or so before returning to the village a very calm man. None of us dared to follow Koko during his rages. It goes without saying that we did not want to have trouble with the spirits. We thought that evil spirits would get off Koko, let go of him, and get us possessed for the rest of our lives. For this reason, we kept our distance from Koko as much as we could. The rest of the time, Koko bothered no body. He was as innocent as a child. Koko also went around to the shops in the village and collected pieces of fabric from underneath the tailors' sewing machines. Over the years, he hoarded so much fabric that it formed a huge heap of cloth by his living quarters inside an abandoned shop in the village marketplace. Koko dressed up in every garment donated to him, as long as it fitted him. At any given time, he might be wearing a bundle of dozen or so garments. It was so heavy that it slowed him down when he walked around. Koko's harmless peculiarities are one of my memories of the village and another reason I chose the name Kokoland.

Kokoland is forty miles south of Sangoor, one of the main cities in western Sudan. The town has shops made from brick and tin, a bakery, and a mill, all built in the 1940s and 50s. The town hosts a market gathering two days of the week, Monday and Friday. Monday's market is lighter than Friday's, when more people gather to buy and sell goods and attend Friday prayers.

There are five distinct boroughs in Kokoland and about twenty tiny villages scattered around it. We lived in the borough of Jabar. The other boroughs were Keekah, Sayir, Hiskan, and government officials' upscale neighborhood, if you like. Several different ethnic groups live in Kokoland, although the town itself is not divided along ethnic lines. However, with the exception of Keekah, where most of the residents are originally from the Tagar region in Sudan, the rest consider themselves Sudanese Arabs.

My family belongs to the Kanuri (Bornu) tribe, and my ancestors came from the area between Chad and Northern Nigeria, so I am not an Arab. I was punished severely for being who I am even though there was nothing in my hand that I could have done to change anything. In fact, not only am I not an Arab, but we were the only Kanuri family in the village. As such, I grew up as an ethnic minority in an environment that did not recognize us as belonging to the area. I experienced all sorts of bullying, discrimination, racism, and hostility.

According to *Encyclopedia Britannica*, "The Kanuri developed a powerful state at the Sudanese terminus of the major trans-Saharan trade route through the Bilma oasis to Libya. This empire, called Bornu (or Kanem-Bornu), reached its zenith in the 16th century. The Kanuri have been Muslims since the 11th century and practice the Malikite code of Islamic law." *Encyclopedia Britannica* also states that "Kanuri, African people, are the dominant element of the population of Bornu state in northeastern Nigeria and also found in large numbers in southeastern Niger. The Kanuri language, derived from Kanembu, was the major language of the Bornu Empire. It is classified as belonging to the Saharan branch of "the Nilo-Saharan" family.

"The current Borno, formerly Bornu, state, northeastern Nigeria, is the central fragment of the old Bornu empire of the Kanuri people. Its name is said to mean (Home of the Berbers)" (*Encyclopedia Britannica*).

Encyclopedia Britanica. (2014, August 31st). kanuri people. Retrieved from http://www.britannica.com.lib ezproxy.tamu.edu:2048/ EBchecked/topic/311571/Kanuri Encyclopecdia Britanica. (2014, August 31st). *Borno*. Retrieved from http://www.britannica.com.lib-ezproxy.tamu.edu:2048/EBchecked/topic/74319/Borno

---

According to oral Kanuri tradition, Sef, the son of Dhul Yazan of Yemen, arrived in Kanem in the ninth century and united the population into the Sayfawa Dynasty. This tradition is likely a product of later Islamic influence. Evidence for the formation of indigenous states in the Lake Chad area actually dates back to about 800 BC, at Zilum.

However, the story told in my family is that the Kanuri in Sudan are descendants of the Bornu Empire, which expanded east to Chad and the Darfur region in Western Sudan. In fact, records show that the Fung kingdom around the city of Sinnar in Central Sudan, founded in the sixteenth century, had Bornu rulers. The majority of the Kanuri in Sudan today are descendants of migrants who, for many centuries, used Sudan as the land route to Mecca for pilgrimage.

Before air travel, the journey used to take years to complete. Travelers interrupted their journeys during the rainy season to farm and stock up on food. Many ended up settling permanently. I was told by elders in the family that the Kanuri migrated to Sudan in larger groups around the 1880s to join the Mahdist revolution and fight the British. Others migrated to provide workforce for the Gezira Scheme founded by the British in Central Sudan in the 1920s to grow cotton. Many continued to move to the area until the discovery of oil in Nigeria. Also, the eruption of armed conflict in Chad in the 1970s blocked the West African–Sudan route, hence reducing the flow of migrants.

Today, the Kanuri are in every region and city in Sudan. Despite centuries of living in the country, to many, they remain outsiders. There are two other West African tribes; the Fulani and the Hausa, who are also considered outsiders. The three tribes together are called the Fallata, and their population run into millions.

After independence from Britain in 1956, the government of the time declared Sudan an Arabic state and sought membership in the Arab League. This move came at the expense of most of the people of Sudan, who are mainly Africans. The Fallata certainly did not help further the pan-Arab banner raised by leaders of the country at that time, so everything African defeated the rulers' aspirations of becoming a full Arab state. The wars the country has been experiencing since its independence are primarily rooted in this identity issue. The Fallata, generally, kept a low profile and shied away from anything that exposed them. Many of them preferred to hide their identity whenever possible or adopt the identity of influential tribes that were more identifying with Arabs. They took this route to avoid racism and discrimination, which I can attest to, in view of my personal experience while growing up.

Even though most Sudanese speak hundreds of different African languages and dialects, in the eyes of the government; the country remains an Arab State. That state of mind of the ruling elites has divided the country into two groups; one legitimate and another, more or less, of second-class citizens. Arabism has contributed a lot to the problem of governance in the country since its independence from Britain in 1956. For example, all of the country's presidents have come from one region of the country, effectively shutting other regions out of senior ruling positions in the government. This has provided a suitable environment for practices such as discrimination, racism, corruption, nepotism, and favoritism, to grow and proliferate rampantly. However, I want to make it clear that this is by no means an attack on certain individuals or specific groups. This is rather about expressing my personal views that the country's problems are rooted in the unresolved issue of identity. I believe that addressing it will guarantee stability and prosperity for Sudan. It is simply a matter of good governance that is based on equality, justice, and citizenship.

Nobody is denying that Arabs are part of the Sudanese component, but the claim that Sudan is an Arab state came at a huge cost to the non-Arabs. This is analogous to the mixed-race citizens of South Africa claiming to be Dutch, although they are, at least, half Africans, if not more. This is why Sudan has suffered nonstop wars for over fifty years, so settling the issue of identity is crucial to peace and prosperity for the Sudanese people. We cannot make progress until we come to terms with who we are and love ourselves for who we are. The few elite rulers of the country took us all hostages to this futile idea of Arabism. They played this role for decades, but in the end, their efforts were to no avail. We should not be surprised why our beloved South Sudan parted ways with Sudan.

It is my hope that this information about my background will make it easier for readers to understand the views I have expressed and where I am coming from. Without this background, some of the contents may not be appreciated.

My fellow Kanuri tribesmen lived a simple and secluded life in the villages around Kokoland. Almost everyone lived off the land. The tools and farming practices they used were both ancient and inefficient. Their lives revolved around rain-fed shifting agriculture. Most of my mother's side of the family lived in two neighboring villages, while my father's family lived in two other nearby villages. I was never enthusiastic about visiting those villages, particularly during the rainy season, because I had to help in cutting weeds in the farms. The labor-intensive work was backbreaking. The same tools are still being used today. Even at my young age, I found it to be very inefficient operation. I hated working in the fields so much it became a major factor in my moving away, later on in life.

There were averages of fifty school-age children in each village, but none of them attended school. That was how the Kanuri maintained a low profile by shying away from limelights such as sending their children to school. Fewer than fifteen Bornu or Kanuri children attended school and only two of them were from my own family.

They were six years my senior. I spearheaded the next group at an immense psychological and physical cost because there were no older students from my family or tribe to shield me from bullying by either the village or school children.

Unlike every Kanuri living in the surrounding villages, my father chose to move to the town. The community disapproved of his action, especially after he decided to open a shop and send his children to school. They thought he was trying to abandon his heritage and be something else. The irony is that the townspeople had the same view and thought of him as a "wannabe" Arab. From that moment onwards, we were outsiders within our own as well as our adopted community. I was a misfit from the very beginning, and that has been the case for most of my life. Not only did I inherit problems similar to those of my father, but I also had additional ones because of my minority status at school. I had to deal with bullying.

The Kanuri community around Kokoland used to hold the view that Western education belonged to the non-believers. They called it *kura kirdiyei*, which means the teachings of the infidels. They thought it was *haram*, or forbidden, for them, being devoted Muslims, to send their children to school. The *fatwa*, or decree, from the community's learned men falsely declared that those who sent their children to school should prepare to take their place in hell on the day of judgment. The fatwa also stated that, "Fathers will grab their children and drag them along into hell fire." It is redundant to mention that there is no such thing in Islam, especially considering the fact that the first word revealed to the prophet was "read." Those were rather the learned men's own peculiar misunderstanding or interpretation of the religion. Most people in the community blindly followed what they were told. The learned men had power and control over the community because they were the only source of knowledge, which they gained through attending traditional Quranic schools. They had stake in maintaining the status quo, but over time, with people becoming more exposed, their powers gradually eroded. Western education slowly pulled the rug from under their feet, and they resented that very much.

In fact the resistance to modern schooling stemmed from the fact that the Kanuri had a well-developed learning system in place. Anything new was viewed with suspicion. Parents would take their children to renowned scholars to receive knowledge. They would study for years until they mastered knowledge by reciting the holy Quran entirely from memory. The successful candidate would be awarded the title of *Gony*, which was a declaration to the entire community of his knowledge and scholarly status. The award process involved the parents organizing a big celebration by inviting the entire community to attend. Learned men from the community who already held the *Gony* title would gather to examine and test the candidate's knowledge for a whole day, reciting the book from memory as well as answering random religious questions. He would be awarded the title if he passed.

In those days, mostly boys attended school. Girls were rarely sent to learn anything. The limited number of Kanuri children attending school demonstrate the impact learned men's fatwas had on people. The problem was that there was no system in place for every child to attend qur'anic school either, so most children grew up not receiving any form of education, whatsoever.

It is amazing that, today, forty years later, there are people who are completely rejecting the concept of traditional education, branding it as an unwelcomed Western cultural invasion that ought to be banned. They remain adamant that Islam forbids it. Sadly, they are resorting to violence to force their beliefs on people. Some members of these groups are Kanuri, my own people. This is not coincidental. It is a problem that has been in the making for a long time. It went by undetected until recently, when it exploded.

My father's life was not an easy one. Venturing into a territory not followed by members of his community came at a very high cost to him, but his stance did not go in vain. The least that I gained from his foresight is the very fact that I am writing this book.

I remember my peers in the village accusing me of being too ambitious. The simple fact that I went to school was considered as something out of my station in life. Many of them though I was not entitled to that. I remember cases when I was being undermined by adults too. The most painful memories for me were the bullying, but I never surrendered. I paid for that in the form of cuts and bruises all over my body. At times, I wished for someone to give me a break. You do get tired of fighting every time you were wronged. It could have been a nice thing if I had an elder brother or boys from the tribe to team up and defend ourselves. It was a jungle there at the boarding school.

I had few options available to me. Either drop out of school and join the ranks of the other children in the villages, an alternative that I rejected at a very early age, or stay in school, be a loner, and fight it out.

CHAPTER 2A

Loss of My Mother

"Jiddoo, Jiddoo, Jiddoo . . . Iyaam baazunah," shouted Zalaan, as he stood in front of his father's restaurant at fifteen meters or so to my left. Zalaan spoke to me in Kanuri, the language of my tribe. The words meant, "Your mother has died." It was around nine in the morning, and my childhood friend Tiffah, his elder brother Ganboor, and I were on our way from school to our homes for breakfast. Tiffah and his brother were not Kanuri, so they did not understand what Zalaan had just said. They started mocking me by repeating the words. They found it very funny, so they kept on clapping and singing, "Jiddoo … Iyaam baazunah," until Zalaan explained to them what had happened. Only then, they realized the gravity of the situation and stopped.

I was seven years old then, in second grade. That morning before I left for school, my mother called me to her bedside and told me to take care of my younger brother and my baby sister. I promised her that I would do so, picked up my schoolbag, and left. She meant to tell me good bye, but I didn't get her message, nor did I understand the full weight of what I had promised her until later. She passed away within two hours from that moment. She was very sick and had been bedridden for several months. Just two months earlier, my father and I accompanied her to the capital, Khartoum, seeking help. We returned without knowing what was wrong with her. I heard some of my family members and her friends say that the cause of her death was *tonuh le-le-noh*, which, in Kanuri language, means, "The moving wound," if there were such a thing as that. Till today, Zalaan remains the man who relayed to me the worst news of my life. His voice echoing those horrible words, "Your mother is dead" continues to give me a chill. My feeling towards Zalaan did not change forty some years later when I met him in Kokoland during a recent visit.

A year earlier, I lost my two-year-old brother Mahmoud to a whooping cough. Twelve years after my mother's death, I lost my baby sister to the same sickness that had caused the death of my mother.

It took two more years before I could find out about the cause of death for my mother and sister. I suffered from the same symptoms for two years, unable to get a correct diagnosis. I had regular attacks, but luckily by that time I was in college in the city and was able to rush to the hospital every time I had an attack. I visited many specialists who could not tell what was wrong with me. One day I collapsed, and my friends took me in a taxi to the main hospital in Khartoum. A medical student examined me and concluded that I had acute appendicitis. He was right. I got it removed, but in the nick of time. I feel extremely lucky. By comparing my symptoms to those of my mother and sister, I believe they both, also, died of appendicitis. I remember they had suffered a great deal before their untimely deaths. These are very painful memories.

Losing a mother, for a seven-year-old child or anybody at any age, is not easy. That caused me to be very insecure and constantly worrisome. The environment surrounding me in Kokoland did not help, either.

CHAPTER 2B

My Biodiverse Home

My backyard was a place for my mother to grow okra, peas, sugarcane, corn, and cucumbers. However, that was only a fraction of what went on around my house. It was a biodiverse environment, which provided a safe haven for many living organisms. Despite the risks posed by some of these creatures, no one bothered. My house in Kokoland was the official residence for almost every tropical insect that you can imagine. I have learned at an early age how to live in harmony with nature.

I built a small chicken house from mud to house all of my chickens, especially the hens with newly hatched chicks, to protect them from dogs, cats, and skunks, which can kill chickens by just releasing their smelly odor. The mud house was also a good place for new chickens I bought from the market so they could get used to the other chickens and adopt them as new flock members. That was how I reduced the chances of new chickens going astray and getting lost in the neighborhood.

I would lock them inside until morning when I prepared their breakfast of millet flakes mixed with water and sand. I would divide the food into three different pans so there was room for each group (chicks, young chicken, and adult hens and roosters) to get their share of the food, particularly the chicks, so the older birds would not harass them. When I fed them grain, I would scatter it in three or four different locations for the same reason. Some of my egg-laying chickens got preferential treatment. They were allowed to sleep inside my hut so they could build nests under my bed to lay their eggs. That way I could tell which one had just laid an egg because they made a loud clucking noise in the morning before dashing out of the hut. The advantage of them being close to me was that whenever I decided to have eggs for breakfast, I knew which chicken nest to pick from. You just do not want to end up cracking or boiling an egg that has already transformed into a chick. I would leave the hut open so they could freely go in and out.

Often, migratory birds such as black cranes, white herons, and house martins would move from the northern hemisphere to the warmer tropics during the rainy season and take up residence in my house. House martins loved to raise their chicks inside my hut for both warmth and protection from the elements. They would arrive early in the rainy season, and I would welcome them by not scaring them off or chasing them out of the hut. They would fly in and out for a few days until they satisfied themselves that there was no danger, and then they would start building their nests by visiting wet areas and picking tiny pieces of mud to bring back to the hut. House martins usually built their nests on the base of the ceiling, which was the shape of an inverted cone. This meant that their droppings landed right in the center of the hut, a few feet away from my bed. That didn't bother me much because the floor was dirt, anyway. It took me only a little time to sweep it out every now and then. Leaving the door partially open allowed the martins to come and go just like the chickens. The door was made of a certain type of thin wood that was bent and woven together. I couldn't have managed to completely seal off the door to keep rats, geckos, or snakes from crawling inside, even if I wanted.

At night, the whole hut buzzed with activity. I would often hear movement under my bed. Every now and then, I would hear the sound of hedgehogs visiting the peanuts sack my father had kept in the room for seeds. Yes, under my bed was the official residence of nursing hedgehog with babies. After each visit to the peanut sack, I could hear the hedgehogs cracking the peanuts at the nest. To avoid making several trips to the peanut sack, some smart hedgehog mothers would build their nests right under the peanut sack and give birth there. In a few weeks, I would see cute and healthy baby hedgehogs roaming the house between sunset and the early hours of the morning, bothered about nothing.

At night, before I go to bed, I would look up at the ceiling just in case there was a snake dangling and ready to drop down on me. Also, in the morning, before I put my feet on the ground, I would check to make sure that nothing was in the way. Cobras often slither inside homes and hide in storage pots made out of clay; their preferred hiding place.

Once it was dark, geckos would sneak out of cracks in the hut to hunt for insects. Spiders would get busy mending their damaged webs or building new ones. Then they would sit and wait for insects to fall in their traps. We didn't know the different spider names because there were so many of them living side by side with us. I didn't know anything about black widow or how harmful it was. I had probably seen them right by my bed and did nothing because it was just normal for spiders to be there. The night also brought out hundreds of fireflies, or *willarum*; meaning the insect that lights, in Kanuri language. They zigzagged up in the air and shone their green lights intermittently, a sight that brought joy to both children and adults.

There was one particular insect with a big, shiny, and inflated belly that I did not know if it was poisonous or not. Like most insects, it would appear in big numbers during the rainy season and cling to straws just a few inches from my bed, but we didn't bother each other. I had no idea where they had come from or what they were doing there. I remember calling it big-belly bug. In fact, most animals' and insects' names were descriptive and mainly based on looks, color, smell, or the sounds they made.

The deafening sound of thousands of frogs living by the edges of hundreds of water ponds echoed all over Kokoland. One group would make a high-pitched sound like the rattling of glasses, another would sound like blowing on saxophones, and a third group would sound like a steamer or a cruise ship's horn.

In the morning, before grabbing the water pot to wash, I would make sure that I examined it just in case a scorpion had crawled through the opening at night while keeping its stinger outside ready to strike fingers or hands that got in the way. Scorpions were not the only thing I would look for. For some reason, fire ants find the inside of water pots an ideal place for taking refuge at night. They would stick together to create a floating ball. In the morning, anyone unaware of their presence would pour the water over his body, along with a bundle of some crazy fire ants, to wash. It would take a few seconds for the ants to spread out in a coordinated manner, and then unleash their poisonous stings, at once. It would take a few more seconds for the person to realize that he was up for a hellish experience.

This was exactly what happened to one guest who came and spent the night at our house. He woke up at dawn to do morning prayers. He washed, then came back and sat down to finish preparing for prayers. He was sitting in front of the hut, and I could see him from my bed inside the hut. I suddenly saw the man four feet up in the air, simultaneously screaming prayers and cussing at the top of his lungs. The ants were attacking him. How he was able to combine prayers and cussing while up in the air was a mystery to me. It showed how severe ants' attack could be. It was both sad and funny, but it wasn't the right time to laugh. The man did whatever was necessary to get rid of the fire ants. He discarded his underwear and frantically brushed ants off his body with both hands. His scream was so loud that it brought my father running to investigate. He found the man in bad shape and he sort of knew what had just transpired. "The culprits must be the wicked fire ants," he concluded. Even though the man was aware of my father's presence, he would not lift his face to have eye contact with him. Showing up at the scene was enough for expressing solidarity with his guest, so my father decided to let him clear up his own fire ant mess. Neither the guest nor my father ever knew that I had witnessed the entire episode. Had I come out of the hut to help, I would have definitely laughed, and that would be disrespectful in view of the situation, so I stayed back and laughed quietly to myself.

It seemed that the regular fire ants bundling up inside washing pots did not carry out a good enough job at inflicting utmost stinging pain on people. There was another type of flying fire ant, indigenous to Africa, I think. As the name suggests, you don't have to worry about finding them, for they roam the air freely and land wherever they wish, and that could be on someone's neck. We dreaded them because they could cause immense damage, if they got inside someone's clothes.

The mornings after nightly rains used to bring out scores of insects, including the dreaded flying fire ants that emerged from tiny holes in the ground. The overnight rain was probably a signal to insect eggs buried underground to hatch, get out to the surface, and fly off, one insect at a time, in a spectacular show of tiny objects filling the atmosphere. By midday, the whole place would be buzzing with activity. The insects presented a valuable opportunity for birds which would be congregating in the surrounding trees. They would be busy all day grabbing insects in the air then flying back to the trees to eat them. It was a panoramic scene of buzzing insects and colorful squawking birds mingled up in the air.

Holes in the house were always a cause for concern, especially the ones close to my bed or around the base on the outside of the hut. They could harbor unwanted guests that could cause serious harm, so it was important to check them out by poking them with sticks and waiting for a few seconds to find out if there was any creature hiding in there. Sometimes I would pour water in the holes to get the same result. Fresh water was scarce, so I resorted to this option only when I had wastewater to spare.

Once, I noticed a suspicious hole on a corner outside the hut. After breakfast, I intentionally washed my hands over it and stood there for a few seconds to allow enough time for the occupant, if any, to come out. Sure enough, a giant black scorpion emerged, but before I could react, it crawled back inside and came back, followed by thirteen baby scorpions. The mother scorpion must have thought that the water I poured in the hole was a sign of the arrival of the rainy season, so she came out to explore and went back in the burrow to tell the babies that it was time to get out and hunt for insects.

Every night I sat a few inches from that hole on a jute mat on the floor and ate dinner. This particular type of scorpion is known locally as the camel scorpion because it is believed to be so poisonous that it could kill a camel. I did experience a scorpion bite, but it was a yellow scorpion, which is not usually fatal.

As you can tell, in Kokoland we were not exposed to risks such as gunshots or car crashes because we had none of that. Risks came in the form of bites from scorpion, snakes, dogs, being kicked by animals, falling off donkeys, or other hazards associated with living in such an environment.

Daytime brought different activities carried out by creatures, most of which were not quite as harmful as the ones that were out at night. For example, in the front of the house, there was a ten foot long pole that was entirely covered with red sand formation. Breaking open a section of the formation would reveal a colony of termites. They used it as a well-ventilated tunnel that provided safe passage when shuttling between their chambers in the ground and source of food, found in the bulbs of the straw that covered the wooden skeleton of the hut. They wreaked havoc on the building and, aided by other elements, it took them only a few years to demolish the entire structure. We would visit the forest to cut down trees and grasses to rebuild the hut. Obviously, the rate of demolition far exceeded the ability of the forest to replenish the harvested trees, which in turn led to desertification affecting the entire region. No one thought of getting rid of the termites because the use of chemical insecticides was an option not readily available to people.

Lizards slowly crawled around the edges of the shade in front of the hut, looking for unsuspecting insects to grab for lunch. Despite the fact that moths blended perfectly with the gray straw, the lizards were able to spot them. They must have the ability to smell them or see their thermal images. Once lunch was secured, the lizards would crawl back to where they had come from until they got hungry again.

Hornets, wasps, and their cousins used tiny pieces of mud to build nests under the shady overhang of the roof, which protected them from the weather. Some wasps produced chemicals that transformed wood into powder, making it easy for them to dig nests deep inside wooden beams and poles to lay eggs. Every time they flew in and out, they caused the wood powder to rain down over my head, beds, food, and everything under the roof. After a few years of nesting, the wasps would have hollowed out most of the wood beams supporting the shade overhang, rendering them too weak to carry the roof's weight. We would use poles to support them for another year or so until it proved too dangerous; then we would demolish the entire structure and rebuild a new shade.

Lazy frogs took up residence under the clay water pot to escape the heat. The dripping water wetted and cooled the ground beneath, making it a comfortable place for them. They would conveniently take their pick of the insects they wanted to eat. Tiny red velvetly rain ladybugs covered the front and back yard grounds, posing no threat to any living creature, I thought.

A chameleon, after deciding that it had enough of living perfectly camouflaged in the leaves of the climbing plants covering the entire hut, would slowly climb down to the ground and start swinging back and forth as it leisurely headed to a new residence on the neem tree some fifty feet away. It would blend perfectly by matching the colors of objects on its way to the tree. It could further protect itself with its ability to look in all directions by moving both eyes independently. Along the way, it would seize flying insects with its long, sticky, and slimy tongue. The rain would also signal to snails to crawl out of the bushes around the straw fence. They would understandably be moving at snail pace to get to their destinations with little to worry about time.

I would often see dung beetles busy rolling their perfectly round balls of "food" from around the donkey's area to a nearby fence to dig a hole and bury them along with their eggs. Later, the eggs would hatch and the baby beetles would feed on the buried food. Dung beetles stand on their front legs and use the back ones to roll the balls backward. Every few feet or so, they would stop and look around for something that was certainly unknown to me, before they continue rolling their balls of dung. I used to watch them with amazed curiosity, but also found it funny that they relied on dung for survival. I hated it whenever I accidentally stepped on them and their precious cargo, especially at night. I would be more concerned about cleaning the dung off my shoes or bare feet than about the possibility that I could have crushed one to death. Later, I grew to respect them after I learned that dung beetles actually navigate their ways by relying on the Milky Way to get to their desired destinations. This shows how little I knew.

Sometimes, swarms of locusts would travel north by the millions, perhaps billions. They would form clouds that would cover the moon light for hours at times. Many of them would crash into objects on their path. Soon, creatures of all sorts; frogs, cats, mice, geckos, and snakes would emerge from hiding and start picking them. I did my part too, picking as many as I could so I could fry them. They tasted like shrimp, and the tastiest of all were the ones heavily pregnant with eggs. That was a good source of protein. I hope I am not upsetting anyone by mentioning this fact. The locusts that were not picked up at night represented a bounty for the chickens to feast on in the morning. Food was scarce and it was customary to see an alpha rooster chasing after a hen holding an insect between its beaks. The rooster, being the legitimate supreme authority, would try to snatch it from the hen. However, that wouldn't be the case on "the morning after locusts." It was time of abundance; hence, there was no need for any chasing around. The birds would gorge themselves with easy picks of locusts. That was how nature provided a source of free food for many living creatures, including me.

The moving shadow of a harrier hawk hovering overhead, scouting for a stray baby chicken, horrified both the chicks and their mothers. Vigilant mothers would make a peculiar sound alarming the chicks of the danger lurking above. They would dash to safety under the mothers' wings or hide under a shade or any physical structure, whichever was closer. They would stay there until they heard signals from the mothers about the disappearance of the danger. Some bold harriers would attack the mothers who, like all mothers, would fight to the last drop of strength to protect their chicks. The chicks were not always successful. Upon hearing the warning sound of a mother, I would, sometimes, rush out to offer help and chase off the harrier by shouting and raising my hands up in the air to make my presence noticed. In many cases, I got there too late. The harrier would have already snatched a chick. It would be air borne and on its way to a safer location to enjoy its meal. Harriers wreaked havoc on my chicken business and I could do little to prevent that. It was frustrating.

The beef jerky we used to spread on ropes to dry under the sun was also a magnet for harriers. It was a processed food that was ready to consume, so harriers preferred it over working hard for their meals. It was unprotected and an easier target to snatch, since they were not met with resistance such as the one coming from mother chickens who were very capable of inflecting severe damage to harriers. Using a dry thorny branch to cover the meat was an anti-harrier organic deterrent technique that worked perfectly well, all the time.

Sometimes, I would hear the playful sound of the neighbor's dog outside the fence, so I would walk out to investigate. On one occasion, I found it teasing a turtle that has gone astray by stretching its front legs and placing them close to the turtle's head. It also lowered its head to sniff the turtle_while wagging its tail. Whenever the turtle tried to change course, the dog repositioned itself to obstruct its movement, so the turtle resorted to the tactic it knew best. It retracted its head inside the shell and played a waiting game. The dog kept on scratching the wet ground with its paws, but the turtle showed no sign of movement. Getting bored waiting, the dog left to look for another source of entertainment. The turtle, upon sensing the clearance of the danger, slowly poked its head out, moved it around to make sure that the_dog was gone, then sped off as fast as a turtle could walk.

My father raised rams for important family or religious occasions. We fed them millet to fatten them. They roamed the backyard, testing each other's strength by fighting fiercely to claim the harem of ewes. They charged at each other from several yards apart and banged their heads together. Nothing could stop them, and if a person got in the way, there was a chance that he or she would end up with a broken arm or leg. The rams' head banging sound was like the sound coming from chopping down a tree in the middle of the jungle. The echo travelled great distances.

Shepherds roaming the land around Kokoland. Photo 2016.

I would frequently hear the annoying bleats of our alpha ram chasing after female goats. The ewes would always run away, but he would keep after them. His loud bleats would encourage the neighbor's ram to come over and try his luck with our goats, and that was when things got really noisy. This would go on for a long time until I grow impatient, walk out, and chase them to the backyard. It was not only the male goat that spent time running after females. The alpha rooster also spent most of the daylight chasing after its harem, but the noise was nowhere as loud as the one made by the male goats.

Around sunset, the doves, the black cranes, and the white herons would fly back from the fields to their nests in the tree in the backyard. The female birds land on their nests, leaving the males fighting over the limited space available, producing a deafening noise. If you combined the the birds' noise with that coming from the village donkeys; you would stand little chance of knowing what was going on around the world.

The village donkeys brayed en masse at about early evening. Their bray was contagious. Once my donkey started, my neighbor's donkey would join and follow suit and before you knew it the entire village would be echoing with the sound of braying donkeys. It was certain that they were communicating with each other. To my bad luck, early evening was also the best time for quality radio reception. My Philips transistor radio was the only window I had to the world. Sometimes my donkey would bray in the middle of the news. I would impatiently wait for it to quit. If there happened to be news about World War III, I would definitely miss it. Then again, even if the donkeys were quiet and there was news about a nuclear war, I would not have known what that simply meant or its ramifications. In a way, such level of ignorance is not bad sometimes, I guess.

At around the middle of the rainy season swarms of mosquitoes would descend on my poor donkey to suck its blood. It would react by trying to wipe them off with its tail, but mosquitoes had learned to avoid landing on areas where they could be reached. The sound of the donkey stamping its back feet on the ground meant it was being overwhelmed by mosquitoes and was desperately looking for help. I would go outside and light a fire, using green grass to produce smoke rather than flame. Mosquitoes hate smoke, so they would fly away and give the donkey a much needed break.

As you can see, it was both chaotic and lively around my house. Domestic and wild animals contributed a lot to my daily routine with their varied sounds, smells, and activities. It was beautiful. I miss all that.

CHAPTER 3

An Unconventional Childhood

Around the time I was in first grade, the first thing I did each morning before I left for school was milking the goats and preparing morning tea. Different goats reacted differently to the process of milking. They were certainly not happy about letting us share their babies' milk, so they did not stand still. Moving around might have been their way of discouraging me from milking them. However, the babies were at my mercy when it came to how much milk I left for them. I think my goats had the ability to withhold some milk, releasing it only to their babies after I had left. I developed a technique that fooled the mothers. Once the milk flow diminished, I patted the udder with the back of my hand, mimicking the pushing of the baby goats as they suckled. This induced the mother to release more milk.

After milking; I would take the goats to the shepherd, leaving the babies behind to roam aimlessly around the house. They would look bored, as if wondering how to spend the whole day waiting for their mothers' return from grazing. They would become happier and more energetic as the afternoon wore on, perhaps sensing that mothers would return home soon with their udders pumped up with milk; a good thing for both the kids and me.

Every morning, before taking the goats to Adam Hussain the shepherd, I would secure our evening glasses of goat milk, ahead of time. I would take a strip of cloth, wet it with some milk, and muddy it with goat manure. Next, I would wrap the nursing mother's nipples with it, and then drive them to the shepherd. In the evening, they would find their way home on their own. They would start calling for their babies once they got closer to the house. The babies would run out to suckle, but, to their disappointment, they would find dry pieces of *manured cloth* wrapped around the nipples. They detested that. They would go around with frustration clearly visible on their tiny faces. Older babies would occasionally pull off the pieces of cloth so they could suckle. To prevent this from happening, I borrowed an "anti-suckling technique" from Khuruj, our neighbor. It involved wrapping an inch-long thorn with the manured piece of cloth, while keeping the sharp end of the thorn pointing downward. In the evening, the mother goats would announce their return, as usual, by calling for their babies from a distance. The babies would then dash out of the house as fast as they could to receive their mothers and suckle, only to be deterred by the manure and the long thorns on the nipples. I just did not feel good about this cruel technique, so I used it few times and abandoned the idea.

Unlike sheep, goats are, somewhat, illusive animals, just like their wild goat cousins. It was difficult for me to catch them for miliking, so I developed another technique to cope with the situation. Every time a goat gave me the runaround, I would go inside the hut, pick up a plate, and drop a handful of sorghum in it. Then, I would come out and approach it one more time, calling, "Hei, hei, hei," while shaking the metal plate. The goat would get curious, stand there, and weigh its options. It would finally come forward, but reluctantly. I would put down the plate on the ground and let it eat the grain, while I got on with milking it. Occasionally, I got lazy, so instead of walking inside the hut to get grain, I would look around and pick up pieces of pebbles or anything that made grain-like sound and drop it in the plate. I would keep the plate at chest-level and shake it. That would leave the goat guessing and wondering if it contained real grain or something else. From previous experiences, it might have learned that pebbles produced a different sound than grain. It would tilt its head sideways in a futile attempt to see the plate's contents. Finally, it would find it hard to resist, so it would come forward.

Adam Hussain, the shepherd, occasionally got sick and failed to show up at the goat yard. Ironically, he would decide to call in sick mostly on market days, especially Fridays. Basically, no one cared much about his welfare, so he helped himself by taking a day off every now and then. I would see him roaming the market place, moving from one shop to another, and begging for groceries. He would also show up in front of our shop and immediately start reciting verses from the Quran.

That was the reward he offered in exchange for whatever people gave him. Our tailor told me that Adam Hussain was a learned man who had studied the Quran and committed it to memory, but Allah punished him by taking away his mind because of alcohol drinking. He was no longer a pure man. Alcohol and the Quran must never mix, he told me. Adam Hussain could recite some Quranic verses, but they were all jumbled up. People took pity on him, so they gave him money and groceries. When he got to our shop, he made his favorite request. My father would ask him, "Adam Hussain, what do you want?" He would always respond, "Onions." While handing out the onions, my father would ask him again, "Why you did not take the goats out today?" Avoiding eye contact, he would respond, "I am sick." We would all laugh, fully knowing that he had decided to treat himself to a special meal that day. Later on, I would see him heading back to his hut with his jute sack hanging on his shoulder. It would be containing dates, okra, tomatoes, cucumbers, onions, and meat he had begged from Buggi, the butcher. I could tell because I could see blood seeping through the jute sack.

Adam Hussain's absence any day meant I had to take the goats back to the house and leave them there until after school. I would then take them out of the village to graze. It was every once in a while activity and I enjoyed doing that. The one thing I liked most was being able to gather buckthorn fruits, which provided supplemental food for both my goats and me. I would shake the tree to drop the fruits, and then the goats and I would race to compete for the best fruits. I would fill up my pockets and sit down to eat, while watching my goats eating, too. I always felt in my gut that there was something wrong about competing with my own animals for the same type of food, but I could not tell for sure what it was. I just did not know any better.

When I visited my grandmother's village, about two miles away, my younger brother Halim shared with me his expertise in bird catching. Certain rules of seniority were observed when it came to distributing fried bird meat among us. Being a guest, I enjoyed certain privileges over Halim and our cousins. The fact that I attended school, while Halim and our cousins did not, raised me to higher village social strata. Attending school meant I could read, write, and speak Arabic; things that were not attainable to children in the village. Knowledge is power, even in Kokoland. The children in the village wore local clothes, so wearing my school uniform of shirts and shorts made me feel special. The fact that I was older than Halim and our cousins guaranteed my privileged status. Naturally, I was very happy with that.

In the Borno/Kanuri culture, younger children were not supposed to call their older brothers by their names, as a sign of respect. They should call them *yayya*, or "big brother." Similarly, older brothers were not supposed to call their younger ones by their names. They should call them *yabeh*, which means "younger brother." Halim, however, rebelled against this tradition and refused to call me *yayya,* even though our elders insisted that he did so. It did not matter much to me, as long as my lion's share of barbecued bird meat was not jeopardized. Fortunately, it did not. When it was time to share the meat, I, being the guest of honor, would sit on a bare bed, while Halim and our cousins embraced the dirt floor. Tradition dictated that guests be treated favorably and generously, so Halim and our cousins abided by those rules, even though reluctantly. I was given the choice portions of breasts meat, while Halim and his contemporaries settled for whatever body parts left. To me, that was fair sharing. To this date, my brother Halim remains resentful of having to put up with those unfair rules and customs. He still talks about it. There could have been some elements of manipulation on my part to gain unjustified entitlements.

My childhood friend Tiffah and I became experts in bird-trap-setting. Adults did not eat bird meat, so we had fun barbequing and eating whatever we caught. It was one of our most favorite pastime activities, but I am sure the birds did not share the same perspective. First, we would get an old flat metal plate and poke holes, half an inch apart, all over it. Then we would weave thread into the holes. We would get hold of horse or ox hair. We would take one end of hair and fold it to create a loop. We would then take the other end and tie it to the thread. Space-permitted, we would tie as many hairs as we could in circular or rectangular formations. We would take the trap and set it wherever we thought we had better trapping chances. We would scatter some seeds in the center of the plate. That way birds would not be able to reach it without passing the loops. Stepping on it or poking their necks through would cause the loop to close and trap the birds. To camouflage the plate, we would bury it under the sand to prevent the birds from detecting it, sensing a danger, and keeping their distance. We preferred to use gray or beige hair as it blended with the earth background. It was easier to get ox tail hair from the butchery place than horse tail hair because there were few horses in town; besides, we did not want to risk being kicked.

Early mornings and late afternoons were the best times for setting traps. Rains during the day meant we had an increased chance of catching more birds as there would be a shorter feeding time. The birds would get very hungry and less cautious when approaching the feeding ground, so we were able to catch many of them. The dry season, especially toward the end of it, was bad for birds because there would hardly be any food left in the forest or farms. At the end of the harvest season, some people would dig underground storage burrows and burry grain to last them until the next rainy season. Other people would build elevated tiny hut-like structures to store produces such as millet, okra, beans, etc. Birds had a way of knowing which storage place was broken open in any particular day to remove food. They would flock to those places in droves to pick seeds dropped in the process. That presented us an opportunity for easy catch. Tiffah and I obtained ox hair by visiting the slaughter area on the outskirts of town very early in the morning because we competed with other children in the village. We always carried sticks to defend ourselves against dogs and village bullies. Vultures and dogs usually got there first and congregated around discarded bones and carcasses. We joined in the frenzy as we looked for oxen tails for our bird traps.

Fried bird meat remains a delicacy forever, as far as Kokoland boys were concerned.

We had another friend, Abbas, who came from the city to stay with his uncle so he could attend the village school. His parents were of the view that his chances of succeeding in life were better if he attended school in the village where there were fewer distractions so he could concentrate on his studies.

Abbas, being a city boy, was clueless about his new environment in a rural setting. Hence, his survival skills were inferior to ours. It was natural for him to consult us for advice about how things like bird traps worked. One morning, Abbas asked us where to find hair for his trap. We told him about the slaughter pit. We also told him that hair from his uncle's grey horse's tail, being long, strong, and easier to use, would greatly improve his chances of catching more birds. Soon after, we heard that Abbas was bedridden. We went to visit him and found he had a swollen forehead with a crescent-shaped mark that was unmistakably caused by a kick from a horse's hoof. He stood behind his uncle's horse, and without any advance warning, reached out, grabbed its tail, and yanked out a bunch of hair. Unfortunately, Abbas was standing at just the right distance to make him a perfect target for a superb horse kick. The horse simply reacted in the best way it knew to protect itself, which almost got Abbas killed. When he recovered, we showed him the right way of pulling hair from a horse's tail. We would calmly approach the horse and rub along its neck and body, then down its back leg. Once we had gained its trust, it would go back to do whatever it was doing earlier, be that eating or relaxing. Next, we would stand to the side, out of range of the animal's hooves, grab a few hairs, and slowly pull them out. That might cause it a sensational feeling, so it would swish its tail from side to side as if swatting mosquitoes or flies. We would repeat pulling hairs out until we had thirty or so.

Abbas was a forgetful boy. The following year, when he came back to Kokoland to attend school, he overheard Tiffah and I talking about the village dogs that currently had puppies. It was very important for us to stay up-to-date on which homes had dogs nursing puppies, because they were very protective. When we roamed the village, we kept track of these danger zones. Over time, we learned to keep a distance of at least thirty meters from the homes with puppies, which was enough space to allow us to escape by hopping a fence or getting into someone's hut so we were not bitten. Abbas, upon hearing us talk about the homes with puppies, decided that he wanted a pet. Without telling us about his intentions, he set out to get one. He picked a house and went straight to the den with one week-old puppies. Their mother was absent on a trip searching for food. Abbas stood there, taking his time to figure out which color of puppy he wanted. He finally picked up one and turned around to leave, only to face the mother just returning from her trip. He was caught red-handed. He dropped the puppy and took off running, but the dog caught up to him. She attacked him, ripping his pants, biting him on his rear end, and scratching his back. He came home in bad shape. We did not find out what had happened until his cousin told us a few days later. Abbas never did really learn how to live in a village setting. He was too much of a city boy. Sadly, our friend Abbas died at a very early age. He was taken by a crocodile while bathing at a bend in the river Nile, in the city of Juba in Southern Sudan. He was visiting his uncle who was a merchant.

Mothers are naturally protective of their offspring, but the ferocity of mother dogs in Kokoland was an exception to this rule. Many years later when I was in London, I saw children on television playing with newborn puppies, right next to the mother dog, which was lying there watching them. It was amazing to me that she lay there so peacefully and unbothered by the children. I always wondered why dogs in Kokoland were so aggressive. I guess it must be the way we treated them, so they responded in kind. It must have been a survival issue for them.

Obviously, spending most of our free time catching birds came at the expense of competing with children in other parts of the world, who might be guided by their parents to prepare for attending Ivy League schools such as Harvard, Yale, Princeton, Oxford, etc. Then again, that was not a concern for us, for we did not miss what we did not know existed. In fact, we were ignorant of so many things.

We called the trapping area *waloofa*, meaning birds' taming ground. We first gained the birds' trust by offering free food for a couple of days without setting any trap. We would go to the town mill and gather up the flour and crushed seeds from the mill floor to scatter on the *waloofa* ground. The way that attracted birds seemed magical. We would literally transform an almost barren land into a feeding ground in just a few days. We would usually choose a place near a tree because birds would not fly straight to the feeding ground. They would first land on a tree to examine the surrounding area to make sure that there were no dangers such as dogs and cats lurking in the vicinity, and then fly down to the feeding ground. We would observe them from a distance so they would not be alarmed by our presence and fly away. We would usually hide in a nearby straw hut and watch through holes we had poked in the walls. Once birds took off and landed with ease, we knew that we had gained their trust and it was time to strike.

We occasionally collected sorghum debris from Dumba's house to use in attracting more birds. She used sorghum for making local alcohol called *mareesa*. Because alcohol was forbidden (haram), collecting the sorghum debris would land us in trouble. We would be punished if we were caught red-handed, so we did that covertly. The *waloofa* area would soon become a place of interest for both humans and animals alike. Birds landing in droves would send a signal to animals in the area that there was food, so they would descend straight to the *waloofa*, causing the birds to fly away. Donkeys, especially, loved the fermented sorghum debris. I think they smelled it from a distance because they usually showed up minutes after we had scattered it on the trapping ground. Goats, dogs, cats, and chickens also congregated there, and that drove us crazy.

Silence was pivotal for bird catching. If we saw an animal approaching the *waloofa*, we would try from behind a fence or inside a hut to discourage it from getting nearer. We would make a muffled sound just high enough to chase it away, but not too high to alarm the birds on the ground. It was a very difficult balance-striking act. If we appeared on site to chase the animals, the birds would automatically fly away. The animals were hardly deterred or bothered by our muffled voices but, fortunately, scarcity of food always drove the birds back. They took a huge risk coming to our trapping ground. They had few alternative options.

At times the birds would desert the *waloofa* due to no particular known reason. That was when I reached out to a bird attracting secret that worked like magic. It was a bird song that I had learned from my younger brother Halim during one of my visits to grandma's village. It has a haunting effect on birds, leading them to subconsciously descend on the *waloofa* the moment I finished chanting it. I think its magical qualities deprived birds of their free will. It is true. The song (in Kanuri) translates to something like this:

- Are there no birds in the East?
- Are there no birds in the West?
- Aren't there any more *dalma kairos* (bird name)?
- Aren't there any more *gozolima tintins* (bird name)?
- Birds, come on and safely land. There is a lot of seed waiting for you.
- Come on and safely land
- Come on and safely land

The second I finished singing, birds flocked to the *waloofa* from all directions. That was really what happened. No, I take that back. That was what I prayed for to happen, and prayers, understandably, were not always answered. This was the extent to which I went to catch birds. You might wonder why a kid would go through all this trouble to satisfy a hobby. The answer is no, it was not a hobby. It was catching and eating birds for food.

One day I set my traps, hid, and waited. There were no birds on sight, so I left to get a drink of water. Upon returning, I saw several small round figures lying all over the feeding ground. I rushed there only to find twelve or so chicks caught by the traps. They were all dead. I was in trouble, big trouble. I braced myself to face a dire consequence. The situation was aggravated by the fact that the chicks belonged to Ganima, a mentally ill neighbor with an unpredictable mood. The situation demanded quick thinking and immediate action—remove the evidence and bury it. I ran back to the house and made sure that nobody saw what I was doing. I grabbed a shovel and rushed back to the crime scene. I looked around and spotted Ganima's donkey tied to a pole and thought that was the perfect spot. Burying the chicks there would make it difficult for Ganima and others in the neighborhood to discover the evidence. The donkey would step on the burial site and hide any evidence of freshly dug-out dirt. I hurriedly dug a pit while looking in all directions to ensure that I was not caught. I dropped the tiny dead chicks into the pit and camouflaged it with sand and some straw leftover from the donkey's food. I felt so guilty burying those helpless chicks, which had done nothing to deserve such an end. It was my fault. My love for bird meat caused the little chicks to meet such a tragic end. I left the scene, certain that nature would take care of them. Maggots would soon begin the job they did best. I knew if I could survive for a week without anyone discovering what had happened, life would go back to normal, and I could let down my guards and stop worrying. Yes, I forgot to tell you, there were no security cameras, in case you are thinking about that.

Ganima showed up at our house looking for my father. I was sure she must have suspected that the disappearance of her chicks had something to do with me. Portraying the image of a responsible child, I pretended that I had forgotten to get the donkey back from the outskirts of town, so I ran off to get it. I have no idea what she said to my father. In the end, I was not punished or accused of anything, and that what mattered. Had they found out, there could have been many conferences held to discuss how to compensate Ganima, but most importantly how to punish me.

I did not know much about breeding season for animals and birds. By the time I learned about that, it was too late. We in Kokoland did not know that we were collectively causing a great deal of damage to our environment. We saw no problem in hunting animals and birds any season of the year. The region was a rich, biodiverse savanna with huge variety of animals and plants. It used to rain a lot. Millions of migratory birds nested in the area during the rainy season due to the abundance of food and water. Some people caught birds and found rings around their legs with English inscriptions, which I did not know anything about until much later. Those birds probably had been marked by European scientists to track them. To us, catching a particular type of bird depended on whether its meat tasted good or bad. That was it. I am certain we played a part in devastating the bird populations in the area.

Cutting down trees and clearing the land to practice shifting cultivation was the norm throughout the region. It took only three or four rounds of farming before the nutrients in the soil became exhausted. Drastic decline in farm yields would force farmers to constantly clear new areas in the forest. Before we knew it, we had transformed the whole area into a desert. The villages scattered around the town used to be hidden from sight because of dense forests, even though they were only a few miles away. Today they are all visible as far as the eye can see. There are no more trees left for fencing, building homes, charcoal, or for the migratory birds to build their nests. There is little biodiversity left. Some people attribute the degradation of the environment to God punishing people for their disobedience. People are reaping the results of their bad deeds, they thought. To many, the situation has nothing to do with the ecosystem.

I, later on in life, learned that everything is relative. As a young boy, I did not miss much living in Kokoland, believing that what we had, or what we didn't have, was the norm everywhere else. Today, forty years later, nothing has changed much. Kokoland is still the same dusty little town with no running water. As you might have expected, there are no paved roads or cars. There is no power, so any electricity-dependent devise or activity that you can imagine is not there, except for mobile phones recently introduced to the area. Yes, there are no televisions or refrigerators either. Simply the basic necessities of life that people take for granted here in the West aren't there. There are more people, but with fewer resources, compared to forty years ago. Despite that, Kokolanders, all along, believed that they were living in a more urban setting than those in surrounding villages. I guess that belief will continue to dominate their thinking as long as they aren't connected with the rest of the world. Once they find out, they will be very angry about having missed out on so much of what the modern world has to offer, for so long. Globalization has not reached Kokoland yet, and some may say this is a good thing, but it will someday. That will be the time when people start raising their demands. The civil wars and civil commotions the country has been experiencing are partly rooted in environmental changes influencing the social fabric and norms.

Donkeys were central to our lives in that rural setting. They were, and still are, the primary means of transportation. No wonder why we didn't go very far. How much can you carry and how far can you go to make a difference in your life, if you must rely on a donkey to conduct your daily business? A man's importance used to be measured by the height and speed of his donkey. The combination of these two factors was instrumental in paving the way to marrying a beautiful woman of a good social standing.

There is a strong bond between a boy
and his donkey. Photo 2016.

There was a strong bond between my donkey and me, much like the one between men and their trucks here in America. He kept me busy most of the time taking care of him, but the dreamer in me found time to wonder about the origins and destinations of the flying objects, which occasionally crossed the sky over the village. I spent so much time with him that, now, I cannot stand the color gray. It always reminds me of a long list of donkey responsibilities, none of which I found to be fun.

In the mornings, I would take my donkey out of the village about a kilometer or so to a grassy area. I would use a long rope to tie him to a shrub so he had a wider grazing range. Being my only means of transportation and shuttling water, his well-being was important to me. I would pay him a visit around midday to make sure he had not entangled himself with the rope because the consequences could be fatal in such a case. Another donkey we owned got tangled up and kept fighting to free itself until it broke one of its front legs. I have never seen an animal suffer that much in my life. No wonder why cowboys shoot their broken horses to end their suffering.

I have learned about time management at an early age in my life. Every day, I had to juggle several activities. That included opening the shop in the afternoon after returning from the farm; fetching water; finding time to play soccer; bringing the donkey back home from grazing; collecting enough hay to last him through the night; and setting green leaves on fire to protect him from mosquitos. If this is child labor, then I lived it. Somehow, I was able to balance all of these activities every day. This delicate balancing act would be shattered whenever a guest or guests showed up, unannounced of course, since they represented an additional burden. It was customary to receive guests with open arms because it was believed that they, indirectly, brought welfare and well-being to the hosting family. This was a divine belief, so it could not be questioned, unless you were asking for trouble with the elders and the learned men of the community. The moment I hear the voice of someone approaching the house and conveying greetings, I would hurry out to receive him. I would automatically run toward the donkey. The guest would dismount and walk to shake hands with my dad, leaving me stuck with the donkey, as if implying that it was the job for which God almighty has created me. I would be stuck with the donkey for the entire duration of the guest's stay at our house.

First I would lead the donkey to take down the saddle, then I would take it to a nearby water pond to drink. Some donkeys were fussy, so they would refuse to drink dirty or muddied water, which meant I had to take them to farther out ponds with cleaner waters. I couldn't blame a donkey for refusing to drink and take it back because its sunken belly would tell that it was still thirsty, and, obviously, there were consequences for my actions. On the other hand, taking it farther out came at the expense of other activities I might have planned for the day, such as a soccer match. That ain't nobody's problem, but my own, so I had to deal with it. After drinking, I would take it to graze by the side of my donkey. That meant I had two donkeys to look after. If there were two guests or more, I would solicit the help of my friend Tiffah. He would come and help me look after them. It was important that we kept the donkeys separated from each other to prevent them from fighting. Donkeys are territorial, so if they could get to one another, they would bite. Some bites could be crippling, and all the blame, as you guessed it, would come my way. In the evenings, we would bring them back to the house and make sure that we tied each donkey to a separate pole in a corner away from each other.

To show hospitality to the guest, I would chase and catch a rooster to kill for dinner. It could be my own rooster I bought for my chicken business, or I could have bought it as a little chick and fattened it to take to the market to sell at a profit. All those plans would be shattered that night and no questions asked. Guests must come first even though they posed a risk to my business. Their unannounced arrival was a casualty for which I did not have any insurance. That night, my bed, my cotton mattress, my pillow, and my blanket would no longer be mine. They would be the guest's and no questions asked either. My rights that night, would be reduced to a bare bed, if any, left in the house and a mat made from palm leaf, if I was lucky. If there were many guests, then I could be settling for the floor, still without showing any resentment, for that was great sin. Once, my brother Aziz and I nagged about surrendering our beds to guests, and my dad took away our fluffy cotton mattresses and made us sleep on mats for a few days. We learned our lesson, so we never resented foregoing our bed rights to guests, ever.

Sometimes, while driving in the country here in America, I would see gray donkeys freely roaming ranches. Such image would immediately invoke all those donkey memories in my head. I would think to myself, "If only you know how much I hated looking after you."

Over time, a special relationship evolved between my donkey and me. He was central to my daily activities. Obviously, one should not expect much brain stimulation, if most of the day is spent around a donkey. However, I must give credit to my donkey for his listening skills. I used his silence to improve my spoken English after I got into middle school. We started learning English in seventh grade. I used to practice speaking on my way to the farm, a distance of an hour's ride. My donkey listened attentively to my newly acquired language skill without any interruption or showing any sign of discomfort from the many mistakes I made and the limited vocabulary I had. I guess he must have noticed that some of the words I used were local words familiar to him, but he never complained. Any time I did not know the correct English word, I invented one or used a local word instead to fill in the many gaps in my sentences. I think my donkey was instrumental to my learning English because of all the quality time I spent riding to and back from the farm. That was when my imagination ran wild and I daydreamed about places and things.

One thing my donkey hated the most was quails suddenly flying off by the side of the narrow trail. In the afternoons, both of us would be exhausted. The slow rhythm of the donkey's walk often lulled me to sleep. Speed wasn't my concern; besides, how fast could a donkey go, anyway. He exerted just enough energy to move his legs forward. He would react to quails by shifting his body in the opposite direction while bringing his speed to absolute zero. He did that in a fraction of a second, which guaranteed my race to the ground. I would be followed by a bunch of farming tools that I would normally be carrying on my lap and the saddle, all tumbling down and raining on top of me. This was the likely scenario every time quails unexpectedly took off a few feet away from us. I never was able to hold on.

Once I hit the ground, my donkey would quickly evaluate the situation to decide whether to stay until I got up, or take off running in the direction of the village. His decisions depended on whether the saddle landed on top of me or stayed on his back. With no load on his back, he would feel light and that gave him a ticket to freedom. He would run at full speed and kick up his heels like crazy, as if telling me it was my turn to carry the load that day. He must have thought that temporary freedom was worth the beating he would receive when I got home. Once he was gone, I would be left with the dilemma of how to carry the tools and the saddle back to the village. It would be too heavy to carry everything at once. Walking away and leaving everything behind was out of the question because someone might pass by and take them, and I would certainly be punished for my negligence. I would wait a little bit longer, just in case someone passed by. Sometimes I got lucky and got help.

Most of the time, I had to deal with the situation on my own. First, I would carry what I could and leave the rest of the items behind. I would walk for a kilometer or so toward the village and drop the items by the side of the road. Then I would go back and gather up the remaining items. That way I would not be far from either place at any point in time, in case someone passed by and thought of helping himself to a free donkey saddle and farming tools. I was not prepared to take that risk. I would repeat the one-kilometer technique until I finally got to the village, then I would leave everything by the first house at the edge of the village and go home to get my naughty donkey and load him up. I, naturally, expressed my anger, but his body language seemed to suggest, "I understand and I don't blame you."

The thing that I feared the most was tumbling down on top of a snake. During the rainy season, shrubs would take over the trail to our farm and only a narrow line of broken grass marked the path. The trail's cooler sand would become a magnet for snakes escaping from hotter areas in the bush, particularly after sunset, when it became quieter. My donkey had great snake detecting abilities. It would, somehow, sense their presence and usually forewarned me by abruptly pulling both of his ears forward. His next step would be an abrupt stop. If I failed to take notice, my body would keep on moving, and the laws of gravity would prevail. I would flip over his neck and head to the ground, with the possibility of landing on top of a deadly snake. The prospect of that happening worried me a great deal. Ali Habib's son, Hussein, fell off a camel on top of a snake, which bit him on his mouth. Luckily, it was not a cobra, so he survived the ordeal. That incident terrified me.

I remember when I was a kid, one of my favorite toys was a piece of a broken perfume bottle I found in our backyard. When I later described the color to my wife, she told me it was purple. I can never differentiate between colors confidently. Like many other things, I did not know the names of colors until later on in life. I used to hold that piece of broken glass up to the sun, close one eye, and look through it with the other eye. I derived immense joy from doing that. My brother Aziz and I used to celebrate when a china plate broke, because we collected the pieces with dull edges and played with them. At night, inside the straw hut where we slept, we would rub the edges of two pieces against each other to create sparks that lit our joyous and smiley faces for a fraction of a second, showing our white teeth, every time we rubbed the pieces together. After we finish playing, we would hide our precious toys in the usual storage place up between the wooden beam and straw, and looked forward to using them the following night, or until we invented another game or tool to play with.

You can tell we did not have stores like Toys 'R' Us and GameStop. Occasionally, we built trucks from discarded wire, which were scarce in Kokoland because there were no industrial activities that produced waste we could turn into toys. The one boy who had access to wire was Tukul, whose uncle was the local judge. He got him some wire from the train station a few miles from Kokoland. We were jealous of Tukul. Being the nephew of the local judge meant he could get whatever he wanted, or get away with anything he did, and no one could lay a finger on him.

My friend Tiffah and I came up with our own plan to secure some wire from the barbed wire fence at the girls' school, to build trucks. The plot was to sneak in a little after sunset, but while it was still bright enough that we could see. If we let it got too dark, we risked being chased or bitten by Hamdan the ironsmith's dog. We could also be punished at home for staying out late. We got to the girls' school as planned, but because we did not have any wire cutters, we used two pieces of stone. Tiffah held one beneath the wire, and I used the second to hit the wire repeatedly so it would heat up and break. We finished with one end and moved about four meters away to start cutting the other end. We figured each of us would get enough wire to make the wheels, chassis, and a box for our trucks. Then we heard a loud bang a few feet from where we were sitting. It was the school guard Dosa who sensed our presence and threw a big stick at us. He must have heard the sound of knocking of the stone, so he came to investigate. We sprang to our feet and took off running. We heard him shout, "You came for the girls. I know who you are. Tomorrow I will tell your fathers and your teachers."

Tiffah and I were in real trouble. It was no longer a matter of stealing truck wire. The whole thing had turned into a life-and-death situation because we had been caught sneaking into the girls' school. I didn't sleep that night and I am sure Tiffah didn't either. I prayed that Dosa was lying about knowing who we were. Then I worried that the school would hire Dajai, the trail hunter, to look for us. He could easily follow our footprints all the way to our homes. I also prayed for the wind to blow overnight and wipe out our footprints. The whole thing was Tiffah's idea, but I did not want to betray him, for he was my best friend. Was staying home the next day an option? No, and the problem would not go away even if we did. I prayed a lot that night. In the morning we did go to school, but I kept looking at the gate, waiting for the guard to show up any time. He never showed up that day, nor the following days. After a week, we reverted to our normal routines, eating regularly again, sleeping at night, and carrying on with our lives as usual. From then on, I avoided having eye contact with the guard anytime we met. I always thought he would stop, look back, and shout, "You!" That never happened. He had lied about knowing who we were. If we had been accused openly of trying to sneak into the girls' school, the community would have shunned us. I was more worried about my stance in the community than the lashes I would have received from the teachers at school and, probably, my dad.

The metal rims of bike wheels were another valuable toy. We rolled them in front of us and used a foot-long stick to push and control their direction. If you happened to have one of these rare rims, other children would befriend you. To own a toy that you could play with and at the same time share it with your friends, in exchange for their protection from bullies, was not a bad deal, I guess.

CHAPTER 4

Life in and around Kokoland

Almost everyone in and around Kokoland worked in the farming business, relying on really outdated farm tools. Different crops were farmed, but there was nothing more tedious than preparing peanuts for planting. To have enough peanut seeds, we had to crack open the peanut shells by hand, one peanut at a time. Holding the peanut between the thumb and the index finger, we would press just enough to crack the shell, but without destroying the seeds inside. Broken seeds would not germinate. To relieve the fingers, which usually developed blisters from cracking the shells, we would switch to using a solid object like a piece of stone or metal, against which we knocked the front tip of the peanut to crack it open. Sometimes we sprayed water on the peanut to soften the exterior of the shell to make it easier on the fingers. Obviously, this was a very slow and inefficient operation, which took us nowhere in terms of how much seeds we could prepare to plant. It was not surprising that what we harvested was limited to what we had planted. Unfortunately, the same method is being followed even today.

Planting the seeds involved an adult, usually the father, digging holes using hoes mounted on long wooden poles. He would walk forward, sideways, in a straight line as he dug holes at distances determined by what was being planted; one foot apart for peanuts, two feet apart for corn, sorghum, millet, and so on. The wife and

Kokolanders continue to use ancient grass-cutting tools in farming. Photo 2016.

the children did the planting by dropping the seeds in the holes and burying them with their feet. Usually, there were more planters than diggers, who worked faster to stay ahead.

The next stage was weed cleaning. For this purpose, we used a metal piece that was about 10x6 inches. It has sharp ends on one side and a circle on the opposite for inserting a wooden pole. Standing up and holding the other end of the pole, the farmer would shove the metal part under the dirt, between the plant rows, and push forward, cutting the weeds by chopping the roots. There were no water towers, canals, or water lines for irrigation systems. It all depended on the amount of rainfall during the rainy season. If it was adequate, then the farmer got a decent harvest. If not, he had to wait for the next rainy season. The same tedious process was also applied in harvesting. The crops were either pulled by hand out of the ground, in the case of peanuts, or cut one bushel at a time in the case of sorghum, millet, or okra. Kokoland was the local trade center, so depending on the time of the year, people from the surrounding villages came to town with their produce to sell. They usually brought fresh vegetables during the harvest season and dried-up products and live animals during the dry season.

This was how people farmed since time immemorial. Because we have most of the population using the same practice to make a living, it translated into a very low standard of living. I thought there was something wrong about settling for Kokoland, for an entire life, so I looked for a place elsewhere. I guess I shouldn't be blamed, should I?

Some homes in Kokoland, especially in the borough of Keekah, fermented local alcoholic drinks called *mareesa* and *aragi*, made from sorghum and palm dates, respectively. Every market day, Angool rode his white donkey to town to enjoy Keekah's famous drinks. He crossed the marketplace passing in front of the shops, concerned about nothing other than getting to his destination, be that Dinga's, Hassina's, or Amta's house, depending on who was raising the white flag that day. The flag was a piece of white cloth attached to a tall thin pole that could be seen from a distance to guide anyone seeking alcohol to the right house. Angool would spend the day at the house, leaving around sunset after alcohol had seeped into every inch of his body. He would usually pass in front of my house and find me sitting and listening to the radio. I remember him producing a snoring sound that was frequently interrupted by jumbled-up sentences that did not make any sense at all. His donkey did a good job getting him home safe because I saw him every Friday.

Kokoland also had its own version of happy hour. Occasionally, someone from out of town would show up in Dinga's house and order the white flag lowered, thus declaring free drinks for all present. The lowering of the flag meant that there was no more alcohol left for sale. Soon the clay pots got filled up to their necks with *mareesa* and placed in front of clients, much to their delight. The men would sit quietly, on short-legged stools, in circular formations, and sip from the drink for the rest of the day. In the end, after downing all that drink, you would see them in semi-hibernation mode with their eyes half-open. Every now and then one of them would struggle to stand up to pay a visit to the loo. His knees would buckle as they find it hard to carry the body, plus the perfectly round-shaped pot belly, the size of the clay pots, stretched to the limit you would think that they could burst for applying the slightest of pressure. He would stagger out of the hut and the few steps to the bathroom would become a strenuous ordeal. In some of the cases, you would think that the men had actual pots strapped to their bellies, only that hidden from sight under their cloth.

Drinking *mareesa* and eating meat go hand in hand. Once I saw men coming out of Keekah, holding empty containers such as bowls, and approaching our shop, I knew they were coming to buy cooking oil. I also knew that Argan must have been selling meat *keeri* (illegally) in one of the houses in Keekah. Normally; people brought empty bottles from home to get them filled, so it was unusual to see anyone coming to the shop with a bowl or a glass to buy oil. The idea was to go back to the borough with oil in one hand and a couple of onions in the other to enjoy some fried meat. Most of the meat came from goats or sheep stolen and slaughtered illegally.

Argan was notorious for selling illegal meat, until he ran out of luck one day. Kokoland was on the trail used by nomad cattle herders on their annual journey during the rainy season. It was common knowledge in town that Argan used the tree cover around two seasonal streams to hide and wait for goats and sheep to pass by. He would catch and kill as many as he could, then lie low until sunset. He would then skin them and take the meat into town on the back of his donkey, under the cover of darkness. Because the area was a trail, animal owners were constantly on the move, so they would not find out about their missing animals until later on when they had reached their destinations. By that time it would be too late to backtrack to look for them. Argan took full advantage of the situation.

Finally, Argan ran out of luck, so he got caught while slaughtering some goats inside a dense forest. That, day the owner stumbled upon him by chance and found that he had already slaughtered eighteen of his goats. In Kokoland, many a times, people who were wronged did not look for justice elsewhere. They took the law in their own hands. Some forms of vigilante justice involved horrific punishment. The idea was to spread the word around to deter potential thieves from even trying. Argan was lucky that the owner of the goats turned out to be a very wise man. Against the advice of his children and family members, he decided to take Argan to the judge in town. It goes without saying that, on the way to town, Argan received a fair amount of blows with fat sticks.

Dallami, the local judge, was a neighbor who had a shop adjacent to my father's. I was there when Argan was brought to face the remaining half of the punishment. The other half had already been carried out on the way. I saw bumps and bruises all over his legs, bald head, and face, which was covered in blood. The backside of his *baft* (coarse cotton fabric) clothing was stained with blood, but I could not tell the type of injury he had received. He was in bad shape. He must have been beaten with a special type of stick called *mudabab,* which was usually covered by oxtail skin. After slaughtering a bull, the tail skin would be peeled off inside out. In place of the tailbone, a stick would be slid into the skin and left to dry, making it a formidable fighting weapon. The colors of the skin added elegance to the stick. Young men carried them around in their wanderings. They also carried knives concealed under the arms.

Onlookers gathered under the tree where Argan was sitting quietly and staring at the ground. He occasionally lifted his head to survey the crowd whenever he sensed someone's arrival. The inaction in Kokoland made such incidents a source of entertainment for all of us, so we did our best not to miss them. A few of the onlookers were friends to Argan, but that day was not one for declaration of friendship or solidarity with a thief. Many knew what Argan did for living, but they turned a blind eye on his illegal activities because they enjoyed the cheap *keeri* meat and free animal intestines they had been getting from him.

Dallami, the local judge, appeared and sat on his crooked bed, so the circle of onlookers closed in on him, with Argan sitting on the ground next to him. The setting was an open court that had little regard for "trivial" things such as privacy and confidentiality. Dallami started interrogating by asking Argan, "Do you confess that you slaughtered all those eighteen goats?" Argan looked down at the ground and produced a murmured inaudible low tone sound that came from deep down his throat. Dallami slightly bent and stretched his neck to get closer to Argan and blasted with a loud and authoritative voice, "What did you say?" Argan lifted up his head while keeping his eyes closed. He opened them with difficulty and it was clear from the intensity of his facial expression that he was reaching to remote corners of his brain to scrape a few religious words to dust and use them to soften the judge's stance on the crime. That way he might be able to convince the judge that he was already on his way to repentance, which could come as soon as he was let go free.

While we all impatiently waited for an answer, he kept quiet and slowly closed and opened his eyes. Every time he did that, he looked as exhausted as someone who had just returned from a long hunting trip, empty handed. He closed his eyes as if telling us that he was going back, one more time, to resume the hunt for an answer inside his brain, just to be sure that he had left no stone unturned. He took a long time squeezing his memory out of any sensible answer or Godly words that he could find to present to the judge, gain his sympathy, and possibly spare him jail time. He miserably failed as his memory did not come to his rescue because there were no Godly words stored in Argan's brain for rainy days such as that day, to begin with.

Argan was bankrupt of any answers. He had no motivation for opening his eyes, so he kept them closed for as long as possible, fully knowing that opening them gave signal to the few dozen or so eyes staring at him that he was ready to speak out loud about his reasons for slaughtering the eighteen goats. He finally decided to confront the situation. He opened his eyes and started moving his lips. Judge Dallami said, "Hmm" (a shorter form of asking someone to repeat what he or she had just said). Argan started talking, but with a soft and subdued voice. He said, "Yes, what can I tell you? In the name of Allah the greatest, what happened was a plight and a destiny; Allah willed so, and Satan whispered to me and played with my mind. May Allah curse Satan, may Allah curse Satan?" He spoke softly and looked desperate. I was surprised to hear Argan speaking like a holy or a Godly man. I had never known him to be a religious man or a mosque goer. That day, Argan was a different person. Miracles do happen in Kokoland.

The judge asked him again, "Did Satan order you to slaughter not one, not two, not three, but eighteen goats?" Argan's lips moved, but said nothing, so the judge continued, "Why did you do it?" Then Argan, after taking a deep breath, spoke, "I swear by the name of God almighty that Satan played with my mind." It seemed that Satan had been playing with Argan's mind for as far as I could remember. I think Satan must have hated that place so much. He was blamed for most problems committed by humans. I don't know of a creature in Kokoland that was more shortchanged than Satan. He was always the short fence over which every Tom, Dick, and Harry hung out their dirty laundry of lies to dry.

At that moment, Argan's friend, Sugud, showed up and pretended as if he knew nothing about the incident, when, in fact, everyone in the village knew that he had everything to do with Argan's illegal *keeri* meat business. He helped Argan by using his own donkey for transportation and distribution of the meat.

The smell of barbecued meat met your nose as soon as you entered the borough of Keekah, especially on Fridays when barbecued meat went hand in hand with alcohol. Smoke billowed above straw huts all over the place, particularly houses that fermented local alcohol *mareesa* and *aragi,* declaring, "Here be alcohol," with full view of white flags hanging high on wooden poles. The barbecue smokes were not consistent with the fact that the residents of Keekah hardly paid visits to the butchery in the center of the market to buy meat, which indicated that something fishy was going on.

Argan must have been in this business for a long time. I came to know of his shady activities after I became aware of what was going on in my village environment. I remember I was five years old or so, and it was after sunset when I heard a wailing sound from the side of Gamzut's house. My mom told me that the man must have died. It was Gamzut, the assistant butcher, who was also Argan's brother-in-law. His job was to assist senior butchers Hardan and Jigir by taking care of the oxen they bought from the animal market in town or from nearby villages. Gamzut would drive the oxen to the slaughter area east of town to prepare them for slaughter. It was a dangerous task as I remember. I had encountered him a few times while he was struggling to control angry oxen. I had to give way by delving into the nearest shelter around. One day things went wrong. An ox he was handling gored him in the chest, seriously injuring him. He was sick and bed-ridden for some time until he passed away that night. It was common for people to ride out their sickness or pain. If they were lucky, they would survive. The local clinic was rarely visited for treatment, especially if it was a minor injury. It was obvious that Gamzut, despite the severity of the injuries he had sustained, did not seek help at the clinic or the city, until he succumbed to his injuries that evening. Some people did visit the clinic, but by the time they did that, it was invariably too late.

Gamzut and Argan were in the same type of business. The difference was that Argan chose an illegal, but lucrative route to conduct his business. He finally fell in the trap and almost paid a price that could have cost him his life. Ironically, his brother-in-law chose to earn his living legally, but that led to his death.

Dallami, the judge, called for Aseel, the guard, who immediately broke the circle of onlookers, stepped forward, and stood at attention. He was in his usual WWII uniform, with an ostrich feather stuck on his helmet. He was ready to receive orders. Dallami told him to take Argan to the prison cell by the courtroom and get ready to accompany him to the city the next day. Aseel immediately bent over and reached for Argan's arm. At that moment, Argan was already struggling to stand up. The beating with the fat stick on the way to town had visible effect on him. It was clear that he was under severe pain. Ideally, he should be taken to the clinic for examination, but I guess he was fine as long as he could walk, even though with great difficulty. Human rights and the Geneva Conventions have different meaning to different people in different places.

We scattered and headed toward our homes, determined to show up at the lorry (truck) stop the following day to bid Argan farewell, on his way to jail in the city. We had something to talk about, until we got pulled out from it by another interesting event in the future. The lorry stopped by the prison cell, so Aseel opened the cell door and led Argan out of it. Every onlooker on the ground and every passenger in the lorry was looking at Argan, who avoided eye contact at all costs. He approached the truck and climbed up with difficulty by stepping on the rear tire, then lowering himself inside. He sat down at a spot people had already vacated for him in recognition of his passenger-of-honor status. Aseel and other passengers got in the lorry, which sped off, city-bound. That was the last time I saw Argan, and I don't have much details on the nature of the prison time he had served.

Every Friday around sunset, my borough of Jabar received its weekly dose of fight between two females, Himairah and Taya, who were neighbors. The fight erupted around the same time every Friday. Alcohol sold at both households triggered these fights. All day on Fridays, local alcohol seekers flocked to both homes to drink and eat barbecued meat, most likely from stolen goats killed by Argan, the thief butcher, above. One of the women, who also happened to be Argan's sister, was the wife of Gamzut, the assistant butcher killed by the ox. As they consumed alcohol, the clients recited poems, sang folklore songs of braveries, and talked, passionately and fascinatingly, about their camels. In many cases, fights erupted and, invariably, resulted in bloodshed from beatings by stick or knife stabbing.

Around late afternoon, and once the drunken clients dragged themselves out of the houses of Himairah and Taya, the climate became conducive for a fight between the two women. Everyone in the neighborhood knew that the women drank what they had fermented, but hardly anybody understood a thing about the reasons for the fights.

The fights would start without warning. We would hear a yell from one of the women, which would be received by a spontaneous response from the other. They would be facing one another, while leaning on their straw fences, separated by a distance of one hundred yards or so. The fights, which came in the form of gruesome insults, went as follows:

Himairah: "Hey you, the daughter of a dog."
Taya: "The dog that rips your heart to pieces."
Himairah: "The gun."
Taya: "The gun that blows your head."
Himairah: "The gun that blows your intestine."
Taya: "I hope your intestine gets ripped off from your tommy."
Himairah: "And you, I hope a knife cuts your intestines to pieces."
Taya: "The blood that chokes you up."
Himairah: "I hope you drown in blood."
Taya: "I hope blood poisons your liver."
Himairah: "You and your red eyes."
Taya: "And you, I hope your eyes get smeared in red pepper."
Himairah: "And you, I hope red pepper burns your heart."
Taya: "The fire."
Himairah: "The fire that makes you and your descendants extinct."
Taya: "The fire that leaves you crippled."
Himairah: "Your bones."
Taya: "Your bones, I hope an axe smashes them."
Himairah: "And you, the axe that chops your neck."
Taya: "I hope a wooden pole pokes your eyes."
Himairah: "The poison that dries up your body."
Taya: "And you, the poison that causes you pain for the rest of your life."

Himairah: "The poison that deprives you of sleep."
Taya: "The poison that dissolves your guts."
Himairah: "I hope you lose your brain."
Taya: "Djinn."
Himairah: *"Djinn al kalaki."* (*Kalaki* is a type of djinn.)

Djinn al kalaki could be the last insult for the night. Nobody knew anything about this *kalaki* type of *djinn.* In fact we did not know a thing about normal djinn, leave alone this *kalaki* one.

I don't know if this was some form of "violent poetry" or what, and if there is such a thing as that. The women would continue this strange fight until the fall of darkness when it would abruptly end the same way it had started, and then everything would go quiet. The conflict never escalated to a fistfight. Everybody in the neighborhood heard it, but they all shunned it aside, considering it a fight between two drunken women, even though the insults were so gruesome. We got a week's break and the same scenario was repeated the following Friday.

Both Himairah and Taya had children. It was not surprising that some of their children followed on their mothers' footsteps. Taya had one daughter, Bunna, who was a first-class bully. No one could challenge her for fear of her mother. The road that led to the village market passed in front of her house. She sometimes made it impassable. I remember I was in first grade, and my brother Aziz was in second. One day we returned from school and found her waiting for us at our house. Our parents were away at the farm at that time. She demanded that we give her some sugar, but we told her we didn't have any. She left, after threatening us that she was going to tell her mother, Taya, the super bully woman. We got so scared that we hid under a bed until our parents returned home. We told them what had happened, but I don't know how they handled the situation.

Another incident took place when I was returning home from the market carrying a few grocery items. Bunna saw me passing by her house, so she appeared, obstructed my way, and said, "You, come here." I stopped, placed my items on the ground, and met my fate. We fought, ferociously, until a passerby intervened, held us apart, and ordered us to go on our separate ways. I remember she tore my clothes and roughed me up pretty bad. I held on to her hair, but I doubt it if I caused her damage as much as she did. Bunna was a couple of years older than me and she was a big and strong girl. Let me tell you something; I was not afraid of her. Oh, I take that back. I was, only, slightly afraid; besides, the man in me would not allow me to unleash my true power to fight a girl. This is just in case some of you are wondering why I was beaten up that bad by a girl.

Himairah, the other super bully woman, also had children. Two of her daughters were twins. Ironically, one of them was a bully, just like Bunna, while the other one was timid and friendly. Twins were believed to possess superpowers. The idea of two persons having photocopy images of each other was considered a miracle, far beyond anyone's imagination. No wonder people thought that they possessed supernatural capabilities. It was believed that twins could pull snakes and scorpions from under their armpits. For that reason, nobody messed with them. Himairah's twin daughters were befriended and treated with respect by children and adults alike. Ironically, Himairah, somehow, managed to send her timid twin daughter to school. She went on to graduate from college and become a prominent figure in her field.

Merchants, including my father, visited the city of Sangoor for restocking. Goods were also delivered by lorry each week. The trucks that served the region arrived on Sundays and Thursdays, carrying merchandise such as sugar, tea, oil, cloth, etc. In addition, they served as a communication medium with the city. Usually, passengers coming from the city were cleaner, better clothed, and better looking than the average person in the village. Even those who went to the city for just a couple of days looked cleaner and happier. They would have had a chance to take one or two showers while in the city because water was abundant there. They might also have had a chance to eat some fruit. Visiting the city was a big deal for me.

The borough of Keekah also supplied porters. Obviously, forklifts were unheard of. Kutal, the chief porter, and his men waited impatiently for trucks' arrival from the city to unload them. The following day, market day, Kutal and his team would happily reload the trucks with sacks of peanuts, sesame, hibiscus, sorghum, pearl millet, charcoal, gum arabica, and unprocessed leather from camel, cow, goat, and sheep skin for transportation to the city. Kutal and his team sang songs of encouragement as they worked. The songs were vulgar at times, to say the least, and would be considered harassment elsewhere, but, somehow, Kokolanders seemed not to be bothered. They were mainly sung around men.

Some men from our Kanuri tribe like Omar and Kuluso, who lived in a nearby village, also worked as porters. Kuluso was famous for winning bread-eating contests. He once ate ten loaves of bread in a single sitting. He used to brag about his strength and carrying abilities. He would lie facedown on his belly and have two-hundred-pound sack of gum arabica placed on his back, and he could still get up, unaided. He enjoyed celebrity status among Kokolanders, even though a short-lived one. I wish I could show him what bodybuilders and Scottish cabertossers could do. Soon his back, legs, and knees started to give out on him. Over time, loading and off-loading those big lorries with sacks of gum Arabica, sugar, salt, grains, etc., did take a toll on the bodies of many porters.

Business savvy female merchants travelled to Kokoland to buy inexpensive butter, live chickens, and fresh produce to take back to the city to sell at decent profit margins. Very few courageous women were engaged in trading activities. They were seen as a challenge to man's world. Wives were not supposed to engage in activities husbands did not approve of. Nothing much has changed over the years.

Water was extremely scarce in Kokoland, particularly during the dry season. I remember, the entire village used to line up every day in front of the flour mill and wait for the green Ford tanker truck, owned by the city municipality, to arrive with its valuable cargo of water for distribution. That old truck with white stripes in the front meant a lot to me. It saved our lives.

I was about five years old then, but I did take part in the stampede to secure one gallon of water, if I could. Upon sensing the arrival of the truck, many living creatures, including flies, showed up on sight to get a sip of the liquid necessary for life. Goats, chickens, and dogs competed with us at the back of the truck, where a plastic pipe poured water into different-sized containers. Considering my age and size, the container I carried was a tin gallon. I remember it was red-colored, with a Shell Oil emblem on its lid. I used to feel good about myself whenever I returned home with that container filled with water. The image, stuck in my mind, of women and children pushing their way and competing with men for water was depressing. It goes without saying that succeeding or failing in getting some depended entirely on who was the fittest. Obviously, there was not enough water for every one and many times I went home empty handed. Every day, the truck would pull away and leave many people standing there holding their empty containers, wearing blank faces, and staring into space. Worry, desperation, and hopelessness was the norm. People would reluctantly leave the place hoping for a better chance the following day. After that, several old gray donkeys with protruding ribs and hips would slowly approach the spot where the truck was parked. The process of filling the containers involved swiftly moving the big hose connected to the back of the tanker to fill up one container at a time. People pushed and shoved for position so that they could be next in line. That resulted in some water dropping and soaking into the sand. The donkeys would congregate at that spot, lower their heads, and lick the wet sand. It was a very sad sight.

Seeing images of refugees congregating around supply trucks always reminded me of my own experience fighting for a gallon of water. The sight of women and children at refugee camps stretching out their hands and begging for a piece of bread, or fighting to hand empty containers up to someone on top of a truck handing out food supplies, invoke haunting memories inside my head.

CHAPTER 5

Excessive Beating: A Preferred Tool to Advance Learning

There were two primary schools in Kokoland, one for boys, and another for girls. There were limited first grade spots to cover the entire region. Besides; the two schools had up to fourth grade. To progress to fifth grade and beyond, children would sit for exams and compete for even fewer spots at schools with higher grades in other towns. For this reason, the few children who attended school felt special. Third and fourth graders bragged about their seniority and showed it by intentionally spilling ink on their shirt pockets. It was an unspoken message to tell others about their belonging in the club reserved to those in advanced levels. That was also a way to separate themselves from first and second graders who were not allowed to write in ink. The fact remains that schooling wasn't something taken seriously by many fathers, and for this reason children easily dropped out.

In first grade, we learned the Arabic alphabet by writing in the dirt outside in the school yard. We would listen to the teacher pronounce the letters and repeat after him. Then he would walk around and show each of us how to write them in the dirt. Except for blackboard and chalk, we did not have other teaching aids. Ballpoint pens were not available then, so we used quill pens.

It was the students' duty to keep the school tidy and clean. Students in each grade were divided into six groups and each group was assigned to classroom clean-up according to a set schedule. Groups in third and fourth grades were also responsible for preparing ink and filling the inkpot on each desk hole in their respective classes. These tasks were supposed to be carried out early in the morning, before the morning assembly bell rang. Failure to adhere to this strict regimen resulted in severe flogging. Who needed that? When it was my turn to clean, I headed to school very early, then went back home to drink morning tea, put on my school uniform, and headed back to school, one more time, to attend classes.

One morning my father came to wake my brother Aziz and me to prepare for school, but my brother was nowhere to be found. My father noticed a freshly dug hole beneath our hut's door, which was made of a certain type of skinny sticks woven together. The wet dirt piled in front of the door had big paw prints on it, which led my father to believe that Aziz was taken away by a hyena. He headed to our neighbor Juku's house to ask for help. Fortunately, Aziz showed up shortly after that. No one knew he had classroom clean-up schedule that morning.

The fact that he left while it was still dark was a sign of how serious he was about his task. Those who failed to show up to clean were flogged during morning assembly. This was a daily routine, so I did not blame Aziz for sparing himself from such torture. It turned out that our neighbor Juku's big dog was the culprit in digging the hole. I heard my father say that the dog must have been after the sack of peanut seeds in the hut. It was planting season. In fact, the sack was pulled all the way to the side of the door from inside the hut, but the hole beneath the door was not wide enough to get the peanut sack through and out of the hut, so, probably, at the break of dawn, the dog abandoned the mission and went home. We never discussed the incident with my father, and I am still not sure if the culprit was the neighbor's dog or a hyena. My father might have decided not to alarm us by talking about different scenarios.

I took school very seriously, so I exerted effort needed to pass my exams and progress from one education level to the next. For example, students from more than ten elementary schools had to compete for forty five seats. It was even tougher to secure a spot in high school and college. Teachers were brutal in the way they punished students who did not do well in tests. Their rationale was that fear would make us work harder. They thought it was better for us to suffer early and relax later. That model worked for very few of us. Most of the children did not fare well at school, so many of them dropped out. In my case, leaving school meant I would face an even bleaker alternative, so I decided to stay put and ride the punishment wave.

The teachers' favorite method of helping us progress in our studies was severe flogging. For a long time, I thought flogging must be the only means of making us understand. It seemed to be the teachers' answer for every situation, whether it was motivating, cajoling, providing incentives, encouraging teamwork, or differentiating between children on the basis of learning capabilities and understanding. Karshu was typical of the children who could not take the beatings for long. He received many lashes every day because he just could not commit the poetry homework to memory and recite it in class, or do his math homework correctly. One day, he received thirty lashes, and that was the last time I saw Karshu. School wasn't meant for him. The headmaster, Mr. Jamoos, was very articulate in inventing strange ways for punishing pupils. His favorite was detaining them at school after classes. He would make them kneel on the concrete floor for hours. Primary school headmaster was the highest authority in town, so nobody dared challenge him.

One teacher, named Sir, had a farm. He planted hibiscus. During harvesttime, he would order us to return to school in the evenings and go to his house to work on pealing the hibiscus rose. It was a very painful process because the plant has some tiny thorns, which caused severe itching. Many of us were allergic to it, but when a teacher asked for some work to be done, we obeyed no matter what. I also remember another incident with the same teacher when I was in second grade. He bought a ram from the animal market in town. I happened to be around, so he called and asked me to take it to his house. I couldn't say "no I can't do it." I used the one technique known for directing the movement of goats and sheep. It involved grabbing and holding the back legs, lifting them up chest level, then pushing the animal forward, forcing it to walk with its front legs. It was a big ram, so I was not able to lift and push it for more than a few feet. It took me over an hour or so to get to the house, which was a matter of half a kilometer from the animal market. Parents did not help much. There was an old proverb occasionally used by parents who took their children to traditional schools to study at the hands of holy men. Their message to holy men connotes, "The meat is yours, and the bone is mine." In other words, they were saying, "Feel free to beat the child into learning." They gave them full power to punish the children in any form they deemed fit. Today, there are fewer beatings at both regular and traditional schools, but, on the other hand, there are widespread child neglect and abuses caused by violence, wars, and poverty.

The condition at school was so bad that many children ran away and never returned. Some concerned fathers dealt with the situation at home by whipping their children pretty badly before escorting them to school and handing them to teachers who whipped them a fresh. Whenever you saw a child being accompanied by an adult, riding a donkey, and heading to school during the week, you knew that child was in deep trouble. Not only would he be punished, but also labeled as a "runner." That meant the entire school would keep an eye on him in case he once again decided to run away.

Unfortunately, there were no bathrooms at the school. Students, especially those who lived at the boarding house, had to go behind the shrubs out in the fields beyond the school fence. The area north of the school was completely polluted, rendering it unfit for anything. However, having to go beyond the school's boundaries gave runners a perfect opportunity to escape. It also presented an equally valuable opportunity for the rest of the children to entertain themselves. The moment a child takes off running away from school, the rest of the children would chase after him like hounds chasing after a fox. Once caught, the runner would be dragged back to school, while screaming, pulling, and kicking to free himself. His catchers would finally hand him over to a teacher, who would flog him severely to deter him from running again. Many determined runners put up with the punishment they received at both ends, home and school, and ran away, anyway, until the parties (school and parents) grew tired and gave up on them.

There were three children notorious for running away from school. Sheikh was one of them. Once, he ran to his village. His father, who had a very weak eyesight, put him on the back of a donkey and took him back to school just around sunset. At the gate, Sheikh slid off the donkey and took off running in his village's direction. The children's screams alerted the father. Angry and embarrassed, the old man left the school and went back to his village. We never heard from him or his son again. To the envy of many runners, Sheikh finally succeeded in staying home.

The decision about returning a child to school belonged to the father. If he happened to be out of town, by the time he returned home, the child would have been away from school for some time. The longer the absence, the greater the chance of dropping out of school.

In my case, I never thought about running away. My father frequently talked about the importance of attending school, just in case I had different ideas. For that reason, any attempt by me to test his seriousness would have been futile and could have probably resulted in flogging, something I did my best to avoid, even though unsuccessfully in a few cases.

My primary school in Kokoland (1967 – 1970). It is clear that conditions have deteriorated over the years. Photo 2016.

My nephew Sarky also used to run away from school. Sarky was particularly renowned for biting anyone trying to capture him. He was wild. The last of the three notorious runners was my cousin Tijani, who lived with his parents in a village about three miles from Kokoland. When he was school age, his father brought him to town to attend school. The boarding school was a place Tijani did not find appealing. I guess he must have thought that it was not normal for children his age to be living on their own, taking care of themselves, and doing stuff such as washing their own clothes. Tijani ran away from school a lot, but his father was relentless in returning him.

Despite receiving his due share of punishment, he was not deterred from running away. Obviously, for him the benefits of being at home outweighed those at school. At home, there was enough food and he had full freedom to do whatever pleased him. Tijani thought that there was no point in running home only to be returned to school. He finally decided to stay away from both school and home, choosing instead to go "wild." The last time he ran away from school was during the rainy season. His village was surrounded by a dense forest. He decided to take refuge there. The school authorities thought that his father had given up on him and decided not to bring him to school anymore. On the other hand, his father thought he was at school and that he had given up running away. Tijani enjoyed his newly found freedom living in the forest for a month or so. He would spend the entire daytime there and sneak into the village at night after everyone had gone to sleep. He would sleep in a deserted hut by the edge of the village, known to be harboring a cobra. He was lucky he never encountered the deadly snake. At dawn, before people woke up for early morning prayers, he would quietly leave the village and return to his beloved forest.

A woman in the village, named Akilah, found out about Tijani's secret, but decided not to reveal it to anyone, not even to his parents. According to her, forcing a child to attend school was cruel and inhumane. After all, as far as she was concerned, school was forbidden (*haraam*) anyway, so why should anyone be forced to go there? Schooling was an infidels' idea, and she could not understand why Tijani's parents took him there. Not only did Akilah keep Tijani's secret to herself, but she helped him enjoy a comfortable life in the wilderness. After sunset, she would sneak out of the village in search of the boy. Once she got out of sight and satisfied herself that no one could hear her, she would call out for him. Tijani would then emerge from behind a bush or a shrub, first revealing his head. After making sure Akilah was the one calling his name, he would respond by saying, "Ya," just loud enough for her to know his whereabouts. She would bring him food, usually a bowl of porridge and okra soup. That was takeout in style. She would sit on the dirt and wait patiently for Tijani to finish eating his one-course meal. The woman would then pick the empty bowl and, without saying a word, head back to the village. She would repeat the same ritual the following evening. Drinking water was not a problem for Tijani because there were many ponds around the area.

It was the rainy season, so everybody in the village left, shortly after sunrise, for work on nearby farms and stayed there until the afternoon. That gave Tijani an opportunity to sneak into the village. He would go straight to his house and look for food to replenish his body energy. One meal a day was not enough. After eating, he would sleep until it was about time people returned from the farms, then he would go back to the forest, only to repeat the same scenario the next day. His mother noticed something strange happening in the house. Food was going missing from her cooking pots. She also noticed the presence of marks on the bottom of the pots that looked as though someone had dragged little fingers to scrape food residue from the pots. The marks looked as if they were left behind by a child. "But, in God's name, who could have done this?" She asked herself. She told her husband about it, so they decided to find out. One day, they stayed behind at home. Sure enough, as soon as Tijani thought the last person had left the village, he snuck into the house and went straight to the *Tukul* (small cooking hut) looking for food. That was when his parents closed in on him and stood by the hut's door. *Tukuls* don't have windows, so Tijani was trapped. His father, with a whip in his hand, told him to get in front of him and follow the trail to school. For the entire distance of three miles, every time he slowed down, his father caught up and whipped him across his back.

After each lashing, Tijani would jog faster to create a gap between them. It took only a few yards before his father caught up and gave him another lash. They got to school and headed straight to where the teachers were gathered. Tijani received his last lash, which forced him to poke a hole in the straw shade and push his body through. He appeared suddenly in front of the teachers, who sprang to their feet, ready to flee. Needless to say, he also received punishment from the teachers. That was the last time Tijani ran away from school. It was finally obvious to him that it was not worth running anymore. In fact, Tijani stayed put at school, progressed, and graduated from college.

CHAPTER 6

Elvis Presley Mistaken for Yuri Gagarin

Information about what was happening around the world was scarce in Kokoland. My father was one of the first to own a Philips transistor radio. It was a huge box (2' × 2' × 2') standing on four legs. People sat around it and listened to programs broadcast from the capital. I had no idea how the radio worked, but my father's explanation that there was a man inside did not add up either. By the late 1960s, small radios replaced those big and bulky ones. My father bought me one, which became my window to the outside world. It was one of the best gifts I ever received, and it was instrumental in transforming my life. The radio provided valuable information about a world I could only imagine.

The signal was relatively strong in the mornings and evenings. The evenings were of special interest to me because of the wider range of radio stations available, including Radio Monte Carlo, the BBC Radio, and Radio Voice of America, which, in particular, played a pivotal role in shaping my future. I used to look forward to 7:00 p.m., when I could listen to foreign programs. I would place my bed in the front yard and wait patiently for sunset. I would lie down facing the star-filled sky and listen to the radio. I would roam between stations, depending on what programs were being broadcast. I knew all the schedules by heart. BBC broadcast political affairs in Africa, which I knew something about. I relied on Voice of America for news about issues outside of my world. I did not understand most of the topics because my vocabulary was limited and my knowledge of what was happening around the world was near zero. At that time, I had never been to the city. Of course, you need to bear in mind that the word city is a relative term. I found the program about listeners' requests for Western music especially entertaining, even though I did not know who those singers were, or in which language they sang.

Radio Monte Carlo brought a different type of joy and entertainment. The way the female broadcasters talked was angelic and heavenly. They always left me wondering how they looked. I knew, for sure, that our village women did not sound like them. While I lie there, listening to the stations, I would create my own imaginary world, building on what I had heard. Most nights, I would go to sleep without switching off the radio; a task that my father happily rendered on my behalf. Dry batteries were very expensive.

We had a neighbor, named Sammane, who owned a shop in the market. He had no children, so he sometimes relied on me to bring him lunch from home or take his donkey back to his house when he returned from his farm. He was never happy with my free service. He expressed his anger by trying to beat me anytime I got close to him. Once, he sent me to get his torch (flashlight). He thought I was late and tried to slap me on the head, but I dodged his blow. I learned to keep my distance. You might expect me to have gone and complained to my father, but I did not.

The only time Sammane showed any satisfaction with my free service was one day when his niece Razinah frantically called for me to come to their house, which was separated from ours by a straw fence. I came running, and she told me to rush to the market and tell her uncle Sammane that a boa snake was inside the cooking hut, swallowing the chickens. I flew to the market to tell him. We both hurried back to the house, where he grabbed his shotgun and shot the snake. It was a large yellow snake, about eight feet or so, with a bulged belly from the chicken it had just swallowed. It was customary for dead snakes to be taken out of the village to be placed on top of ant-mound. I called my friend Tiffah to help me do that. Word about the incident spread in the village, providing fertile ground for superstitions and rumors. Some suggested that it was a spirit, or djinn, because boas had no business being in the village. Others said someone who wanted to harm Sammane must have sent it. The fact that it was hiding in the kitchen hut, hunting down the chickens, was a matter of buying time until nightfall, when it would convert into a djinn an attack Sammane. Someone asked me if we had destroyed the snake's eyes after dropping it at the ant-hill. When I told him we did not, he said Tiffah and I should brace ourselves for an attack from the snake's relatives. He said they would be looking for it all night. Once they find it, they would look into its eyes, which would show images of the person(s) who killed it. They would copy the images into their own eyes, then look for the culprits and bite them to death. These peculiar ideas might have come from brains that could have learned to program computers, but it was a different era and place. Obviously, we did not have *National Geographic* magazine or television channels to inform us what boas could and could not do.

We did not sleep much that night, as you can imagine. The very first thing Tiffah and I did in the morning was to head out to the ants mound. To our relief, we found that the snake's flesh was gone. All that left was a curled-up skeleton. We wondered if the snake's relatives had come and stored images from its eyes before the ants consumed its flesh. For some time I was bothered by the thoughts of that snake. I worried that its relatives continued searching for it. I imagined them everywhere. I looked in every direction when I walked Kokoland alleys and avoided venturing out at night. Unfortunately, we could not talk to adults about our fears because they were the primary source of these types of irrationalities. Besides; they believed in them even more than we children did. There was no hope.

Sammane died soon after that incident. He rode his donkey on one hot summer day and went to inspect a piece of land he was preparing to farm. He had a full blown heat stroke, which led to his death. Some people were quick to attribute his death to the boa incident, exclaiming "what heat stroke?

An incident that took place a few months earlier with Sammane connoted qualities of bravery. Sadly, he did not live long enough to enjoy fame. People in Kokoland spoke about Sammane riding his donkey home from a faraway village. It was around sunset, and he was crossing a dense forest when he noticed a man following him from a distance. Whenever he slowed down or stopped the donkey, the man would do the same and hide behind a tree. He was certain that the man was planning to rob him once it got dark. Sure enough, after sunset, the man caught up with Sammane and demanded that he give him the money he was supposedly carrying. Sammane stopped the donkey. He then turned around, raised his hand, pointed a dark object he was holding in the man's direction, and shouted, "I swear by the name of Allah, if you make any move, I will blow your head to pieces. Move and walk in front of me." The man did exactly what he was told. When they reached Kokoland, Sammane ordered him to head straight to Dallami the local judge's house.

At the judge, Sammane dropped the black object supposedly resembling a gun that he used to threaten the robber. The judge, upon closely examining the object with his flashlight, found out that it was a front leg of a dead goat. It turned out that the robber was Ringam, a Kokoland resident known to everyone in town. Even though Sammane refused to press charges against him, the damage was already done. Ringam just could not continue living in Kokoland when every man, woman, and child knew him for being threatened with a leg bone from a dead goat. The incident represented an inexhaustible reservoir of anti-Ringam derogatory song material for the village girls to draw from, for eternity. There was no place for Ringam in Kokoland, so he absconded from the village for good. It was rumored that he did try to return to the village after many years. One day, he wanted to sneak back without getting spotted, so he waited in the outskirt of the village for sunset. To his bad luck, Tiris, a hearing-impaired man, saw him as he was returning from his farm. He recognized him, even though Ringam was hiding his face with his turban, except for his eyes and nose, so he ran up to him. He raised his right hand above his head and created a repetitive snapping sound with his thumb and middle finger to remind Ringam of an event that has taken place a long time ago. Using sign language, he said to him, "Aren't you the coward man threatened by Sammane with a leg of a dead goat, a long time ago?" Ringam thought to himself, "There is no hope," turned around, and left. That encounter sealed every plans he had for returning to Kokoland to live a normal life. People didn't believe Tiris, but he swore by the name of Allah that he saw Ringam, recognized him, and spoke to him in person, before he ran away. Naturally, Tiris used sign language to swear, just in case you are wondering.

Sammane did not live long after his encounter with Ringam to enjoy fame for his bravery. My father took me to visit him in the hospital, and that was the last time I saw Sammane. I have lasting memories of the man, both good and bad. Just a week or so before his fatal stroke, he and my father moved out of Jabar, our neighborhood, to another part of Kokoland closer to the market. We were neighbors again. Many people in the village believed that Sammane's new house was haunted. It was known for unexplained deaths of its residents. Sammane was the latest casualty. As you can tell, we had all sorts of causes for death that could be anything, but scientific explanations such heat stroke.

I remember, Sammane and his senior wife, Zohoor, frequently visited doctors in cities as far as Khartoum for fertility treatment. They were not successful, so Sammane took his second wife, Haninah, but with her too, he was unsuccessful. Rumors got to Kokoland that the waters of a geyser that erupted near the city of Gadharif, in Eastern Sudan, had miraculous healing powers. People believed that it could heal the sick and the disabled, regardless of the nature of the sickness or disability. Thousands of people from all over the country descended on the geyser seeking treatment. Sammane and his senior wife Zohor were among them. Soon the place became a source of waterborne diseases from contamination, and many sick people picked up additional sicknesses. The government intervened and closed down the geyser.

Gagarin was our village's John Travolta. He worked for Sammane, selling water. He operated a water tanker pulled by a horse. His horse was a valuable source of hair for our bird traps, so we maintained an excellent relationship with Gagarin. We never told him we pulled hair out of his horse's tail, but we thought a good relationship with him would prevent him from complaining to my father or, most importantly, Sammane, if he found out. Gargarin's water tanker carried over sixty gallons. He used to spend the whole day running trips to and from the water reservoir about three miles away. He had a well-built body, which we attributed to his special daily diet of dates, milk, and ghee (butter). He had come from the city, so he could have been lifting weight, but I doubt it if at that time anybody in Kokoland knew what weight lifting was.

Gagarin's true name was Awadh. The name could have come from someone who had been following world affairs. He might have come across the word Gagarin in the news, liked it, nicknamed Awadh after it, and the rest of us in the village followed. This is what village people do. Believe it or not, there were trend setters in Kokoland. The Russian astronaut Yuri Gagarin orbited the planet Earth in 1961, but that information did not get to the village until several years later. All we knew was that Gagarin was an international celebrity, but we did not really know why he was famous. To show respect for his celebrity status in the village, we decided to bestow that famous name, Gagarin, on Awadh, who was famous for being an excellent dancer.

Whenever Gagarin danced, he twisted and shook his body. He was famous for keeping perfect rhythm. Somehow, we confused Yuri Gagarin with Elvis Presley. As children, we had no idea who the two men were, anyway. We very much trusted our elders' knowledge, assuming that they knew better. Years later, I found out that Elvis Presley, the king of rock and roll, was also a dancer, so I was able to connect the dots. Awadh must have seen Elvis dancing in a movie theater in the city, copied his moves, and demonstrated them to us in the village. I doubt it if anybody else in the village ever knew the connection. Growing up in a remote village, then later finding out how different it was from the rest of the world, can make you unsure about many things you have been told. You would constantly be verifying information, asking yourself questions, and wondering what else you thought you knew, but it might be wrong.

Nevertheless, Awadh Gagarin was a great source of entertainment for the village because he was unconventional. Normally, people performed their different tribal dances at weddings, but, with Gangarin in our village, things were about to change.

The post-harvest season, October to January, was the time for celebrations. Revenue earned from selling farm produce was spent on weddings, buying clothes, or securing a newer model of transportation; a faster donkey. Village wedding celebrations were special events. Any family planning a wedding could ask Zumbah, the café owner, in advance, if they could borrow his crooked benches the night of the wedding. The benches would be lined up in an open yard and reserved for the elders and village dignitaries. Mats made with palm leaves would be spread out on the ground in front of the benches for women and girls to sit on. The center of the mats were usually reserved for village divas such as Um Shol and other singers and drummers. The boys had no special place to go. We would be roaming around everywhere until someone ordered us to sit on the dirt in one place so we would not spoil the party.

Parties began with people flocking to the wedding place. Guests were received by household members and family friends, who would invite them to take a meal. Men would be seated on the dirt in circles, in groups of five or six. A flat metal plate, about two feet in diameter, containing food, would be placed in the center of the circle. When they finish eating, we, children, would hand them soap and pour water on their hands to help them wash. After that they would walk to Zumbah, who would be standing behind a table. A kerosene lantern would be placed on one side of the table, and an open plate and a glass jar on the other side. The plate and the jar were there to drop in them coin and bank note contributions. The coins were kept in the plate and the notes were stuffed inside the glass jar to keep them from getting blown away by wind. Zumbah's brother Abdullah would be sitting beside him, with a pen and a notebook placed in front of him. That was the "moment of truth" when men paid their social dues and debts owed to the wedding family. It was an open court where community members received instantaneous judgment about how generous or miserly they were. The women would be sitting on the mats, observing and taking note of the tiniest of details. Men would reach into their pockets and take out their wallets, which were usually made from unprocessed goatskin. They would take out whatever they had decided to contribute and hand it to Zumbah, who would yell, "Shooooobash!" at the top of his lungs to draw everyone's attention. After that, he would start calling out each man's name and his contribution. After every one of Zumbah's announcements, the women would yell in one voice.

The women yelled by holding the thumb and the index fingers together. They would raise their hand closer to their lips and produce a "Yooooi" sound that was repeated many times in a span of just few seconds. The sound was made by breathing out while vibrating the throat.

There was a correlation between the length and the loudness of the yelling, and the amount of the contribution each man made. The longer and louder, the better, so it could be a source of pride for the man, or an utter embarrassment, if it was a subdued and short *yooooi* yelling. The women remembered how much each man paid. Special attention was given to men who made their contributions in coins. They received a barely audible yelling, a sign of disrespect as well as disapproval. To some people, these events represented passports that allowed them to marry up and climb the social ladder. Others were demoted for good. Abdullah would record each contributor's name and the amount he gave. Later in the night, when contributions drew to a halt, he would total the numbers and give the final figure to Zumbah, who would yell, "Shooooobash!" for the last time. He would then announce the total amount contributed that night, drawing a prolonged yelling from the women. The men would start whispering to each other, debating which wedding in the village raised the highest amount of money that season, compared to previous ones.

My wife could be the first woman to yell in public here in America. She once yelled at an event in an indoor stadium at Texas A&M University when our son won a triple-jump tournament. She screamed her yell without any advance notice, scaring the hell out of people around her. I saw some of them reaching out for their cell phones to dial 911 before realizing that there was no real danger. One man standing next to her told her that he liked her yell and asked if she could do it again. When he told my wife that he didn't think he could yell, I intervened and told him not to even try because yelling is an activity reserved for women, only. Men who try to do it, even jokingly, will forever embarrass their families.

My wife yelled for the second time when her presidential candidate won the elections. It was around midnight when the results were announced. She was very loud, and I think our close neighbors must have heard her. I told her that people do not know what to make out of her yell, so she had better stop doing that, and she agreed. That promise is holding so far, but I doubt if it will last for long. I am certain that someday she will get excited about something else and will yell again.

As the elders ate and prepared for celebration, we children roamed the area aimlessly. We made sure that we carried around sticks to protect ourselves when the inevitable fights broke out for no known reasons. The kerosene lanterns helped us forget our boredom. They were borrowed from shop owners after closing their businesses for the night. We were attracted to them the same way as moths and other insects that hovered around them. Because there was no electricity, those lanterns could make or break the celebrations, so the wedding organizers heavily guarded them. However, we took our chances and circled around them. We could not resist doing that for two reasons. First, the nights were usually cold, and we sought the warmth from the heat emitted by the burning kerosene. Second, the lanterns were made of a ball of bright, reflective silver-colored, metal. Mirrors were scarce in the village, so we used the lanterns to view our crooked and elongated faces. We also amused ourselves by stretching out our tongues, widening our eyes, and making other silly behaviors. We would get so captivated by the lantern that we would totally forget about the guard, who would be walking around carrying a thin and flexible tree branch to use as a whip. By bending over and bringing our faces closer to the lantern, we risked exposing our backs. The guard had to make a split-second decision. Should he hit one of us on the back with the whip and risk knocking down the lantern, plunging the place into darkness and putting an end to all the festivities?, or should he simply shout and chase us away?

Chasing us had proven to be ineffective because we always returned and raised the risk of knocking down the lantern as we jockeyed for the limited space around it. Therefore, the guards, usually, preferred to use the whip on the low hope that we would be scared, so we would stay away.

After tallying the contributions and judging the men and their merits, it would be time for partying. That usually started with local songs, which appealed to everyone in the village. Young men would start exhibiting their dancing skills to score points against peers and, most importantly, to draw girls' attention. At that time, someone would shout, "Where is Gaga?" (This was Awadh Gagarin's shortened nickname.) People would start looking in all directions for Gaga, who by then would be standing nonchalantly in a dark corner, intentionally shying away from the limelight. Another man would call out, "Gaga, where are you? Come over and show us your arts" Initially, Gaga would object to dancing when people approach and beg him to do so. They would grab his arms and try to lead him into the dance floor. He would resist by leaning backward, trying to free himself from the many men surrounding him and holding on to both arms. They would arbitrate for a few minutes until Gaga got satisfied that all attention was on him. Then, he would agree and slowly emerge from his dark corner, just enough for his presence to be noticed by the women, who would be quiet and waiting for him to take over the arena. More people would congregate around him, insisting that he got down to the center. Having reaffirmed his social and celebrity status, he would slowly walk toward the women who would start drumming to produce rhythms for songs synonymous with him; Gaga. Next, they would start singing those songs especially reserved for him. Although the rhythms were similar to those in Elvis Presley's songs, as I found out later, the words were definitely local. Awadh usually wore crisply ironed elegant, but very tight, pants, short-sleeved white shirts, and polished black pairs of shoes; clothing that was uncommon as well as unattainable to almost all of us in the village. He warmed up by alternately tapping the front of his shoes against the floor, maintaining a strict rhythm. Once he secured the crowd's full attention, he went into action.

The whole crowd would be ready for a spectacular show, including Maryood and his friend Sandah, who could have been drowning themselves in local drinks the whole day in preparation for the party. By the time they showed up at parties, they would be awash with alcohol. We always wondered how they managed to make it to the party venues, in the first place. They would usually stand by each other's side, barely maintaining their balances. They would repeatedly lean forward and backward every few seconds. Sometimes they would fall facedown or on their backs when they had consumed alcohol beyond their tipping points. Their eyes took ages to open and shut. They would be looking deep into the crowd, but seeing absolutely nothing. They would occasionally start fighting with themselves by talking hostilely to no one in particular.

The situation would quickly turn into a fight directed at anything in front of them, be that a person, a table, a tree, or nothing. It really did not matter much to them. At that time, two men would approach from behind and wrap their arms around them and hold them tightly. That way, Maryood and Sandah could both be led away from the party grounds to their respective huts without being able to resist or swing blows in all directions. They would start snoring in a matter of seconds. In the morning, they would have zero recollection of what had happened the night before. That was how party organizers could stop party crashers like Maryood and his friend Sandah from spoiling once in a while precious party moments that we all waited for impatiently.

Gaga went into action by leaning forward. He would battement one leg to the front while keeping it slightly bent. He would also keep one arm dangling loosely by his side, while stretching the other arm forward, with the hand bent and the fingers pointing downward. He would make a head gesture you would imagine he was looking down, but, in fact, his eyes looked straight into the horizon. They pierced through the standing crowd and beyond. At that moment, Gaga would be "spirit ridden," a phrase we commonly used to refer to anyone behaving abnormally. Next, the women would beat the drums, even louder, producing Gaga's favorite rhythms. He would respond in style. He would start shaking his legs and hips, while maintaining a strict rhythm. It took me over twenty years to find out that Gaga's moves were Elvis's. He was perfect in every move he made, exactly copying Elvis, except for the head and eye movements. Gaga was a black man and his hair was naturally Afro, so swift movements to his head did not produce corresponding movements to his hair. You might have rightfully guessed that he did not have blue eyes. Gaga was both talented and lucky. His face was riddled with tiny round scars indicative of having survived anthrax. Rumors circulated in the village talked about the low survival rate of people who got infected with anthrax. It was believed that the few lucky ones who survive it would go on to become very famous. Gaga was one of them.

When Gaga shook his hips and legs, some people expressed disbelief, while others read prayers. Yet, other people who visibly looked worried, commented that it was a sign of the end of times, as predicted by the ancestors, when men danced like women. Almost everyone wore local clothing made of *baft* cotton. Traditionally, men wore a long robe or shirt (called *jellabiya*) that hung to the ground. Wearing pants was generally considered a "womanly" behavior and was not acceptable. Men dancing while wearing pants was also unacceptable. Shaking the legs while wearing skinny pants that revealed the body's contours, especially a man's buttocks, was like the straw that broke the camel's back. Only women were allowed to shake and dance with their hips and buttocks. In some places, males wearing pants aren't allowed to lead prayers, even today. Some people thought Gaga had brought a curse upon the village. Elders and conspiracy theorists went as far as spreading rumors that he had been sent by people in the city to change the village's way of life and cultural fabric. Others thought he was a phenomenon that must be confronted and fought against. Those village conservatives thought Gaga's behavior was anti-establishment and outright blasphemous. However, if what he was doing was so bad, why were people there watching him in the first place? Truthfully, everyone enjoyed Gaga's show very much. He was the best thing in town. Years later, while living in San Francisco Bay area, I read a little about Elvis's time and about the hippie subculture and events that took place in Berkley during the 1960s. Gaga was instrumental in bringing some of that to Kokoland.

The village women provided Gaga with several different beats, and he danced to their tunes. We gave names like "twist," "jerk," and "horse" to some of the beats. We gave these names without knowing what they really meant and whether people elsewhere used the same names. I found out much later that other people performed these dances by twisting the body, shaking and jerking around, and jumping up and down. It was natural that the village elders expressed concern about Gagarin's influence, because these types of body movements were not normally known or used for expressing feelings and emotions. This imported American culture was just too much for Kokoland.

Awadh Gagarin crowned the nights with one special last performance. He would bend his knees, lean his body backward until the back of his head touched the ground, then reversed his move until he stood up on his feet again. He never lost his balance. We attributed Awadh's flexibility to his nightly ration of dates, milk, and butter. Some young men tried to copy Awadh's moves but failed miserably. There was a huge difference between being an athletic city boy who has had exposure to foreign movies and Elvis Presley's moves, and being a country bumpkin.

Even though Awadh Gagarin did not orbit the earth like Yuri Gagarin, he did orbit Kokoland with his cart selling water. Most importantly, he played an instrumental role in transforming Kokoland into appreciating the art that he introduced. He laid down a solid platform for many Kokolanders to appreciate music, dancing, and fashion, the Kokoland way. Gagarin inspired me to raise questions about what else existed outside of Kokoland that I did not know of. He helped me set out on a journey to find out.

In one of the village parties, Jidairi showed up drunk as usual and carrying his WWI shotgun. He could hardly walk. He went straight to the center of the dance ground, and people immediately started praying, for obvious reasons of course. Jidairi raised the gun ready to fire, but it jammed as was the case most of the times. He lowered it down, bringing the trigger closer to his face to tamper with it into functioning. At that point, the gun barrel was about the level of people's heads. The safest thing to do was to flee the scene. People bent down to lower their bodies as close as possible to the ground, but their effort trying to avoid getting accidentally shot by Jidairi was compromised by the very fact that Jidairi himself was a very short man, and hence closer to the ground. With their behinds facing the women and girls sitting on mats on the center, they scattered in all directions. Men were supposed to be brave and stand in the face of danger to protect their women at any cost. That night many men decided to forego bravery for another night. Some women covered their faces with their *saris*, when others covered their ears with their hands. One of the party organizers stepped forward to help Jidairi, just in case he lost his balance. You might wonder why Kokolanders put up with all this risk. This was because very few people in the village owned shotguns, and Jidairi was one of them. Owning a gun propelled a man into a celebrity status. In addition, the number of gun blasts during a wedding party was a statement about the social status of the people getting married. Drunken Jidairi with an unreliable shotgun in hand was a recipe for a major disaster, but, despite that, people were ready to put up with it.

Finally, Jidairi managed to fire his gun. The blast caused an instantaneous eruption of howling of every single dog in the village. Pigeons escaped from their holes and flew overhead, mingling up in the sky with birds that took off from nearby trees. They knew that they were in an imminent danger, so they frantically changed directions before disappearing into the dark sky. The number of shots fired was one of the indicators of the success or failure of the wedding. People also took pride in the number of gun owners who showed up at their wedding. Luckily, we never had an incident until automatic guns such as AK-47s were introduced. After that, there were many tragic incidents resulting from misuse of automatic guns because people did not understand how to operate machine guns.

After each gun blast, the women yelled like crazy. The gun blast, coupled with the yelling, drove the dogs even farther away. For Kokoland dogs, guns brought pain and suffering, and every shot fired might mean death of a member of the dog community. Older dogs seemed to have a way of telling their puppies some tragic stories about guns because younger dogs screamed louder and for a longer time. I don't blame them. Whenever word spread in the village about a particular dog with rabies, a police officer from the city was dispatched to deal with the situation. People knew that a bite from a sick dog required an immediate medical attention of fourteen injections around the belly button. Such medical service was available only in the city. There were also records of people bitten by sick dogs, but they failed to seek help. They ended up catching rabies, which led to their deaths. Unfortunately, the process of tackling the problem of sick dogs involved the killing of healthy dogs that just happened to be in the wrong place and time. Some dogs were known all over town for being very aggressive. They guarded their houses, literally, with their teeth, preventing people, especially children, from passing. After each police campaign, they would become timid and appeasing people. That would be the case for some time until they forget all about the police gun ordeal and revert to their old aggressive behavior.

The police officer's gun blasts would lead many dogs to escape from the village to take refuge in the forest until the campaign subsided or hunger drove them back into the village. Some dogs would resort to desperate measures to hide themselves, be that inside huts, any hut, or seeking protection from people even when they were strangers. During one of these campaigns, a dog ran right inside our classroom when class was in session. It was a life-and-death situation. After the campaigns, children were the ones charged with the responsibility of dragging the dead dogs to the outskirts of the village to burn the bodies. I must admit that the whole operation of hunting down sick dogs was very cruel and inhumane.

One evening my father walked home from the shop and showed us his right leg, which was covered in blood and had a big chuck of flesh dangling from it. He told us that he had been bitten by Harira's dog, which had rabies. Luckily, the following day was a market day and there was a truck leaving to the city, so he managed to get there in good time for treatment. My younger brother Halim also got bitten by our neighbor Sammane's dog. Although the dog was not sick, it was known for being extremely aggressive. When it attacked and bit another child named Suleiman, Sammane's nephew, Muaz, shot and killed it.

Over time, some village teenagers picked up few moves form Awadh. They sometimes came out of their shells and danced side by side with Awadh in the center of the dance floor. They were the next generation to carry the torch. Some young men like Kheir did well and impressed us all, whereas others like Karfa were disastrous. Bad dancing cost dancers dearly as their image in girls' eyes would be demoted to junk status. Karfa committed many blunders, which made it very difficult for him to shake off the stigma of being flat. In fact the village girls officially called him "Mr. Flat". Karfa overestimated his dancing skills and made the mistake of his life by sharing the floor with Gaga. He was a young man who had no rhythms whatsoever, leave aside competing with Gaga. Karfa's reputation was dealt a fatal blow.

You must remember that Kokoland girls were scarce and illusive as well as being night creatures like bats. Village parties were the only thing that drew them out of their homes. As such, some of us went to a great extent to harness attention from them whenever a brief window of opportunity presented itself. This was very relevant to the case of our friend Karfa. He concluded that enough time had passed and people had forgotten about the embarrassment he had caused himself sharing the dance floor with Gaga. He decided to do something about it to regain his confidence during one of the parties, which were hard to come by.

The sweat from the girls' hands beating on the goatskin drum would make it dull and low in sound. To remedy the situation, we would rub the drum surface with sand, which absorbed the moisture. Then the drum would be exposed to low temperature to tighten the skin surface. It would be lowered on a lantern to trap the heat emitted inside the drum, but not too low to cause the lantern to go out from lack of oxy-

Goatskin drum used by Kokoland girls.

gen. It was important that it stayed lit, or there would be no party that night. It was a delicate process that required someone with the right skills. Karfa, in a desperate attempt to regain recognition from the girls, volunteered to heat the drum. He had no previous experience doing that, so he decided to try it his own way.

Perhaps he wanted to invent an ingenious new way for heating drums. That way he would impress everyone, but especially the girls whom he desperately wanted to please. Karfa picked up the drum from the girls, flipped it upside down, and placed the skin-side about one inch away from the lantern. Few seconds later, we heard a cracking sound. We all looked in Karfa's direction and saw him holding one half of the drum in each hand. It was simply too much heat for the drum to bear, and the laws of physics took care of the rest. With no drum, the party was over before it got started. Many people looked down at the ground, searching for an open space to spit, a sign of utter disgust. Others cursed him, his ancestors, and the day he was born. That was the only drum the village had that night. It was purchased from the city especially for that occasion. We returned to our respective homes, dragging our feet with disappointment. Those party gatherings were the only chance we had for mingling with girls to show off.

Karfa was the type of person who never repents from his sins. He was notorious for repeating the same mistakes. During the following school holiday, he came up with a different idea. We were gathered at a party place when he suddenly stood up and asked everyone to be quiet. He moved closer to the lantern and removed a piece of paper from his pocket. Murmuring engulfed the whole place. People lowered their heads in disappointment and gazed at the ground, as if looking for a tiny coin that they had dropped on the sand, which required a lot of concentration to spot. Poor Karfa had a talent for ruining parties. He began to tell us about his journey by train to the capital, Khartoum, and he would like to share that amazing experience with us. As he read from the paper, people started to desert the place. Upon finishing his story, he reached into his pocket and pulled out a second paper, which, he said, contained classical Arabic poetry. He continued to read from it until very few people remained.

They stared at him in silence, but with visible disgust. Bear in mind that many people in Kokoland were not educated. The vast majority of them had not even attended first grade; besides, Arabic was not their mother tongue. So, obviously, understanding and appreciating poetry written in classical Arabic was a long shot. The whole thing was a fiasco. Karfa was a victim of a system that promoted elitism. It was not surprising that he did not know when, where, and how to practice it, if at all. Kokoland, certainly, was not the place for that.

As I mentioned earlier, children's presence at parties was considered by adults as a source of annoyance because they listened to no rules and ran all over the place. Their absence was preferable, but they showed up anyway. The party organizers stood guard holding whips, ready to handle children who got out of control. They whipped the backs of unlucky children, with such enthusiasm.

I remember how my friends and I used to take risks and hurry to where the women and girls were sitting. We would stand there just long enough to perform *abishri*, once or twice, then run away before someone whipped our skinny backs. *Abishri* was carried out by holding tightly together the thumb, the pinky, the ring finger, and the middle finger, while keeping the index finger loose. You would then raise your hand in front of you, slightly above your face, and drop it down fast, as though hitting something. This sudden move would bring down your index finger slamming onto the four fingers being held together, producing a cracking sound. That was our way of expressing interest in girls. We would walk up to the girl of interest and perform *abishri* a few times over her head.

In contrast to women yelling to express happiness during weddings, men's response to grand events was giving a very loud scream, called *rorai*, which surprisingly resembles the word roaring. Besides performing *rorai* during weddings, men did it at other events such as the birth of a male child. Sadly, in Kokoland, the delivery of girls went by silently.

Abishri was a very risky business because rejection was abundant. I have seen many instances when young men's night was totally ruined because their *abishri* performance was not well received by their girls of interest. Their efforts went by without getting the loud yelling of approval. As far as I was concerned, being a young boy, my presence or absence at parties did not make much of a difference, for nobody took notice of what I did anyway. I was nothing more than an object that moved around and obstructed views. One day, I gathered courage and decided to perform *abishri*. I waited until the girls started singing a nice song with good rhythms. I targeted one girl, then I stepped forward. I held my stick in one hand and prepared my other hand's fingers to perform *abishri*. I always carried a stick, which I used in case I encountered a stray dog on my way home after the party, but most importantly, I needed it if some children decided to pick up a fight, which was not uncommon. A stick in hand was a deterrent, so kids left you alone.

I walked toward my target girl, with my eyes glued to her, while keeping immaculate rhythms in total sync with the drumbeats. I was halfway on my journey when I noticed that the very girl I wanted to impress with my *abishri* was leaning her head sideways to have a better view of a couple of boys I had left behind in the crowd. Obviously, she was not interested and had no time to waste on me. I asked myself, "Should I continue or should I go back? If I go back, could I ever recover from this blow?" In few seconds, both my heart and my rank in society sank and hit rock bottom. I became so depressed, but I really should not blame the girl. Why would a pretty girl be interested in a skinny boy wearing an oversized *baft* cotton *jellabiya* and slippers, carrying a stick in one hand, and coming over to do *abishri*? I occasionally borrowed and wore my father's skullcap to add a touch of fashion to my looks. I was wrong, and that cap sealed my fate that night. It was so big that it left enough room at the back of my head to fit another skull. It was ugly. I felt as if I had something written on my forehead that read, "No promising future with girls." I was not fashionable at all. I hated the feeling that I meant nothing, even to Kokoland girls. All of these thoughts crossed my mind during the one second it took me to move one step forward.

I decided to continue with my plan come what may. Once I reached the girls, I stood there and cracked two *abishris*, then turned around to rejoin the male crowd on the other side. Embarrassed and humiliated by the girl's action, I crouched down below the crowd's eye level. I scurried through the crowd into the darkness behind them and sat down to lick my wounds. It took me some time to recover. Finally, I got up and slowly snuck back into the crowd and poked my head forward. I looked in peoples' faces to make eye contact and find out if anyone took notice of my embarrassing moments. I satisfied myself that was not the case, so I blew a sigh of relief. It took me many parties before I could regain enough confidence to try another *abishri*.

Kokoland elders resisted anything foreign. They wanted to preserve the village lifestyle and culture. In the 1950s, the British colonial administration planned to build a railroad extension to connect the region with markets in the rest of the country. They wanted to pass the line by Kokoland and build a train station there because of its location as a hub for agricultural products. The village elders were called for a meeting and consulted about the benefits of the railroad in helping with development of the area. You would think that was a no brainer. No, you are wrong because the elders completely rejected the idea. They argued that the railroad would lead to moral disintegration of Kokoland. Moral standards were measured by the level of conservatism exhibited by Kokoland women, and the elders believed that trains would bring to the area people who would not uphold the community's values. They prayed and offered sacrifices so there would be no train station in Kokoland. Their prayers were answered, as no train station was ever built.

An incident that took place many decades later, reminded me of Kokoland elders' rejection of the railroad idea. The mayor of a large U. S. city also rejected an offer to host Winter Olympic Games in his city, arguing that would have a negative impact on the community. He managed to convince enough city residents to vote against the proposal. Decades later, he was asked if he stood a chance of winning a bid to host the games in his city. His response was, "When hell freezes over."

Gagarin's influence opened our eyes to the possibilities of new clothing and new music genres. The village parties were based on traditional folk music, and each tribe performed its tribal dances. Slowly, a new phenomenon known as *rabbah* grew popular. It first appeared during the mid-1970s, about the same time hip-hop and rap music developed in the United States. *Rabbah,* like rap, uses rhythmic beats and rhyming speech that was chanted. I have always wondered if Kokolanders really invented rap. Probably, it was just coincidence similar styles of music developed in such diverse parts of the world. By that time, a new generation of Kokoland partygoers had also evolved. It was a group of us middle and high school students.

As such, parties and weddings had to accommodate two groups; traditional conservatives, who were mainly village youth and older people, and younger generation of progressive students, if you like. The first part of the evening was dedicated to the first group, who danced to local drumbeats and folk. Next was students' turn to dance to music from cassette players, which was very much resented and detested by the conservatives, fully believing that it would transform Kokoland to the worse, but forever. As amazing as it might sound, Kokoland did have class wars.

Occasionally, the two groups crossed boundaries, and that led to friction. Sometimes, older men attended parties organized by teenage students. The men were used to local drumbeats, so they would find it difficult to keep up with beats from cassette players. They would temporarily forego the traditional dance styles they knew best and put genuine effort to emulate the students' foreign style of dancing, newly introduced to Kokoland. Because the whole thing was trial and error learning, the men would start shaking and moving their bodies in all directions, but soon find themselves gravitating toward what they knew best; stamping the ground like mad with shoes made of unprocessed cow skin. Soon, dust from beating on the ground would billow up, and the girls in clean saris would start murmuring and covering their faces, in an attempt to avoid the dust. The girls' action would infuriate the men who would feel both unpolished and unwelcomed. They would become agitated and ready to fight.

Village conservatives, especially, disapproved of students (boys and girls) dancing in pairs. They held the view that such behavior was anti-norm and un-Islamic, so they initiated fights that erupted often. Upon sensing imminence of a fight, A village wise man would intervene by calling out, while using his hand to give directions, "All men stand on this side, and students and girls move to this side." The students were ordered to join the girls' camp because they were known for settling disputes through dialogue, logic, and peaceful means, just like girls. People thought force was the best answer for settling disputes, particularly when girls were involved. Real men fought with knives and thick sticks, but students talked their way out of troubles, so they were viewed as harmless as girls, hence they were told to stand side by side with them until things got sorted out.

We used to name all foreign music *jas,* confusing it with jazz, but I think we did a pretty good job, butchering only part of the word. The same way we confused Elvis with Gagarin, we could have confused James Brown with Bob Marley or Mick Jagger. We were literally in the dark due to lack of both knowledge and electricity, and that was why people from the city had the upper hand, being more exposed to outside world. *Jaloa* music from Zaire infiltrated Kokoland from the south. The fast-beat presented a middle ground between traditional and Western music. Obviously, there was no room in Kokoland for groups such as Abba, singing The Winner Takes it All, Money Money Money, or Boney M., singing Malaika. However, we students, by pretending that we knew every single group we played and understood all their songs, we created and enjoyed a false notion of authenticity and sophistication. What mattered was that people in the village did not know that we were clueless as they were about everything Western. On party nights, we happily pitched in and raised enough money to buy batteries for our cassette recorder so we could dance all night. It was a lot of fun.

CHAPTER 7

Fashion and Barbers-Gone-Doctors, the Kokoland Way

Warning: There are sections in this chapter containing graphic description of cruelty to humans and animals, so readers' discretion is advised.

My friend Kapsoon and I would often sit on sand dunes in the moonlight and talk about girls. Kapsoon lived in the city, as did my other friend Abbas, whom I wrote about, earlier. He used to visit Kokoland during school breaks to help his uncle Sammane, who also happened to be Abbas's uncle. At night, we would sit and talk about our day's imaginary adventures with girls. We both knew damn well that we were lying to one another, but we did not care, anyway. Each of us knew exactly what the other was doing during the day because the whole village was less than a mile in diameter, so every move was spotted right away. Girls were kept inside homes and rarely allowed to venture out. We saw and met them in our imagination and talked about our false experiences in the moonlight as if they were facts. Actually, we went daydreaming at night.

Once we progressed to high school; we gained some status in the community, so we were able to organize volunteering activities such as adult education and theatrical programs to enhance literacy. However, we also had a few ulterior motives. Those activities added legitimacy to our efforts of bringing girls out of their houses without the parents' objecting to the idea. We taught some lousy classes, but we had quality time with girls. Some village boys objected because we enjoyed special status more than they did, so fights occasionally broke out. We invited troubles upon ourselves, but we thought it was worth it.

As I previously mentioned, I belong to the Kanuri tribe and for that reason some people believed that I was not supposed to dream big or indulge in things like expressing interest in girls from certain tribes. That was a risky prospect, which I learned about the hard way, one day. I went to a party and, while I was dancing with some of my friends, I made eye contact with Sabiha. She looked at me and smiled. I thought she offered me an entry visa into her heart, and that would solve all of my emotional issues for good, so I decided not to miss that lifetime opportunity. The problem was that, even though we (boys and girls) lived in the same village, it was as if we belonged to different planets. We had little idea how to deal with one another. I thought a single smile from a girl was enough to create a foundation for a relationship that could immediately be propelled into the next level. There was no time to waste, so I wrote Sabiha a letter the very next morning. That turned out to be a very big mistake.

In the villages around Kokoland, neither eye contact nor any other form of contact with girls was allowed. Upon deciding that it was time for a son to get married, a father would quietly conduct his own search for potential bride. After identifying one, he would ride his donkey and travel to the village to meet the girl's father. Such trips were usually successful and the marriage would take place in a matter of few weeks.

Sabiha had only smiled at me, but I got carried away and wrote her a letter. My mistake, I gave the letter to to a neighbor; a boy named *Karitha* (disaster),to deliver it to her. Instead, he took it to a pack of enemy boys who happened to be congregating at the village well. Not only had I committed an act the bullies considered condemnable, but they also had the evidence in their hand. Punishment was inevitable. Luckily, because I was leaving to school in two days, I stayed in my house and ventured out only a few times before I left.

God saved me from a certain disaster. I would have paid a heavy price had the village bullies caught me.

To my young Kanuri boys who lived in the surrounding villages, Kokoland was Paris or London, if you like. It was their primary source of inspiration for fashion and music. They copied new trends in dancing and played music the language and the meanings of which they did not understand, so they butchered them to suit their own village taste. They thought they copied from the master, but the truth was that we in Kokoland also did our own butchering. One thing I must give them credit for is their ability to accurately copy the beats and rhythms. Some nights, I could hear the sound of the impeccable goatskin drum beats coming from far away, whenever the wind blew in my direction.

In Kokoland, our sense of fashion was horrible by all accounts. It was more of a fiasco than fashion. I think the fact that we did not have large mirrors was a factor in that because we really did not know how we looked. We only had access to very small Chinese mirrors, just wide enough to see one eye at a time. We tilted our heads and moved them around so we could see one eye, then the other, then the rest of the face. Because we could not see the full face, at once, we had to learn to remember how one side looked while looking at the other half. I am not exaggerating.

We also used lantern gas tanks and truck side mirrors to view our faces. The side mirrors were mostly off limit because they were above head levels, besides, truck driver assistants would not allow us to get closer without chasing us. I remember visiting the barber tree for haircut very few times a year. The barbers had the largest mirror in Kokoland. It was about eighteen by twenty-four inches, and had a big chunk of one corner gone. It had a diagonal crack from the top left corner to the bottom right corner, and it did a pretty good job distorting figures.

As a child, I had a Mohawk style of haircut, which I thought was very cool. Sometimes, I had it shaved off but left two distinct bunches of hair, one on the front of my head and the other on the back. The first thing I checked any time I had access to a mirror was my Mohawk. Once I got to school, it became a source of embarrassment because Mohawk haircuts were considered old-fashioned as well as a sign of being a villager, which is who I am, even today, anyways.

Our best opportunity to view full figures of ourselves was during the rainy season when the water ponds were full. On a sunny day, we could see our entire figures, but unfortunately, when we were at the pond, we were not always dressed in our best clothes. Because we went there to fetch water, we usually wore the dirtiest clothes we had. That way it did not matter much if they got muddied. Washing clothes was a nightmare. We were never reckless with our clothes, besides we didn't have many spare ones, and, for that reason, we saved the best of our clothes for important occasions.

It was a blessing that I could not see how I looked. I might not have liked it. I am proud of our traditional dress, which every person in Kokoland wore. There were two types of garments made from either baft (cheap coarse cotton fabric), or poplin (a little bit more expensive fabric). One garment, which was just long enough to cover half of the legs, is called *arraagi,* and was worn for casual events. The other one covered the entire body all the way to the ankles, called *jellabiya*, and was worn for special occasions. They were very comfortable dresses considering the hot weather. We boys wore the shorter version most of the time. Were they fashionable? I thought they were okay, but I might be wrong.

We broke from tradition after Awadh Gagarin exposed us to new forms of clothing that included shorts, shirts, and pants. I was eager to transform my style from wearing local clothing to *afranji*, which means foreign or European. How could I impress girls with an *arraagi* extending down half of my skinny legs, a cap double the size of my skull, a red pair of slippers, and a stick in my hand? It was a nonstarter. Changing my clothing style to pants and shirts was a huge transformation for me. I was very excited about that, but I did not know how to do it. Ready-made clothes were rare, so I had to rely on local tailors to do their best to stitch fashionable pants and shirts for me.

In the early 1970s, Japan invented synthetic fiber used in the production of cloth. Shops in Kokoland started displaying a wider range of synthetic cloth of many different colors. Before that, the types of cloth available to us were primarily made from cotton, carrying names such as bafta, poplin, dabalan, etc. However; with the importation of synthetic products, it became possible for us to access a new collection of fabrics such as smoking, silk, crimbleen, and triveira. People were very happy about that because the new fabrics lasted much longer than cloth made from cotton. Also, because washing became an easier task, which meant shorter cleaning time, less money spent on soap, and less time spent on ironing. It was an important juncture for me as far as fashionable clothing was concerned. I was captivated by the new color diversity. One drawback to synthetic fiber was that it often produced static electricity when rubbed against the body or touched a metal object, resulting in a light electric shock. It also trapped heat, especially during summer. The names of some of these fabrics, such as smoking, were accurate descriptions of how people felt them during summer. However; the diverse selections they offered made up for the disadvantages.

Kokoland landscape was mostly brown and gray, so any different color was appreciated. Because my father had a shop, I had easy access to as many colors of the new fabrics as I wanted. Our tailor Ghanim was a true artist. Soon, I owned new styles in a full spectrum of colors. I had pants and shirts in yellow, purple, brown, green, orange, and blue. I knew nothing about proper dress codes. Looking back, I think some of the colors I wore did me a disservice. They were more appropriate for warning than attracting girls. No wonder why I had bad luck with girls. As far as the color gray is concerned, I have little love for it, even today. I had enough of it because gray donkeys were everywhere in Kokoland. They were a constant reminder of my daily donkey responsibilities.

Some people did have artistic (fashion) temperament. A man named Abkitir, for example, was one of them, but his efforts were undermined by a combination of factors such as lack of resources, being in the wrong place and among people who had little understanding or appreciation for style. Abkitir owned a camel, which he rode off to town on market days. He also used it for transporting sacks of peanuts, sorghum, and hays. Upon unloading his cargo, he would go to Jibreel's restaurant and change his clothes before returning to roam the market and show off to village women. He would wear a crisply ironed white *jellabiya* and a turban, which he casually placed on his right shoulder. That was how he made a fashion statement. More people came to Friday markets, so Abkitir changed his clothes twice that day to impress as many women as he could. I understand Abkitir's predicament now that I have observed musicians and celebrities changing clothes several times during concerts and award ceremonies. Abkitir was one camel-riding celebrity. I wonder what his chances in life could have been had he lived in Hollywood.

I noticed that people from my Kanuri tribe who possessed artistic talents tended to desert farming and gravitate toward activities such as barbering and tailoring. I also noticed that some of them exhibited panache in the way they dressed, walked, spoke, and carried themselves. Those who worked in the tailoring business were creative in making designs from their own imaginations. Sometimes they were aided by foreign pictures, which found their way to shops in Kokoland via packing materials used in packaging fabrics. The glamour and celebrity status associated with tailoring attracted one young man named Gaddoom. He abandoned farming to become a tailor. He ended up a casualty, as he just could not do a good stitching job. His designs turned out so ugly even for Kokoland taste and standard of fashion. People made fun of the young men who wore new styles of pants and shirt designed by Gaddoom. He had great difficulty in getting shirts' collars right. It was obvious that he wasn't going to survive for long. Lack of customers forced Gaddoom out of stitching business. He reluctantly reverted to what he knew best, but hated the most; farming.

Unlike Gaddoom, Sabir was renowned for his artistic skills in creating fashionable designs, especially made for Kokoland's teenage girls. He was nicknamed Abu H. because of his Casanova status. "Abu H." stands for "Father of Hawaa" or "Father of Eve." Whoever gave him that nickname also meant to say he was a man who loved to be surrounded by women. When I recently returned to Kokoland, I went to visit with him. I had not seen him in over thirty years. I assumed that I could start our conversation from where we had left, decades earlier. I was wrong because, "Too much water has flown under the bridge" since I saw him last time. I found Abu H. had turned into a holy man. I wrote about my awkward encounter with him in the last chapter; 20.

It took until the mid-1970s for some distorted stories about America's hippy era to get to us in Kokoland. For example, we referred to big Afro hairstyle as the Beetles. At that time we did not know anything about the Beatles as a rock band from Liverpool in England, so we most probably confused the Beatle's hair style with Afro. Most likely, someone picked up these jargons from the city, brought them back to the village, and dropped them on our laps, without any orientation, and the rest was history. I for one, and until I ventured out of Kokoland, thought that the Afro hairstyle was literally named after the black beetle commonly found in the area. How more confused could I be?

We also wore style of pants called Charleston. They were similar to the bell-bottom pants worn in America and Europe decades earlier. The width of the pants' leg-opening was a factor in determining a teenager's level of coolness. We also called them fans because they moved like fans when we walked, stirring up a lot of dust. We were truly Kokoland's version of hippies, even though we knew little about the movement; besides, being thousands of miles from Berkeley, California.

Wearing big hair in Kokoland meant inviting undesirable elements such as dust and lice. The plastic combs we used were no match for our dense African hair. It was common to see us using combs with several teeth missing. Some of the broken teeth would disappear in our dense hair until we accidentally find out someday while taking bath. Water was a scarce commodity, so taking bath everyday was a luxury we could hardly afford. We perspired a lot as a result of heat, especially at the neck, so the area around our shirt collars quickly got dirty, and Kokoland girls hated the smell of sweat mixed with dirt. In case you are thinking about deodorants, we did not have that either. Should we worry about drinking water or deodorants? To keep the collars clean, we wrapped them with handkerchiefs, which became the first line of defense against sweat and dirt. The colorful handkerchiefs, besides keeping our shirts cleaner for longer periods before we washed them, also added a touch of style that helped advance coolness. Washing clothes was one of the most laborious and taxing activities. As you can tell, girls can make boys inventive, and we in Kokoland were not an exception to this rule.

One problem with my newly acquired collection of rainbow-colored Charleston pants was that I grew taller, faster than I could afford to replace them. I resorted to unstitching the cuffs on the trousers to gain an inch or two in length, but I still outgrew them and ended up walking around with my ankles exposed. I had the same problem with my long-sleeved shirts, so my lower arms stuck out beyond the ends of the sleeves. My hands and legs grew faster than the rest of my body. That was a serious problem for me because it was much harder to be fashionable and look cool while wearing clothes that you had outgrown.

As if too short pants and sleeves were not enough trouble for me, shoes with tall blocky heels became very popular in Kokoland. We called them tanks. At the age of fifteen, I was already six feet three inches tall. Adding shoes with four-inch heels to my long legs, short pants, and sharp colors created a nightmarish combination. It was both uncool and hazardous. My center of gravity was way high. Every time I lost my balance after stepping on an uneven ground or in a pothole, I risked tumbling to the ground. This was very dangerous, especially when crossing city streets with fast-approaching traffic, a situation I experienced more than once. I was lucky that my mishaps were limited to coins falling out of my shirt's front pocket and rolling into the street. My tank shoes and long legs also put a lot of stress on my knees, which were still stretching and growing. I used to feel immense knee pain when I went to bed. I needed more time to rest so my knees could adapt, but that was almost impossible to achieve. I had to get up early and take care of my responsibilities, such as opening the shop, fetching water, and collecting grass to feed my gray donkey. Thus, I rarely got enough rest.

When I got to high school, I became exposed to real fashion. The school was located in the outskirts of the city, so I had many opportunities to visit the city over the weekends. Those visits helped me learn more about the difference between Kokoland and the rest of the world. Movies gave me some idea about life elsewhere, but the problem was that I did not really distinguish between fact and fiction, so I took all movies seriously. It took me some time to understand the difference between movie categories such as drama, comedy, action, science fiction, horror, etc. For a long time, I used to believe that some movies did more harm to society than good and wondered why they were made in the first place.

Somehow, I convinced myself that I was setting precedents in

Donkeys continue to be a vital means of transportation, especially in rural areas. Upgraded versions of donkey-pulled carts are being used in the outskirts of cities.

fashion, but please don't be too hard on me, as I didn't know better. My school friends Musa and Maaz occasionally asked me if they could borrow my shorts and shirts to wear them over weekends when they travelled to their villages. I grew even more confident that my taste in fashion was trusted. Why not? I was the first teenager to introduce Adidas shoes to Kokoland when I returned from the city. That was in 1980. My white Adidas with green stripes was a qualitative transformation in shoe fashion. I was also the first teenager to introduce the Congoli style of dress to Kokoland. Congoli meant pants and shirts made from the same fabric. The style must have found its way to us from Congo, as the name suggests.

As I mentioned earlier, cutting hair and tailoring were the two trades that attracted people with artistic inclination. There was little else to do. The Kokoland barbershop was nothing other than a tree, under which Kolo Al Hallag (Kolo the Barber, in Arabic) and Mohammed Wanzam (Mohammed the Barber, in Kanuri) set up their business, every market day (Mondays and Fridays). During the rest of the week, they roamed the nearby Kanuri villages responding to calls to attend Kanuri events. The tree was the barbers' place of business for decades. Surprisingly, they did not think of building a mud shed to house their business. Cutting hair under a tree is a bad business model.

Mohammed Wanzam possessed other skills too. He was a linguist. Even though he was illiterate, he set trends by introducing new phrases into the Kanuri language, which were copied by others. I noticed him pronouncing names and words with a twist to add some level of sophistication. The way he laughed was indicative of a man very confident of himself. He walked differently from other people and he exhibited panache in the way he carried himself.

Not too far from the barbers' tree, Amu Barakat set up his donkey-grooming business, yet under another tree. Nobody wasted money on grooming ordinary, gray, load-carrier, dumb, and slow donkeys. In contrast, slim and speedy donkeys, usually used in transporting people, were lined up to receive quality grooming from Amu Barakat. Freshly groomed donkeys were vital components of a man's journey to fame. When the owners of these special animals talked, ordinary people listened. Beautiful donkeys added status to their owners. I must say that Amu Barakat's grooming abilities were fantastic. Not only did he transform the donkeys' looks, but also made a huge difference in the lives of many Kokolanders.

A donkey trader from a far region, hundreds of miles away, visited Kokoland once a year with tens of donkeys. He usually showed up on Fridays, market days, to sell as many donkeys as he could. He took a spot near Amu Barakat's tree. It was a once-a-year opportunity for those who were looking for speedy donkeys. People rushed to the spot to be among the first to pick the best donkeys. It was also an opportunity for Amu Barakat to groom many donkeys on that day. He used to groom way beyond sunset. It was black Friday as far as Amu Barakat was concerned.

A relaxed setting for haircut and toenail clipping.

Barbers, besides cutting hair, provided medical services as well. There was a medical clinic in town, but it was rarely visited by my Kanuri people from the surrounding villages. They believed that going to doctors was a sign of having little faith in God. They argued that everything that happened to human beings was God's will. My father used to persuade them to visit the clinic, but they always held firm to their beliefs. They counter argued, "If doctors have the ability to cure people, then why do they get sick, and why do they die?" They further argued that every time they took a patient to the clinic, he or she didn't make it, so they thought there was no point in going through the trouble because the outcome would be the same anyway. My father told them the problem was that they resorted to the clinic after the damage was already done. They relied on local medicine made from leaves, herbs, bushes, and roots. The treatments did not work most of the time because they were based on trial and error. When the patient's condition deteriorated and reached a critical point, barely holding on to life, he or she would be put on a donkey's back and taken to the clinic. It would usually be too late for most patients.

My elder sister, Fantah, lived in a nearby village. One day my father, on his way back from a trip to another village, passed by to see her. He found her very sick. He told me she was surrounded by many bowls containing different local medicines. He immediately took her to the clinic for treatment. She recovered and, later on, told me if it was not for my father's unexpected visit, she could have died. My father thought that, apart from her sickness, the combination of the different medicines, alone, could have killed her. Sadly, the outcome was different in the case of my cousin Kassab who died from kidney failure after taking some local medicine. Kokolanders' lack of understanding for health issues was especially hard on young mothers. The death rate among young women during delivery was very high. This was a combination of poverty, marrying at young ages, and a lack of proper medical care. The proceeds from the sale of this book will go toward the creation of a health and vocational center to address some of these very issues.

Kokoland barbers filled the vacuum created by the limited health care available to people. They offered *hijamah*, a treatment given to those who suffered from exposure to extreme heat. Like most people, those who suffered from severe heat stroke rarely visited the clinic to seek help. They would lie in bed inside a hut and take local medicines. The lucky ones recovered, but many either died or survived to live with some form of disability. Abba Numah, our tailor Mai's brother, lost his vision right after taking a bath with cold water, upon returning from his farm on one hot summer day.

For hijamah purposes, the barbers used a small funnel-shaped metal utensil that has two-inch-diameter opening and a four-inch-long thin metal pipe attached to the side. The barber would begin treating patients complaining from heat exposure, first, by shaving the back side of the head. Next, he would use a razor blade to make several small cuts on the shaved area. He would then cover the area with the *hijamah* utensil. He would chew on a piece of paper, then place his mouth on the pipe and start sucking air out of the utensil, and that would cause it to stick firmly to the back of the head. He would use the chewed paper to plug the pipe, then move away. The patient and the barber would randomly pick up a topic and talk about it for the next half an hour or so before the barber returned and carefully pulled away the utensil from the patient's head. It would be full of chunks of dark blood, which he would shake off on the ground a few yards away. He would use his foot to cover it with dirt. The patient would get up, reach into his pocket, and pull out some coins and give it to the barber. I never ever saw Kolo or *wanzaam*, the barbers, check to see how much money they were paid. They received the money with one hand and used the other hand to cover it before depositing it away in their pockets. How much the patients paid was entirely left to their judgement. It will be nice if we have the option to decide how much to pay for health care here in America.

There was a less gruesome form of hijaamah, called *um foulah*, which means "peanut-size wounds." It was used for treating muscle aches. An empty glass container was used for this process. First, small pieces of soft dry pulp, peeled from a stalk, were placed inside the glass jar and set on fire. The jar would quickly be flipped and placed over the location of the aching muscle. Smoke and humidity would fill the jar as a result of the fire going out due to lack of oxygen. That reaction also caused the jar to stick to the body. It would be left there for about half an hour then removed. The treatment would leave behind brown-colored blisters on the skin that looked similar to peanuts, hence the name *um foulah* or peanut wounds. Then, the barber would carefully pop the blisters with a needle. The patient would get up, pay a few coins, and leave.

Dry straw tissue was also used for a procedure called *um dabar dabar*, which means "the mother of all wounds." This was not for treating health problems. It was rather a useless practice carried out by children to test the extent of their bravery and tolerance for pain. Basically, it was self-inflicted burn. It involved lighting one end of an inch long piece of straw and placing it on the arm. The process was repeated several times to show who, in the end, had more burns. The wounds would heal and leave behind round marks that looked like cigarette burns. This was just children daring each other to prove who was the bravest. It was not an initiation ceremony or anything like that. My brother Halim, who currently lives in London, has *um dabar dabar* marks on one of his arms. He told his trusting English friends that the marks were a result of a fierce encounter he had with an African lion. He likes to joke around.

Not too far from the barbers' tree, you could occasionally see a group of four or five men trying to pin down a donkey to the ground to administer treatment for heat stroke. Because donkeys played such important roles in people's daily lives, their owners, supposedly, took good care of them. Without giving the donkey any advance warning to prepare for what was coming, the young men would attack it and hold it down. Out of shock, it would begin kicking as though it was a matter of life and death. Sometimes, the men would get overwhelmed by the donkey's resistence, so passersby would stop and lend a hand, even without being asked. What else there in Kokoland to do, anyway? One man would hold up the donkey's head, while another open its mouth. A third man, holding a sharp metal object in his hand, would approach and start piercing the donkey's upper jaw, repeatedly. The idea was to release bad blood from the animal's head. After that, they would let go and move back. The donkey would stagger away while trying to control its balance. The whole thing was cruel. The same procedure was applied for treating less serious donkey illnesses. For flu-like symptoms, tea made from local herbs was poured through donkey nostrils.

Kolo, the barber, had a secret for treating toothaches. Going to see a dentist was not an option for Kokolanders because we had no dentists in town. Once, my father had me take my brother Aziz to see Kolo at the barbers' tree. Aziz had been complaining from toothache for a few days. Kolo always administered his secret toothache remedy in a secluded area away from the barbers' tree and the eyes of the curious. Per Kolo's instructions, the three of us went back to our house. He asked for charcoal to be burned in a clay pot, usually reserved for burning frankincense. He looked inside his old leather bag and took out a small cloth sack containing some dried roots. He picked up some of it with his fingertips and sprinkled it on the charcoal fire. Next, he asked Aziz to bend over, open his mouth, and inhale the smoke coming from the burning roots. He also covered Aziz's head with a bed sheet. We waited for several minutes until we heard popping sounds, just like popcorn. Then he lifted the sheet from Aziz's head. Sweat and tears ran down his face from the smoke. Kolo lifted the pot, brought it close to his face, and gazed inside it. Then he showed it to Aziz and asked, "Can you see the tiny white maggots?" Aziz looked for a while then finally nodded, thus affirming Kolo's observation. I became curious and wanted to have a look at the maggots that had fallen out of Aziz's mouth, so I said, "Can I also see? I was expected to say, "Yes, I also saw the maggots." In fact, I looked all around the burning pot for any sign of fried maggots, but I did not see any. The pressure was mounting on me to give a positive answer. When I sensed that Kolo was about to move away the bowl, I said, "*Ya*, here they are." With a smile, Kolo told Aziz that he was cured and that all the maggots that had infested his tooth were gone and he would soon be fine. He then got up and returned to his business under the tree. I looked at Aziz and found him putting his hand on his swollen cheek. His eyes were red from crying and the smoke. There was no way he could have seen and recognized burned maggots under those conditions, so he had lied about that. His toothache worsened, and my father had to take him to the city to get his tooth removed. While he was in the city, he probably got the opportunity to enjoy a piece of cake or some fruit. Going to the city was a good thing. I thought that it might be worth having a toothache of my own.

There were two types of shops in Kokoland. Small canteens, which sold dry food items such as sugar, tea, coffee, and dried herbs, and larger shops, which carried food items on one side and fabrics on the other. The latter group also had tailors sitting in the front, ready to stitch fabrics purchased from the shop. My father's tailor, Ghanim, was a true artist. He had a great sense of humor as well as the ability to stitch clothes for women to their complete satisfaction. For that reason, he had a large customer base, which sought his service all the time.

Ghanim had a bike. There were only two bikes in Kokoland, one owned by him and the other owned by Jidairi, the gun owner

I previously talked about. To the amusement of everyone, Ghanim performed acrobatic stunts with his bike, but he acted as if the bike was behaving on its own. He used to show concern about his bike's uncontrollable behavior to convince us children that it was occupied by djinns and spirits. After every stunt, he would whisper verses from the Quran, pretending that he was reading to expel the djinns and free his bike's "soul" from them.

Like the barbers, Ghanim had some medical knowledge. In Kokoland, many people had diverse skills because we did not have licensed professionals, as you might have guessed. Amu Ibrahim suffered from a disease called Madura foot cancer. It was some sort of cancer that caused one of his feet to swell many times its normal size. This disease causes the surface of the foot to become riddled with deep holes that fill with watery pus, causing it to resemble a termite chamber with ventilation holes. This is why it is known to the Kanuri as *kongoo-lah*, which means "termite chamber." Amu Ibrahim lived in Port Sudan, over one thousand kilometers from Kokoland. He was told that Ghanim was the only man who could cure him and save his foot, so he travelled to Kokoland to see our tailor. Amu Ibrahim's condition kept him from moving about freely, so I was assigned to look after him. I brought him food and water and collected the empty dishes. I occasionally brought him bath water, which was a scarce commodity in Kokoland. Soon a friendship developed between Amu Ibrahim and me. In fact, I somehow ended up owning Amu Ibrahim's troubles, which I did not mind even though it added more responsibility to my already full plate. He was Ghanim's patient, but I rarely seen him tending to this poor man's needs. His meals came from our house, something my father personally attended to, making sure that I had taken food and water to Amu Ibrahim on a daily basis. For the entire six months duration of Amu Ibrahim's stay at our house, I never saw Ghanim treating him. His foot was constantly wrapped with a piece of cloth, which was always wet with blood and pus draining from it. The strong odor was evident from several meters away.

Amu Ibrahim always received me with a big smile. I visited him frequently and kept him company. He used to prolong my stay by telling me interesting stories, even though sometimes I wished if I could leave sooner to go and play soccer or set traps to catch a bird or two before sunset. One afternoon, I brought him food and found that he had crawled out of his hut and sat in the straw shade in the front. After he had done eating, he asked me about school, and I told him it was fine. He told me if I worked hard at school, then I would grow up, become famous, and be able to wear shoes with heels that made a unique sound when I walked on hard surface like tile. I had no idea what kind of shoes he meant. Using his right hand's index and middle finger, he drew dot marks on the sand by walking the two fingers while saying, "Tock, tock, tock, that is how you will walk on tile." That act brought a big smile to my face as I started imagining things, places, and being among famous people. The problem I had not seen any famous people apart from my teachers. Besides; I did not have the shoe type he was talking about, nor did I hear any sound from my shoes when I walked over hard surfaces. I had never seen tile either. My smile faded away when I looked down and my eyes fell on my dilapidated red slippers. The reality of my situation hit me hard, then.

My feet were constantly ashy, something I was very used to, especially during winter when I declared war on water. Because I had no access to warm water, I stayed away from taking shower for as long as I could, until someone, most probably my elder sister Fantah, decided that I was dirty enough that I needed a bath, urgently. We played soccer bare-footed, so most of the time my feet were covered with dirt. I made a mistake by describing them to members of my family that they were as gray as ash and looked like fish skin. They brought up the subject every now and then by asking me, "Tell us about your tilapia-like ashy feet."

I always had, only, two pairs of footwear; slippers and a pair of plastic shoes for school. I changed into my slippers as soon as I returned from school so that my plastic shoes would last longer. I wore my shoes until they developed holes in the heels. I would tie my broken slippers with a nylon rope to extend its life until I got a new pair. For treating cracks on my plastic shoes, I would heat up a knife and place it carefully between the two cracked parts just long enough for the plastic to melt down. I wouls remove the knife, then press and hold the two parts together. The plastic would cool off and the two pieces would stick back together without leaving noticeable repair marks to attract my friends' attention. My friend's living condition was hardly better than mine; nevertheless, it was important to keep up appearances, just in case they tried to play class game. Prolonging shoe lives was necessary because we just could not ask for and get new shoes whenever we wished. We had to earn them the hard way, so forget about owning new Nike releases for the simple sake of collection. Besides; walking barefooted was not an option due to the hot ground and the thorns scattered everywhere, so I had to take good care of my shoes. Wasting things was not even possible for me. You see, I have embraced the slogan, "Waste not, want not" at a very young age.

The condition of Amu Ibrahim's foot worsened, and his general health deteriorated, so he finally decided to leave for the city to seek proper treatment. One Thursday, a truck arrived from the city and I, being curious like anyone else in the village, went to investigate. I was surprised to see Amu Ibrahim with his foot amputated. I had mixed feelings. I was happy to see him, but sad that he lost his foot. He was much cleaner, much happier, and could easily move with his artificial leg. He returned to say thank you and good-bye. He stayed with us for a few days and left for his city, Port Sudan, on the other side of the country. I never saw or heard from him again.

Another barber, named Dungus, also came to Kokoland from a nearby village on market days to cut hair and offer hijaama treatment. Unlike Kolo the barber and Mohammed *wanzaam*, Dungus was a disaster, as far as my mother was concerned. Sometimes, especially during slow business days, my father would ask Dungus to accompany him home to give us haircut. They normally showed up at the house unannounced, and my mother was never happy about that. He was offered a meal or coffee, depending on the time of day. My mother, like many people in and around Kokoland, believed that Dungus was a sorcerer. She thought that he was harmful to us, her children. Because we were the only Kanuri family living in Kokoland, anytime we heard voices of people speaking the Kanuri language in the vicinity, we knew that they were heading to our house. My mother could distinguish Dungus's unique and loud voice from among any group of people approaching the house. Once certain that Dungus was coming home, she would panic and start shouting at us to make ourselves invisible. While signaling to us with both hands to disappear, she would also recite verses from the Quran to neutralize Dungus's black magic effects on us. We would run in the opposite direction of the house's entrance. Because there was only one entrance to the house, we would use a small hole under the straw fence dug by scavenging neighborhood dogs. Through that hole, we would go dashing toward my friend Tiffah's home. We would continue hearing my mother reciting verses from the Quran, only louder and louder, to make sure that Dungus heard her clearly, just in case he was intending to play "magic games" with her children. She would respond to my father's inquiries as to our whereabouts by telling him that we were somewhere in the neighborhood playing, but never gave him further details. We would return home after making sure that Dungus's annoying voice was nowhere to be heard. My mother made sure that we went for haircut at the barber tree only on days when Dungus was not around.

Warning: This section contains graphic description of acts that some of you might find to be cruel to both children and adults. I request that they are to be viewed within the cultural context of the place, but, by all standards, some of the acts remain unacceptable, abusive, gross, and not funny, and I am not advocating any of it. I am rather stating facts about incidents that I have personally experienced. By doing so, I hope I am not offending anybody.

Barbers were among the first people to get invited to Kanuri events such as weddings, births, funerals, boys' circumcisions, etc. The presence of many men in one place also presented a valuable opportunity for haircutting, shaving beards, and performing hijamah. Barbers performed circumcision on seven year old boys at special village ceremonies. It is needless to say they did not use anesthesia. Very few people around Kokoland took their boys to the clinic to have them circumcised under relatively safe and pain-free conditions. It is not surprising that village boys did whatever it took to avoid going through the nightmare. Like barbers, village elders did not help alleviate the boys' fears. It was common to threaten to invite over zombies and *wanzaams* (barbers) to handle those who disobeyed orders or got in troubles. Children feared *wanzaams* more than zombies because they (*wanzaams*) were known for inflicting real pain. They might have heard stories from elder boys about their circumcision ordeal with *wanzaams*. Children less-feared zombies and less-worried about the psychological pain caused by listening to scary stories about them. They would be fine as long as they stayed away from zombie territories; darkness.

This is not funny, but it was quiet common to find village jokers who liked to mess around with naughty children, normally boys. There might be a situation whereby kids could be fighting one another or playing roughly and would not stop when told to do so. That would be an ideal moment for a village joker to intervene. He would jokingly say to the elders around something like, "You just wait." Then, he would abruptly get up and start walking toward the children. Pretending to be holding something, he would bring his hands up closer to his mouth and blow a couple of times, supposedly, on a razor he was hiding. Without directing his talk to any one specific child, he would shout; "trap him and bring him over to me." By acting crazy and moving frantically, the joker would signal to the children around that he was holding a razor and that he was ready for action; circumcision. The children, each fearing for himself, not knowing which of them the joker meant to trap, would take off running in all directions as fast as they could, heading toward their mothers for protection. Elders would laugh and joke about it even though that entertainment came at the expense of striking fear in the hearts of the children. It is not funny at all.

In a different scenario, the joker might calmly get up and, again, without directing his talk to any one specific child, would loudly say something like, "Let me go and get the wanzaam." He would put on his shoes and start walking away pretending to be on his way to the wanzaam's village to get him over so that he could carry out what he knew best. In seconds the place would be deserted from children.

Wanzaams and village children were natural enemies, and that was understandable. Circumcision is not a joking matter and children did not take it lightly.

Wanzaams also performed tribal scars on bellies and faces of newborn babies. This was done on the seventh day of a child's birth. The scars were usually five pairs and each was about one-inch long. They were administered on the chest and the belly. I can speak about this with total confidence because I have my own belly scars.

The Kanuri have their own unique style of facial scars. One scar comes down from the forehead and ends at the tip of the nose, thus dividing the face into two halves. Each cheek is marked with three, four, or, sometimes, five vertical scars. There is no one standard length, width, or depth for these scars. That is determined by the wanzaam who performs the ceremony and his unique individual cutting style. Some facial scars are visible from a distance while others are so thin and can barely be observed. That reflects the wanzaam's experience, as well as his level of enthusiasm and loyalty to the Kanuri tribal culture and traditions. I think a wanzaam's advocacy of tribalism can be measured by his exaggerated style of extra-long, extra-wide, and extra-deep scars on someone else's face. There is an old Sudanese proverb that says, "On a skin that is not yours, you can drag a branch of thorns, if you like." I personally think that this proverb advocates selfishness, but, of course, it goes without saying that it alone doesn't sum up everything about the Sudanese people.

Once a person receives facial scars, he or she will be stuck with them forever. No technology out there that can remove them. The tradition was widespread, but it is dying out and younger generations no more carry these marks of nobility. Many of my older family members have facial scars, especially the main one on the center of the face, which we jokingly named "The Center of Africa."

My father once told me a story about a Kanuri man named Haj Ali, but he doubted that it was a true story. Haj Ali was a prominent member of the community and was known all over the region. I happened to know him personally. He had extra-wide facial cars. It was rumored that when Haj Ali was a young man, some tribesmen came from out of town to visit his father, who was not at home at the time. It was believed that he failed to meet the guests cheerfully and refused to talk to them in Kanuri language. Upon his father's return, the guests complained about the humiliating manner in which his "city" boy received them. They told him that he acted snobbishly, treated them with disdain, and appeared unimpressed by their village looks and unfashionable tribal scars. That was a great sin for which Haj Ali received a severe punishment. The father decided; he must be scarred. The father tricked Haj Ali by inviting a few men, including a *wanzaam*, to the house for a meal, but without telling his son the reason for the unjustified invitation. At zero hour, the men jumped on Haj Ali and pinned him to the ground. Then, the *wanzaam* approached and administered extra-wide scars on Haj Ali's face. The father's rationale was that his son could run away, if he wished, but he would never be mistaken for a different identity. He would remain a Kanuri for as long as he lived. As you can see, some people could go to great extents to prove a point. It is immaterial whether it was a true or false story. The fact remains that Haj Ali had extra-long, extra-wide, and extra-deep scars, regardless of whether he had them when he was a newborn baby or as a young man. The whole story could be nothing more than a dark humor adopted by elders to remain in control by scaring children into upholding tribal traditions, staying obedient, and being in check. That is to say, there were consequences for acting cheeky with the tribe's elders.

The most gruesome thing I saw *wanzaams* do was an act also carried out on the seventh day of a child's birth. It was also the same day for naming the baby, giving him or her haircut, and administering tribal scars. I saw a *wanzaam* using a piece of wood the size of a spoon handle to pin down the child's tongue. Then he used a razor blade mounted on a straw to cut something from the child's throat. It was a bloody scene. I witnessed that incident once, but never dared to ask anybody for clarification. I tucked it deep in my memory and kept it there. In all probability, the same act might have been carried out on me the same day I had my belly scars. I really have no idea why it was done, nor what purpose it served out.

The question that comes to mind is why would anyone think that it was a good idea to scar a seven days old baby. I might sound critical of my own people's tribal heritage, but I certainly don't mean to offend any culture, mine or others'. Who am I to do so? People have to decide for themselves as to what traditions to follow. Nevertheless; we should never subject children to some of these acts so called ancestral heritages. Fortunately, some negative traditions are fading away, but sadly we are experiencing other forms of abuses caused by poverty, wars, violence, human trafficking, child labor, etc. We still have a long way to go.

CHAPTER 8

Darsail: A Primary School From Hell

At times, little knowledge can be very confusing. My brother Aziz was one grade ahead of me. He and his friend Abbas, when they were both in first grade, advised me on how to prepare for first grade, the following year. They emphasized that my success would be guaranteed if I paid attention at school and took good care of my studies. They told me I could advance from elementary school to junior and high secondary schools, and from there, Aziz told me, I could progress to the mosque. I was baffled by the nature of progress that would take me from a primary school in Kokoland to secondary schools in, certainly, better towns or cities, only to find myself back studying at the mosque in Kokoland, built with local wooden poles and millet straw, if I was lucky. I was six years old then, but I could tell that did not seem like progress to me. I was disappointed by the prospect of coming back to Kokoland, much more than the idea of studying at the mosque. To be honest, Kokoland elders did a lousy job building a straw shack and naming it a house of worship, when they could have afforded a better and a lasting structure. During the rainy season, the palm leave prayer mats were always wet due leaks from the caved-in straw roof. The sandy areas between the lines of mats were irregularly dotted with half-inch-deep holes caused by water dripping from the ceiling. No one could escape the brown stains, especially those who came to prayer dressed in white *jellabiya* (garments). I guess I had my reasons for not being impressed. I later on found out my brother had confused the word university with the word mosque. Both words have the same meaning in Arabic; "a gathering place."

The idea of boarding schools with hundreds of young children living in one place is a difficult concept for some people to grasp. My wife was visited by her cousin Adibah for the first time at her boarding house when she was in high school. Adibah was quiet and somewhat subdued, so my wife asked her what was wrong. Her response was, "Who is going to marry all these girls?" Obviously, she had neither seen so many girls in one place, nor did she have an idea that there were high school boarding houses for boys. I happened to be one of those boys, who ended up marrying her cousin.

Following the death of my mother, my brother Aziz and I had no one to look after us, especially when it came to meals. My elder sister had already married and moved to the city. Things were particularly bad when my father had to leave with his merchandise to markets in nearby towns, so he approached Mr. El Tayeb, the school principal in Darsail, for help. Darsail is a town about fifteen miles from Kokoland. Mr. El Tayeb agreed to take us in to stay at the school boarding house. My father was very appreciative of that help. Living in Darsail may have been a lifesaver for us, but it had many drawbacks too. We faced so many challenges.

We did not have electricity, so our main source of light was the sun. Tough luck for us if we failed to finish our homework before sunset. We usually woke up around 5:00 a.m. to study, finish homework, and memorize Arabic poem or verses from the Quran. Failing to recite correctly from memory or failing a math test had severe consequences, which came in the form of flogging. It is hard for someone who has not experienced this type of punishment to appreciate its severity. I used to wake up with severe abdominal pain, worrying about what fresh hell the day would bring, be that caused by teachers or fellow bully pupils.

My old boarding room in Darsail, primary school
from hell (1970-1973). Photo 2016.

There were five boarding houses and each one housed about twenty-four pupils. Some of our beds were made of metal frames with rope nets weaved across the frames. Those beds were at least thirty years old. It was part of furniture supplied to the school when it was built by the British during the 1940s. Invariably, each of these ancient beds had a hole somewhere, but we managed to maneuver our tiny bodies around them so we could sleep. The metal beds were usually reserved for senior pupils (grades four to six). The other beds were made from local wood and had cracks everywhere. You cannot think of any shape that is more crooked. We did not have mattresses. In the beginning of the school year, each pupil was given two dilapidated thirty-year-old wool blankets. We used one as a bed mat and the other as cover. They were dirty, smelly, torn along the edges, and riddled with holes, all over. I doubt it if they had ever been washed, certainly not during my three years at the boarding school.

Every morning, four pupils cleaned the boarding room, two cleaned the inside and the other two did the front. Inside, one pupil would lift the beds, one at a time, allowing the other pupil to go underneath and use a ragged piece of cloth to sweep the floor. The area in the front was twice the room size. We used our own hands to clean that area. We would put our tiny hands together and spread our fingers half-inches apart to create rakes out of our hands. One person would stand in one corner of the area, bend over, and start raking the dirt, one square foot or so at a time. He would be raking while moving his feet side ways to shift his body in a straight line. The other pupil did the same thing. Together, each time, they would rake two feet by thirty feet or so (the length of the area). Then they would go back and repeat the same process, perhaps fifteen times, to cover the entire are. Hazards associated with this work included cuts from pieces of old rusty blades, needles, or wires, as well as stepping on and touching saliva that was spat out by children with severe coughs. Obviously, we did not know what tetanus meant. We did get sick, but we rarely visited the clinic. We sought help only when we were bedridden and could not function anymore. The one fever we knew was caused by malaria. For other types of sicknesses, we reduced our activities and rode the pain until we recovered. Raking the floor was also a weapon used to punish those who did not obey orders. Due to our bad luck, both Aziz and I lived in the same boarding house as Habib, who was the pupil in charge (the alpha), as well the school's superbully.

Once, my father and a group of friends went on a trip to a nearby village, Nabag, to pay tribute to relatives following the death of a family member. On the way back, their truck got stuck in mud so one of the passengers climbed a tree to cut down some branches to lay on the track to help free it. The man lost his grip, fell, and injured himself seriously. They took him to the clinic in Kokoland, but to their surprise, the place was packed with angry people. Mr. Samuel, the South Sudanese medical assistant, called my father and warned him of an imminent threat from a plot put together by members of the Bibi tribe against the Kanuri in retaliation for the murder of a man named Suleiman, a few hours earlier. All hell broke loose. The situation was tantamount to the Bay of Pigs crisis, as far as Kokoland was concerned.

Earlier in the day, a fight broke out between young Kanuri men, some of whom were my cousins, and young men from the Bibi tribe. It resulted in the stabbing death of one man named Suleiman. Suleiman happened to have a son my age, named Azrag, who attended school in Kokoland. It was unfortunate for me that Azrag also had cousins who attended my school in Darsail. Habib, the alpha and the superbully, was one of them. Habib and friends started talking about retaliating for the death of Suleiman. In those days, retaliation for the death of a tribe member was a common practice. It didn't matter who was the person being targeted for killing. It was immaterial if he was closely related to the killer or not. Anyone from his tribe would do. This practice was known as *Tha'ar*, an Arabic word for revenge killing.

I remember, one of our neighbors, a young man named Barood, was in the Bibi camp when the fight broke out. Customs dictated that he should have stood his ground, defended the girls, and honored his tribe, but he could not take on the heat of the fight. He fled the battle zone and took off running toward Kokoland. When he got to town, he had completely lost his composure and could not say anything comprehensible or sensible when people asked him about what had happened. In the midst of sobbing and hallucinating, the only sensible answer he could give was, "They are all dead, everyone is dead." Barood became the joke of town. Women knitted derogatory songs defaming him for betraying his friends and letting down the tribe's girls. He could not take on the heat from the stigma either, so he ran away from town. He disappeared for over ten years before returning to Kokoland. Life was never the same for Barood. He lived a subdued and an overly quiet life, avoiding any gathering where there was a slightest chance for evoking those painful memories. I have written more about Barood's incident fleeing the battle ground in chapter 12.

Word spread quickly around our school that my brother Aziz and I were designated as *tha'ar* targets for Suleiman's murder. It was rumored that our cousin Hamdan was the one who stabbed Suleiman under the arm, causing him to bleed to death. Unfortunately for my brother and me, the head student in our room, Habib, was also the leader of all the Bibi boys at the school. Revenge killing was usually carried out by adults, but children copied what they heard at home from their parents and other adults in their villages. We were branded as the Kanuri boys whose cousin killed the Bibi boys' cousin. They ganged up on the two of us and made our lives hell. We were constantly antagonized and bullied. Every Bibi boy in school turned against us, but the most severe animosity came from four particular children, namely Jamur, Karim, Khatir, and Habib (the alpha bully in our room). Habib used raking the area in front of the boarding room, with our bare hands, as I have described above, to avenge his cousin's death. He forced us to rake the floor any time of the day he wished. If you happened to see us raking the floor at times other than in the morning, you knew that we were being punished. This torture went on for two years. Finally, Habib completed sixth grade and dropped out of school because he failed the test for transitioning into middle school.

Now, looking back, I think Habib could have been suffering from some form of psychotic disorder because of the sadistic tendencies he had. One night, he ordered all of us in the room to bring our shoes over to him and pile them by his bedside, which we did. He told Sabri, one of the boys in the room, to sit on a bed a few meters away from him. He started throwing one shoe at a time at Sabri, hitting him on different parts of his body. When he finished throwing the shoes, he ordered us again to collect and pile them up so he could continue throwing and hitting his target, Sabri. There were three rounds of shoe-throwing at Sabri. The rest of us huddled in the farthest corner of the room, barely visible because there was only one kerosene lantern in the room, which was owned by Habib. We sat and watched, unable to do anything to help Sabri. In another incident, Habib gathered the peelings of cucumbers, placed them on top of his kerosene lantern until they got very hot, and then pressed them against Sabri's hands and arms. Sabri screamed, while Habib laughed loudly and uncontrollably, clearly entertained by the younger boy's miserable condition. Sabri was a timid child, and his response to any situation was crying. Many children picked on him. I am still haunted by these terrible memories.

We could not complain to the teachers because we were afraid of retaliation by the bullies. The teachers never came around the boarding house to inspect. After the end of the school day, the laws of the jungle prevailed. We lived by rules created by the bullies, based on their physical strength and power derived from members of their tribes or boys from their villages. God help you if you have none of that. My brother and I were on our own.

My brother suffered even more than I did. Habib used to beat him repeatedly, whenever he felt like it. Sadly, I could not do a thing to stop that. I was not able to confront Habib and the many boys from his village. Our situation was aggravated by their belief that we, being Kanuri, did not belong there. It was also considered cowardly to complain to the teachers. Complaining to our father was out of the question because we were afraid of something bad happening to him, if adults became involved. Our father was our only source of security, and we worried about losing him, so we dealt with the situation on our own. The outcome for my brother Aziz was disastrous, as you will read about it later on. He just couldn't continue taking the beating.

The big tree on the right is the same tree Habib and friends used for trapping dogs in the middle of the night, in the early nineteen-seventies. Photo 2016.

Sometimes, Habib and senior boys from other boarding houses would catch and beat stray dogs. The big neem tree behind our boarding room was their staging area. At night after supper, usually during full moon, they would place a tin under the tree and fill it with garbage and remnants of porridge. They would get a rope, tie a cord with a loop on one end, and tie the other end to a branch to keep it dangling down, with the cord hovering just on top of the tin. One boy would climb the tree and wait quietly for stray dogs attracted by the food smell to appear. As soon as a dog put its head through the cord to snatch a chunk of porridge from the tin, the boy up in the tree would pull on the rope, tightening the cord around the poor dog's neck. Its frantic and desperate attempts to free itself would only tighten the cord further, making its situation even worse. Then, Habib and his friends would come running out of their hiding places and start beating the dog with big sticks, all the while laughing at the dog's howling in pain. The noise brought some children out of their rooms to watch the horrible and scary scene unfolding in front of their eyes. Some stood in dark corners and watched from a distance, while others congregated at room windows. After satisfying themselves, Habib and his friends would run away and signal to the boy up in the tree to release the rope, allowing the dog to escape with the rope hanging from its neck. No one knew how many dogs survived or died from their terrible ordeals. We did not dare tell the teachers. None of us wanted to be implicated in the crime or summoned to the teachers' office to tell what we saw, nor did any of us wanted to answer for Habib and his gang.

Habib was not just a master at beating children and dogs. He also thought he was a scholar. One time, he ordered us to gather around him. After telling us that we knew nothing about anything, he began disseminating knowledge. He asked, "How big do you guys think the hydrogen bomb is?" We all kept quiet because no one dared to volunteer a response that might lead to beating or hand-raking the front yard. He continued his lecture by saying, "The hydrogen bomb is smaller than a grain of pearl millet, but it can kill many people." That was the end of the lecture. I thought it was a valuable piece of information because I knew little about nuclear bombs. However, he got me wondering what is the relationship between a grain of pearl millet and the nuclear bomb, and how something that tiny could kill many people. I cherished this valuable piece of information for a long time, until I read about Colonel Paul Tibbets, the *Enola Gay*, and the bombing of Hiroshima. I remember cursing Habib a lot that day. As it turned out, the phrase "nuclear bomb" translates, in Arabic, to something like "gain bomb." Habib chose pearl millet, the smallest grain size known to us, to show the bomb's effectiveness. There is a Sudanese proverb that translates to something like, "Having half vision in the land of the vision-impaired is tantamount to full vision." Habib was both our torturer and enlightener. We accepted that fate as we were helpless and equally clueless. He most probably learned about the Hiroshima and Nagasaki bombs of WWII in the news. He then localized it and passed it on to us to confuse us, over and above the confusion we already had from everything around us.

Years later when I was in high school, I heard the news that Habib had gone crazy. One night, he and young men from his village were gathered around campfire telling stories and laughing. One of them told a funny joke, and Habib burst into laughter from which he never recovered. He literally laughed his sanity away. Considering the earlier behaviors he had exhibited, I was not surprised at all.

Mr. Muaz had monopoly over school supplies to both primary and middle schools in Darsail. Somehow; he managed to repeatedly win and secure government bids for as long as I could remember. It must have been a lucrative business, so he did whatever it took to win them. The arrival of his truck at our school at the beginning of each school year brought about tremendous joy. It came loaded with sorghum flour, dried okra powder, dried meat (of unknown type or source), cartons of sardines, Dutch cheese, and sacks of powdered milk. We were told that the sardines, cheese, and milk had come from the United Nations Educational, Scientific and Cultural Organization (UNESCO). Because we could not read English, the middle school boys told us that the writing on the milk packages read, "For dogs and little horses." I don't think that was true, and we did not care whether the milk was meant for children, dogs, or ponies. We thanked UNESCO a lot for supplementing our daily diet. We were keener about knowing how many cartoons of UNESCO items were off-loaded than anything else, because that determined how long the rations would last during the school year. It was usually not long. We were served three meals, which consisted of porridge made from sorghum and dried okra soup, occasionally cooked with dried meat. That was our daily food regimen. Malnutrition was common among us even though we were unaware that we had it. I sometimes visit my boys' school here in America to have lunch with them. I see some children throwing half of their lunch in the trash bin, and I wonder, "What on earth is happening?"

I love eating sardines. My family members here in America carried their own diagnosis and attributed my sardine-eating condition to some type of phobia caused by food deprivation. They think the damage to my soul is irreparable and that it is hopeless to try to change my eating habits. My son told me that he just could not understand why I am still eating stuff that, he thinks, tastes like wood chips. He suggested that I should relax, let go, and try new things, but he doubts whether I will ever break away from the "chronic inhibitions" I suffer.

The food storage was a (4x4 meters) room with no windows. During summer, the temperature often rose to 110 degrees. That level of heat created a wonderful environment for maggots and mice to proliferate. It was common to spot maggots floating in our meals of okra soap and porridge. We knew that, we saw that, and we ate that, day in and day out, pretending they never existed. We had few options.

Occasionally, our cherished sardine cans would overheat, explode, and produce intolerable odors. A teacher would order us to sort the good tins from the bad ones. He would tell us to remove the cans that had already exploded, as well as the ones that had expanded and were about to explode. We generally did a good job, but we used our own standards for what was good and what was bad. Some cans might not have passed the teacher's standard for good cans, but we thought they were still edible, considering the alternative food made of dried okra soup and porridge. Food poisoning was a risk we were prepared to take so we did not go hungry. We took the real bad cans away and buried them. It saddened us a great deal to see all that food gone to waste.

Sardine, if available, was usually served for breakfast, after the second period. After breakfast, we would go back to class and turn the room into an extremely fish-smelling place. The school roof was made of tin and there were no fans or air-conditioning. During the summer, by midday, the classroom would become a furnace. There were forty-five or so of us in each classroom, and together we literally polluted the air inside with smell of sardine. In fact, that did not bother us much, since we were the source of the smell. There is a proverb from Kokoland that says, "A hyena doesn't find his den smelly." Some of our teachers, especially the ones from the city, looked down on us and expressed disgust from the sardine odors the forty-five of us collectively produced from our breaths and hands due to not being washed properly. After breakfast, we would go to the water-tree to wash and drink. There were half a dozen or so open barrels (drums), lined under a neem tree, filled with water for drinking, washing, and bathing. We would scoop water from the barrels to drink and sit nearby in the dirt to wash our hands. There was no soap, so we would grab dirt, pour a little water on our hands, and rub them together to remove the sardine oil before fully washing them, but that did little to help remove the strong smell. There was horrible odor around those drums, but we were used to it, so we did not bother. During the dry season, the water area also attracted frogs, lizards, and insects that took refuge under the barrels, probably to cool off from the summer heat and also to drink.

It is worth mentioning that every one of us living in the boarding house aged between six and twelve years. There were no parents or adults to guide us, so right and wrong matters were left for us to decide.

At night, after we go to bed, mice would take the room over and happily zig-zag across the floor, picking up crumbs we had dropped during the day. Sometimes things got so bad that we had to take action against the pests. We got rid of them, first, by removing the beds from the room, then flooding their holes in the room corners. We would wait with sticks and hunt them down when they pop out of the holes. That gave us some peace of mind, but that did not last very long. Mice are known for being fast reproducers, so we had to administer the same treatment every few weeks or so.

Our beds were lined up very close to one another. That made it easy for bedbugs to move from one bed to the other. They were masters of blood sucking. Once we were asleep, they would attack our exhausted bodies, picking and choosing where to dine at leisure. To get rid of them we would remove the beds and leave them outside in the front yard, all day under the summer sun. We would beat the ropes on the bed frames with sticks to shake off the bugs. They would drop on the ground and start running away in search of cooler places, but the sand was too hot for them, so they would succumb to dehydration from heat. We occasionally got hold of powdered bug poison, which we scattered in between the cracks of the wooden beds. The poison did kill the bugs, but caused serious side effects, such as eye infections, stomach upsets, flu-like symptoms, and other respiratory problems, so we avoided using it as much as possible. There was no adult supervision and we had no advance knowledge of how to handle such poisons or knew anything about their side effects.

We also suffered a lot from lice infestations. We got rid of lice in our clothing by exposing them to heat, the same way we did with bedbugs. Once we return from classes in the afternoon, we would take off our clothes and spread them out on the ground under the sun. Then, we would cover them with hot dirt and leave them to bake. Hours later, we would pull the clothes from beneath the dirt, shake them off, and dress in them again. Washing our clothes was a luxury we could not afford all the time. As you can see, we resorted to environmentally friendly methods to deal with our problems with bugs. We would occasionally use soap to get rid of head lice which were superb at moving from one head to another. We wrestled a lot to pass time and test each other's strength. We butted heads when we wrestled, and that provided an excellent opportunity for head lice to move and take up new residence. Every Saturday morning, we went through a round of health inspection. The teacher would carefully examine our heads to find out who had head lice. Lice eggs formed lines of tiny white objects clinging to the edges of the hair. The border between the hair and the skin on the back of the neck was usually covered with dirt and salty sweat, which, I guess, provided abundant food for the eggs once they hatched into little lice. You could tell we were infested with lice by the abrupt and unsynchronized movements of our hands to scratch different parts of our bodies. The waist was the preferred hiding place for lice because the underwear we wore had stretchable rubber waistbands that prevented it from slipping down. It was an ideal area for lice to live and lay eggs. This was why you would frequently see children placing both hands on their waists and twisting their underwear repeatedly to cause them to rotate around the body in a desperate attempt to get rid of the lice and the unhatched eggs.

Fingernails were essential tools for scratching, but long nails presented a health hazard. It was important that we struck a balance between having nails that were short enough to pass the weekly inspection on Saturdays, but long enough to carry out the important job of scratching. I used to think that fingernails were there for the sole purpose of scratching bodies. I had no idea that there is a beauty dimension to them, so pardon me. Dirty uniform, dirty underwear, dirty hair, or dirty fingernails brought the person a minimum of five floggings.

In my opinion, lice and bedbugs are very intelligent creatures. It was easier for us to detect their movements at night when it was quieter, than during the day when we were on the move, which made it difficult to feel their bites. When we went to bed, they seemed to keep a low profile until we were deep asleep. Then they ventured out to bite. Upon sensing the slightest of movement, they would take off running to hide in our clothes, the bed cracks, and ropes, only to come out when we were still and soundly asleep again. That would go on until we succumb to a prolonged sleep, leaving them to roam our bodies freely. In the mornings, the crime scene, represented in our bodies, the cloth we were wearing, and the blankets, would be tainted with blood stains. It could be a result of greedy bedbugs sucking more blood than their bellies could take, and hence releasing some of it on our clothes, through their rear ends. It could also be an outcome of us subconsciously reacting to bites, while we were deep asleep, by turning our bodies and, in the process, crushing them to death under our weight, and spilling their blood.

One day, one of my boys brought up the subject of lice they had discussed at his school. I casually responded by telling him that I used to have lice all over my clothes and head when I was a little boy. A few days later, he told me he had confided to his teacher that I was the only person in the family who had lice. After that, every time I went to his school, I made sure that I had a fresh haircut, in an attempt to defuse the lice myth, just in case I encountered his friends or teachers and they looked at my head to verify his claim. I think the damage has already been done.

In the mornings, we drank tea made with UNESCO powdered milk. The tea was our only source of sugar. The same plates used for serving porridge and okra meals were also used for serving tea. We would place our metal cups in a line and wait for Habib, the sick super bully, to pour, supposedly, equal tea quantities in each cup. The plates were old and rusty. They all had black rings in the bottom, a sign of wear and tear. We placed the cups and plates on the ground, and that was how dirt got in, if they happened to have holes. This is an important clarification in case you are thinking why we did not place them on tables. What tables?

We learned not to dig too deep in the porridge so we did not end up swallowing porridge mixed with sand. The rust from the bottom of the plate dissolved into the tea, leaving a heavy concentration of black liquid at the bottom. We jockeyed for position to place our cups close to the plate to be among the first to get tea. The concentration of rust increased as more tea was scooped up. Latecomers got more rust in their tea than tea. We would carefully lift up the cups so as not to stir the rust. That degree of care was also extended to the way we tipped the cup to drink the tea. At each sip, we carefully looked at the bottom of the cup to make sure that we stopped sipping soon enough to avoid swallowing any of the rust with the tea, but without leaving any good tea behind.

We used to get very hungry between sunset and supper, particularly during winter when the few grams of porridge and okra we were given became as valuable as prime steak dinner. As we waited for the supper bell, we sat and leaned our backs against the boarding room walls. Some of us hummed, while others talked to friends. You would occasionally hear a boy walking around and calling the name of a friend. This was the only way we could communicate on those dark nights.

Jockeying for position in the line to pick up a plate was extremely important. Just like placing our cups in line for tea, being first in line gave us an opportunity to walk into the kitchen and choose a plate with more porridge and okra soup. That way, each one of us in the group of five or six sharing the plate, could get more porridge. If we joined the line late, we ran the risk of not getting a plate at all. Sometimes our female cooks, Umbototo and Al Bannor, did not prepare enough plates for all the pupils. In such cases, the heads of boarding rooms would go around and place children who did not have a plate with other groups. Invariably, by the time they joined their new groups, the porridge would already be gulped down. They would find themselves staring at empty plates. Can you imagine going to bed without having your share of porridge with okra soap?

Makeen, his brother Hakim, Saoori, and Radhi were four pupils at Darsail elementary school, known for having huge appetite. They were given a derogatory name *sawaeer*, which literally meant "those with rabies" because they ate a lot. This group of *sawaeer* celebrated the weekends because many children from nearby villages went home to visit, so there was more porridge to go around. Radhi, in particular, was known for eating so much that he would not be able to get up on his own, unless somebody pulled him up. On the other hand, Hakim was known for going around and scratching off tiny bits of porridge residue hanging on the bottom of plates. Children would leave one small bite of porridge as a reward for him so he would return the empty plates to the kitchen on their behalf. That was how he got twenty or so additional bites each day of the week.

We usually sent one person from our group to stand in line and get our group's plate. Then we would choose a spot in the open, or under the tree that was used by Habib and friends to trap dogs, to sit down in the dirt to eat. There were no lights, so we ate supper in the dark. To my bad luck, Makeen was in my group. He was excellent at eating more than his fair share of food. He maximized that by taking bigger bites and eating faster than the rest of us. By the time we finished eating, he would have had about double of what the rest of us had. We were very frustrated about our inability to keep up with him.

This is not the end of the story with Makeen. One evening, he invented an ingenious technique to cheat us, even more than he used to, out of our share of food. That night, we chose to sit closer to the kitchen where we could faintly see each other's faces in the flickering light emanating from the wood fire in the kitchen. One boy in the group noticed that Makeen's hand was not reaching his mouth all the time. Every other time, his hand stopped at his chest and went back to the plate for another bite. Upon paying closer attention, the boy discovered that Makeen's bite that disappeared at his chest level went into something he was hiding inside his *arragi* (supersize T-shirt). The boy shouted at Makeen, "What are you doing, you dog?" Makeen tried to get up and run away, but we were able to tackle him down. We found out that Makeen had his morning teacup hidden under his clothes and was dropping every second bite into it. It was more than the rest of us could bear, so we gave him the beating of his life, right there.

Our response to Makeen's greedy behavior turned out to be a serious tactical mistake. It kind of back fired. We attracted the attention of other children, who gathered around to find out what was happening. Unfortunately, beating Makeen and making a fuss out of the issue deprived us of the opportunity for getting rid of him by quietly transferring him to another group. Everyone living in the boarding school knew about his dirty tricks and would no longer accept him as a group member. We were so frustrated because we had no idea for how long Makeen had been cheating. With his wicked tricks, which were a combination of his speed and the cup under his shirt, he could have easily been eating one-third of the porridge in the plate, something like ten tablespoon-size bites of porridge out of approximately thirty bites in total. That left the rest of four or five of us the remaining twenty bites to share. Under normal circumstances, a boy like Makeen could progress to become a renowned problem solver. His technique of "a cup under a shirt" was a genius idea. Sadly, no one around could see his potential, certainly not us in his group. Who cares? Makeen's greed came at our expense, and we hated that. We were about only one thing; survival. *Sawaeers* were bad. We detested them so much that we created a song to undermine them. It goes, "We pray to God not to make us *sawaeer* like Makeen, tanga-ranga."

Another boy named Yonis also played dirty tricks. He would approach children, who would be eating, with his right hand stretched forward. He would be tucking his thumb under his four fingers, which he held tightly together and slightly bent downwards to appear as if he was holding something in his hand. He would say, "Please let me soup-up my dry porridge bite." He was alluding to having a dry bite of porridge in his hand that he just wanted to soften by mixing it with little okra soup. The truth was that his hand was always empty. That was a trick he used to fool the children into allowing him to put his empty hand in their plate and get away with a chunk of porridge and okra. Yonis's trick was known to many, but it sometimes worked, particularly with first-grade children, who paid a huge price for their lack of experience. Watching annual hotdog eating contests always makes me think that any one of the *sawaeer* at our primary school could easily win such contests.

Many a time, we ran out of the rations that we received from the UNISCO, way before the end of the school year, and we were left with limited daily portions of porridge and dry okra meals served three times. To supplement the shortage, we invaded the nearby forests in the evenings to gather wild fruit. There were no low-hanging fruits, so we had to either climb the trees or throw stones or sticks to knock them down. We always paid attention to the bushes and watched out for scorpions, cobras, or other types of snakes. Huge thorns protected most of the wild fruit trees.

One evening my friends and I went to the forest, collected some baobab, tamarind, and other wild fruit, and headed back to the boarding school just before sunset. We wanted to get back in time for the evening attendance assembly. We came across the road that trucks used to get to and from the city. We got curious when we heard the engine sound of a truck approaching from a distance, so we stopped to find out if there were passengers we knew. It turned out that the truck belonged to Uncle Zari, the only Kanuri in the area who owned one. We waved at the passengers as the truck passed. Instead of continuing its journey, it stopped. I was surprised to find out that my father was one of the passengers. He was returning from the city with merchandise for the shop. It was a nice surprise. My father and the passengers, most of whom I knew, gave us palm dates, mangoes, bananas, oranges, guavas, and money before continuing their journey. We sat down right there to sample our bounty from the city, or from heaven, if you will. That was the first time some of my friends had ever tasted some of these fruits. As we ate the bananas, we used a technique to get as much nutrition from it as possible. We pressed the inside part of the banana peel tightly against our lower teeth and scraped it downward to get at the peel's soft inner tissue before discarding the skinned-off peel. We never wanted to waste anything that was edible.

We got back to school with full bellies. You might think that we no longer needed the wild fruit and that we might have thrown it away. No, we did not do that because we had other plans. We carried it back to school and generously gave away some to our friends. We also gave some to other children to create new pacts to keep bullies at bay. When the inevitable fights break out in future, our friends wouldn't hesitate to stand by our side. Giving wild fruit for free also forged closer relationships with old friends so they shared with us any supplies they got from home. Nothing was given away genuinely for free in Darsail the school from hell, where we traded favors to survive. I guess strategic planning is a principle I am familiar with since a long time ago.

To this day, I still remember how that unexpected bounty of fruit tasted. It gave me an unparalleled satisfaction, and it also nourished my body. When you are very hungry, you don't care whether you are eating an apple or an onion. They will both be welcome treats. I also have a memorable experience with bread. It took place when I was about five years old. The same Uncle Zari, the truck owner, drove to our farm village to load my father's harvest of peanuts for that season. As the porters worked, Uncle Zari asked his assistant to get up the truck and get me a piece of bread from the storage box. That was the tastiest bread I ever had. There was no bakery in the farming village where I was born.

During harvest seasons, we would go to Friday markets, carefully guarding our half or one-penny coins, to buy cucumbers, corn, sweet canes, boiled peanuts, etc. As for the dry season, when we could not gather wild fruits from the forest, we would go to farms that had already been harvested, and dig out peanuts left behind in the ground.

We figured out that hard-packed farm grounds retained more peanuts than soft and sandy soil, so we carefully picked the right location to dig. Because farmers harvested peanut by using their hands to pull the plant out of the ground, how much peanut they harvested depended on the type of soil. Much of the harvest remained in the ground and went to waste. It was a very inefficient operation.

When I told my children that I used to eat wild fruit, they responded, "Don't you know that wild fruit can be poisonous?" I told them I did not know that when I was a child, and even if I had known, I would not have resisted eating it. Wild fruit was important for my survival. If I got sick after eating something, I avoided it the next time we went foraging in the forest.

As you can tell, we were very poor children. Ironically, despite that, we were a source of income to some village women. Everything in life is relative. With half a penny, we could buy a tomato or peanut sandwich from Macky's sister. We avoided buying any food in the presence of other kids for fear of ending up making enemies, unnecessarily, in case we refused to share it with them.

As soon as you handed Macky's sister your half a penny and received your sandwich, you got surrounded by children with hands stretched out, urgently begging you for a piece. Each one of them would be saying, "Addeeni" (meaning give me some), repetitively and loudly to grab your attention. You would look deeply into their faces, carefully assess the situation, and decide who should get a piece and who should not. Your decision would primarily be based on who had given you a piece of bread in the past and who was likely to give you something in the future. You also had to be sure about your risk tolerance, if you decided against giving a piece to please a bully. By the way, all of this strategizing, maneuvering, and making decisions under stressful conditions was about giving away a tiny piece of bread the size of a peanut or less. You have to be careful not to be carried away; otherwise, you will be left with nothing for yourself. If you concluded that the children begging you were of no past or future value, you would take off running. They would chase after you with their hands still stretched out, yelling, "Addeeni, ana addaitak!" which means "Give me some, haven't I given you before?" Running away was not always safe either. You could find yourself in a hostile territory infested by a gang of bullies, or end up bumping into another bunch of children, and that could double your risk many folds. What an awful nightmare! As you can tell, we were hungry all the time, since the food rations we received was not enough, as I explained above. Here is the bottom line; when you see a bunch of children with their hands stretched out, chasing another child holding a slice of lime, begging him for a drop of lime juice, you know they are extremely hungry.

Because of my Kanuri background and history, I took every opportunity I could to assimilate and gain acceptance from children at school. Sometimes my efforts to achieve such a goal were compromised. One morning my grandmother walked into my classroom unannounced, thus rendering my endeavors for integration fruitless. While the teacher was talking, he saw an old woman standing at the door, surveying the class. The teacher stopped, and the pupils stared at her. Then she pointed in my direction and spoke in Kanuri, saying, "Sayyidna areh," which means "Our lord, come over."

Grandmother called me "our lord" in the Kanuri language, because I am named after my grandfather Mustafa, who held the title of *Gony,* which, as I described earlier, was given only to holy men who could recite the Holy Quran from memory, so she never called me by my name, as a matter of respect. In fact, in the Kanuri tribal customs, husbands and wives never call each other by their given names. They usually use the names of their firstborn sons or daughters. To draw each other's attention they would say, "Father of so-and-so" or "Mother of so-and-so." At times, they use gestures or ambiguous sounds to draw each other's attention. I heard my father use terms such as "By the way, I tell you, so-and-so" to start a conversation with my stepmother. She also started talking to him abruptly without any introduction to the intended subject.

Majorly embarrassed, I silently begged God for mercy. Grandma was here at school! She happened to be visiting my aunt Maryam in a nearby village, and they both decided that it was a good idea to pay me a visit at school and bring some wild fruits. When they got to the assembly area in the center of school, Grandmother told my aunt, "You wait here and let me go and get *sayyidna*." She started with first-grade classroom, surveyed it, and walked away without saying a word, leaving the teacher puzzled. I found out about it later on from the teacher. She moved on to the second and third-grade rooms and did the same thing. I imagine she left while muttering to herself, in Kanuri language, something like, "Na allan babu," meaning "he is not here," until she found me in fourth-grade room. I rose from my chair and went to her. I stood no chance to stay seated, hide, or remain anonymous. The whole class, including the teacher, burst into laughter. I knew that my story would soon be known throughout the entire school, so I braced myself for a semester of mockery. This was the kind of thing students chewed on for eternity.

Grandmother greeted me in our Kanuri dialect while I was still a few feet away from her. This only confirmed to everyone that I was not an Arab. The damage to my efforts for assimilation was done. She held my hand and rubbed my head while leading me toward the schoolyard. Rubbing my head was her way of showing sympathy toward me for having lost my mother, her eldest daughter. I walked without looking back, certain that the teacher and the entire class were looking at us, amused by what had just transpired.

When we reached the center of the schoolyard, we found my aunt Maryam sitting on the ground. She greeted me, and we all sat down. They opened some cloth bags containing boiled and dried peanuts, baobab fruit, and sesame paste mixed with sugar. Wonderful, I thought to myself, but then I started worrying about the time. In about fifteen minutes, the bell would ring, and all the classes would leave for breakfast. There was a chance that the entire school would congregate around us. Of course, the bell rang, and I resigned to my fate. Three hundred students from the six grades emerged from classes and many of them passed by where we were sitting. They joked and laughed, but I avoided eye contact. I decided to forget about everything for the time being, leaving it for later. I spent quality time with Grandma and my aunt until they decided to leave. I accompanied them to the school gate and bid them farewell. I thought it was nice to have school visits from family members, but sometimes that came at a cost, which is fine.

Neither Grandma nor my three aunts recovered from the loss of my mother. They always showed sympathy toward us. My mother's friends, some of whom I did not know well, also expressed their sadness. Market days were particularly difficult for me because whenever my mother's friends spotted me, they called and asked me to come forward so they could express some *sympathetic rituals*. They would start talking to me in Kanuri in a low and a sad tone. One by one, they would rub my head, while saying, "Yayo, kingi Allah ye. Ya ngodoi, adumah dinao. Aduma Allah ye sirao," which means "Poor little creature. This is life. This is God's will." I would stand there calmly as they grieved. I used to be a total wreck inside. They would fantastically ruin my day by evoking memories that I had bottled up and tucked away deep inside my brain. I would remain in that down mood until the occurrence of a joyful event such as my friend Tiffah passing by and asking me to go and set bird traps.

The fasting month of Ramadan presented an opportunity for us at school, but it also posed a challenge. As a ten-year-old boy, I was not supposed to fast, but due to lack of supervision, I did anyway. We competed with each other to see who was stronger and could withstand thirst and hunger from dawn to sunset. I must say it was not an easy thing to do, but looking back, I believe it has contributed toward enhancing my willpower and self-control. We saved our daily food rations and ate it when we broke fast at sunset. It is needless to say, we did not have microwaves. What is there to microwave anyway? Sorghum porridge and okra? We picked up tiny pieces of charcoal from around the kitchen and lit up fire to cook millet-flour soup to supplement our poor evening meal. We used empty sardine and cheese cans as our cooking pots. After eating, we felt good about satisfying our egos that we were tough and could withstand thirst and hunger.

Rapty was a Greek man who moved to Darsail and adopted it as his place of residence and business. He was the contractor who delivered water to the school using his old red Ford tanker truck driven by Ishaag, a young man from the nearby village of Hajjah Harirah. One day, Ishaag delivered a large empty container and dropped it by the water barrels under the tree. Because it was different from the other barrels we had, several boys grew curious and came to investigate. They discovered a brownish butter-like stuff at the bottom of the container. One child licked some of it and told the others that it tasted sweet. In a few minutes, there was a frenzy of children feeding on the stuff. Soon, they all fell sick with severe diarrhea. Luckily, the situation was not fatal, and they survived. I myself tasted the stuff, but I could not tell what it was, and my gut feeling told me it was not edible. Despite the severity of the incident, no teachers showed up to investigate, and most likely nobody told them about what had happened. Events like these did take place from time to time, and it was a miracle that the side effects we suffered as a result of food poisoning caused by eating expired sardine, or injuries we sustained from fights were not life threatening.

We wrestled a lot in our free time. We bumped our heads to tackle one another, and that was how we exchanged lice. Kids with surplus lice passed them on to those with lice deficiency. As you can tell, we were very generous children. We also played soccer using colorful tennis-size balls, which fitted our budgets and level of energy, very well. We certainly did not have the energy to kick full-size soccer balls; besides, we could not afford them anyway. We had our own rules for soccer games. We had one playground where several teams of up to ten children per team played simultaneously. We distinguished each team's ball by its color. We constantly bumped into one another, but that never bothered us because it was just part of the game. Both wrestling and soccer games were mostly practiced at the beginning of the semester when we were relatively fresh and healthy, having just returned from our villages where we were on school breaks. However, I would not say home was better than school for all children. Despite the bad living conditions, some children were better off at school than at their homes. We wrestled less frequently as the semester progressed because of lower energy levels.

It would be well into the rainy season when we returned to school in August for the fall semester. By that time, our playground, which was located outside the school fence, would be overwhelmed by a wicked thorny plant called *Tribulus terrestris*, or goathead. We would cut the grass and clean the ground so we could play soccer, but the plants, especially goathead, would have already shed their seeds on the playground, making it impossible to completely do away with. Each goathead seed has three thorns, with one of them always pointing upward, ready to cause severe damage to any bare foot that stepped on it. No plant seeds caused us more pain than goathead. It was known to have been used as weapon by some African tribes to fend off other attacking tribes. They dipped the seeds in poison and scattered it in the enemy's pathways. The goathead seeds are similar in appearance to caltrops used by ancient armies to scatter in the paths of enemy cavalry and even by modern armies or police to puncture tires, for example.

We played soccer games barefooted. In few weeks, we would have cleaned the playground from goathead seeds. They caused a lot of pain when we stepped on them while chasing the ball, but we did not mind at all. The joy we derived from playing soccer game outweighed the pain. The area around the playground remained intact with goathead seeds everywhere. It was a big problem to retrieve the ball when it was kicked far away from the main playground. We could have easily put on slippers before we went to get the ball, but we were very impatient and did not want to waste any valuable playtime. We often hopped on one foot, hoping to halve the pain, while retrieving the ball.

At night, we suffered excruciating pain from all the thorns we had carried in our feet while playing soccer. It usually took two to three days for the pain to subside. Certain trees have up to two inches-long thorns. They usually pierced through the foot and broke. The wound would become infected and, I guess, in other parts of the world, that would call for surgical treatment, but we dealt with the situation on our own. It was common to see a child limping or hopping on one foot due to injury. We used long needles to dig out the thorns. We helped each other in removing smaller thorns that were considered a mere inconvenience. As for the ones that were deeply buried in the foot, we trusted nobody, but ourselves because it involved deep digging and bleeding. It was not easy to pull them out, so we resorted to a different technique to solve the problem. We would insert the back end of a needle in between our front teeth and gum, scrape out remnants of food, which would naturally be mixed with some bacteria, and stuff the wound with it. In a day or two, the spot would swell up from infection. Then we would use both thumbnails to squeeze the wound, forcing the thorn to pop out of the foot. We believed the "medicine" we applied had magical effect. It created pus, which made it easier for the thorn to slide out of the foot. The truth is that the body could have reacted in the same way, without any intervention from our end, had we waited for the same period of time; a day or two. What did we know? In a way, ours was rather an organic technique for solving the problem. It was way cheaper than visiting the emergency room, which we did not have at that time, anyway. It is till the case today, forty years later.

We removed only the thorns that caused us unbearable pain. We let our bodies tackle the less harmful ones. The body would build a fence (callus) around the thorn and isolate it from the flesh. A few days later, the pain would fade away and the thorn would eventually dissolve in the body, I think. Some may wonder why we did not wear soccer shoes. It was because we did not have soccer shoes. In fact, we did not know they existed; besides, affordability was another issue. We mostly wore slippers and we did not want to risk damaging them while playing soccer. This is to avoid being pulled out by the inspection teacher on Saturdays for punishment, in case we showed up barefooted. In addition, to avoid being reprimanded by our fathers for being reckless with our shoes and failing to make them last the entire semester, come what may. If you happened to flip over my slippers, you would find hundreds of thorn tips stuck there. Those were shorter thorns that did not find their way to my feet. The problem was that the quality of slippers was bad and they broke easily, forcing us to live with the consequences. The shoes often separated where the plastic piece went between the great toe and the second toe.

I used my slippers until the heel area wore thin; then I tiptoed whenever necessary to avoid thorns. I prolonged their useful life as much as I could until a circular hole emerged at the heel, rendering them totally unwearable. It would be time for recycling. When I was younger, I used to carve wheels for my toy truck from the parts that were not completely worn out. I would poke a hole in the center and use razors to cut along the edges to make designs that left track marks on the sand, just like tires. I used to drive my play trucks on sand dunes. I walked sideways to avoid stepping on the track marks. I very much enjoyed looking at the long trail marks I left behind. What can you do when you don't have Toys "R" Us store?

The upper side of my feet, like most children, resembled a grayish or brownish jute mesh. They had near-perfect grids created by cracks in the skin, resulting from a buildup of dirt and Vaseline. We used Vaseline during winter so that our feet would not look so ashy. The beige-colored bottoms of my feet were riddled with tiny dark spots all over, caused by the holes I had dug to remove thorns. Because I played barefooted, the holes filled with dirt, creating a beautiful design of a beige surface covered with black dots.

I remember wearing bandages wrapped around my legs and feet, most of the time. They covered wounds I had sustained mostly while playing soccer. I was very skinny and my wounds took a long time to heal. Obviously, the food was not nutritious enough to expedite the healing process. Lack of care and dirt did not help, either. We took bath once a week, if at all, and that, certainly, made the situation even worse. Once, I spotted maggots around the edges of a bandage that covered a deep wound on my leg. The wound would just not heal and kept growing. I was lucky that it was time for the semester break. I went home and my father took me to the clinic so it got treated. It left a huge mark on my left leg. I seriously injured my toes numerous times as I played soccer. I would limp for weeks until they healed on their own.

There are scars all over my body, including the tribal ones on my belly. My children were always curious to know what really caused them. I transformed my boring answers into bedtime stories about a false heroic encounter with a pack of six hyenas that I single-handedly defeated. At times, pigs do fly, especially in our home. I told them that once, while I was on my way to the village, returning from the farm, soon after sunset, I came face to face with a hyena that suddenly appeared and grabbed my left leg. Seconds later, another hyena appeared, jumped at me, and bit me on my right arm. I chose my left leg and right arm for the sake of consistency because there are big scars, supposedly, caused by hyenas. I continued my fake story by telling them that I looked back and saw four more hyenas running toward me to join the other two. I jumped up, freed myself from both hyenas' jaws and started running. All along, I was keeping a tight grip on my big stick, which had a metal bolt mounted on one end. The bolt was of the sort used for tightening big truck wheels. It was common to mount damaged bolts on sticks to use as defense weapons.

I ran as fast as I could and the hyenas chased after me. The gap between us grew narrower, then, luckily, I saw some shrubs by the side of the road, so I ran, hid there, and waited for them to pass by, while holding my stick up in the air with both hands ready to strike. When the first hyena got closer, I jumped in front of it. It charged at me, but I was very quick, so I hit it with full force on the nose. It howled loudly and fell to the ground, then the one behind it charged at me, and I gave it a powerful blow on the back sending it tumbling to the ground. The remaining four kept on coming at me, one after another, and I knocked down each one of them. The battle lasted a mere five minutes or so, and I found myself towering over a pile of six hyenas lying on the ground and could barely move. For the sake of my story, how tall I was at ten was immaterial. I limped home and told my father about my near-death encounter with the hyenas. He told me we descended from brave souls, so he was not surprised that

I stood my grounds and fought ruthlessly, the same way my ancestors did.

In the morning, people heard about my story and decided to verify it by going to the incident place to see for themselves. They found the six hyenas in bad condition. It was visible to everyone that they were injured, but did not sustain life threatening injuries and it appeared they will recover in few days. My story was credible and everyone in the village was satisfied with it. The boys in the village hoisted me onto their shoulders and carried me all over the village, and the village girls emptied whole bottles of perfume over my head and clothes.

That was the story of my heroism. It would have been nice if it was true, but it served its purpose anyway. I don't think I have ever seen my six and eight-year-old boys happier and prouder of me as their dad. In fact, the closest thing I had to an encounter with hyenas took place when I was about seven years old. A pack of hyenas attacked at night and killed a neighbor's donkey. The neighbor's house was about two hundred meters from mine. Who said Father Christmas is an imaginary character? My boys were so happy listening to my fake bravery story, so I better remember the details because it will be a matter of time before they ask me to tell it again. They will quickly detect any flaws or deviation from the original story, and that will put my credibility at stake. Mark Twain said, "If you tell the truth, you don't have to remember anything." I guess, if you tell a lie, you better remember everything, just in case you have to tell it again, someday.

At school, we had limited protection from diseases like malaria. When we fell ill, we resisted the sickness until our bodies gave up and we stayed bedridden. In the mornings, we would drag ourselves to the assembly area before classes, register our names, and walk to the clinic, a quarter of a mile or so from school, to receive treatment. If our conditions worsened, then someone would be dispatched to the market to send a message to our fathers to come and take us home. I used to get malaria at least once a year. I remember, a couple of times, lying down in the dirt, under a tree waiting for a truck to carry me to Kokoland. There was no such thing as special care. You would get sick, endure the pain, and recover, if lucky. I survived my illnesses, but my mother, younger brother, younger sister, and few of my friends did not. These are very painful memories.

One of the school bullies named Yonis and I got into an argument over an issue. One evening after sunset, but before supper, I heard the voice of Agrab (scorpion) calling my name. It was dark so that was the only way we could communicate with one another. I responded to his call and after finding me, he told me that Yonis wanted to see me at a secluded area behind the classrooms, away from everybody. I knew right there that I was in for a fight. There was no way I could have declined the "invitation," or Agrab would tell the whole school that I chickened out. He was known for knitting plots and carrying dirty messages. I followed Agrab to the specified location and found Yonis standing there. He immediately attacked me and we wrestled for some time until I was able to push him down to the ground. I sat on his chest and choked him hard. Agrab witnessed everything. I got up and left, fully satisfied and confident that I had scored points against him. Sadly, there were no witnesses, apart from Agrab, to record my victory over Yonis. Defeating him in the absence of other witnesses would not do much in preventing future fights. It was important for children to see for themselves that I could take on a bully like Yonis. That was how I could have raised my rank and gained more respect. It was a jungle out there.

As soon as I reached the boarding room area, the supper bell rang, so I ran to get me a good spot in line. While standing there, I suddenly received a severe blow to my chest, which brought me tumbling down to the ground. It took me few seconds to realize what had happened. It was Yonis, who, hiding under the cover of darkness, threw a brick at my chest, hitting me so hard that it knocked me down breathless for few moments. Then he jumped on me and punched me repeatedly. The blow was so severe that I was gasping for air. I was fighting for my life. The children congregated around us and recognized who we were. To every child who witnessed the incident, I was clearly being beaten up pretty bad and was defeated. The points I had scored earlier did not count anymore because no one knew about it except Agrab, Yonis, and me. The physical damage that I sustained was dwarfed by the psychological one. My reputation and standing in school was at its lowest point. If you were defeated, according to the school's unwritten rules, others would be motivated to test your abilities so they could enhance their own status. I knew it would take a long time before I recovered from both damages.

That night, I went to bed with excruciating pain in my chest. I could barely breathe. In the morning, I woke up coughing blood. You might think I went straight to the clinic. I did not. That would have only added salt to my psychological injury because the children would know how badly Yonis had beaten me. There are always people who play it dirty. As I grew older, I began to understand the importance of developing a strategy before going to battle. Propaganda and choosing the right battle ground are two important factors in winning wars. I did not know how to use them effectively at that age. Yonis picked the first location so no one would see if I beat him. As far as everyone else was concerened, Yonis was the victor. Yonis and I were in the same eating group, so at breakfast, the first meal after the fight, we sat around the same plate to eat. That morning, his gestures and body language clearly exhibited an image of someone who had victory under his belt. He was acting too cocky. In my case, I was more concerned about getting well. It took at least a week before the pain in my chest subsided. I don't know what lasting damage the blow had left, but I bet there is one.

Our school had a different attitude toward bullying than you could find elsewhere. Fights between children were a source of entertainment for the whole school. Some fights started with children poking one another on the chest with their index fingers. It meant that they had no real intention of fighting and most probably they were not too sure about the strength and fighting skills of one another. There was no use for escalating the fight and risk losing to the other party. To avoid that risk, they would continue poking each other, hoping for a miracle to save them from an uncertain outcome. If they were lucky, a wise and a mature child, which was a rarity, would intervene and stop the fight before it got worse. Both challengers would happily accept the older child's decision to separate them. They would walk away, but loudly bluffing and cursing each other to show that they were totally unafraid and ready to continue fighting, had it not been for the intervention. Each one of them would be implying that he was deescalating the fight as a sign of respect for the wise boy and, certainly, not out of fear.

Because fighting was a source of entertainment, the likelihood of a promoter showing up was also a real possibility. Bullies did all they could to encourage fights. Jumaa was one of those readily available fight promoters who offered their free services to children who were about to settle a dispute. He would approach them, bend down, and grab some dirt in his hand. He would then stretch out his arm and open his hand, exposing the dirt. His hand would usually be about chest high and held at equal distances from the two opponents. Next, he would start shaking his open palm, slightly, while singing, "The soup is burning my hand. Who is brave enough to take it away from me?" By that time, a crowd of onlookers would have gathered, and the opponents would be at a point of no return. All the ingredients for escalating the level of violence were there. Suddenly, one of the opponents would gather some courage and quickly put his hand beneath the bully's hand, knocking it upward in the direction of his opponent, showering his face with dirt. That was when the real fight began. The shouting from the crowd of children would be deafening. It was usually hot, so both fighters would be sweating. They would be wrestling to the last drop of energy they could squeeze out of their skinny bodies to keep themselves standing up right. The one who hit the ground first would run the risk of his sweaty face being smeared with dirt, or he could literally be forced to eat dirt. Nothing was more humiliating than being seen spitting dirt out of your mouth. For that reason, the opponents fought ferociously.

Losing or winning such battles reshaped our ranks and were valuable opportunities for evaluating each other's strength. When it was obvious that there was a winner and a loser in the fight, someone from the crowd, which by that time would have been fully entertained, would intervene and break up the fight, saying something like, "The winner takes it all and the loser is standing small." It was important to have a backup plan in the form of an older brother and children from your village or tribe to avoid being picked on.

The absence of such support undeterred bullies and made one totally exposed to them. My bad luck was that I had none of that kind of support available to me at times of need, which were so many.

Both Yonis and his friend Hakim came from the city to live with us at the boarding house and attend primary school in Darsail. I always wondered why their parents chose to send them away from the city to a village. During school vacations, they both left and went back to the city while the rest of us disappeared into the bushes. When school reopened, we always enjoyed a few weeks of exciting tales from the city. Yonis and Hakam told us fresh stories about going to the cinema and watching American movie heroes like Ringo, Django, Sartana, and Shami Kabour, from India; names none of us had ever heard of. Much of what Yonis and Hakim told us did not make sense because we had never been to movies. We were nothing more than a bunch of naive village children because we took whatever they told us for granted. I especially enjoyed listening to Yonis's stories, even though we were, officially, enemies since the night he hit me with the brick. I enjoyed the sound he used to make with his mouth imitating the sound of a hero's punches landing on a bad guy. Only Yonis could make that amplified punching sound. The truth was that, deep down, I resented the fact that my stories from the village were neither a match, nor as attractive as my opponent's. How could I compete with him when I spent most of my school break with my gray donkey? Who would find it interesting to listen to a story about a gray donkey, especially when most village children had donkeys of their own? I did not know much about the spaghetti westerns and their heroes until I was much older. I made sure that I watched the 2012 movie *Django Unchained*, starring Jamie Foxx. Even though this movie was very different from the Django of the seventies as told to me by Yonis and Hakim, it brought back many good, bad, and ugly childhood memories.

One day a fight broke out between Yonis and Hakim for no apparent reason. It took place under the neem tree by the water barrels. I don't remember any reason for that fight other than Hakim trying to assert his authority as a dominant player in the school. Hakim won because Yonis did not lift a finger to show that he was ready to fight. No doubt, I was fine watching my enemy being beaten up. In fact, Yonis tried to appease Hakim, but Hakim had other motives. He wanted to practice fighting skills he had seen in cowboy movies in the city. I finally found out about this many years later when I had a chance to watch Western movies, which I still love to watch, even today. In preparation for the fight that day, Hakim even wore pants designed like the ones he had seen in the movies. As Yonis sat on the ground, Hakim slowly walked up to him, bent down, yanked him up by the collar of his shirt, and punched him on the face. Yonis screamed from both fear and pain as Hakim looked around to see who was watching. I think he wanted to make sure that there were as many children as possible witnessing Yonis's humiliation. His ultimate goal was to satisfy himself that everyone in the school saw how formidable he was. By then, the crowd had grown so large that shorter children had to jump up to try and get a glimpse of the action. Hakim made eye contact with every one of us in the crowd, and then turned back to Yonis. Yonis retreated, but the circle built by the crowd left him no opening to escape. Hakim started punching Yonis fast and hard with both hands, while making punching sounds with his mouth. He also murmured words that I thought were English, but who could be certain and tell. Later on, I learned that had nothing to do with English. By that time, Yonis was heavily bleeding from the mouth. Babikir, who was one of the most respected students in the school, emerged from the crowd. He stood between the two, separating them with his hands and signaling to everyone that the fight was over. It was about time we all dismissed, including Yonis who found in that a window of a valuable opportunity to disappear, hurriedly. Hakim had reaffirmed his fighting superiority. He stood around for some time enjoying the looks of admiration from the kids. He made strange gestures none of us knew anything about. He shifted his weight from one leg to the other as he put one forward and pulled the other back. He also rubbed his lower lips with his tongue, and looked at the crowd out of the corner of his eye, while tilting his head slightly to one side. I think those gestures were exclusive to Hakim. He made them as an extra bonus for those who stayed around after the show was over. I never saw any Western movie hero making movements like that. We were truly country bumpkins who could easily be persuaded to think that something as ugly as beating Yonis in that horrific manner was not only okay, but also worth-watching for entertainment. It was not fine at all. It was a jungle out there and we hardly had any supervision. Once Hakim fully satisfied himself that he had accomplished his goals, he walked away without saying a word. The crowd was happy to break the circle and make a room for him to pass.

For a long time, I thought God gave those punching skills to city boys, or perhaps to Hakim alone. It took me until I watched movies such as *Dirty Harry*, *The Magnificent Seven*, *The Good, The Bad, and The Ugly*, and others, to fill in the gabs. Hakim was not invincible at all. He was a big lie.

After I had a chance to visit the city, I found out that Western movies were a big thing there. A friend told me of a moviegoer who was so into those types of movies that he, once, came to the theater dressed in full cowboy gear, wearing loose pants (fashionable at the time), boots with spurs and rowels, a cowboy hat, a cigar, and a horse saddle that he carried on his shoulder. I have yet to find anybody who freely promoted American pop culture more than what that young man did. Watching movies gave me a chance to escape the realities of life in Kokoland, even though temporarily. Whenever I came out of a movie, I felt sad because I was leaving behind beautiful people, scenery, and imaginary worlds that were far beyond my reach. I also felt bad because I did not get many opportunities to go to the city, nor did I have enough money for movies.

As you can tell, Darsail was a true jungle. Teachers rarely came to investigate what was going on. There was one incident with a first grader that I will never forget. I think the boy had a problem with his eye site. He could barely see. Some kid found out and told other kids about the boy's disability, so they turned him into a source of entertainment. I remember for a couple of days, around sun set, the boys would gang up against the little boy, grab his cloth, hit him at different parts of his body and run away. The boy could not see, so he would be bumping into objects, and the other boys laughed every time he fell down. The boy disappeared shortly after the incident. He probably went back to his village and told his parents about what had happened to him, so they decided to keep him home. I was young too, but I knew what the boys were doing was very wrong. I was sad and helplessness that I could not do anything to protect the little boy. The problem was that I could not protect myself, leave alone extending help to others. Darsail was truly one hell of a school from hell.

CHAPTER 9

Bullying Redefined

The Kanuri were known throughout the region for being religious people. They generally upheld their religious teachings by praying regularly and refraining from drinking alcohol and cigarette smoking, beside following other commands. They minded their farming business and did not interfere in other people's affairs. Not sending their children to school was one way of keeping to themselves, so they would not be seen by the so called more legitimate tribes of the region as claiming what was not theirs. Besides; they believed that school was an institution created by the infidels to lead their children away from the truth path. Only a few people from my family broke away from tradition and sent their children to school. My uncles had many sons and daughters, but none of them attended school, not even first grade. This was at a point in time when the central government was paying for all school expenses from primary to college. It took decades for people to realize the importance of education, but, to many, the damage caused by illiteracy was irreversible. The Kanuri's God-fearing way of life led local tribes to believe that they had special powers bestowed upon them by their knowledge of religious secrets and that they could perform miraculous acts. On the other hand, their timid, appeasing, and compromising approach to life made them an easy target for dominant tribes such as the Bibi. I think they were mainly hampered by the lack of education, coupled with cultural and language barriers, which made them keep to themselves.

As I mentioned earlier, after the death of my mother, my father arranged to transfer my brother Aziz and me to Darsail Primary School where we started fourth grade. The move was hellish. Life at our new school was one crisis after another. The bullying we suffered was unbearable, especially the one caused by children from Bibi village, as I have written above. The only other Kanuri child at the school, besides my brother and me, was Ali. The Bibi children told others at the boarding house that my brother and I had the ability to change into hyenas at night. They warned them not to have anything to do with us. A boy named Karim was the lead antagonist. He mimicked the sound of hyenas every time we crossed paths. Whenever he made eye contact with my brother or me, he would laugh and say, "Please don't eat me," and the rest of the children would laugh too. He would tell others that our "red eyes" was a sign of our ability to change into hyenas at night, so they must take care and avoid us as much as possible.

Some tribes believed that the Kanuri were sorcerers who used black magic on people. Although this was a very offensive accusation, none of the Kanuri would say a word about it because of their peaceful way of life and the language barrier. They prayed frequently to fend off injustices and ill-treatment from their adversaries.

One day, rumors broke out in school that a Kanuri man in Darsail had casted a spell of black magic on a little girl. The claim was that the man, using his eyes, was able to suck out the little girl's guts. Those allegations caused a crisis of epic proportion for my brother and me. Some children responded by harassing and beating us because we belonged to the Kanuri tribe.

Usually the punishment for a man accused of committing such crime was death, especially if the victim died. The only way for him to escape the punishment was by restoring the victim to his or her good health. Normally, the accused sorcerer would be brought and forced to reverse the magic. The girl might still die, even though the cause of death might have nothing to do with black magic. However, that was the way unexplained phenomena were interpreted at the time. In most cases, the poor men accused of committing such crimes would not be able to express themselves and communicate their thoughts well due to language barrier, as I mentioned. Consequently, they would mostly fail to defend themselves. Luckily, the school closed two days after the incident, so my brother and I were able to travel to Kokoland unscathed. I don't know what happened to the girl or the man. I returned to school the next semester and had to deal with more pressing new problems.

My father told me about a dispute that took place between a Kanuri man and his wife. They decided to go to the local court to seek judgment. The man asked his wife, "When we go in front of the judge, could you please tell him about your grievances and mine as well?" Her response to him in Kanuri was, "Yo ingila zauro," which means "absolutely no problem." In fact, she did just that. They stood in front of the judge who asked her to speak first, and she did. The judge then turned to the man and asked him to speak about his complaint. The man turned to face his wife, then spoke at length (in Kanuri language). When he finished talking, his wife turned to the judge and explained, in Arabic, what he had told her. The judge could not make sense of the comic scene unfolding in front of his eyes. In fact, he did not believe that the woman could have told the truth about what her husband had requested her to say, bearing in mind the fact that they were there standing in front of him because they sued one another and were seeking judgment, each for himself. He solicited the help of a translator, so he asked a Kanuri man sitting on the bench among the public, to translate and tell the husband what his wife had just told him (the judge). The man spoke to the husband in Kanuri and, to everyone's surprise, confirmed what the husband had exactly asked his wife to tell the judge.

I guess this was an example of an absolute loyalty between husband and wife. The whole thing defeated the very fact that they were in dispute to the extent that they had to resort to court to seek resolution. My dad told me that the judge, with his wisdom, decided in favor of both of them. He used accommodating language rather than legal arguments to settle the case. I doubt it if there was a legal precedent that he could have used for settling this case. The judge probably felt that those two innocent human beings belonged to one another, so he decided not to fault either of them. He told them to go back home and try to work it out and come back in a few months to tell him how things went, either way. They accepted the verdict and left the court room very happy. They went to the town market, bought some groceries, and headed home. The husband was seen leading the way and the wife trailing him by a few feet; a sign of total obedience. What a waste of tax payer's money?

One child at school, named Jamur, occasionally used to pick up dirt, bring it up close to my nose, and say, "Smell this dirt. Is this your grandfather's land?" I guess that could be something he had heard adults talking about at home in the village. Jamur's act was obviously an, unwelcomed, open invitations to fight, and I never shied away from accepting it. The common belief that the Kanuri possessed supernatural powers passed down to us from our ancestors was something I occasionally used in times of need. Children used to sing a mocking song about Kanuri's supernatural abilities which rhymed like this: "Barnu [Kanuri] barnook, a tree without roots, if five of their men tie you down, fifty five men won't manage to cut you loose."

To survive, I had to either fight, or use deterrent tactics. Constant fighting could be exhausting. It would drain you both physically and mentally. You would constantly be developing strategies, but you just could not guarantee a favorable outcome all the time. If you lost, it caused more fights because it gave other children the opportunity to evaluate and test your fighting skills. It gave them the confidence to bully you and score points that enhanced their own social ranking. Therefore, it was important to have other defense mechanisms. You wanted to avoid fighting as much as possible. Because I was a Kanuri, it was assumed that I could use religious secrets combined with tree roots and animal parts, to inflict harm upon children who bullied me. This was a powerful deterrent measure that was presumably at my disposal to use during those dark days. Coincidentally, this was happening to me around the same time nuclear bombs were used as a deterrent by world superpowers to prevent a third world war. As absurd as this comparison might sound; those horrible days at school were equivalent to living daily under the threat of a third world war of my own.

A few times, I resorted to my presumed religious secrets and employed bluffing as tactics to defend myself, even though I wasn't prepared to have them called. You can tell I was very desperate. Whenever a bully antagonized me in such a way that, I thought, was leading to a fight, I would carefully assess the situation and choose the time and place for battle, preferably around children. I had learned my lesson the hard way from the fight Yonis and I had, which I talked about earlier. It would also be an ideal time for the use of something supernatural, especially when there was a possibility of losing, if I used conventional fighting tactics. Here is how I executed my supernatural fighting plan. First, I would show some fake seriousness and intimidating gestures like biting on my lower lip, nodding my head repeatedly, and saying, "*Istabir,*" meaning you wait." I would say that wile making an *Istabir* gesture by stretching my hand forward, but keeping my fingers tightly held together. *Istabir* alone could suffice and do the trick because it might carry the meaning that my opponent must brace himself for a barrage of black magic attack, inevitably, coming his way, therefore I didn't need to say anything more. Children feared black magic at varying degrees and there was always a boy in the crowd who would be dreading the idea of black magic spilling over and leading to unintended consequences. Sometimes guided missiles stray and hit wrong targets. The boy, out of fear and desire for leaving nothing to chance, would step forward and explain things to my opponent, on my behalf. He would tell him, "Hey, you better be careful. This boy's father is a holy man. If he complains to him, that will be "your sunset." Sun-setting meant harm from black magic was certain to befall the boy. That was enough warning to diffuse the tension. Bluffing worked every time I used it. The boys probably knew I was bluffing, but no one wanted to risk challenging me because I had never been tested in the past. No one dared to be the first person to venture into such uncharted territory and get exposed to black magic of all kinds. It was a question of fearing the unknown.

It was common for Kanuri to wear charms. They were a combination of Quranic verses, tree roots, and herbs, wrapped in goatskin. Charms were worn by both adults and children. To tell you the truth, as a child, I did have charms of my own, which I wore around my arm beneath my sleeves. That was a better place to hide such secrets. I could have worn them around my neck, but the visible thread or leather cord would have given away my secrets. Everyone believed that charms had special powers. They protected you from evil spirits, made you smarter, and helped you do well at school. Charms could also be used as tools to stall the progress of competing students by affecting their performance on exams, their grades, and ultimately their rank in class, which mattered most. Charms simply needed to be rubbed on the competitor's head, and his brain would be "blocked," and cease to function smartly, as far as school work was concerned. The person would not remember, surprisingly, a thing when taking exams. The process was called *kadook*. If someone got *kadooked,* exam results were certain to be bad. *Kadooking* would cause everything the student had learned to evaporate, especially math. I remember those who claimed to have been *kadooked* always made a big scene ahead of exam times. They made sure that as many children as possible knew about their predicament. That way, they would already have justification for not having done well in exams when the results came out. It is needless to say that most of the students who claimed to have been *kadooked* had a history of bad results. Not a bad way for putting the blame elsewhere on some supernatural powers.

I also remember boys who claimed to have been *kadooked* always choosing a time about an hour or so before sitting for exams. That was the time we sat quietly on the ground outside, leaning our backs against the class wall, waiting for the bell to ring so we could go inside and write the exams. We crammed answers to questions we highly expected to appear in the exams. Those were called "spotting notes." The process of cramming those notes at that limited time before exams was called "saddling-snack." The quiet and timid image of pupils resembled the image of donkeys and horses given snacks to eat so they would stand still and make it easy to saddle and load up, hence the term saddling-sack. That was the best time for pupils who were unprepared for exams to claim that they were being *kadooked.* They would argue that they were magically deprived of their mental ability to rehearse and retain their spotting answers to pour onto the answer sheet. This is how they paved the way for their expected bad results. What a waste of energy. You would imagine they could have gotten better results had they channeled that effort toward studying and preparing for exams.

I prayed for a safe end of semesters to have a break from school and all the bullying, hunger, punishment by teachers, lice, bedbugs, etc., that I would have endured, but the problem with school breaks was that they had their own sets of hazards. Fights between children took place regularly. In most cases, they were quickly settled and everyone moved on and dealt with the new school order and the reality of having a new winner and a new loser. In other cases, they would resort to de-escalation and the use of the famous word *istabir*, or you wait, tactics before walking away. Besides intending to solicit help from supernatural powers, that could also mean putting the fight off for another day when they would be better prepared. In both cases, they could be buying time to get help from whoever came forward first, be that human friends or the djinns, so that victory would be guaranteed. Sometimes postponing a fight could also be due to fear of being punished by teachers in case it got reported. As far as I was concerned, being a minority, it did not matter much if I fought right there or put it off for later, since I had no one to back me up. For some reason, I did not count too much on djinns coming to my rescue at times of dire need.

The last day of school was also reserved for settling scores between students who competed with one another academically. Those who fared well at school were targeted and beaten up by those who did not. School breaks were generally viewed as liberating times because school rules did not apply any more. They were a relief for me as long as I could safely reach the town market center. The distance was one kilometer, but it was a treacherous one because it would be riddled with bullies.

Finally, it was the last day of my fourth-grade school year. That morning the bell rang, so the entire school assembled in the school yard. Each grade lined up in front of their respective classroom and waited for the teachers to assemble at the school theater. Beginning with first grade, each class head teacher called out the names of pupils, starting with the one who scored the highest grade average. Upon hearing his name, the pupil would run to the teacher to receive his grade certificate, along with the admiration of the teachers and some of the pupils. Those whose class rank was not among the top ten were usually unhappy because only top ten pupils received applause in recognition for their hard work and good performance. That was why some pupils took out their resentment on the students who did well. In my case, despite everything at school, I worked hard and always secured my place among the top five. I did not have alternative options at my disposal. Some children held the last rank in class, exam after exam and year after year. They were often called the class's "brake coach," like coaches at the rear end of trains used for speed-control. Everyone knew who ranked last in each of the six grades. School children sometimes paraded them all the way to their homes by walking behind them and singing a special procession chant; "Losers must be beaten up with slippers." There was a chance that they were further humiliated by their parents for doing so bad at school. Nothing good could come out of calling the name of a child in front of the entire school to tell him he was the dumbest in his class. You can imagine the lasting psychological damage those children could have endured. Many of them did not show up at school the following term. They dropped out and looked for something else to do in life. They only created room for new class lasts and brake coaches, so the sad parade saga continued. It was a brutal environment.

After the name of the last student from sixth grade was called, the principal stepped forward delivered his semester-end speech, and wished us a wonderful break. Once he declared the dismissal of the assembly, all hell broke loose as everyone scrambled for the school gate. Doing well in my rankings made me a legitimate target for beatings. That was my unwanted reward. I had to chart a safe route out of school or form an alliance with a group of friends who were in the same predicament. However, the latter option was not always readily available to me.

I will never forget that morning of the last day of my fourth grade school year in 1971. I left the schoolyard and hurriedly returned to my boarding room. I kneeled down and pulled out the metal suitcase from under my bed, then I headed in the direction of Uncle Gony Hamza's home. My suitcase was made from a very heavy iron so it could not easily be broken into. Its Chinese-made lock gave me additional assurance that my belongings were kept safe and not stolen. On the other hand, its heavy weight was a problem for me that day. It slowed me down enough to the point that I had to take rest breaks every few yards to change hands. When I got to a narrow ally, halfway to my destination, I heard a voice behind me say, "Hey, you, stop." I looked back, and I saw Salim, his brother Ali, and three other youth whom I did not recognize. They certainly did not attend school because there was only one primary school in town and I would have known them, if they did. I knew that the moment of truth had arrived. I placed my suitcase on the ground and braced for a fight; I had no other choice. I never shied away from fights brought upon me, even when the odds of winning were extremely unfavorable. Salim said, "Why were you acting cocky at school the other day?" Then, his brother Ali said, "You Borno [Kanuri] killed our uncle." This meant I had to prepare myself to pay a heavy price for two crimes I had not committed. I had only a few seconds to prepare to defend myself. The two boys ran at me and the other three followed on their heels. When they got closer, Salim stopped and grabbed a dry branch, covered in sharp thorns, from the fence by the side of the road. They got to me, and we collided. I knew they were there to kill me. I blindly punched and kicked even though I received five blows for every one they received from my end. I also received severe blows from the thorny branch on different parts of my body. The battle went on for several minutes. I did not fall down, but I was bleeding from my head, my nose, my lips, and my back. In the midst of the fight, I saw Suleiman standing between the gang and me. I had no idea how and when he got there. Suleiman was one grade senior to me, and he happened to live in the gang's neighborhood. How much longer could I have survived is anybody's guess, but I knew I would go down fighting. Suleiman was finally able to push us apart and break up the fight. The gang could have overpowered both of us, but they decided to stop fighting. They might have feared that if they continued and injured me badly, they would not have gotten away with it because Suleiman was a witness. They walked away and left me catching my breath. Suleiman helped me remove some of the thorns stuck in my back and clean off the blood, then he left and continued his journey to his house.

My body ached all over. I was fortunate that no sharp objects like knives were used in the fight. Nevertheless, the branch had inflicted serious damage on my body. It came from a tree with thorns curved like fishhooks. Once they grab onto a piece of cloth or skin, it will almost be impossible to get them loose. Pulling them out with force causes even more damage because they will also pull along a piece of skin or clothing. I guess that is how trees protect themselves from being eaten by goats and other animals. The thorns were so effective that people used them in making fences to keep animals at bay.

I had bumps and bruises all over my body. I was able to remove the visible thorns from my hands, my legs, and the parts of my back that I could reach, leaving the rest, which broke off deep under my skin, to be dealt with later. The ones on my back that I could not reach, remained there forever and dissolved in my body, over time. There was no way I could have solicited the help of anybody to get them removed. There would have been many questions about what had happened to me and who caused it, so leaving the thorns in my body was the better option. The bumps on my lips and my head are still there and they constantly remind me of that horrible day. I don't know what could have happened that morning, had it not been for Suleiman's sudden appearance. I was fortunate to have survived that ordeal.

Some of the fights between children had fatal results, even though this was uncommon. A year later, when we returned to school after summer vacation, we found out that Fathi, the brother of one of my classmates named Mahmoud, had been stabbed and killed by another student named Adam. Both Fathi and Adam were in fourth grade when this happened. Fathi constantly harassed and antagonized Adam. They both shared the same road walking to their houses. Fathi beat Adam whenever they met. Adam grew intolerant, so when Fathi confronted him one day, as usual, he stabbed him with a knife he had been concealing under his clothes.

When I was in college, a colleague of mine found out that I had attended Darsail primary school and wanted to know if I knew a young man named Adam Z. He told me that Adam had moved to his village, got married, and became the village tailor. Adam decided to move away from Darsail after serving a jail sentence in a juvenile detention center in the city. He must have decided to start a new life, so I did not tell my colleague about his past that he had committed a murder crime.

As indicated above, I was on my way to uncle Hamza's house. However, I wanted to avoid questions about the bruises over my face, so I decided to change course. I picked up my metal suitcase and headed to the town center where I left it with Musa, a shop owner who was a friend of my father. I told him that my father would pick it and bring it home the next time he passed by on his way from the city. Unfortunately, the case got stolen before my father could get it. Months later, I found Abdullah, a fellow pupil, wearing one of my garments. I told my father about it. He decided not to press charges when he found out that Abdullah was an orphan living with his grandmother. Because of my father's decision, I lost every piece of clothing I had owned, so, naturally, I did not care much about Abdullah's family situation. At that age, I did not fully understand my father's act of compassion and sympathy for Abdullah.

I travelled on to Kokoland, but I never told my father about the fight in Darsail. I kept my distance from him so he wouldn't notice the bruises on my head. Even if he found out, I would have gotten away with it by giving him excuses such as "I fell from a tree and hit some branches," or "I got kicked by the donkey," and so on. We thought it wasn't a manly thing to tell our fathers about fights between us children. That was our business and we were the ones who must handle it. Mothers were the last to know about their children's fights. Anyway, at that time, my mother had already passed away, so that option was not available to me, even if I wanted to tell her.

I was bullied so much because of my slim physique. I was targeted more frequently than other children. Fighting was the preferred way for attaining seniority. If you won a fight you would gain respect from the children, but, of course, you would not be left alone, since you would be challenged at your new rank. That was also the case if you lost because you would be viewed as weak and an easy target to beat. You would represent an opportunity for children seeking to enhance their own chances of climbing up the power ladder. The school arena was filled with constant struggle for power. I never invited troubles upon myself, but they always found their way to me, leaving me no option but to stand up and fight back. Sometimes I won and at other times I lost. I was a minority at school as well as among my own Kanuri people. I was seen as too ambitious and some people did not like that, so they volunteered to put me down back in my right place. Perhaps I would have been less bothered had I been timid. Many kids, both at school and in Kokoland, did not like the fact that I was a Kanuri boy who attended school and, justly, expressed his indignation whenever treated unjustly. I paid a heavy price for my stances and for who I am. I have battle marks all over my body; a constant reminder of those dark days.

Fights were instigated by two different groups; school children, as previously described, and village children who did not attend school. The village fights were especially problematic due to their unpredictability. Village children did not worry about the consequences of fighting because they didn't have much to lose. They were not concerned about getting punished by teachers for mistakes they had committed. They strongly disapproved of the fact that I attended school, so they were more aggressive in their attacks. I could be walking the street home and minding my own business. That was not enough for keeping me out of trouble, if I met bully boy Bahar and friends. They never needed reasons for picking up a fight.

One day, my father sent me to get him a cup of tea from Omer's café. When I got there, I saw a group of six children from the village sitting on the ground in the afternoon shade of the building. One of them was Saleh, another bully who was also friends with bully boy Bahar. They looked at me and talked among themselves for a moment, then I saw one boy named Eid get up and walk toward me. He stood a few yards from me and said, "Hey, what do you think you are?" I asked him, "What do you mean? but he hit me with an object before I could even complete the sentence. It was a knife he was hiding in his pocket. Blood gushed out of the left side of my head and ran down my face, covering my shirt. News got to my dad who rushed to Omer's café and led me to the clinic. I received several stitches then I was taken home. I was very sick that night, both physically and at heart, but especially at heart because I was taken by surprise and I could not defend myself. At that moment, the problem was out of my hands. It become an intertribal matter because it had resulted in blood-spilling.

One Friday, after I had fully recovered from my injuries, my father took me to Uncle Ramadan's shop where fifty or so representatives from my Kanuri tribe and the boy's tribe were gathered. Uncle Ramadan, the shop owner, who was also a much respected community leader, spoke first. He asked me to come to the center where the men were sitting so they could see my wound, which was clearly visible, being in the center of a shaved area of my head. Next, he asked me to leave, so I went back to our shop, leaving my father to negotiate a settlement for my injuries. That was the last time this subject came up between my father and me or any other family member. I never knew what the gathering discussed or the form of settlement they reached. It must have been agreeable to both tribes because the issue did not escalate into a tribal conflict. I learned to keep the memories of those dark times tucked away in a far off corner in my mind. I occasionally visit them, but I leave hurriedly.

Bullying was not reserved for children alone. Adults also bullied. Whipping was the preferred method for punishing children and teaching them lessons about the importance of keeping out of trouble. An adult had complete authority to punish a child who committed a mistake, irrespective of whether he were the child's father or not. I think the saying "It takes a village to raise a child" must have been coined in Kokoland. The difference in Kokoland was that

"It took a village to whip a child." Some adults eagerly exercised the right to take part in raising children, as was the case with one of my father's relatives, named Kazallah. This Kazallah man strongly believed I was a spoiled school-going child and that I needed whipping to force and tame me into becoming a better-behaved kid. I knew his feelings toward me all along. He particularly resented the idea that I was attending school, but he could not convince my father to agree with his views and take me out of school, so he waited for an opportunity to get me.

One day, I went to visit one of my uncles in a nearby village. As the following day happened to be a market day, father expected me to come early in the morning to open the shop and help him handle customer orders. In the morning, on my way to Kokoland, I spent some time in the forest to cut some wood to carve a boomerang, so I was late. I arrived at the shop and found my father and Kazallah. They both exhibited body language indicative of their disapproval of my late arrival. It was obvious to me that my father had told Kazallah about my failure to show up earlier, and that was enough reason for him to lend my father his full sympathy and support. After all, the general view held by adults was that "the children of the day" were disrespectful and don't listen or obey their elders. I went inside the shop and assumed my responsibilities. Out of nowhere, a blow landed on my head, followed by a couple of slaps to my back and neck. I was taken by surprise and had no idea why I was being punched. I fled the scene and left Kazallah behind me shouting and saying how spoiled I was and that I always gave my father a hard time by not helping him in the shop. Kazallah acted to show full solidarity with my father. I was never on good terms with him, so his behavior was not unexpected. The opportunity to discipline me presented itself that morning and he took full advantage of it.

It was perfectly understandable that Kazallah chose the tool he knew best. You might be surprised to learn that I was not mad at my father for allowing this man to beat me. This was a calculated balancing act that my father must have given a serious thought. He really had only two choices. He could have objected to my beating and ended up facing the fury of the entire community, which would have branded him as someone who lacked the skills necessary for raising children, or he could let me live that one time "punishment by proxy" experience. I could tell from his facial expressions that he did not fully approve of the idea of beating me, and that alone was enough solace for me.

The bullying I was exposed to was an overflow from the ill-treatment my father received from the community. He chose to farm near the village of Hikam, my birthplace, in an area by a seasonal stream known for fertility of its soil. He had many successful harvest seasons, so he was able to save enough money to open a shop. His success earned him animosity from some community members. One particular man named Kinnah, expressed open hostility toward my father. Kinnah showed up at our shop one Friday afternoon, during the harvest season. The market was packed with shoppers and traders. I was about eight years old at the time. For reasons unknown to me, Kinnah started threatening and exhibiting hostility toward my father, who told him to leave the shop, but he refused. My father walked out from behind the groceries table and confronted him. He pushed Kinnah out onto the shaded verandah in front of the shop and walked back. Kinnah followed him inside the shop and continued arguing, but more aggressively. It was clear that he was intending to hurt my father.

The argument escalated to a new level. Kinnah lifted up an axe he was holding and was about to strike my father, but he was not fast enough. My father was faster. Kinnah came tumbling to the ground. Blood was all over his clothes. In a few seconds, it was all over. Kinnah lay on the ground, motionless. Here, I intentionally decided to withhold account of what had exactly happened as I don't feel comfortable divulging it. News about the incident spread in the market like wild fire and hundreds of people rushed to the scene to find out. There was a deafening noise from the collective voices of men arguing. Emotions ran high and tempers flared as people divided up into two camps, one supporting my father, which was mainly comprised of Kanuri people, and another supporting Kinnah, made up of people form his village and the surrounding area. It was a chaotic scene that was about to turn into an intertribal conflict. In fact few skirmishes did break out, but fortunately wise men from both camps intervened and the voice of wisdom prevailed. Kinnah was carried to the clinic where he received treatment for his injury and regained consciousness. All I was concerned with was his survival. If Kinnah had died, I would probably have lost my father, even if he were proven not guilty. The incident was self-defense, but local customs could demand *tha'ar* or revenge killing, out of the law, had Kinnah died.

Members from both communities met and levied a fine on my father. The details of the settlement was not known to me, and I did not care. I just wanted to forget all about the incident. Even though Kinnah survived, members of his tribe threatened to retaliate. It was rumored that they were determined to prevent my father from farming his land the following year. I was so worried. The prospect of losing my father by the next rainy season turned my life into a living hell, and there was nothing that I could do, besides waiting. I wanted to bring up the subject to discuss it with him, but I was certain he was going to tell that it was a matter for adults, only, to handle. Luckily, the rainy season came and passed without an incident. I shoved the horrible matter into a remote corner of my mind and never discussed it with anybody. My father took his thoughts with him to the grave, most probably thinking that I have no recollections of what had happened on that infamous Friday.

There are painful incidents in my life that are represented in the death of my mother, the death of my baby brother, the death of my baby sister, and the bullying I had suffered, but the following two incidents are equally painful.

I was ten years old when one morning my baby sister wandered away and got lost. It was the rainy season and Kokoland was filled with people from out of town. I was terrified that someone had snatched her and feared that I would never find her. My father and my elder sister went to nearby villages looking for her, whereas I stayed behind in Kokoland walking around in the neighborhood and asking people if they had seen her. I desperately looked for her throughout the morning and the afternoon. I finally received the news that someone had spotted her at the flour mill. I rushed there and found her sitting with our neighbor, Hajjah Asha, in her place of business, under the neem tree, where she sold roasted peanuts. Hajjah Asha heard the news about my missing sister while she was on her way to the market. At the flour mill, she saw a woman from out of town waiting for her sorghum to be ground. She also noticed that the woman had a little girl sleeping in front of her on the ground, covered with part of her sari. When the woman made a slight move, she pulled away the sari, revealing the little girl's face. It was my baby sister. Hajjah Asha immediately confronted the woman and told her the girl was not hers, and that the entire village was looking for her. The woman took off and by the time my father got there, she was long gone. That incident worried me a lot and I became so protective of my sister, promising myself to do whatever possible to keep her safe. Sadly, she passed away after falling sick with appendicitis. I could not come to terms with her death. Her loss filled me with pain every time I remembered that.

The second incident is about my brother Aziz, who literally became insane when we were in fourth grade living in the boarding school, in Darsail. One early evening, he began to exhibit abnormal behavior. For no reason, he started chasing children. Soon word spread around school that Aziz had gone mad. Wherever he went, he became a source of entertainment for children. Some of them would entice him to chase after them, which he did. The rest would be shouting and running after him. Then another group would approach and distract him from the first group, so he would leave them and start chasing the new group. I also ran, aimlessly, with the children, hoping for some miracle to happen to stop the chase, since I could do absolutely nothing to prevent it. The children made a deafening noise as they chased Aziz and that attracted even more children to the scene. Not one teacher came out of the teachers' residence to find out, even though they were less than two hundred yards away. That tragedy went on until sunset. I was extremely sad. That night was one of the longest nights of my life, dwarfed only by the night of the day I lost my mother. I stayed awake, most of the night, thinking about what I should do the following morning. I hoped that Aziz would recover overnight so our lives would return to normalcy, if there was such a thing as that in Darsail. I was less concerned about daily hardships I faced, such as beatings, bullying, hunger, mice, lice, bed bugs, and racism, as long as my brother and I were sane.

In the morning, I was greatly disappointed at finding that Aziz's condition did not seem to have improved over night. I woke up and saw him sitting on his bed, which was separated from mine by four beds. He was bent over with his head between his knees. He was hunched up as small as he could. I waited until the other children woke up before I approached his bed and sat beside him. We did not say a word to each other and I noticed he was keeping his eyes half shut, as if thinking intensely. He was withdrawn, dejected, and worried. Aziz needed help, urgently.

Aziz did not leave his bed to get dressed or show any interest in going to class. In the afternoon, I went to the town center and sent a message to my father to come to school. He showed up the following morning and I was called from class to brief him about Aziz's condition. I had seen my father worried and sad many times before, but his face looked entirely different that morning. He softly said good-bye and took Aziz home to Kokoland.

Aziz's school era was over. Sadly, he never fully recovered from his condition, even though my father spent years taking him to hospitals and holy men. Some of the treatments recommended by holy men included depriving him of certain types of food and drinks such as tea. There were other more severe treatments involving things like flogging, which some people believed it to be effective in chasing away evil spirits. The idea behind food deprivation and flogging was that the pain inflicted on the sick person's body will make him an unattractive place for spirits' residence, and hence forcing them to dismount and move away from the body, resulting in the person's full recovery, or so it was believed. The flogging we received at school was viewed as a means of encouraging us to do well and progress in life. I have issues with such an idea, but I can understand that and can live with it, so long as I am in my full mental capacity. However, beating a sick child to cure him from a mental illness is a very painful thing to swallow. Aziz continues to struggle in life even today. I am lucky to be in a position to extend him my support every now and then. I will continue to do so.

At school, math was a great challenge to Aziz and he was not good at memorizing Arabic poetry. He fumbled in class when asked to recite the poems. The punishment he had received was severe and inconsistent with the "crime" he had committed. He was constantly beaten by teachers, as well as the head of our boarding room, Habib, and other children. He received more beatings than I did. I sometimes escaped punishment by being "philosophical" in explaining myself. Of course, using philosophy was an attempt to outsmart the bullies, but the technique did not always work, particularly when I did well on exams. There was always the risk of getting beaten up on school breaks, as I described earlier.

Aziz was three years older than me, but because he had to repeat classes, we ended up in fourth grade at the same time. He is actually my half-brother and the youngest of three children. He has two older sisters. He was named after his grandfather Aziz (nicknamed Merchant Aziz), who was the richest man in the region during the 1950s and 1960s. The story goes that my father wanted to marry Merchant Aziz's daughter, who happened to be sought after by many young men in the region because of her beauty and her father's wealth, I guess. However, my father, being an orphan and poor, stood little chance of beating out the contestants and winning her heart. When he was eighteen, he lost both of his parents within a span of six months due to an epidemic that devastated the region in the 1940s. He told me he won the contest because a well-respected learned-man named Sayidna Gony Al Waly stood as godfather and helped him by speaking to Merchant Aziz on his behalf. His victory created a great deal of animosity and resentment from those who viewed themselves as more worthy of Merchant Aziz's daughter.

Years after my father's marriage to her, she became insane. It was widely believed in the community that some of my father's enemies used black magic to cause Aziz's mother to lose her sanity. One of my uncles told me that a black male goat was buried alive as part of the evil rituals. Aziz was just a baby when this happened. My father married my mother a couple of years later. Aziz lived with his mother and grandfather until our father brought him to Kokoland to live with us so he could attend school. Learned men from the community attributed Aziz's mental breakdown to having been breastfed for longer than the two years allowed by the Quran. They argued his mental condition was passed on to him from his mother via her milk. I believe that the beatings and the hardships at school were more likely to have contributed to Aziz's breakdown.

I remember two instances when Aziz directed his violent behavior toward me. I had no idea what prompted him to attack me. The first incident took place in Kokoland after my father had taken him out of school because of his condition. I had gone home on a school break. He made a slingshot from rubber bands with the ammunition made from tiny pieces of wire. He cut the wire into one-inch pieces and bent them into "V" shapes. One morning, while Aziz and I were sitting about ten feet apart in front of our father's shop, I noticed that he was extraordinarily quiet. I did not want to stir up any trouble, so I also kept quiet and did not bother him. He abruptly turned around to face me and raised both his hands. The next thing I felt was a stinging pain just under my left eye. It took me a few seconds to realize that he had used a slingshot to hit me, and that he had meant to harm me. I got up and left the place. After that, I did my best to avoid being alone with him. We slept in the same hut, so I was naturally worried about being around him. I did not tell my father about the incident because he already had enough worries dealing with Aziz's situation. There is a tiny scar on my face, which constantly reminds me of what had happened that day. A week or so before the end of the school break, he attacked me again. That morning, he exhibited some aggression toward me, so I decided to take precautions, sine I did not know what he was planning. I walked over to a neighbor's shop and sat there. I also kept watching just in case he decided to come after me. A few minutes passed and I saw him get up and walk away. I thought he had gone inside our shop. Out of nowhere, he appeared in front of me, raising the metal yardstick we used for measuring fabrics. I swiftly lifted my left hand just in time to shield my head from the blow. Luckily, it landed on my arm. Our neighbors and people around intervened and separated us. Our father was out of town at the time. I did not tell him about this incident, either, when he returned home few days later. I left for school and I doubt if anyone ever told my father about it. Those were the last two violent encounters I had with Aziz. Time progressed and we went our separate ways. These two incidents were among the many factors, which pushed me away from Kokoland. I never thought I would end up this far.

Saturdays were always hazardous. We had a minimal chance of getting through the day without a beating of some sort. We could be singled out by the morning inspection teacher for failing to get a haircut, having long fingernails, or not bathing. As soon as we heard the morning assembly bell ring, we would all rush and line up in front of our respective classrooms. The inspecting teacher would emerge from the teachers' office and start walking in front of the columns, inspecting one student at a time. He would examine us from our hair, which would mostly be red-colored due to some sort of nutritional deficiency, all the way to our feet. He would carefully look at our chests to decide if we had recently bathed or not. If in doubt, he would lick his index finger and rub it against the suspect's chest. That action would leave a differently-colored spot on the skin, compared to the rest of the chest, which meant the child had not taken bath for some time. The scrubbing of the chest with the wet finger would form dirt rolls sticking to the finger. If still in doubt, the teacher would bring his index finger closer to his eyes to examine if there were tiny rolls of black-colored dirt hanging on there. That would seal the child's fate that morning. He would be told to step forward to be flogged.

Some children were known for not taking baths, so they were routinely flogged. Those of us who bathed regularly, about once a week, wondered what was wrong with them. I have no idea why would anyone choose to be flogged for not washing himself when there were plenty of other reasons for which one could get lashed or beaten up. What is so difficult about bathing once a week? We were all generally dirty, but some children were noticeably dirtier. They always had black dirt build-up on their chests and necks.

We also folded up our shorts as we stood in line to reveal the lower edges of our underwear for the teacher to determine if they were clean or not. Many things might have happened over the weekend, which could have prevented us from coming to school clean enough to pass the inspection test. We sometimes forgot about washing our school uniforms, but we mostly failed to wash them due to carrying out other activities such as working on the farm or fetching water. None of these activities left enough time for anything else. Sometimes we would wash our clothes, but forget to bring them inside the hut at night. In the morning, they would be soaking wet due to rain or morning dew. Ironing wet uniforms to dry them was another challenge we had encountered regularly. We would wait in line for the only charcoal ironing machine in the boarding house. At times we ran out of charcoal and were left with a cold ironing machine. No more charcoal meant I had to go to school wearing wrinkled clothes.

Again, uniforms that were left on a fence to dry overnight could be eaten by goats. Goats were notorious for their love of eating clothes and homework notebooks. That really got us in trouble. They love clothes made out of cotton. I often had to chase after them to pull a notebook, a vest, or an underwear from their mouths. It was not uncommon to see me racing a goat to our backyard fence to get there first to grab my cloth that I had hung to dry. Many a time the goat would get there first and start chewing. I would be fighting hard to pull the cloth out of its mouth to save what I could, while it would be biting hard, keeping its grip and chewing as fast as it could. The ferocity with which I fought the goat was a function of whether I had spare underwear to wear to school that day or not. There was another hazard posed by sudden whirlwind (twister). It would pick up clothes that were hung out to dry and drop them in faraway places. I would go from one neighbor's house to another, asking, "Has anyone seen my underwear? Did the whirlwind drop it here by any chance?"

Some of us were less fortunate and did not have the luxury of owning spare underwears. Going to school with dirty underwear was a risky thing to do, but going without one, at all, was a lot riskier, as my friend Garba learned a hard lesson from doing that, one day.

In my case, inspection teachers never pulled me out for being dirty, even though my feet were never clean enough to pass the test. With their grayish and brownish look, they blended well with the color of the ground, making it difficult for the teacher to recognize anything different about them, so I was able to escape punishment for having dirty feet.

One Saturday, while we were all standing at attention in lines in front of our classrooms, we heard a row in the headmaster's office. Soon after that, we saw Malik (a sixth grader from the village of Salam) running away from the headmaster's office. He was being chased by Mr. Tayfoor, the school headmaster. In a sudden move, Malik turned around and punched Mr. Tayfoor in the stomach, causing him to fall down to the ground. Two teachers ran after Malik and tackled him. They dragged him to the center of the schoolyard and called out for four of the school's strongest children to come forward. They stepped out of their lines and were immediately ordered by one of the teachers to carry Malik *four-eh*, which means being carried facedown by four people, with two holding the hands and the other two holding the legs. They pulled him up until he was lifted about two feet off the ground. Then the teacher approached with a camel whip. This is a special type of whip used by camel herders. Naturally, if it can cause enough pain to bring a camel into obeying its master's orders, it is certain that it can cause devastating damage to a child's body. Because punishment came in the form of flogging our behinds, it left welts and broken skin, and frequently drew blood. Even the lightest of flogging made it impossible for anyone to sit on his behind. I went through many sleepless nights worried about the possibility of flogging on the following day, particularly when I had math exams and Arabic poems or Quranic verses to recite from memory.

The teacher approached Malik and began flogging him with the camel whip. Malik shrieked and screamed at the top of his lungs. The whole school stood there and watched in horror. Malik twisted and jerked his body in agony. He tried to pull his hands and legs free, but to no avail. The teacher continued flogging him. I counted something like thirty lashes. Toward the end, Malik barely responded to the flogging. His screams faded away and turned into faintly moans. He completely stopped kicking and pulling. The teacher ordered the children to put him down. Malik lay flat on his belly, unable to move. The teacher told us to dismiss, so we started walking. We glanced back in Malik's direction as each grade marched toward its respective classroom. I saw him, first, crawl then get up and, with great difficulty, stagger toward the boarding rooms. That was the last time I saw Malik. He was dismissed from school for punching Mr. Tayfoor. We never found out the reason he was called to the headmaster's office.

Flogging was a daily phenomenon, but *four-eh* was reserved for the worst offenses. Witnessing such horrific punishment alone can leave a lasting effect on any child. One can only imagine the impact on the person being punished. In another incident, a pupil named Aron from the village of Timah, was called to the teachers' office for some reason. According to eye witnesses, the teacher flogged him with the camel's whip until he soiled himself. Everyday life in Darsail Primary School filled us with fear and anxiety because anyone could be next in line for some form of punishment, for one reason or another.

The level of punishment in terms of number of lashes varied from one teacher to another. Some teachers, I am certain, had psychological problems that was manifested in the way they punished children, which in many cases were carried out for trivial reasons undeserving of any form of punishment, let alone severe. Our math teacher, for example, was known for his ill-temper. He used to throw books at students and hit them for giving him wrong answers.

Mr. Hajar was another ill-tempered teacher. He was always in a bad mood and got easily frustrated or angered for the slightest of reasons. There were five periods per day, two before breakfast and three after. It used to get very uncomfortable during the last two periods due to high temperature. One day in class, Mr. Hajar threw a piece of chalk at me while shouting, in absolute disgust, "Shut your mouth." The chalk landed inside my mouth, went down my throat, and choked me. I pulled it out of my mouth and continued the class. That day Mr. Hajar looked extraordinarily angry and agitated, so everyone was quiet because we did not know if the situation would escalate into flogging or not. I ate sardine for breakfast that morning and sat in a tin-roofed class with a hundred degrees temperature. What is so unnatural about yawning under such circumstances? The problem I had with this incident was that Mr. Hajar's father and my father were business partners. When my father enrolled my brother Aziz and me in the boarding school, he introduced us to Mr. Hajar and asked him to be there for us in case we needed his help. That was not forthcoming because we did everything we could to avoid any encounter with teachers, since the outcome was, invariably, not in our favor. There you are, a chalk in my throat from my "supposedly" mentor for the simple reason of yawning in class. I was deeply hurt by his action and felt he was not worthy of my father's trust. I searched my soul to find if I carried a grain of respect for this teacher, but I could find none. Years later, I ran into him at a wedding party in Kokoland. At that time, I was in high school preparing to take the national university exams. Upon seeing me, he commented that I would never make it past secondary school because "universities are no places for party goers like me," he said. He told me that the success of his younger brother Jallab was the outcome of hard work and not going to parties. I resented his comments. What did Mr. Hajar know about my future? Years later, I learned that he had become an alcoholic, and was taken to a holy man for treatment. The irony is that he might have been forced to sip from the same bitter flogging medication he had been administering to us, which was a common treatment as well as punishment for drinking alcohol. Nevertheless; I must admit that not every teacher in Darsail Primary School was abusive. Equally, there were teachers who were models for kindness, dedication, and commitment to seeing us succeed. I'm grateful and have full respect for them.

We developed a technique, which we called "doubling" to reduce the intense pain from flogging. Every time we had a recitation session, we ran the risk of being punished, so we prepared for flogging ahead of time. In the morning, before leaving for classes, we would wear two to five sets of underwear and shorts to create a thick layer of clothing. It did not matter whether they were dirty or not as long as the top clothing was clean. The technique did work, but we could not fool all the teachers all the time. Sometimes the teachers would suspect that something was not adding up, especially when the sound of the whip landing on the child's behind produced a muffled sound like that of beating on a mattress. Doubling was a risky exercise. At times, children gave away their secret when dust erupted from clothing they would be wearing, every time the whip landed on their behind. The teacher, upon finding out, would ask the child to remove all the layers of clothing, except the last one. He would then double the punishment because of cheating. That was not enough for some overzealous, for the wrong cause, teachers, who would also call for four strong children to administer "four-eh" punishment, as described in Malik's case above. Children were forced to adopt such cheating tactics to reduce the intensity of pain. Were they to blame?

One night a group of children resorted to what was tantamount to a criminal behavior to rid us all of flogging with the camel whip. They broke into the office where the whip was kept, stole it, and buried it outside the school fence. In the morning the headmaster appeared and addressed the assembly, while fuming with anger about what had happened the night before. He threatened to flog the entire school, if we failed to flush out the culprits. Most of us stared attentively at the ground, avoiding eye contact with the headmaster as much as we could. Every few moments, we would take a glance at his site to assess the situation, and then revert to staring at the ground afresh.

An eye contact with the headmaster was a call for trouble. He might call you to step forward to tell him what you knew about the incident. If you spoke the truth, you ran the risk of being beaten up by the children for betraying the entire school. If you refused to say anything, you ran the risk of flogging, possibly *four-e*h style. The best strategy was to gaze at the ground for as long as it took, or until the danger dissipated. That strategy did work. Finally, the headmaster threatened us one more time that he was going to find out who took the whip and that all hell would break loose when he did, so we had better be prepared. His last words before disappearing from sight were "You will see. Dismiss." I said to myself *hillak*, which is a Sudanese Arabic word for, "We cross the bridge when we get to it." We all hurriedly walked away to our classes.

The burial of the whip gave us a break until a teacher travelled to the city and got a replacement. Absence of a teacher from classes for a couple of days was a bad sign because, in all probability, he would return from the city with a whip held under his armpit. Teachers were the highest authority in town; therefore they received a special treatment. When they travelled, lorry drivers picked them up and dropped them off at the teachers' residence by the school. They did not have to walk to the town center like everyone else to catch a lorry. The rare and far spread out sound of a lorry stopping by the teachers' residence was a phenomenon we hardly missed, especially if the lorry was returning from the city. That meant it was dropping a teacher, so we made sure we were there to see if he was carrying a whip or not.

If the teacher showed up empty handed, we would stay up a little longer that night to celebrate the fact that we would have more school days free of camel whip, the most hated torture tool. If he returned with one, we would go to bed earlier than our normal bedtime, out of worrying about what the next day would bring. Ironically, sleeping early supposed to mean getting more rest, but, as far as we were concerned, it meant we were worried to our cores that we could not function anymore. We wanted to sleep early so we could free our minds from thinking too much about tomorrow, hence less suffering. Sadly, that also meant allowing bed bugs and lice more time to suck our blood and lay more eggs, which ultimately meant more suffering. We never could win in Darsail Primary School from Hell.

Teachers rarely visited our boarding quarters. However, school rules demanded that any time a teacher called out, "Boy!" we should run like crazy to find out what he wanted. You would see many children running toward a teacher until it became clear that one child had gotten there first, so the rest would go back to whatever they had been doing earlier. Occasionally, the headmaster would come out of his residence in the afternoons, stand there for a few minutes, and look at us in the distance, goofing around. We would keep an eye on him and be ready to dash toward him as soon as he called for us. Sometimes he could merely be scratching his potbelly, but we would rush toward him thinking that he was silently calling for help using hand gestures. It was difficult to tell what was going on from a distance. We would run toward him, until we got to a point where we could clearly see and tell what he was actually doing and what his intentions were, then we would decide whether to stop or continue running. We most probably suffered from nearsightedness, which could have been caused by malnutrition; a condition that all of us definitely had. We ran toward the fuzzy image of the teacher out of fear of group punishment. Sometimes a teacher would come out of the teachers' residence at night and start flicking a torch (flashlight), indicating that he needed someone to come over to render a task. It would be dark and there was no way he could tell who did and did not respond to his summon, but we still ran, anyway, as soon as we saw the flashlight. There was always a chance that we might all be punished the next morning, if nobody responded to his call. There was also the possibility that someone might, rightly or falsely, report names of those who ran away and disappeared under the cover of darkness as soon as they saw a flashlight flicking. As you can tell, there were defectors among us, so no one wanted to run the risk of single or collective punishment.

My brother Halim, who was two years younger than I, was our grandmother's favorite. He lived with her in a nearby village three miles from Kokoland. After the death of our mother, Grandmother adopted him as her son. He lived like a prince and no one dared to touch him or refuse him any demand. He had many goats, which were the center of his life. Unlike my situation, milk was readily available to him any time of the day. I thought he was living in absolute heaven. My father wanted to enroll him in school when he was old enough, but Grandmother did not want to let him go. She clung to him desperately arguing that it was her duty to look after him. Our father did not want to upset her, so Halim was able to escape going to school and spend a few more happy years with his goats, which he enjoyed very much and continues to speak about them up to this day.

Grandmother finally relented and let Halim go to school. One fine morning, my father brought him to Darsail, the boarding school, to be with Aziz and me. He was fresh from the village. He spent all that day telling me about his goats. The only language he spoke was Kanuri, which was mostly unheard of around school. By the comfort with which he spoke to me in Kanuri, I could tell that he thought the entire world spoke a single language; Kanuri. To Halim, what was normal in the village should also be applicable elsewhere without any reservations. He was completely unaware of his environment and his standing as far as the rest of the world was concerned. Our grandmother had insulated him from life's hazards. Of course, he had no idea how much damage he had caused to my efforts to assimilate and gain acceptance. He completely tarnished my image that I had painstakingly rebuilt after Grandmother came and pulled me out of class. I had barely recovered from that incident when Halim showed up. I lost all hope in ever convincing the school children that I was an Arab.

Halim told me about the Kanuri names of his white goat (Bollum), his red goat (Kimirum), his goat with the loud voice (Gundarum) and his very smelly alpha male goat (Luk), and so on. He told me how much he missed them and seriously worried about their well-being during his absence in school. He even sang special songs about his goats. Halim took breaks between songs and sobbed.

Obviously, he was not only grandma or home sick, but also goat-sick. He dearly missed the village and everything there. He always talked about Grandma and how well she treated him, being her golden grandchild.

Both of my brothers were musically challenged. Halim sang about his goats and Aziz sang about his grandfather's camel. The sound made by that camel was probably all the music Aziz had ever known by the time he came to attend school in Kokoland. His grandfather owned a traditional mill that produced sesame oil. The sesame seeds were poured into a giant wooden mortar that was turned by a camel going around in circles to grind them. There was a giant wooden pestle inside the mortar, connected by a long wooden extension to the harness on the back of the camel, which walked around the mortar, hence turning the pestle. The pressure created by the weight of the pestle squeezed oil out of the seeds. At the same time, the friction of the wood surfaces rubbing together created an irregular droning sound as the camel circled. Out of sheer boredom, the camel also produced sounds while it monotonously walked around the mill. Those sounds went on for most of the day, and they could have been the only two musical tones my brother Aziz was ever exposed to. He sang one tone on and on until he grew bored, then he switched to the other tone and sang it for an equally long time. He alternated between these two tones for hours, which threatened to drive me crazy. They were the most boring sounds imaginable. The only break I got was during the day when we were at school. I think my brother Aziz could be the only person ever to mimic the sound produced by a traditional oil mill combined with the sound of a bored camel used as the power source. He could have been a contender for The Guinness World Records.

The use of camel-driven mill to produce sesame oil. Photo 2016

The children in the boarding room congregated around us to celebrate the arrival of our (Aziz and I) younger brother, Halim. He spoke in Kanuri and I translated what he said into Arabic. For some time, we were a source of entertainment for the school. Few children, inadvertently, learned some Kanuri words, which they repeated for days without knowing what they really meant. Halim also told me how much he feared dogs, and I told him I didn't blame him. I was not surprised that there were no dogs in his village because many Kanuri, both adults and children, were afraid of them.

Nobody could mess with Halim when he was under Grandma's watchful eyes. He got upset for the simplest of reasons. He would immediately walk and sit in a place that anyone passing by could easily see him. He would then begin complaining by humming his crying-song, "Udo udo do, udo udo do," which meant "me, me, me" in Kanuri. Thinking about it now reminds me of Toby Keith's country song "I Wanna Talk about Me." He would repeat that line for hours, just so he could get as much attention from people as he could. One by one, people would inquire about what had befallen Halim. He got great satisfaction from hearing comments such as "You guys, why are you doing this to Halim?" Most of the time, he cried "Udo udo do, udo udo do" for no reason. If a pothole caused him to trip, it was all that was needed to trigger hours of fake crying.

Fortunately, Halim got distracted easily, so he would stop his monotonous crying-song. Obviously, he was topicless. A hen showing up in front of him and scratching the ground in search of a piece of grain or an unlucky worm could catch his attention. He would forget everything if a rooster appeared and started chasing the hen. Halim would then spring into action and take it upon himself to defend the hen by throwing some chunks of dirt at the rooster. I would be sitting some distance away from him, praying that the chicken incident would make him forget what he was doing. If I were lucky, a caravan of ants led by a proud ant-general would, enthusiastically, march in front of Halim in an elegant formation. They would be on their way to attack Grandmother's grain storage, without being invited to feel free to help themselves. They would travel back and forth to the grain storage, happily carrying their loads, one grain at a time. Watching ants work was the secret to keeping Halim captivated for a long time.

I would avoid eye contact with Halim, hoping he would forget about whining. However, if I caught him off guard and we did make eye contact, his body language would tell me that he was searching his brain trying to remember what he was doing. He might succeed in remembering where he had stopped, but by that time, his tears would have dried up, so it would be time for replenishing. He would start using the backs of both his hands to squeeze his eyeballs ferociously in a futile effort to produce tears. Squeezing his eyes mostly reddened the veins, so it appeared as if he had been crying so much that his eyes turned into pepper-red color. Then he would drop his hands and look in my direction as if saying, "Look at me. My eyes are red and tearful and I am still under stress, so what do you think?" The squeezing would cause his eyes to turn red, but produced no tears. His brain would find no credible evidence of stress, hence would conclude that there was no justification to instruct the eyes to continue wasting a valuable resource, so they would cease producing tears. I would get up and leave him half-convinced that he had my sympathy. Sometimes he would restart the "udo, udo do" saga, but soon realize that the rhythm was broken. He would frantically try to remember it so his hums could be in sync, just like before. That way, people could continue noticing his agony. Grandmother would show up and say, "For God's sake, I don't like it when you do this to my boy." She would not be blaming someone or directing her speech to a particular person. She could be saying that even when there was nobody around. Grandma's intervention would give Halim a reason for a new round of humming, only this time with renewed energy. His wails could be heard over a wider area of the village, as if he were trying to set a new record.

Grandma brought back Halim special teacups as a gift when she returned from a pilgrimage to Mecca, but he kept them all to himself. Sharing was not Halim's cup of tea. He had full right to the goats' milk. He looked far healthier than both Aziz and me, even though, to console myself, I thought his healthy looks came at the expense of the goats' kids. When we visited Halim, we did share some of the milk, but we were at his mercy as to what milk quotas we received. Halim's bed was strategically positioned inside the hut. It was placed adjacent to a sack full of boiled, salted, and dried peanuts; his favorite snack, even today. The positioning of the bed near the peanut sack was for convenience purposes and ease of access, whenever he wished, even at midnights, and no questions asked.

Halim was central to Grandma's life. She listened and paid a great deal of attention to him whenever he spoke in his spoiled, useless, and strange fashion. She looked at him and listened with admiration, but whether his speech was substantive or not was immaterial, as far as Grandma was concerned. Every child in the village used the word "ummi" to call their mothers, but Halim had his own version for the word mother. He twisted the word and called Grandma something like, "Emi." The way it sounded depended on his mood at any given time. Aziz and I received only a fraction of the attention Halim got. We rarely had conversations directed to us. We felt we mattered less, but I, personally, didn't have problem with that.

In all fairness to Grandma, she was one of the kindest, happiest, and most humorous persons I had ever known. I had my fair share of gifts from her, but there was one special gift that I will never forget. Upon returning from her second visit to Mecca, she got me a *kiskittah* (a leather cowboy hat). It was an exotic thing, so I cherished it a lot. However, I had mixed feelings about putting it on or not. Even though I was five or six years old then, I felt that a cowboy leather hat, my extra-large *arragi* (traditional dress), and my ashy dirty bare feet, formed a disastrous combination. It took me four decades to be in a position to do justice to cowboy hats by having the confidence to put them on without the need to explain myself. Many things need to be put in place for a cowboy hat to be considered as well-fitting. Now I own few hats and I love them. The fact that hats are out of fashion is something for others to worry about, but not me. I have some catching up to do.

I looked forward to ending one particular visit that I paid to Grandma and Halim in the village so I could head back to town. Before I left; I surveyed the village for the last time. Honestly, there was not much that could please the eye, but it was and remains to be Grandma's village that embodies many of my childhood memories. I saw "African engineering at its best" as my dear friend Kenny Mahogany, from San Francisco Bay Area, jokingly put it whenever he saw an unsuccessful design, be that a car, a building, or a dress. He would follow his insults by commenting, "No offense, so don't take it personally." Kenny was brutally sarcastic. Obviously, I don't intend to offend my own people, but the extreme rural-ness of the place was difficult to deny. In the distance, I saw a group of goats standing on their back legs and stretching upward as far as their body could reach, trying to get to the tops of shrubs and bushes to nipple the softer parts. Nearby, I saw a gray donkey tied to a tree, standing with its head hanging low, and both eyes shut, probably thinking, "What is life is all about and why am I here?" Crickets from the big trees by the edge of the village produced a nonstop, high-pitched, and irritating sound, most likely caused by fanning the wings to cool their body from the midday summer heat. In one corner of the house stood a wooden structure elevating Grandma's storage container, which was made of meshed straws, for storing dry black-eyed pea, dry okra, bushels of sorghum, all kept for harsher times, which were about every day, anyway.

Grandma's Village. Photo 2016.

Under the wooden structure, a middle-aged red rooster stood guard, displaying his colorful tail. He kept an eye on his half a dozen or so harems which had dug themselves depressions on the ground to rest and cool off, while enjoying the sense of security Mr. Rooster happily provided. He proudly looked at them and told himself, "Life is great." The irony was that Mr. Rooster's life on earth could be numbered to any day a dignitary guest visited Grandma. That could be as soon as the following day, when Grandma would hint to Halim and his best friend Yourei to do justice to the guest or do injustice to Mr. Rooster, depending on how you look at it. They would happily adhere to Grandma's instructions so that in the process of showing hospitality to the guest, they would also have their share of chicken that night. Unfortunately for Mr. Rooster, that scenario could bring an end to his empire built by blood and sweat. Pretty soon, the power vacuum created by his absence would be bridged by neighborhood roosters moving in from Buraima's or my brother-in-law Arabi's homes, to claim the kingdom, along with the harems, but without spilling a drop of blood, except for Mr. Rooster's.

In Grandma's village, it did not really matter if the time was now, last year, or next year. The whole surrounding provided another meaning for the term rural living. Nobody in the village seemed to miss living elsewhere, as if people knew nothing about else-where's very existence. I said good-bye to Halim and left. What I really meant was, "Halim, go on and enjoy your high-class living." I headed home to Kokoland quite satisfied that I was not going to miss a thing. My problem was I seriously thought that Kokoland was the better alternative to Grandma's village, but the reality was that, in the grand scheme of things, they were the same. In fact, I too did not miss living elsewhere, just like the people in Grandma's village, for I also did not know that elsewhere existed, either. Clearly, I was making a fuss over nothing.

I wanted to continue writing about another bullying incident, but I digressed for a while and talked about my Grandma and my dear bother, Halim. As I mentioned earlier, bullying came in many forms. At times, I got bullied at places when I least expected. Upon arriving at the outskirt of the village, uncle Zari made sure that he blew his old Bedford truck horn that produced intricate musical sounds, declaring to Kokoland residents his arrival from the city. It was time for the once-a-week entertainment session that many people in the village had always waited for impatiently. There was little else to do. Passengers returning from the city invariably brought happy news about city life. Naturally, news was conveyed verbally because I hardly seen anyone carrying newspapers, besides most people did not read. Uncle Zari was the only truck owner who battled the muddy terrain to connect the village with the city during the rainy season. Usually, the owners of the remaining two trucks would remove the tires to protect them from damage caused by weather. They would replace them with barrels that carried the truck body until the end of the rainy season when they put back the tires and resumed operation.

I grabbed my *cartabbo* and headed to the town center. *Cartabbo* was made out of a stick and a big discarded bolt that I had obtained from my uncle's tool box. It was a formidable fighting tool that was rarely being used because of the serious harm it could inflict on a person. It was a mere deterrent weapon, if you will. It was important that you carried your weapon to the market because you never knew what could happen. Uncle Zari's truck was a magnet for both good and bad boys.

Most important, we used um *cartabbo* for downing baobab fruits that could be hanging a couple of hundred feet up the tree. It was an effective tool for aiming and hitting the fruit because the heavy bolt would drag the stick in a straight line, making it easier to hit the fruit. In contrast, boomerangs, because of their curved shape, got stuck in the tree branches, more frequently. The bolt would drag the *cartabbo* down to the ground, and we were happy about that because metal bolts were hard to get. Besides; climbing up a big baobab tree to recover a boomerang stuck in the branches was a dangerous thing to do, as one boy named Ubgrain found out the hard way. Luckily his injuries were limited to a broken arm.

I got to the town center and, like everybody else, took a tour around the truck. I slowly walked and bumped shoulders with other boys who were also there for the same purpose. We were more focused on the people who just returned from the city than paying attention to our steps. Village dignitaries sat in the front seats because they could afford to pay additional fees. Usually three to four people, size-permitted, occupied the seats on the right hand side of the driver. The rest of the passengers travelled in the cramped back of the truck; men standing up and holding on to the metal grid of the truck body and women sitting down in the center on top of merchandise. That was why many people lost their lives in the event of an accident because they got pinned under truckloads of heavy merchandise such as sacks of sugar, sorghum, gum Arabic, etc. Trucks (Lorries) were the only means of transportation, so they were used for carrying goods, people, and animals, all in one place.

People descended from both sides of the truck so, to capture everything, we walked around in circles until we saw a more interesting sight or person, then we stopped. We mostly congregated near the front seats of the truck to be among the first to know if there was good or bad news, depending on how you look at it, especially if there were new teachers on board transferring to the village primary school. It mattered a lot to know if they were the type that whipped children into learning, or used softer approach, which was hard to come. Finally; I stopped at a point where I had a clear view of a more exciting, once-a-week, action taking place. I lowered my *cartabbo* to the ground, placed both my hands on the other end of the stick, and kept watching people disembarking from the truck and off-loading their belongings.

A boy named Musa Kindi Kindi stood a few feet to my right. I noticed that he was looking at my *cartabbo* and half-smiling for no apparent reason. He was plotting something which hatched out a few seconds later. In fact he had decided to own my *cartabbo* against my will. He took advantage of the relaxed and happy mood around the truck and, without warning, grabbed my *cartabbo* from my hand when I least expected. He then turned around and knocked me on my left knee, momentarily crippling me. That brought me down to my knees and he took off running toward his house in the southern edge of the village. The son of a (gun) zapped me with the very tool I was carrying to protect myself from such types of attacks. I could not chase after him, so I kept on looking at him as he ran away and slowly disappeared.

I sat there until the pain subsided down enough for me to walk home. I slowly got up and, with difficulty, lingered my way home.

I did not go to the clinic to seek treatment for fear of being accused of getting myself into a fight that led to my injury. In Kokoland, it was not uncommon that the victim got further-victimized. Besides, Kindi Kindi was not attending school, so complaining to a teacher to get him punished was out of the question. He had nothing to lose or fear.

I was not surprised that Kindi Kindi resorted to this easy, but wicked way to own himself a *cartabbo.* He did not want to spend time going through the trouble of visiting a nearby forest to cut the right size stick to mount a bolt on, or cut a branch to carve himself a boomerang. He thought that owning mine was the easiest of all. I had known kindi to be a very lazy boy just like his friend Allori. In the few times he and his friend came to offer help in the farm as day laborers, they caused more damage than good. Their ultimate goal of going to the farm was to get back home as soon as possible. For that purpose they worked recklessly the moment they set foot in the farm. They buried as much peanut seeds as each hole could take, did that as fast as they could, and ate as much as their tummies could bear, so we would run out of seeds and go home as early as possible. We did not worry about how much they ate because there was that much uncooked peanuts they could have eaten before their stomachs gave up.

I lingered for few more days and recovered, or so I thought. Nowadays, decades later, I continue to feel pain on my left knee, especially during winter. It could have been caused by one of the many falls from donkeys, wrestling, or playing soccer, but I suspect that it was Kindi Kindi's blow that caused it. That was the last time I met Musa Kindi Kindi. He avoided me until I left to school in few weeks' time. We parted our ways for ever. He went on to become a soldier and years later I heard that he got killed in the battle front during the civil war between north and south Sudan.

CHAPTER 10

My Water and Chicken Businesses

At the age of ten, I discovered the true purchasing power of money, so I decided to embark on a wealth-generation odyssey. I created and successfully ran three small businesses to help secure my school uniforms and some pocket money. They were a candy business, a chicken business, and a business selling water. Candy and water were scarce commodities in Kokoland, and for that reason my profit margin was high. Even though I ran my businesses only during school breaks, I was able to generate enough profit to pay for my school supplies. My candy business was nothing more than a wooden box, which I placed in front of my dad's shop so his customers could also buy from me. I did compete with my dad who was also my wholesale supplier. He gave me bags of candy on credit, which I sold, paid him what I deemed a fair price, and kept the remaining balance as my profit. My biggest sales were on market days, especially Fridays. Toward the end of the day, parents bought candy to take to their children in nearby villages. I could also afford to give away free candy to my cousins and to their friends. Every time I visited Grandma in the village, I brought along lollipops, mint candy, and bubble gum to give away.

My location also attracted businesswomen who sold milk and milk-cream. Kokoland was a trail for nomad cattle herders who crossed it on their seasonal north-south migration. They moved north during the rainy season to avoid the deadly Tsetse fly and returned to the south during the dry season. Those were good times for my business. On market days, the women would light a campfire beside my candy box to boil milk cream, which they poured into bottles. They lined up the bottles for sale at prices based on size. Female merchants from the city flocked to Kokoland to purchase milk cream, unprocessed leather, charcoal, live chicken, sheep, and other agricultural products to take to the city and sell at very high profit margins.

I bought bottles of milk-cream whenever I had extra cash. As a favor for giving them free space, the women sold me the cream at lower than market price. I then turned around and sold it to the merchants from the city at the regular price and kept my profit margin, without lifting a finger. The women also offered me free yogurt, the best organic yogurt you could ever get.

I also ventured into chicken business. I bought young chickens, took them home, and released them in the yard. I fed them for a period of two months or so, then took them back to the market, and sold them. My chicken business did not do well for two reasons. First, I released the chicken to roam the neighborhood freely and that was how they got exposed to chicken diseases such as flu, which spread around far too easily. Once one chicken got sick, it took only few days for the entire flock to get wiped out. As you can tell, I had no idea what poultry farming was. It was not worth trying to sell sick chicken because every chicken buyer knew how to find out if a bird was sick or not. They would rough it up or squeeze its legs to see if it quacked, which meant it was healthy. If it kept quiet, they would get up and walk away without saying a single word, leaving you and your sick chicken pitying yourself. Some people tried a more humane technique. They would pull up the chicken to get it stand on its legs, then they let go. If it dropped down, that meant its legs could not carry the body weight, which meant it was sick.

The second reason why my chicken business did not do well stemmed from the serious hazard of guests showing up at our house, unannounced. Their arrival, particularly at night, meant the loss of one or two roosters, guaranteed, and that took a great toll on my business. Guests did enjoy the chicken barbeque, but I refused to take part and have some. That was my way of expressing disapproval of losing some capital against my will. My objections did not matter much, anyway, because guests always came first.

As far as my candy business was concerned, the two main causes of devastation were shoplifting and goats. I usually sat in the shop verandah to guard both my candy and my dad's shop. That way I was able to address customers' needs at both businesses. You can tell that multitasking was second nature to me, at ten. Problems occurred when I went inside the shop to handle transactions such as selling clothes, which involved price heckling, and measuring. The process took a considerable amount of time. That presented a valuable opportunity for shoplifters and goats, which, together, accounted for most of my losses. One time, I came out of the shop and found a kid standing by the candy box. He could not explain to me why he was just standing there. I repeatedly asked him if he wanted to buy something, but he kept on shrugging his shoulders without saying a word. Upon close examination, I found out he could not speak because he had his cheeks filled with bubble gum. In fact, I could visibly see pointed round shapes on each cheek due to lack of space inside his mouth. He was a greedy kid. I caught him red-handed, so he just stood there looking at me, but unable to speak. I thought of telling his dad, which could have resulted in harsh punishment; flogging, but I decided not to do that. Anyway, beating was a service that was readily available in Kokoland whether kids asked for it or not, so why bother adding more misery. Besides; candy was a scarce commodity. It was my mistake that I left it unguarded and the kid stumbled over it. He had just found a treasure. Funny enough, from his looks he did not seem to be worried about the possible consequences of his actions. He must have thought it was a risk worth taking. Kadees was another kid who was specialized in stealing palm dates. He had his own technique for doing that. On market days, he used to target onion merchants, who also sold palm dates by pouring it on jute mats, on the floor. Kadees, who would intentionally be roaming the market, bare-footed, would pass by and knock few dates with his feet, pretending that was an accident. He wouldn't bend down to pick them up because the merchants would find out. He would use his big and index toes, in each foot, to pick two dates at a time. He would walk away a few yards then bend down and pick them with his hands. People knew his tricks and what he did, but didn't bother. They could have given him free dates, had he asked for some, but he chose that route. When I returned to Kokoland, decades later, I found Kadees roaming the market bare-footed, the same way he did when we were children, only that he had become mentally incapacitated.

My candy business flourished to a point I thought it did not make good business sense to purchase finished products to sell at relatively limited margin. It was time to produce locally. Giving away valuable resources unnecessarily was a bad business practice. I sold five pieces of palm dates for half a cent and I gave one additional date as a bonus to motivate customers to return and become repeat business. Some bullies like a boy named Abdulla tried to intimidate me into breaking my price model, but I refused to budge, even though that could have resulted in a fight when we met en route to the water pond a few miles away from Kokoland.

I stumbled on one man who claimed to possess candy-making skills. "Superb," I said. I told my dad that his candy prices were no longer attractive and I was at a point in my business that dictated the need for taking bold strategic measures. He accepted my argument, but he convinced me to buy the raw material (sugar) from him. I agreed and was able to negotiate a lower price for each pound of sugar I bought. When you are the only candy maker in town, you can dictate your own terms. I took the candy expert to my house and set up a candy manufacturing plant that certainly fell short of any quality and hygiene standards you could think of. I got him some charcoal, a stove, a pot, and five pounds of sugar. I also stuck a six-inch nail, at eye level, on the pole in the center of our shade built from millet straw. We were ready for candy production. First, he boiled the sugar until it turned into liquid. Then he removed the pot from the stove and kept it for five minutes. When the liquid sugar turned into sludge, he took it and hung it on the nail and started pulling and twisting to create a rope-like formation. The wooden beam holding the roof was also a residence for many insect species.

One particular moss made holes inside the beam and converted the wood pulp into a yellowish and powder-like stuff. Business was usual for the insects above our heads getting in and out of their residence. Every time they left or returned to their holes or when my candy maker pulled down the candy sludge, the whole shade shook and the yellowish powder came raining down on us and on the candy material. It created yellow dots all over the surface of the light beige-colored candy, enhancing its looks, and probably, adding flavor to it, even though coincidentally. Monopoly and the lack of health inspection services in Kokoland was certainly a recipe for bad candy. Now I have grown to appreciate the contribution health inspectors make to our well-being.

We then cut the candy to one-foot long pieces. We left it to cool and dry then further cut it into two- and four-inch pieces. I sold the pieces for half a cent and one cent, respectively. A few weeks into production, we introduced the concept of proper coloration. We boiled hibiscus and mixed it with the mold to produce a two-colored candy, which called for doubling the price. I enjoyed full market monopoly. My product was locally manufactured, locally marketed, and locally consumed, therefore no money wasted on shipping. Besides; in the land of no candy, anything that looked like candy and tasted just like candy, was considered candy, and, therefore, marketed and sold like candy. It did not really matter that it most probably contained tiny insect remains.

Boys showed up at my business place either to buy or steal candy, if an opportunity presented itself. I could live with the shoplifting because I could offset my losses by charging higher prices for my candy. Another big portion of my losses was attributed to some crazy Kokoland goats. They figured out that there was an easier way of making a living off the market rather than off the nearby forest, so they developed a habit of invading the market, especially on market days. They took huge risk from beating by traders who displayed their goods on the floor. Just like the kid above, the goats must have come to terms with weighing their options carefully and deciding it was worth it.

One gray goat that belonged to a man named Said was notorious for attacking food items displayed for sale. She would come charging into the market center where traders, both men and women, would be sitting in the dirt, guarding their sale items lined up in front of them. The overall view was a mosaic of colors formed by the men's white clothes, the women's saris and the variety of merchandise on display. Those items included dry okra, sorghum, onions, sun-dried tomatoes, peanuts, peas, sesame seed, etc. Gray goat used to rush in and take everyone by surprise. She attacked produces that seemed to be less guarded. She could figure out who was paying less attention and targeted his items. That way she was able to put those few seconds to a maximum use. She loved dry okra and onions, so she spent more time grabbing a mouthful of the food. She would usually rush in with an open mouth, sink it in the food item of her choice, and start biting rapidly. The movement of her lower jaw shook the entire head in a fast and mechanical manner. At the same time, she would be fully alert to detect any source of movement which could mean a beating of some sort. Her actions brought about three reactions from the traders. Some of them shouted at her, others raised their hands up in the air to chase her away, and the rest reached for their shoes or sticks to give her a blow. This is why she limited her attack to any given food item to few seconds, then took off. As she crossed the line of merchants, hands went up and down creating a wave movement similar to the one made by fans during soccer games. They also murmured words and you could hear the name of Said, the owner, being mentioned repeatedly. Nobody was happy with him for failing to control his goat.

My third type of business was selling water. As I indicated earlier, water was a very scarce commodity in Kokoland, so it fetched premium prices. It was a lucrative business that attracted many young boys. All it needed was a strong donkey, a water container made from tarpaulin, and a will to labor like crazy shuttling water from nearby ponds to Kokoland. If you did just that, you would not only be in business, but also fast on your way to fame and richness. Things are relative in life, aren't they?

There was no water tower or a pump, so running water in homes was out of the question. The only source of water was a fifty-meter deep well which catered to the needs of few households in the village. The water was salty and the well ran dry frequently. People had to wait for hours so a few gallons of ground water could seep and gather at the bottom of the well. When it was time to start pulling out water, people simultaneously dropped their buckets down the well. The well itself was narrow (about five feet in diameter), so some robes got entangled. It took time to sort things out, then there would be no water left. It meant few more hours of waiting for another round. Sometimes frustration led to big fights, considering the prospect of going home without water. Donkeys and goats roamed around the well, desperate for a sip of water, but they hardly got any sympathy from the people. You could see the carcasses of dead animals scattered around not too far from the well. Our neighbor Haj Salman used to spend most nights at the well just to return in the morning with a few gallons of water. People spent nights at the well falsely thinking that fewer people would show up so they could fill one or two jerricans. The truth was that everyone adopted the same tactics and in the end, they all showed up at night. That was also to avoid the heat during the day.

People in villages around Kokoland relied on water from wells they had hand dug with shovels in streambeds. After the rainy season, they would continue drinking from ponds, which kept rainwater for some time, depending on each pond's size and the number of people and animals that drank from it. Before those ponds dried up, people, in each village, would call for a meeting to agree on a plan for digging wells in nearby streambeds. All men took part in this collective effort. Some sections of streams had shallow ground waters, which made the digging job easy, while others called for sinking deeper wells to get to the water.

The well-digging process was an entirely labor intensive operation that relied on simple digging tools. Upon reaching ground water some ten meters or so deep, a thick robe woven from a certain grass type would be placed in circles, starting from the bottom of the well and moving upward. The robe would hold the wet sand from gathering at the bottom, preventing the well from crumbling. The robe would also work as a filter, which allows relatively clean water to seep through. People drew water from those wells for both human and animal consumption. The water was far from suitable for drinking; nevertheless, people drank it and left their kidneys to carry out the heavy filtering duty, I guess.

Few yards away from the wells, animal owners built round formations of mud plates that were two feet high by ten feet in diameter. They tediously pulled water from the wells, one bucket at a time, and filled up those mud plates for their animals to drink from. The number of plates built and how many times over they were filled each day depended on the number of goats, sheep, cattle, and camels a family owned. It also depended on the number of able men in each family who could do the job. It was common for people to spend nights after nights pulling up water to be ready when the animals showed up in the morning. Because of the very high temperatures in summer, animals, especially goats and sheep, needed to drink every day, whereas cattle could go for two-day intervals without drinking. The wells needed overhauling every few weeks, throughout the dry season. As time passed, the ground water travelled down deeper. A meter or so would be dug deeper down to catch up with the receding water. New grass robes were placed around the well's new depth.

The whole process of digging and maintaining wells was very hazardous. Well diggers would mark a place to dig, but they might not exactly know how deep they needed to go, or if there was water, at all. Every year, few people lost their lives or went through near-death experiences caused by crumbling wells. There was little chance that a person would survive the ordeal of a well crumbling over him. The community elders would consider the well to be his grave. They would perform prayers and throw a cloth coffin in the well and cover it with sand. That was the best they could do to give the person a proper burial, considering the circumstance of his death, and also to bring closure to his family. People had no choice, so they went through the same tedious and dangerous well-digging experience, year after year.

Despite the difficulties people faced while digging and maintaining them, wells were considered common properties for anyone fetching drinking water. Regardless of who owned the well, people, especially women, were allowed to fill up their jerricans anytime, without questions asked. Tress-passers did stir up troubles when the water was drawn for the purpose of selling in Kokoland. Village people did not have much sympathy for Kokolanders who violated their water rights.

Not too far from Kokoland, there used to be a densely wooded area with a stream running through it. There was also a big reservoir, which was the main source of drinking water for people in nearby villages, for many months after the rainy season. Cattle owners who owned large herds constantly shuttled up and down between the reservoir and their camps. There was hardly any time for the cattle to graze, nor was there any cattle feed nearby. This situation compelled herders to travel long distances with their herds. In the process, many animals did not make it to the next rainy season. The government of the time (around 1965) embarked on a project to widen the reservoir so it lasted the entire dry season. Because both people and animals drank from the same open-source water, the government decided to build another reservoir and barbed wire fenced it to prevent animals from drinking from it. It was linked to a well sunken outside of the reservoir from which people drew water. The water was relatively cleaner in comparison to the open reservoir. However, the depth of the well and the distance people had to travel, coupled with the congestion around it, especially after the open reservoir had dried up, all discouraged people from continuing to use it. Some people reverted to the old tradition of well-digging at streambeds closer to their villages, whereas others went back to drawing water from the same, easily accessible, open and muddy reservoir.

Using donkeys to haul water. Photo taken in 2016.

It was my responsibility to provide drinking water to our house. I was very young, so it was hard for me to pull full-sized buckets of water from the well to fill up a thirty-gallon tarpaulin container. The process also involved carrying the bucket some fifty feet or so, then lifting it up to pour the water in the tarp container on the back of a donkey. Because many people drew water from the well, we had to keep the donkeys at a distance, which meant taking longer trips back and forth the well before we could fill up the tarpaulin container. There were rocks placed around the well. It got muddy and slippery, and that caused many people to fall down and sustain serious injuries while carrying those heavy ten-gallon jerricans. Sadly, people laughed whenever someone fell down. They screamed the word "fallas," meaning "ran out of strength."

Like many people, I found it convenient and more practical to fill my container from the open reservoir. I led my donkey deep inside until the water got to his belly. Then, as he took his time drinking, I filled the container by lifting the ten-gallon tin, only half filled, since I did not have the strength to carry it up if it was full. One of the most stomach turning images you can ever imagine was something donkeys always did. They were notoriously known for the habit of defecating and urinating the moment they stepped in a pond or a still water. That was the first thing they did, guaranteed. My donkey was not an exception to this rule. This presented a predicament for me and other kids my age. Filling the containers from the area around the donkey meant, in absolute terms, loading up water that contained high concentration of donkey dung and urine. On the other hand, stepping further in the pond to fill up the tin with relatively cleaner water exposed me to the risk of falling in a deep hole and drowning. I was always mindful of what had happened to Shaban, the local clinic's medical assistant, who nearly drowned in the same pond. He went there to hunt for wild geese. He shot a few, so he swam to retrieve them, but he got exhausted and could not swim back out of the pond. If it was not for Kalomi, the fisherman, who happened to be in the vicinity, Shaban could have drowned. Between the two options, I settled for the former one. Drinking dirty or polluted water is, anytime, better than running the risk of drowning while fetching cleaner water. The truth is that members of my family and I drank water containing donkey dung and urine for as long as I fetched water. I am sure they did not get a break from drinking bad quality water when I was away at school. It was unlikely that those who sold them water cared more about their well-being than I did.

As I mentioned earlier in Chapter 3, the thing I feared the most was tumbling down from my donkey and falling on top of a snake, but I equally dreaded under water snakes. They are known for their venom and fatal bites. For this reason, I was mindful of them whenever I stepped in the pond. I always remembered an incident that had happened to the son of Gambo, our neighbor at the farm. He went to collect drinking water from a nearby pond. When he stepped inside the water, something bit him on his toe, so he lifted his foot out of the water to find out. There was a big snake hanging from his toe. He screamed, so we all ran toward him. When my dad and I got there, we found the boy's father rubbing the toe with some green leaves and reading prayers. We stood there for a few minutes until he fished what he was doing, then he said, "Nothing, yes, nothing," which meant he had a secret snake medicine and that there was nothing to worry about. The boy got up and went about his normal business. I understand if you think the snake was not poisonous, but I was always worried about stepping on one, regardless. The fact remains that I had to do what I had to do to bring drinking water to my home.

After filling the tarp container, I would seal it with pieces of jute that I usually cut from old jute sacks. I would slowly lead the donkey out of the pond and head home. I would come to the pond riding, but on our way back to Kokoland, the donkey, being heavily loaded, would not be able to carry one additional pound, so riding was not an option. That was my daily routine during school breaks, which took only few weeks before my body gave in. It was a very exhausting job, considering my age at late primary and middle school years.

I held my breath and prayed for a safe delivery of the load to the house. Potholes and dry mud on the road presented huge risk. The donkey could trip, fall down, get hurt, and damage the tarp container. Once on the ground, it would not be able to stand up on its feet with the load on its back. First, I would release some water to lighten the load and help it stand up. If I failed, I would release an additional amount and try to push it to stand up. If I released the whole load and the donkey still could not get up, it meant I had a bigger problem on my hands. The donkey might be seriously injured. If the tarp container broke after impacting the ground, it took only few seconds for the water to run off. That day I would go home without a drop of water. Occasionally, the donkey would get up with some water in the tarp. Returning to Kokoland with less than the full load meant I had to run an additional trip to compensate for the loss. I carefully weighed my options. It all depended on whether the donkey tripped and fell down at a point closer to Kokoland or to the water pond. If it was nearer to the pond, I would go back and fill up again, provided the tarp container was safe and I still had some time before it got dark. As you can see, tripping of a donkey required countless strategies to minimize the damage or enhance the outcome. The given thing was that it came at some cost all the time. To mitigate the risk emanating from that, we visited the water pond in groups of friends. Together, we helped a fallen donkey to get up without releasing a lot of water, provided that it was not hurt.

Some children were extremely cruel to their donkeys, especially when they tripped and fell down. They would beat them so hard to force them to get up, and also to make them walk faster. In most of the cases, those donkeys were underfed and could barely walk while carrying heavy load of water on their backs. One particular boy, named Bade, always carried a stick with a sharp end, which he used for poking his donkey on its back around a wound that was beneath the saddle. The donkey would speed up few yards from pain every time he poked it. That way, Bade could get to the water pond and back faster, so he could make up to three trips a day. Many of us believed that he created the wound purposely.

Bade also told us of another technique he had invented. He swore that it worked whenever he applied it on his donkey upon falling down to the ground. It involved holding the donkey's tail by both hands and pulling it upward to force it to stand up. A donkey's tail dangles downward, so pulling it upward, naturally, caused it tremendous pain, which would force it to stand up to relieve itself from the pain. He told us if this technique did not work, then he, as a matter of last resort, would bite the donkey on the tail. He claimed that simultaneously biting and pulling the tail would send shockwaves of pain through the donkey's spine, which would jolt it into standing up. The problem with Bade's technique was that if the donkey was injured as a result of tripping and falling down, forcing it to stand up would only cause additional injury. This was a horrific thing to do, by all standards. Many of us did not approve of the way Bade treated his donkey.

In my case, with help from my dad, I was able to take good care of my donkey. I never subjected him to such horrendous cruelty. In fact, I fed him millet, mixed with salt. Millet was not readily available to many people, yet I fed it to my donkey as a token of appreciation for the great service he rendered. I also treated him with melons and watermelon shells, neatly chopped to small pieces and marinated with salt, a delicacy he enjoyed eating so much. He was the corner stone in my water business and a breadwinner. On the other hand, I was resentful of the fact that he kicked me a couple of times for no reason, despite the due diligence I exerted in taking care of him. That resentment lasted until recently after I learned from my 10-year-old son that Abraham Lincoln too was kicked by his donkey unconscious and was in a coma for two days. When donkeys were capable of subjecting someone like Abraham Lincoln to the same treatment as my humble self, it means that my resentment was misplaced, so I rested my case when I heard the story. Who am I to complain? I looked into the matter and found out that it was a horse that kicked Abraham Lincoln. This is an important correction, just to be fair to donkeys.

Sometimes the tarp container leaked water due to aging, which meant the loss of a valuable cargo. The first remedy we all resorted to was pouring a couple of hands full of dirt down the tarp. This technique worked in the cases of slight leakages. For more serious ones, we relied on another solution. We used the bark of one particular tree, which we dissolved in water to get a thick and slimy soup-like material. We would carefully pour it inside the container and shake it well to spread the liquid all over, sealing the gaps causing the leak. We would then fill it up with water.

All living creatures in the area descended to the pond to drink, so the water we drank contained mud, donkey urine, donkey dung, cattle dung, bird poop, dirt, frog eggs, baby frogs, slimy bark soup, and numerous other organic elements, to name a few. In the end, we drank anything, but water. It was some kind of soup, which hydrated our bodies. This is not to forget that primary school children who lived in the school boarding house also flocked to the same pond every Thursday afternoon to wash their clothes and bathe. They did their washing a few feet from the pond shore. Naturally, dirty wash mixed with soap found its way to the water from which I filled my container.

Reaching Kokoland safely was not the end of the story. Getting to my house was one thing and emptying the container was another. The fence gate of my house was so narrow for the donkey to get through. That meant I had to empty the container, half a tin at a time, and carry it to the water pots fifty feet or so inside the house. We could have widened the gateway to make my job easier, but we did not.

The rainy season presented an excellent opportunity for me as I was able to draw water from nearby ponds fed by rain water. My travel time fetching water for the family was reduced to a fraction of the time I spent collecting water from the reservoir during the dry season. This left me ample time to play soccer and also to make some money.

Hajja Safiya was an elderly woman who lived in our neighborhood. She was famous for brewing local alcohol. I saw in Hajja Safia an ideal candidate for my water business. I approached her with a proposal to become her sole water supplier, promising to be prompt and dependable in adhering to my delivery schedules. She agreed without hesitation.

Out of the many ponds and water holes around Kokoland, I carefully visited the ones that were relatively distant from human settlements, preferably the ones by farmlands. They contained cleaner water, in comparison to other ponds, because animal owners could not get to them without destroying farms, which was a call for fights that in many cases resulted in serious injuries or death. I was able to provide my family a relatively purer water that contained less dirt. However, I could not do anything about the frog eggs, baby frogs, algae, and thousands of tiny microscopic creatures undetectable by the naked eye. After all, it was the rainy season, so water-dependent creatures took full advantage of the short window of opportunity to reproduce when there were abundant food supplies to feed their offspring. Dirt and mud were the least of my worries. Before I poured the water in the pot I placed a cloth mesh on the mouth of the water pot to filter the insects. Anything that could find its way through to the pot was tolerated. It was not uncommon to find seaweed, algae, and larvae inside drinking containers. Despite frequently suffering from waterborne diseases, my family members and I were lucky to have survived.

My religious teachings forbid me from drinking alcohol or aiding anyone making, marketing, or selling it. However, I complied with the first part of the teachings; drinking, and turned a blind eye on the rest. I visited Hajja Safiya, obtained from her a brewing schedule, on which basis I delivered the water quantities she needed.

The demand for her drinks peaked on Fridays and Mondays. Both days are market days, which drew many people to Kokoland. You've guessed it right that the intention of everyone visiting Kokoland wasn't always to do Friday prayers. Hajja Safiya did not care much about the source of water I supplied. What mattered to her was any liquid with which she could brew alcohol (*mareesa* and *aragi*).

Despite that, I just could not draw water from Tabojah, a pond that was a stone's throw from Kokoland's borough of Keekah. The water was filthy and contained high concentration of waste. While I found it unethical to deliver Hajja Safiya water from Tabojah pond, I did not go far and out of my way to fetch her relatively quality water compatible with that I delivered to my house for drinking. I supplied her something in between. Hajja Safiya paid me the equivalent of one cent for every ten gallons of water I delivered. I thought that was enough incentive for me to avoid supplying her water from Tabojah, as a matter of ethics, but not enough for venturing too far away from Kokoland. Was it possible that some kids drew water from Tabojah and sold it to other alcohol brewers in Kokoland? You bet.

Nearby ponds, including Tabojah, were our community swimming pools during the rainy season. No wonder my friends and I suffered from skin diseases and got fevers frequently. We were fine as long as we could walk around. We were taken to the local clinic only when we were bedridden, a sign to parents that things were at a tipping point. I used to suffer from severe headaches and nose infections many years after I left Kokoland. It turned out that I had very dirty ears. The doctor was able to dig out loads of stuff that had accumulated over years of bathing in muddy ponds. My childhood friend Tiffah complained about the same symptoms. I tipped him of what it was, so he too got his ears cleaned of mud and other stuff.

For every full tarp container delivery to Hajja Safiya, I got paid six cents. I made two to three deliveries a week. My average weekly earnings was fifteen cents. I was very content with what I made until I moved out of Kokoland. That was when I realized that relying on a donkey for transportation or selling water to generate wealth would not get me, or anyone else for that matter, far or rich.

Occasionally, low sale volumes of alcohol reflected negatively on my water business. I delivered half of my load, which meant I had to market the rest of the water to other people in the village. I went around and knocked on the tin jerrycan six times, to signal to households having water shortage. People came out of their homes and called me to drop my load, after verifying the pond source of the water. I always told them the truth. Based on that, they would decide whether they wanted to use the water for drinking or washing. It all depended on their social status. Ironically, Kokoland too had class system. The five primary school teachers and the medical assistant who lived in the government officials' neighborhood considered themselves classier than the "commons" living in other neighborhoods. On the other hand, Kokoland residents thought that they were superior to those who lived in villages around Kokoland. How ironic?

My contract with Hajjah Safiyah, coupled with my candy and hapless chicken businesses, landed me comfortable earnings, which helped with my school uniforms and stipends for supplementing the food shortages I experienced at boarding school.

I guess I have just redefined the term clean drinking water. I explained to my family members that, considering where I come from, it is waste of money to buy water filters on the premise that tap water in America is not clean enough for drinking. Really? Give me a break. I paid a heavy price for getting them to know of my different definitions and standards for things. They thought I will be fine with lower standards of products and services, and I still would not miss a thing. I heard my wife many times say, "This food has gone bad," and my son's response was, "Don't worry. Leave it for Dad. He will eat it." How cruel? My son believes that if I take part in sardine-eating contest anywhere in the world, I will win.

As mentioned earlier, Kokoland is a migration trail used by nomad cattle herders. My brother Aziz and I saw an opportunity in this seasonal migration. The women brought along with them empty snail shells, which we bought for dirt cheap price. We carefully trimmed the shells' tops and turned them into *gargoors* or spinning toys. It took special trimming technique for the shells to spin smoothly and for a longer time when played on the sand. We used date seeds to carry out the first round of trimming. We would hold the bottom of the shell with one hand and the top edge between the date seed, the thump, and the index finger of the other hand. We would then press hard and slightly tip the hand holding the top edge to break small chunks of shell. The hard date seed helped with breaking the shell easily and also in protecting the fingers from getting injured by the sharp edges. We would repeat the process until we had trimmed the shell top into a circle. Then we would spin it on the sand to see how smooth it ran. To get the best result, we would place the shell under a piece of cloth to see the edges that were visibly long and pointing outward, which we then trimmed, using our teeth. We sold them to village boys as processed or modified products, charging prices many times the original cost. We stored some and sold them, at even higher prices, during the dry season and after the nomads had left the area. This is Business 101, right?

Abu Ali, the village blacksmith, stepped in to get a share of the lucrative opportunity to sell spinning toys. He made them from tin to last longer, but his invention had a devastating effect on the village children. It caused severe damage to fingers, so parents complained about that and he stopped making them, leaving the market for my brother and me to monopolize.

Abu Ali's invention caused an outcry in the village because the way we played the game involved punishing losers. We played in teams of two to five children. We would hold the bottom of the *gargoor* tight between our thumb and middle finger. We would then twist the two fingers, anti-clockwise, and let go as we pulled our hands downward, fast. That action caused the *gargoor* to spin on the sand. As it span, we would slightly knock it on the base with the tip of the thump, causing it to flip and turn upside down. If you were successful in flipping it over, you punished your opponent (if only two of you playing), or the person sitting to your left (if more than two playing). The person being punished would flip his palm face down and rest it on the ground, using his thumb. Then we would play the *gargoor* the same way described above, but this time aiming at the back of the opponent's hand. There would be a knocking sound if the *gargoor* landed and hit a finger bone, causing the person to raise his hand up in the air out of pain. We agreed in advance on the number of knocks for every successful flip, but it was usually one knock. Abu Ali's metal *gargoors* caused serious harm to children. It left bloody wounds, so parents complained about his harmful product and forced him to stop making them.

Aziz and I also figured out that cattle-nomads, especially the Fulani, loved crafts made out of beads. We collected tin pales, used in wrapping tea boxes coming from China and India, from my dad's shop, and used them in making wristbands. First, we would cut the pales into seven or eight-inch long pieces. Then we would curve them into wristbands. After that, we would wrap them with beads in thin nylon beading threads to create colorful designs such as diamonds, squares, and other shapes. Do my brother and I qualify to be among the first recyclers? This might as well be our inadvertent contribution to the well-being of the planet, I guess.

On Mondays and Fridays, we displayed our crafts alongside my candies and sold them at prices of our choice. At times, we charged ten cents per piece. Can you imagine? We were rich. We also made comps by slicing bamboo wood into thin straws, then cutting them into six-inch-long pieces. After that, we would sharpen one end of each straw and hold twelve of them together with copper wires, creating perfect comps. We also sold them on market days with my other stuff. I bet that product diversification does enhance sales revenue.

We also invented a mouse trap, which worked for a brief window of time. That was our contribution toward dealing with mice infestation, which almost took over our shop. The drawback to our invention was that the number of mice we trapped overnight was determined by their number inside the trap when one of them bit on the onion-bait and triggered the door shut. If there was only one unlucky mouse inside the trap at that moment, then that was what we got for that night, and the rest of the mice continued to wreak havoc in the shop. I must admit that our invention was not efficient at all. In fact, it could not cope with the mice's reproduction rate. It presented little threat to the colony residing inside the shop.

That was the case until a Chinese-made trap appeared in town. The new trap could hold as many mice as possible, as long as there was room inside. The trap gate was designed like a platform, which was kept shut by a metal weight hanging on a four feet long solid wire, connected to the metal platform. Once a mouse stepped on the platform, its weight, being heavier than the metal weight, would push the gate downward, causing the mouse to slide to the bottom of the trap. It would go straight to the piece of onion we had placed inside the box, while paying little attention to the fact that the metal weight had caused the gate to shut behind it. More mice would keep on sliding in as long as there was room inside the box. Sometimes we trapped more than a dozen mice. In the morning, we would take the trap to the center of the market and release them. That was enough distance from the shops so their chances of escaping was slim, especially considering the fact that there would be kids and adults surrounding them. What happened next was unpleasant, so there is no need to mention it here.

By using the more efficient Chinese traps, we did observe a decline in mice population inside the shop. In fact Chinese products slowly pulled the carpet out from beneath my feet, as far as my business was concerned. Comps and handicrafts made out of plastics flooded the market, so my business could no longer compete. I am certainly not new to the idea of Chinese products taking over locally-made ones. On the other hand, people were very happy that they had access to stronger Chinese-made plastic robes, compared to the ones locally-made from baobab tree barks. They no longer worried about their donkeys cutting loose and spending time looking for them, when they were supposed to be working in their farms. People were also happy with plastic robes which they used for drawing water from wells. They were less worried about losing the buckets, which piled and blocked the bottom of the well. They less-frequently overhauled wells by going through the dangerous work of lowering someone down to do the cleaning job. They grew more confident doing that, compared to the days when they used baobab robes, which easily snapped, causing serious injuries and sometimes death. Kokolanders thought that Chinese products were a blessing.

CHAPTER 11

Health Myths and Traditional Medicine

Health care in and around Kokoland was at bare minimum, if at all. There was one small clinic, which catered for the needs of the entire region. People sought its service in emergency cases only. My Kanuri people, who lived around Kokoland believed little in modern medicine, considering it an extension to Western value system. There was little awareness about the importance of visiting the clinic. Infant mortality was high due to death caused by childhood illnesses such as measles, whooping cough, chicken pox, jaundice, and skin diseases, to name a few. Death of young women while giving birth was prevalent. The Kanuri married away their daughters at a very young age and in most cases below the age of fifteen. That posed a huge risk to them when giving birth, particularly during first deliveries. There were no trained health-care workers or midwives. Most birth complications led to death of both mother and child. In few cases, pregnant women were taken to the clinic, but it was usually too late. The lack of health care and adequate means of transportation (mainly relying on donkeys) affected the survival chances of pregnant women and their unborn babies. This was a huge problem, which I observed first-hand growing up.

Whenever my dad got a chance, he spoke to the community about the importance of visiting the clinic to seek help. He frequently found himself at loggerhead with village leaders, particularly the community elders. They looked at him as someone who abandoned his heritage only to come back to challenge their authority and question the way they lived, so they mostly refused to take his advice. Some argued that there was no point in visiting the clinic, since most of those taken there ended up dead, anyway. Others also argued that there was no hope in seeing the medical assistant because he himself would get sick and die, someday. To them, all was in God's hands. If God wanted a person to get sick, he would, and if he wanted him to die, he would, period. People saw the whole thing as destiny and that no amount of human intervention could change the outcome. The problem was that they were oblivious to the fact that most of those taken to the clinic were in advanced stages of illness. Sadly, in the case of women and children, they had no say in visiting the clinic or not. The decision rested in the hands of the father; the head of the household.

The remedies for treating illnesses involved the use of alternative medicine and prayers. Tree roots and branches were readily available, so they formed the bulk of medicinal recipes. The problem was that those herbal medicines, on their own, could kill people because no one had any idea how they worked inside the body. Some were toxic, poisonous, and triggered fatal allergic conditions. One of my nephews died from kidney failure resulting from taking a mixture of herbs and gum Arabic. My father once paid a visit to my elder sister in a nearby village and found her very ill. She was surrounded by half a dozen bowls containing different local medicine for her to take. He told her that, apart from her sickness, consuming that many different roots and herbal mixture, alone, could have killed her. He took her to the clinic and, fortunately, she fully recovered to tell me her story, decades later. She told me she was so lucky that my dad showed up unexpectedly. If it wasn't for that, she would have ended up dead, she said.

The problem with recommendation given by community elders of what local medicine to take could have been pulled off the top of hats. To start with, the nature of the illness might not be known, leave alone giving the right prescription. If someone became ill, members of the community would flock to his house to wish him good health and pray for his fast recovery. They would ask about the illness and if he ever tried so and so. They would suggest that a particular medicine was taken before by xyz and it did work, so he, too, should try it. That was it. Few moments later, another person would show up and give another recommendation of roots and leaves, while, adamantly, arguing in favor of using his recipes and no one else's. A third person would come up with another treatment, and that could be animal parts. Soon, there would be a dozen or so bowls of different local medicine to take. Some would suggest the best time for taking the medicine to be first thing in the morning. Others would insist that the person should fast for a whole day before trying the medicine. Yet, others would recommend the exact number of days the treatment should last. Some people would go as far as prescribing the type of food that should be eaten while taking the medicine. Everybody helped in his or her own way of treating the illness and, in the process, he or she would gain recognition within the community, especially if there was full recovery. It did not matter if the person recovered on his or her own or not. Every bowl owner would claim credit for that. It was likely that they would go on and prescribe the same treatment to other people in the future, quoting their past success record. The exact type of illness might be immaterial. I must state here that I am by no means trying to undermine my own people. What they did was, probably, to the best of their knowledge and was done with good intentions in mind. However, the results in certain cases were disastrous, as I have seen that in my own family members.

Everyone in the community was a farmer, so most people were familiar with the vegetation in the area. That was why they had some general knowledge about traditional medicine. The truth was that few people had proven cures for specific illnesses. They kept their knowledge a secret in the family and passed it down to younger generations. Such people were well sought after, so they travelled from one village to the other providing their services. The Mandarai brothers, Hamid and Ali, had cure for snakebites; however, Al Haji Yuram was unlucky. He died from a cobra bite before receiving help. I doubt it if anyone had an effective anti-venom treatment.

I recently received the news that my friend Butri had died from a rattlesnake bite. Butri became a doctor during the three decades I was absent from Kokoland. He did not receive any formal education or training. Over the years, he developed skills for giving injections and dispensing off first aid medicine. Practice makes perfect. He roamed the villages providing his valuable services, so people called him Doctor Butri, and he happily responded to their calls in a heartbeat, while fully enjoying his doctorial life. Basically, he grew to believe in his fake credentials. Butri just stepped in to fill a huge gap that existed in health care. Could he have misdiagnosed or given wrong prescription, which could have resulted in serious side effects? Very likely.

There were people who questioned Butri's credentials because they knew that it would require some formal education to become a doctor. There was a second group that did not believe in Western education or Western medicine, anyway. For this group the death of Butri must have strengthened their argument that he, despite being a doctor, could not save himself from death. However, the one thing for sure is that many people in the community will miss him and his valuable services.

The barbers or *wanzams*, as I have written about earlier, also played their physician role by filling in the gap created by lack of trained health-care providers. They combed the area delivering their services at village events. They shaved heads and beards, treated toothache and sunstrokes, and made Kanuri tribal scars on faces and bellies of seven-day old babies. Most important, they circumcised boys, of course, without anesthesia. I doubt that they ever knew if anesthesia existed by then. Even if, they had known, they would have kept quiet for fear of running out of business, in case people learned about it.

One would imagine that, over time, local and traditional medicine would give way to modern medicine. The reality is that more people are resorting to local treatment due to high medical costs and decline in people's living standards. In a recent visit to Kokoland, the bus driver stopped at a small village on the way, for a short break. A man carrying a small suit case boarded the bus and started announcing to the passengers that he had medicine for treating diabetes, blood pressure, cancer, heart diseases, migraine headache, lung decease, and sterility. You would wonder how he could carry all these medicines in such a small case, and if there was enough time to conduct the diagnosis needed before making his recommendations, bearing in mind we stopped for a mere half an hour break. Miracles do happen in my homeland. Few passengers reached out for their wallets and bought some tiny bundles, which contents I could not tell. The doctor-patient conversation was conducted quietly in observance of confidentiality. That was not a bad thing, considering the circumstance that we were inside a bus. In fact, nowadays it has become a more acceptable practice to have traditional medicine providers in locations nearby hospitals. It is a clear sign that there is room for their business. Those who could not afford the costs of doctor visits will settle for the less expensive types of health solutions, just around the corner from hospitals. Whether these treatments work or not is another thing. "Something is better than nothing," one of the bus passengers sitting next to me argued.

I had my lion's share of childhood diseases. There were immunization programs for few illnesses such as measles, meningitis, and chicken pox. In other cases, children got sick and, if lucky, recovered on their own and waited for the next round of illness. There was a high mortality rate among children. Health authorities used to visit Kokoland every year to offer limited help. Somehow, the common belief among people in those days was that immunization was not good for children. I really don't know how they reached that conclusion. Parents, especially in villages around Kokoland, upon learning about the arrival of the immunization team in town, would tell their children to run and hide in the forest and return only after the "danger" had disappeared. Children felt good about what they did and bragged about their skills in eluding the team. Were they to blame?

I was immunized a few times, but had no idea what for. I fell sick with malaria, chicken pox, measles, pneumonia, whooping cough, skin disease of the scalp, and appendicitis. Malaria and whooping cough were the two most killer diseases, which wreaked havoc among children. Against the odds, I was lucky to have survived whooping cough, which was known for low survival rate. Sadly, my baby brother Mahmood was one of its victims. I was about five years old, but I vividly remember how he suffered before we lost him one morning when he was only eighteen month old. Those were very painful memories and they remain so today. I was also lucky to have survived appendicitis. For over two years, I suffered from the swelling of my appendix. I repeatedly visited doctors who always told me that the results of the analysis were negative despite the severe pain I was enduring, so I stopped seeing doctors. Instead, whenever I felt pain, I would rush to my residence, stay in bed, and fight it for a whole week or so, until the inflammation subsided, only to go through the same ordeal in a matter of one month or so. In one attack, I took a cab to the hospital. A trainee medical student examined me and suspected that I might have appendicitis. I was lucky to get it removed just in time. I wouldn't have made it, if I wasn't living in the city and had access to emergency that day. My mother, brother, and baby sister were not so lucky. Only after the removal of my appendix, I could connect the dots and draw comparison between my mother's, my baby sister's, and my own symptoms. Sadly, it was too late for them. They both died from burst appendices. Another family member, my uncle Ibrahim, also died of a ruptured appendix, as I found out way later.

After the death of my mother, my elder sister took my baby sister to live with her in the city. She used to get very ill, but no one knew what was causing that. One day, she had an attack, so I went to see Dr. Ismail, who was a neighbor, to seek help. I knocked on his door and told him that my sister was very sick and needed immediate care. He told me to wait. I waited for over half an hour and knocked again, but he did not respond. I heard an ABBA record playing, so I knocked the door one more time to express the urgency of the situation. This time, he scolded me from behind the door for not being patient enough to let him get dressed. I decided to leave. I went back to my sister's house and waited for him, but he never showed up. I was planning to leave to the city in the morning, on time to be at school for exams, so I left. I told my elder sister to take good care of her. Few days later, I got the tragic news that my baby sister had passed away. I believe the cause of her death was a ruptured appendix. I could tell because I went through the same experience, a couple of years later, and was able to compare hers and my mother's symptoms with mine. Looking back, I should have never left Dr. Ismail's house. I should have been more patient and waited longer, or looked for another doctor. That decision filled me with guilt and pain every time I remembered it. As you can tell, my decision to seek help from the doctor by knocking on his door instead of going to the emergency room was not right. The problem I did not know any better. I was not familiar with the concept of emergency service at that time, being from rural Kokoland.

Malaria medicine was not readily available those days, so people resorted to local treatments made of acacia fruits, hibiscus, baobab fruits, and tens of untested experimental medicines. People thought there was a positive correlation between bitterness, or sourness of the medicine and its effectiveness, hence speed of recovery. I caught malaria once or twice every year, usually during the rainy season, which was perfect time for mosquito reproduction. At the boarding school, every morning, tens of sick children dragged themselves out of bed and met at the schoolyard. They registered their names and, with great difficulty, marched to the clinic, half a mile away. The children's ages ranged between six and thirteen years, but there was hardly any supervision from the teachers, so they catered for themselves.

In case a child was too sick to walk on his own, two of his friends would shoulder him to the clinic. It would be a cause for concern if he could not get out of his bed. We would inform a teacher and a message would be dispatched to his father to come and get him. I went through this experience a few times when I fell ill with malaria and had to travel to Kokoland. Walking to the town center to catch a lorry was another challenge. It meant struggling for a mile or so with fever and body temperature above one hundred degrees. It was a very difficult thing to do. I remember a few times lying down in the dirt under a neem tree, waiting for a lorry to take me to Kokoland, but without being sure if it would ever show up that day or not. If I was lucky, I would travel for an hour standing on my feet, while subjecting my joints to double pain from the illness and the jolting of the lorry navigating through one hell of a bumpy road. Malaria is known to cause excruciating pain to joints, so you can imagine. For those of you who are wondering where the ambulances were, my answer is, "We can't think of eating cake when we don't have access to bread." I certainly did not know such things as ambulances existed. Malaria also shuts down appetite for food and drink. I just took the pain for a week or so, recovered from it, and waited for the next attack. If I were lucky, the combination of the severe headache, the fever, and the loss of appetite, would let me get away with half of my weight, which was half of my age's normal weight, in the first place, anyway. I was very skinny.

Another problem with malaria is that the fever and high level of temperature mess up the brain. In severe cases, one loses his mental capacity. A few times, I lost consciousness and started hallucinating. People used to say, "The malaria has climbed his head," to describe anyone who was going through such a condition.

There were three instances when malaria "climbed" my head. The first time, I was in first grade. I lost consciousness and woke up to find myself dangling from the window of our mud hut. I saw my blanket on the ground, outside the hut. I unconsciously dropped it, probably planning to catch up with it and continue walking or something. I woke up to my sister grabbing me back inside, just in time before I jumped. The second time, I got very sick while I was away at school. I remember having a severe fever that night when I went to bed. I gained consciousness in the middle of the night and found myself in an unfamiliar place, certainly not my boarding room. I realized that I was standing by the barbed wire fence probably trying to get out. It was pitch-black night and there was not a single light glittering anywhere. We did not have electricity, anyway. I scrambled my way back to the boarding room, luckily, without encountering any zombie, the creature my friends and I dreaded most. I heard a story of a child who drowned in a pond not too far from the school. It was rumored that he was sick with malaria and he sleepwalked from his house into the pond and got drowned.

I was a teenager when "malaria climbed my head" for the third and last time. I remember having a hot body temperature and I was slowly losing my brain capacities, so I fought hard to control it and stay alert, but I finally lost the battle. I started talking rubbish for a few seconds and then I went blank. I couldn't remember what I said thereafter. My stepmother heard me talking to myself, so she came to my rescue. I gained my senses without knowing for how long I had fainted, but I noticed a strong smell of fragrance on my nose. My stepmother probably knew about perfume characteristics of restoring consciousness. I slowly dragged my feet to the clinic and received malaria medicine.

As I mentioned earlier, before malaria drugs became available, people used local medicine and followed all sorts of recommendations to treat the disease. I remember one of those recommendations was to jump in a pond very early in the morning. I personally tried this a couple of times. I was told that the vapor emitted by my feverish body, after emerging from the pond, was a sign of recovery. This is why the Kanuri word for fever is "smoke." They will tell you that a person has a "smoke" if he is suffering from a fever, probably not being aware of the fact that fever is the side effect of something else. Naturally, taking a bath reduces the body temperature, but it does nothing to the infection in the blood. This misconception might have led to the death of many people who settled for a jump in a cold pond-water in the morning, rather than seeking proper malaria treatment.

Later on, malaria medicine became more readily available, as long as people were willing to go to the clinic and pay the price of the four shots of tetracycline, quinine, or other types of malaria drugs. Some malaria medicine caused severe allergies and non-stop itching, which lasted for days. This could equally be painful; a fact that augmented the argument of the non-advocates of modern medicine. For that reason, even less people visited the clinic to seek treatment.

One crazy recommendation for treating measles was the squeezing of onion into the eyes of the sick child. I was in first grade when I fell sick with measles. I vividly remember receiving this horrible treatment suggested by a neighbor, but I don't think it worked. After two days of absence, I insisted on going to school, even though I could barely stand up, due to high fever. The morning assembly bell rang, so I went and stood in line with my fellow first graders. In each grade; there were forty-five or so students, who stood in two-line formation for inspection. Usually, the teacher would start inspecting the first grade. He would inspect the front line, then the back line, before moving to second, third, and finally fourth grade. That day, against all odds, Samuel, the medical assistant appeared and walked behind the teacher. When they got to where I was standing, they both stopped. I could barely open my eyes to see what was going on. Samuel closely looked at my face, then ordered me to step out of the line, so I did. After the inspection was completed, there was a dozen or so of us pulled out of the lines, all sick with measles. We were taken to the farthest straw shack and got quarantined. I stayed there until I fully recovered after a week, then I was released. Every day, new kids quarantined, as others were released after recovery. That went on for some time until the epidemic was brought under control. I remember being told that measles caused vision impairment and that I had to agree to take the onion liquid eye drops, if I wanted to preserve my eyesight. I had no choice but to accept. I'm glad that I insisted on going to school, where I was diagnosed and properly treated by Samuel. I don't know what could have happened, if I did not. It was rumored that my friend Hamza's mom failed to administer the onion medicine on him when he fell sick with measles, so he ended up losing one of his eyes. It was also rumored among us, children, that Hamza's mom, ate the onion she was supposed to use for treating her son. This is unfair to Hamza's mom and I don't think it is true. Children can be brutal, at times. People casually recommended forms of treatment they thought would be effective in certain cases. Such advices were taken and implemented regardless of the consequences. If they worked, fine. If they didn't, that was fine too. It was also fine if they caused side effects, since no one was held negligent.

Jaundice was locally treated by administering two pairs of one-inch-long cuts in both arms, using a sharp blade, or, in extreme cases, a hot metal object. Jaundice, locally called "the yellowing disease" is known to be caused by excess material called bilirubin that circulates in the blood when the liver fails to filter it out as a waste. I am not sure if such operations were effective or not, but there was a strong belief that the success rate of treatments with fire was high. The argument was that "tough illnesses needed equally tough treatment", so fire was the answer. A close family member had arthritis, which caused him severe pain in his limbs. He went around asking people for treatment until he found someone who claimed to possess secret knowledge for riding him of his condition. He told him he needed fire-burn administered to his lower back. Accordingly, the practitioner heated a piece of metal until it was red hot, then stamped it on the man's back, just as he told him. The man's daughter told me that the brutal image and smell of the burning flesh were so unbearable for her that she fainted. She said she cried for days, every time she remembered the incident.

It was believed that exposing children to dew vapors caused seizure. The treatment involved the use of one particular type of tree, native to the area. A flat board and a stick from this tree were used to make a friction-based fire. Then, the hot edge of the stick would be placed on the forehead-center of the baby suffering from seizure. The burn would leave a penny-size circle on the forehead. I remember witnessing this treatment being administered on a close family member when I was a child. I don't know if she was cured or not because she died from a different childhood illness at a very young age. This was another form of fire-based treatment.

Animals also had their share of these crazy recommendations. Nasser's dog, Sumbul, fell ill, so someone suggested that she too needed hot-iron-mark burns in certain areas over her body. Sumbul was a nonchalant, peaceful, and a very quiet dog that, unlike other ferocious Kokoland dogs, bothered nobody. She always lay down curled up in her usual place, under a neem tree in front of her owner's shop. I remember the morning when the man showed up with a stove and charcoal, which he placed a few feet from Sumbul. She innocently looked at him not having the slightest clue as to what was coming her way. I was watching from our shop, a distance of a hundred feet or so. The man lit up the charcoal and placed a metal bar on it until it turned red. He suggested to another man to use a nearby wooden stool to pin down Sumbul to the ground to prevent her from fleeing or biting. They approached her and she thought they were going to pet her or give her some cookies, but then they simultaneously acted. Upon one man pinning her down with the stool, the other man placed the hot metal on the side of her body that was exposed. She howled so loud that other nearby dogs, figuring out that something terrible must have happened to a fellow dog, also started howling and running away. After that, they let go of her and she took off running away as fast as she could. Sumbul was not diagnosed before the treatment to know the cause of her illness. The principle used was, "Burn her first, maybe she will get well." Sumbul was never the same dog again. From that moment onward, she always maintained her distance from people and exhibited aggressive behavior whenever someone got near her, but it was too late anyway. The damage was already done. She died shortly after that incident. The whole thing was so cruel and I will never forget it.

Burns were administered on donkeys too. They, sometimes, sustained wounds due to carrying heavy loads without proper cushion separating their backs from the wooden saddle. For treatment, the area around the wound would be burnt to prevent the wound from spreading. I am certain that there exists a better cure than burning to cure.

Al baseer is a title given only to those who fix broken bones. The word itself means "the visionary." He stabilizes broken arms and legs by using pieces of wood. The full recovery of a patient depended on the type of his injury and its severity. You must understand that there was no such thing as holding someone responsible or accountable for anything going wrong. Both patients and family members accepted negative treatment outcomes. The assumption was that patients were treated in good faith with the view to helping them recover from their injuries. Everything was in God's hands, so losing a limp or life during treatment was considered fate or destiny. It was immaterial even when the treatments was administered on a trial-and-error basis. In fact many of the *Baseers* were nothing, but enthusiastic members of the community who were bold enough to step forward at times of crisis, such as in cases of major accidents, to give recommendations. People did not know any better, so nobody questioned or challenged their fuzzy recommendations. If *Al Baseer*, or, better put, if the patient was lucky and the treatment worked, then *Al Baseer* would be considered the community's expert in broken bones. From that moment onward, any accident of similar nature would be referred to him. In most probability, patients' recovery was due to a self-healing process, especially in children and simple injury cases.

In more serious cases of injuries to limps, for example, the bones would heal, but the limps would fail to function normally. Sometimes persons with broken arms that did not heal properly were taken back to the same *Baseer,* the visionary, who badly treated them in the first place, to try to correct the deformity. Sadly, the process might involve the gruesome act of intentionally breaking the arm one more time to re-fix it, properly. This was particularly the case with children. I heard that the visionary would distract the child, then grab the crooked arm and, literally, break it. The child would most likely be in a worse condition than before. In the cases of open wounds; recovery was unlikely due to infection. It would be too late for patients when taken to the hospital for treatment. Amputation might become inevitable.

One of my cousins broke his arm, so he was taken to the visionary to get it fixed. The arm healed, but he could not stretch it. He was a perfect candidate for a second time arm breaking session, but he, luckily, escaped that ordeal. He continued to live with his disability. Our tailor, Mai, who lived in a nearby village, had an accident on his knee. He did not visit the clinic to seek treatment. He labored under pain for over six month, drinking from bowls containing mixture of roots and wild fruits. The pain finally subsided, but he too could not stretch his leg anymore. He also lived with that disability for the rest of his life. His brother, Abbanumah, returned from his farm on a hot autumn day and took a bath with cold water. He fell sick and lost his eyesight. Ironically, the visionary could not treat him for loss of vision. He lived vision-impaired for the rest of his life. People, basically, rode the pain and lived with the consequences, which were, in many cases, permanent disabilities and sometimes death.

One of the most bizarre practices carried out by some *Baseers* to treat children's broken arms involved the use of baby chickens. I have no idea how this practice came into usage, but anything was possible in Kokoland. After killing a baby-chicken, removing the feathers, and cleaning the internal organs, it would then be wrapped around the child's broken arm. The hand would be held up at chest level by a piece of cloth or thread hanging from the neck. It would be kept that way for a week or so. The dead chicken would then be removed and the child would have a healthy arm again, or so it was believed. If the arm turned out crooked, then it was tough luck. The next patient might have a better chance for a full recovery. God help the child if he happened to have an open wound when the risk of amputation would be imminent, especially having his wounds wrapped in a dead chicken.

People were very superstitious. The idea of treating broken bones with baby chickens could have evolved according to the following scenario: "A man was sitting in front of his hut, when his young boy came running to him and crying. He told him that he fell from the donkey and broke his arm. Coincidentally, a baby chicken appeared and passed in front of the man at the same time his son was telling him of the accident. He saw a message in the timing of his son sustaining injuries and the coincidental appearance of the poor baby chicken. "Baby chickens are a good treatment for broken arms," the man concluded. Next thing, he killed the baby chicken and wrapped it around his son's broken arm. A neighbor saw the child walking around in the neighborhood with a baby chicken wrapped around his arm, hanging from his neck. He might not have any idea about what had happened, but that image alone was enough for him to conclude, "Baby chickens must be the ultimate treatment for broken arms." The neighbor had just become a potential future specialist in broken arms. It was likely that, in the future, if he heard people talking about a child who broke his arm, he would be quick to suggest the baby chicken treatment. He would inquire, "Have you tried a baby chicken to treat the arm?" If the answer was no, he would say, "What is wrong with you people? How come you did not administer the baby chicken treatment?"

Baseers were health experts, by hook or by crook, but were there true *Baseer* experts who knew exactly what they were doing? That might have been the case. I recently saw a video showing a tribal healer repeatedly hitting a patient real hard on the head to rid him of his headache. I thought to myself that humanity still has a long way to go. Few weeks later, I read a piece of literature, which talks about trepanation; a surgical intervention used in ancient times to, literally, drill or scrape a hole into the human skull for the purpose of extracting the stone of madness, or something. I immediately changed my mind and said to myself, "Humanity has come a long way."

One person from Kokoland named Kokab told me about another story involving cruelty to both humans and animals. First, I didn't believe him, but he insisted that it was true. It, again involved the use of fire to "burn in order to save." He told me that one day he took his dog and set out to hunt squirrels. The dog spotted one and chased after it until they both went out of sight. Kokab caught up with his dog only to find him trapped deep in the middle of a dense shrub known to have hook-shaped thorns. If persons or animals got entangled in one, it would be very difficult to break free without sustaining injury to the skin. The dog was screaming and the squirrel was nowhere to be seen. Kokab told me that squirrels were known to use a certain technique to get away from dogs chasing them. When they get close to a bush, they would flip their bushy tails to one side and take the rest of the body in another direction, tricking the dog into following the tail and slamming into the bush. Upon freeing itself, the squirrel would be long gone.

Kokab's dog fell into the trap and could not free itself. He tried to help, but he couldn't. He then remembered a story his dad had told him about a man returning to his village from a marketplace. A lion chased him and he could not find a place to hide inside, but a thorny shrub. The lion could not get to him. It waited for hours then left. The man, unable to free himself on his own, did not show up at the village, so people went out to look for him. They heard his screams for help and rushed to his rescue. They found him entangled in the shrub. They tried their level best to free him, but they could not due to the pain that was caused by the thorns every time he made the slightest movement. Then a wise man spoke. He said, "It was hardship [the lion] that forced this man into such an awkward plight. Only an equally harsh treatment that will set him free; fire. Set the shrubs on fire. He will come out, God willing." The man had to choose between burning alive and enduring the pain from the thorns. The "wise man's" recommendation worked. The man did come out. Kokab executed the bush burning technique giving his dog the same two choices, and, like the man, the dog chose the latter option. Anyhow, I doubt that these two stories from hell were true, but people found them quite funny and amusing, despite their cruelty. However nonsensical this may sound to some, they remain pass time story types told around camp fires in Kokoland. What else was there to talk about?

One early morning, Fanami, a close friend of my dad, rode his donkey and headed to a marketplace some distance from his village. On the way, he fell to the ground and broke his neck. Some nomads found him and alerted the people in a nearby village. They declared him dead and carried him back to his village. Tradition dictated that burial must take place as soon as enough community members had gathered, so in a matter of few hours Fanami was buried. I walked the same trail Fanami had used, to visit family members in a nearby village. For some reason, whenever I passed by the spot where he fell down from the donkey, I asked myself the question, "Was Fanami really dead when they buried him? Did he die instantly?" For some reason, I continue to believe that he survived the fall because the place was sandy and he fell only a few feet to the ground. I wished there was a health expert in the village to give a second opinion before burying Fanami. Looking back, I think there were some fatalities that might have resulted from negligence, mishandling, and lack of experience. They were preventable.

I was in fourth grade when I injured the lower part of my left leg while playing soccer. I was living at the boarding school at that time. Due to lack of care, the wound kept expanding. Some kid suggested to me that I should get hold of a discarded AA battery, break it open, and use the black carbon stuff as medicine. He told me to bandage the entire wound so it would heal fast. I followed his instructions, verbatim, and the result was disastrous, as you might have already guessed. The wound area was about double its original size in a matter of few days. Things got out of control, so I had to travel back to the village to seek help. After many antibiotic shots, the wound healed, but left behind a deep scar. In fact, my legs are riddled with many scars as a testimony to my treacherous journey. Some of them were the results of accidents, while others, such as the one I described above, were caused by sheer stupidity. I avoid wearing shorts to save myself the trouble of answering to my kids the question, "What happened to your legs?" They look bad, real bad, but they provide a reservoir of ideas for fake stories such as my (above) encounter with the pack of six hyenas, which my boys love listening to.

My boys constantly reminded me of what I had told them about my childhood, growing up in Kokoland, that the only thing I owned was a gray donkey, and that there were no paved roads, cars, or traffic lights. There was no way I could pull off stories involving accidents to give justification for my scars. For that reason, I stopped talking about anything involving technology in Kokoland and resorted to blaming hyenas as culprits. In the process, I also took the liberty to make a hero out of myself by casually throwing statements such as, "I single-handedly defeated a pact of hyenas." The official story, as it stands now, is that hyenas caused my scars. I will deal with the situation, there and then, when my boys grow up, read the book, and find out about the hyenas' innocence. For the time being, Father Christmas stays real. I, being an African dad, am not clued in about my children's education style, which is based on critical thinking, use of logic, and problem solving. Where I come from, a child with an inquisitive mind is considered argumentative, disrespectful, and must be whipped so he could better behave. Yes, it is true that we do things differently, but, on a serious note, I don't whip my boys, just in case you are thinking. I don't want any trouble.

One of my friends had his brother come over from Africa to visit. They talked about their childhood stories, reminding each other of the days they went hunting for rabbits and how good rabbit meat tasted. The children were listening. In the morning, one of his boys, ready to leave to school, called him and whispered in his ears, "Don't let my uncle eat my pet rabbit."

As far as mental illness was concerned, it was considered to be something beyond anyone's scope of knowledge or understanding, so it was attributed to the spirits. The terms, "He has wind" or "He is windy" were used in the Kanuri vocabulary to describe someone suffering from mental or psychological disorder. This was because spirits were believed to be illusive by nature, just like winds. In fact, it was also believed that spirits or djinns were the ones who caused twisters, so people prayed whenever spinning winds suddenly erupted. The prayer recited was, "Prophet Mohammed is here, don't pass by us." It would be repeated until the wind has completely passed through. Anything to do with spirits was beyond visionaries' or *Baseers'* scope of expertise. This zone was left entirely to holy-men to prescribe treatment according to their knowledge of illnesses caused by spirits, or according to their whims, as was the case in many situations. Knowledge-based treatments included offering of prayers, burning and inhaling mystical charms and frankincense, and denying patients the access of certain types of food and drinks, especially tea, for unknown reasons. Whim-based treatment included extreme prescriptions such as whipping and chaining. It was believed that harsh treatment was a good tactic for forcing the spirit to dismount and abandon the possessed person's body. The pain inflicted on the body would make it an unattractive place of residence for the spirit, so it would depart. Of all mental illness treatments, whipping, I think, is the most painful one. It has both physical and psychological impact on the patient. One of my relatives, Falta, had her share of whipping, but on top of that, she had her hair shaved by her brothers to humiliate her and to bring her under control, even though her illness was something entirely out of her control. She was sick, for God's sake. I was about eight when I experienced these draconian measures used in treating Falta. Today, after all these many years, nothing much has changed. We still have not realized the importance of adopting science-based approach to treating mental illness.

One day, I overheard one of my aunts confidently describe a certain emotional condition by saying, "It must have been caused by *Kalom Tada-Rum*." The words sounded like a title of an article in a reputable scientific journal, such as The Christian Science Monitor, talking about a breakthrough in cancer treatment. In fact, *Kalom Tada-Rum* is not entirely void of science. It is a Kanuri term used for describing emotions shown by an overprotective and worrisome mother who loves her children excessively, especially if she has only one child. There is nothing wrong in that. The words *Kalom Tada-Rum* translates to something like; "The gut that is solely responsible for making a mother exhibit a protective type of behavior." The problem was in the confidence my aunt had shown when diagnosing the condition, which left no room for doubting her conclusion that a gut was the brain controlling all aspects of mothers' love for their children. She was referring to the sensation of butterflies in the stomach. In fact, there was some truth in what she said.

For a long time, Kanuris held holy men in high regard for assuming the role of knowledge gatekeepers. They entrusted them with the responsibility of upholding communities' moral code. They were also considered to be God fearing and good worshippers, so people followed them blindly, accepted their opinions, and relied on their judgment for settling disputes between community members. They did a fairly good job playing that role. As time progressed, society also progressed, and the village's old social order became less appropriate for present times. As a result, the principle of self-check adopted for upholding good citizenship and acceptable behavior, which was relied on for organizing communities since time immemorial, was violated. The problem was that self-accountability did let people get away with murder. Nowadays, not every holy man is considered pure and honest to gain people's absolute trust, solely on the basis of superficially carrying themselves as God-fearing personalities. The younger generation is defiant of the old customs and laws governing behavior and hierarchical structure of communities, which gave elders the upper hand in running all aspects of village life. They no longer believe in their absolute authority. Information technology is providing alternative sources of knowledge and is playing a big role in eroding powers bestowed on holy men and elders.

In the autumn of 1979, word spread in the city about a holy man who was a telepath or a mind reader. Local papers extensively reported on the case and many people flocked to his place of business to meet his holiness to be blessed and get treated for their illnesses. A receptionist met and interviewed the patients, then compiled a report about their conditions. The patients were first seated, then called, one at a time, to meet the holy man. They were led through a corridor to a dungeon-like half-lit room where the holy man would be sitting on a mat on the floor. Sitting on the floor was a sign of humbleness and holiness. It sent a message to the patients that his holiness refrained from indulging in luxurious style of modern living such as sitting on porch leather sofas. That way he could practically show people that he was not much interested in anything that is finite and lasting, including life on planet Earth. He would rather work for the here-after. He would greet each patient respectfully using a low tone of voice, forcing them to reciprocate in kind. He would then take the patients by surprise and tell them in detail about the complaints that they had reported to the receptionist, earlier on. Mysteriously knowing what was in the patient's heart and mind was truly a sign of absolute holiness and nothing short of that. Since he could tell all about the past, he could also foretell what could happen in the future. Having captured the trust and admiration of his patients, he would prescribe for them treatments, usually charms folded inside paper, to wear around their necks, arms or waist, or to burn them and inhale the smoke, according to certain regimen. Patients were generous and happy to pay for the service. Fees paid were based on prescription given, severity of cases, and the nature of patients' wishes.

One day, a patient went to visit the holy man to seek treatment for a condition he has. Upon arriving at the place of business, he recognized the man at the reception, who happened to be a former coworker, but the receptionist could not tell who the man was. He carefully listened to him, seated him for some time, and then sent him to meet the holy man. To the man's surprise, the holy man also turned out to be another former coworker. The three of them worked at the postal service handling telegraph communications. What the holy man and his receptionist were doing was that they were using telegraph technology to transmit messages between themselves. The holy man was able to fool his unassuming victims into believing in his telepath abilities until that infamous day, when his coworker showed up. He claimed to be the man who could foresee the future until his time to go to jail materialized that day.

These are few examples of bizarre ways of treating illnesses, but people were mostly fascinated with the use of fire. They believed that there was a positive correlation between pain and recovery. The severity of the pain inflicted by the use of fire or the bitterness of the medicine consumed, led to better results. The problem with traditional medicine was that it lacked any form of accountability for mistakes committed by the visionaries, *Bassers*, or holy men. It would be tough luck for the patient if the treatment resulted in his demise due to organ failure or any other side effects. People branded anybody questioning the patient's fate as a person of a weak faith. Faith was central to people's lives, so challenging someone's beliefs in a community led by holy men was suicide. For this reason, people settled for anything to avoid such types of consequential accusation. Having said that, I believe not every holy man in Kokoland was out there to con people. There were those who genuinely tried to do good, so they helped in the best possible way that they could.

CHAPTER 12

Village Superstitions and Some Cultural Aspects

In the Kanuri culture, black cats were considered to be a sign of evil spirits, especially if seen around sunset. Some people thought that they were djinns who transformed themselves into cats to hurt humans. I think Kokolanders would have found it strange that people in other parts of the world were so fine with black cats that they gave them living space inside their homes. Kokolanders would chase away black cats so they end up taking refuge in the wilderness. Then again, when they see them in the wild, they would wonder why they were there. They would conclude that they were truly djinns, fueling the belief that normal cats don't roam in the wild. The whole thing would become a self-fulfilling prophecy.

As indicated above, I used to be very ill with malaria. The infection affected my brain, so I hallucinated a lot. I would temporarily lose my brain capabilities, scream, and fight, trying to escape from black cats, which had frequent appearance in my hallucinations. I remember my parents used to get so worried whenever I told them about black cats attacking me. They believed that spirits and djinns have a lot to do with my illness, so they took me to holy men for treatment. By the time I was ten or so, malaria medicine became available, and attacks from black cats subsided. Poor cats have been falsely and unfairly accused of being culprits. I always wondered why people in Kokoland hated black cats, in particular. The irony is that every person living there is black. Where did this prejudice against our own color come from?

Many children, particularly from the villages around Kokoland, have died from childhood diseases. Simple preventative measures, such as mosquito nets, could have helped a lot. The introduction of malaria medicine did make some difference. Today, the health condition, especially in the case of malaria infection, is way better than forty years ago. In the process, black cats also benefited by shouldering less blame.

Super-naturals were central to Kokoland's belief system. Science was unheard of, so unexplained phenomena were always attributed to super-naturals. The spirits and the djinns had roles in people's daily life. Zombies also intervened and became part of the formula. Just like everywhere else, zombies appeared only at night. In the case of Kokoland, they lived by the giant baobab trees. For this reason, the trees commanded special respect from people, both young and adults. Their huge sizes provided room, enough for hiding zombies, spirits, and the likes. As children, we did everything we could to stay away from them. If we happened to be walking at night and the trail passed by a baobab tree, we made sure that we read every prayer we had committed to memory. We read them loudly, just to be sure that the zombies heard us, so they would not risk attacking us and get themselves hurt by our strong spirituality, which could be a temporary measure dictated by the moment and circumstances. In most cases, such types of instantaneous and urgency-based spiritualties disappeared soon after the dissipation of the danger. We made certain that we passed the trees as fast as we could. Zombies also took residence at the village's graveyard, from which we kept our distance, no matter what. Zombies are bad, very bad.

A baobab tree from the outskirt of Kokoland.

One morning, my childhood friend, Tiffah, came running to my house to tell me about an incident that took place the night before. He told me that our neighbor Saleh got beaten up by a zombie at a nearby baobab tree, a mile or so from the village. Coincidentally, the tree was named after our neighbor, Hajjah Maseera, who also went by the name Maseera-the Spirit Ridden. Tiffah told me he did hear horrific screaming coming from the tree side. He said that men rushed to the scene to help and found Saleh in bad shape. He was trembling and speaking incoherently, while pointing at the baobab tree. They calmed him down so he was able to speak clearly. He told them that he was on his way to the village back from his farm. At that spot near the tree, a gigantic naked figure, wearing a big bushy hair, appeared all of a sudden from under the baobab tree and rushed toward him. The figure started beating him with a huge stick it was carrying. The beating continued until the voices of men approaching forced the figure to disappear under the shadow of the baobab tree, leaving no footprints or any marks to follow. Using faint flash lights, people could see the signs of beating all over Saleh's body. Everyone concluded that he was beaten by a zombie.

Keeping a tight grip on their flashlights, in one hand, and big sticks, in the other hands, raised above their heads, ready to strike at any moment, a few men took steps toward the tree, while intently gazing on the ground, to see if they could spot zombie foot-prints, but they soon abandoned the idea. It was a good thing that the zombie decided to leave, instead of confronting them when they arrived at the site, so why bother chase after it. Kokoland men claimed bravery, heroism, and knighthood, when it came to fighting other men. However, zombies were a different ball game altogether, so nobody dared to venture beyond the baobab tree to try to hunt it down. There was an unspoken consensus about the risk involved in running after a zombie, so they hurriedly grabbed Saleh, who was still trembling from fear, and carried him back to his home. Faki Bashir, the holy man from the neighborhood, was called to administer prayers and burn charms and frankincense for Saleh to inhale to help him regain his composure and lost mind. The beating left behind visible wounds all over his body, but that was less of a priority. It was important that Saleh did not lose his mind permanently.

Both Tiffah and I were fear-stricken and worried to death because our neighborhood in Kokoland was officially declared a zombie zone. In some parts of the world, such an official declaration would render cities and neighborhoods concerned totally uninhabitable, and that has disastrous consequences on real estate value. However, in the case of my Jabar neighborhood, our straw-based huts were of limited value, to start with, so talking about loss of property value was the least of anybody's worry or concern. Nevertheless, the neighborhood classification as zombie zone had a tremendous adverse impact on our freedom of movement. We observed a self-imposed curfew for as long as we thought that the danger had persisted. All of our activities were limited for times between sunrise and sunset. My donkey lost weight due to a daily loss of an hour of feeding time. It took me longer to take him to a grazing area on the opposite end of the village, away from the zombie zone near the baobab tree. I also made sure I brought him home well before sunset, causing him the loss of a valuable grazing time. The zombie had helped enhance my behavior ratings as far as my dad was concerned. He appreciated the fact that I took the trouble to go as far as I could to find greener grazing pasture for the donkey. I left him wondering what happened to me and what could have triggered such a sudden improvement in executing my donkey-responsibilities. He must have thought to himself, "What a reliable boy I have. I'm very proud of him." Zombies could do miracles, I tell you.

It turned out that the real zombie was falsely being accused of beating Saleh. It was rumored in the village that the beating was a criminal act carried out by a human zombie, who turned out to be one of Saleh's adversaries. The man held grudges against him over one girl. Saleh's story was all over town and in the very first wedding event, the girls came up with a song portraying him as the most coward man of all times. Saleh was completely dropped from their radar, forever. No girl in Kokoland would accept a coward man for a husband, so he might as well be dead or out of sight. He opted for the latter. Saleh abandoned his ancestral land and ran away, never to be seen again, nor did anybody know of his whereabouts. I still vividly remember his constantly smiley face.

Even though baobab trees were the preferred residence for spirits, we were occasionally attracted to them because of their sweet fruits, which we could not resist. We carefully weighed the risks and gains before we got closer to the trees. We chose smaller trees nearer to the village and went to down the fruits during broad day light so that people from the village could hear us, see us, and come for help in case of a zombie attack. We always kept our distance from big baobab trees, which were further away from the village. At nights, I did not venture away from the inner boundaries of my straw-fence; making sure I was always closer to a human and a lantern. I found millions of excuses for not leaving the hut, not even for a visit to the loo or to drink water. Everything could wait until the morning when I could see clearly. Those were special zombie times, which called for unconventional measures. Zombies could certainly cause behavioral changes. What do you expect me to do when my entire outlook of the world came from adults who, too, believed in zombies?

I later rationalized the zombie phenomenon as having something to do with the lack of electricity. Zombies and electricity were two mutually exclusive creatures. The village's whole culture, folklore, and mythology could have been different if we had electricity. It meant we could have had power to operate TVs, radios, cassette players, etc. We could have been more informed about what was going on elsewhere. Besides; we could have streetlights so we could see at night. Darkness freed our minds to imagine the wildest of things.

For lighting, we used lanterns locally made of empty cans filled with kerosene. We would put a twelve-inch-long cotton thread inside the can and pull it out through a narrow pipe welded to the can lid, until we had an inch or so, which we then lit. It was very problematic to light your way outside of the hut in a zombie-infested area. The slightest wind would blow the light off leaving you a sitting duck, vulnerable to attacks from zombies and ghouls. However, the fact remains that I could not see beyond two feet radius, using those lanterns. Despite that they were my primary lighting source for studying and doing homework, throughout most of my school years.

The introduction of dry battery-operated flashlights, to some extent, helped with the darkness situation, but they were very expensive, considering people's income level. Mostly, adults were the ones who owned and kept them for emergency use. As a kid, if you happened to own a flashlight, you waited until your dad discarded his batteries so you could take them for your own use. By that time, the batteries would be so week that visibility would be limited to inches. We, Kokoland kids, knew exactly where we stood in society, so the fact that we were a second priority did not bother us much. In fact, I found the use of flashlights with new batteries an unattractive preposition, anyway. On one hand, I thought that their strong lights solved the darkness problem, but on the other hand, that led to another problem. If you happened to be walking in the wilderness, the moment you switched on your flash light, you exposed yourself to bad elements such as zombies, spirits, ghouls, dogs, wild animals, and muggers. By holding the flashlight in your hand, anyone of these elements could determine your location with precision. This was the reason why I was not very fond of using torches in the wilderness, but, then again, I ran another risk of stepping on deadly snakes, which usually slithered out of the bushes to lie on the trails to cool their body temperature. I twice encountered deadly snakes, but luckily I was not bitten. It is ironic that a simple decision such as choosing between light and darkness could be an act requiring this much careful balancing effort.

My aunt Rahima, a certified mid-wife who lived in the city, had a theory about albinism. She adamantly believed that albino kids were born to mermaids and that they had nothing to do with human beings. One of my cousins, Asim, is an albino. Whenever he showed up at any gathering where my aunt Rahima was present, the entire mood changed. Her face would drop, and, with extreme sadness, she would say, *"Baddalo Wallahi,"* meaning, "I swear, they exchanged him," citing that Asim is not the original human child born to his parents. Asim would be standing right there in front of us, in flesh and blood, but to her he is absolutely a mermaid child. I can only imagine how psychologically devastated Asim would be.

The begging question is why would mermaids take a human child and give away their own. No one dared to challenge my aunt Rahima's Mermaid Child Exchange Theory. We all shied away from any form of confrontation with her because of her authoritarian style in dealing with people. Why was she so? Being the most enlightened (educated) person in her generation within the family, she assumed leadership role and decided to tell everybody what to do. People sought-after her guidance and advise on barrage of issues. Mind you, Aunt Rahima had not been to school, but she received training and mid-wife certification. Bossing everyone around was a logical conclusion as far as she was concerned because everyone else in the family was less literate than her.

Aunt Rahima had great respect for mermaids. She never mentioned the word mermaid, to avoid angering them. She only used the third-person plural pronoun "they" when referring to mermaids. Consciously or subconsciously mentioning words such as spirits and mermaids was a risky business, even to informed and clued city dwellers like Aunt Rahima. We succumbed to her orders and kept quiet whenever Asim, the son of mermaids, was present. We stayed that way for as long as it took, until some incident broke the silence. We would slowly excuse ourselves and leave, but making sure we told her that we would be back to visit the following week. Expressing our intention to revisit aunt Rahima shortly was important, considering her highstanding within the family. It was also a technique we used to obtain her blessings and approval for our departure. Aunt Rahima was an autocratic woman by nature.

People in Kokoland also had a special respect for bats and chameleons. Illusiveness of bats, being creatures of the night, and the ability of chameleons to alter their colors freely as and when they wished, could have been factors in the respect they commanded from humans. My friend Mario, a fellow citizen, whom I met at school in the United Kingdom, told me about an experience he had while visiting a place back home called Sun Market. It was an unregulated market, located in the outskirt of the city, notoriously known for selling crazy stuff. He said he came across a street vendor who sold dry leaves, roots, and animal parts. Among the animal remains, he found a dry chameleon. He asked the man about the use of dead chameleons. The man told him it was good for bringing love into a man's life. He would become attractive to women who, under the influence of dry chameleon magical spell, would be head over heels about the man. The women would totally be deprived of their free will. He asked him, "What do you do with it?" The man replied, "You eat it." He asked him, again, if he could eat from it. The man said yes, then broke a piece and ate it. The irony is that some people believe that eating dry chameleons could bring love into their hearts, yet other people, elsewhere, believe

A vendor displaying his merchandize in an unregulated market for selling leaves, roots, and dry animal remains.

that giving diamonds as a gift has the same effect. Could chameleons be a good substitute for diamonds? Why not? They are readily available in nature and can reproduce at a faster pace. Unlike diamonds, they don't require millions of years of immense heat and pressure to form. What is wrong with people? I am serious.

As kids, we also believed that chameleons possessed strong jaws and magical gripping powers. This is a serious misconception about a creature that doesn't even have real teeth, other than a long slimy tongue. We used to believe that it was impossible to break free from chameleon jaws before hearing the braying of a wild zebra. Projecting chameleons as scary creatures can be useful for protecting them, but I doubt that was anybody's intention. My friend Gana added another layer of mystery to chameleons' mythical powers. He told me that in case a zebra's braying was not forthcoming, then the alternative option was to try to reach out to a close female relative and yank a bunch of hair from the back of her head, then the chameleon would let go. You can tell we did have fertile imaginations in Kokoland. It just cannot get more superstitious. It is easy to believe that these myths have come from someone who had been smoking something he was not supposed to, had it not been for the fact that smoking was a rare behavior in Kokoland. Chameleons are creatures wrapped in mystery. They voluntary change color to camouflage and blend in their surroundings. That might be the reason why some suggested that the best thing to do was to eat them so they could acquire some magical chameleon powers for themselves. I guess adding love to the formula would make it an attractive preposition for love desperados. They would not hesitate to eat chameleons, for love sake.

Here is another story about bats. My childhood friend, Tiffah, once, told me that the powder of dead and dried-up bats could also bring love to a man's heart. The chameleon prescription of the street vendor was to eat it. However, in my friend's case, the bat powder was to be administered in a different way, which I am not going to reveal here. I have no idea where he got this crazy thought from. This book is already riddled with embarrassing stories, but this one about bats dwarfs all of them, so I decided not to elaborate on it.

One day, during high school break, a man approached me at my dad's shop and claimed he possessed supernatural powers. He offered to multiply any amount of cash we had, many times over, for a fee. Yes, for a fee. Does this story sound familiar? One thing I noticed about the man was that his looks were not compatible with the massive money making abilities he claimed to possess. I expressed some interest, but did not give him a conclusive answer, so he sat quietly and waited, while portraying an image of a holy man who had all the world's patience and humility. We drank tea and he left, only to show up the following morning, hoping to find out if I had amassed the cash for him to multiply. I told him I was not interested in doing that, but I would like to know if he had any other secrets. He immediately responded by telling me that he had a proven secret for winning girls' hearts. He was a holy man, so it was a no brainer that he could easily find out about a high school boy's weakness. I did not believe his claims about money, but I was quick to come onboard when it came to girls. I guess rationality goes out of the window when the matter concerns teenage boys and girls. Was I young and foolish? Yes, absolutely.

We talked about his fees, which I did not haggle over much, fearing that he would change his mind and deprive me of a life time opportunity for acquiring love secrets. I hurriedly paid him the money, so he handed me some roots to chew according to certain regimen. He also handed me two additional items, and each was folded in white cloth. He told me to wait until it was sun set, then go to one intersection of roads, dig a hole in the center of the intersection, and burry the two objects, while making sure that nobody saw me. The girl of my interest daily crossed the intersection on her way to and from her house. The idea was that she would inevitably step on the buried items, immediately triggering the love magic. The man also told me that, once I had buried the objects, I should leave the place hurriedly and walk to my house without ever turning around to look back. He said, "God willing, she will seek your love the moment she steps on the buried secret." He told me to just sit and worry about nothing, since love would certainly find its way to me. He took his money and disappeared.

I followed his instructions verbatim, so I went home and waited for "the eggs to hatch", but nothing happened that night. Next day, I waited "till the cows came home" in the evening, but, again, nothing happened. The third night, I heard the sound of some movement along our fence. I loudly thought to myself, "Halleluiah! The magic is working. She took a couple of days just to be sure about her feelings toward me, but she is finally here. She is signaling to me her arrival." I sprang to my feet and ran outside the house to receive her. What I found was the neighbor's stupid donkey pulling and munching on the dry millet-straw my dad had recently used to patch a fence hole created by neighborhood dogs. Upon sensing my presence, the donkey looked at me for a second, with both ears pointing in my direction. Concluding there was no danger to worry about, it went back and pulled a mouthful of straw and continued munching. I went back inside the house totally disappointed that I did not even bother chasing the donkey away, fully knowing that it would damage the fence, rendering my dad's efforts useless. Those stupid donkeys were central to everything I did, including my love life.

I waited for that girl for a long time. Not only that her love did not come searching for me, but I also did not see her ever again, not even a single time after I had buried that useless voodoo stuff. It was a taboo to open and examine the contents of any wrapped secret given to you by a holy man. By doing so, you express loss of faith in the magic's ability to deliver the intended goal. Once you open it, you render it ineffective. It bugged me a great deal that I did not know what I had buried. This predicament reminded me of one of the greatest lines in a speech delivered by the late President Reagan who said, "Trust, but verify."

Few weeks had passed after the burial of my love secrets, but still nothing happened, so I started doubting myself. I began to look for excuses why my dream did not materialize. I finally concluded that the holy man had misunderstood my request. He also had me worried that he might have understood the opposite of my intensions. I genuinely started believing that he mistook my request for asking him to make the girl vanish instead of magically leading her to me. I thought to myself, "He must have given me an anti-love treatment, which led to the disappearance of the girl." From that moment onwards, the passage of every single day convinced me that I was right about my conclusions. I grew more certain that there was a communication error.

I became distraught and in total denial. I thought to myself "I must hunt this man down, come what may, so he could correct the fiasco he had committed by giving me the wrong love recipe." I started looking into the faces of strangers travelling through Kokoland, hoping to meet the holy man. I theorized that he could be using Kokoland as his stopover while moving around promoting his bonzi schemes. I prayed for our roads to miraculously intersect somehow someday, but that dream never materialized. Rationality and love can hardly cross paths. There is a Sudanese proverb about the extent to which a person could go to find a lost valuable item. It says, "Desperation can lead a person to open a cow's mouth." This is just in case there is a chance that the item he is looking for is, somehow, in the cow's mouth.

Crooks tricking people into believing that they could magically multiply their money, many folds, is not a new thing. Recently, I have been receiving overseas phone calls and e-mails from strangers, which started with statements like, "Hi, I'm so-and-so, the chief of continent of *xyz*. You see, I have $500 million which I would like to share with you fifty-fifty if you do so and so." Does this statement ring a bell?

As I mentioned earlier, science and scientific interpretations of uncommon phenomena are nowhere to be found in Kokolanders' vocabulary. Every unexplained phenomenon was attributed to the spirits, the djinns, and the devils. A man, named Bajoory, was one of the wealthiest people, if not the richest man, in the region. He owned thousands of cattle. Bajoory's problem was that, despite his wealth, he dressed in rags and walked bare footed. Unlike nomads, whom were well known all over the place for their generosity, he was a miser. He was so miser that whenever he heard the sound of people approaching his cattle camp, he would pick up his spears and head in their direction to meet them further on up the road before they got to the camp. He would then ask them if they had seen any lost calves on their way. He did that to avoid serving them food and drinks in case he waited for them at the camp. He would convince them that he was a man on a mission, so they would not blame him for not receiving them hospitably, which was the norm among people. Why would Bajoory behave in such a way? People believed that he owned none of the cattle under his possession. They belonged to the djinns and he was a mere guardian who looked after them. He could not take any action without consulting with his masters, the djinns, people believed.

The devils lived everywhere in and around Kokoland. Activities came to halt upon sunset as the night was reserved for them. They did graveyard shifts. My mom told us to stop playing as soon as the sun went down. If we did not and continued playing, then she would tell us that we ran the risk of "poking the eyes of baby devils", then we would be personally responsible for the consequences of our actions. That was a serious deterrent, for the simple reason that we did not know what those consequences could be. Every time we played past sunset and hurt ourselves, she would tell us that the devil was the one who caused the accident because we failed to listen to her and ended up hurting baby devils, so their parents retaliated. The inability of the naked human eye to see in darkness, causing us to bump into one another and objects, and hurting ourselves, was never a factor. The mentioning of the devil's name was quite enough for taming our wild behaviors, on the spot.

My mom used to sit in the late afternoon shadow of the fence and pound coffee beans in her stylish bronze mortar to prepare her evening coffee. Every drop of the bronze pestle produced a ringing sound that was repeated few seconds later, about two hundred yards east of where she sat. She told me that the devil who lived over there was copying her. She occasionally created complex rhythms when she pounded on the coffee beans and, to my amazement, the devil was able to exactly copy her actions, no matter how complex they were. I was so intrigued by the devil's skills and was curious to find out why he chose to live by the mud house owned by our tailor Ghanim. Anyhow, I kept my distance from that house for a long time and avoided passing by it at all cost. Eco was nothing short of magic that only devils could master. Pulling my legs was so easy for my mom.

One of my close relatives got addicted to local alcohol. I heard some relatives attribute his condition to black magic. They believed that the magic was intended to hurt his elder brothers, but it missed them and fell on him, so he became addict. No one thought that he needed medical attention. It was probable that he also believed in that explanation, so he carried on drinking. This is yet another self-fulfilling prophecy.

The village graveyard was another natural place for restless souls and zombies. I, like every other child in the village, avoided passing by it. The stories we heard about after-death experiences were mind-boggling. Adults did not help much in providing us with any soul-comforting explanations. We were taught about heaven and hell at school. However, there were local flavors and details added to that, which made the whole thing extremely scary. We were told that those who accumulate bad deeds on earth would be punished as soon as they were buried in the grave. "A gigantic snake would appear and strike at the person, sinking him to the seventh earth, below, only to be met by a huge evil scorpion, which would be impatiently waiting for him. It would knock him with its huge needle, sending him right back to where he had come from. The snake and the scorpion would exchange roles and continue to torture the person until the Day of Judgment."

People believed that they could foretell if a person was heading for good or bad times in his grave. As soon as someone's death was announced, young men would rush to the graveyard, pick a grave site, and start digging. The ease and speed with which they could dig and prepare the grave was an indication for how blessed the person about to be buried. If the site turned out to be rocky and hard to dig, that was a sign of a terrible fate waiting him. It was also considered a good luck, if it rained immediately after a person's death and burial. As you can tell, we obviously viewed life and death solely from Kokoland's perspective. Our assumption was that topography, landscape, geography, and weather conditions were uniform worldwide, so death during the rainy season brought more luck than death during the dry season, even though no one had a say in their time of death. Besides; the fact that it did not rain at all in some places, whereas it rained abundantly in others, was irrelevant. As I have mentioned earlier, Kokolanders, all along, thought that they were the center of the universe. Everything was based on their values and belief system.

The general concept of death and dying were bleak, and the views on life were equally pessimistic. During middle and high school in the 1970s, I acquired bits and pieces of information about the cold war and the rivalry between the two camps. My vivid memories about that era were that soon a third world war would erupt and totally annihilate life on the planet. The sketchy information that trickled down left me with many unanswered questions and loopholes. It was not fun, depressing, and frightening because everything I was told, while growing up, revolved around zombies, ghouls, devils, spirits, and, on top of that, nuclear war; a catastrophe I knew would devastate life, but could hardly grasp. A gloomy picture was painted about life on earth, which made it unworthy of living, but the problem was that life after death was equally scary. I though to myself, "Where shall I go?"

Here is a story about a man known for committing bad deeds. He died and was taken to the village graveyard and buried. After returning home from the funeral, the holy man who led the prayers realized that his wallet was missing. He looked around, but could not locate it. He then remembered the last time he had it was inside the grave when he was helping to lay the body to rest. Being certain about that, he asked few people to join him, go back to exhume the grave, and extract the wallet. The men reluctantly agreed, so they all went over and dug up the grave. To the men's horror, four black dogs rushed out of the grave and took off running in different directions, as if chasing something, until they disappeared from site. The holy man and his friends looked down the grave and were petrified with fright when they saw a completely burnt coffin and an intact wallet that had no signs of burns, whatsoever, by the side. They quickly picked it up and hurriedly started to re-earth the grave, then the four dogs appeared in the distance, rushing back toward them. The men were forced to give way so the dogs could go back inside the grave before covering it with dirt.

Such stories usually began with the statement "They said so and so happened," but who were they, where, and when the incident took place was immaterial. You would wonder why the dogs were black, just like the cats, where did they go, and what were they doing inside the grave? Were they punishing the dead man for the bad deeds he had committed during his life? The problem here is that the adults who told the story also believed in the details as much as we did. The message conveyed by including black dogs, burnt coffin, and unburnt wallet was that bad people would get punished inside their graves, whereas the righteous ones would go unscathed. The unburnt wallet was a tangible proof that its owner was truly a holy man.

Could such stories have been knitted by some people with ulterior self-promotion motives? Whatever the reasons, the end result would be some form of an impact on children's attitudes toward life in general. Because of such inputs and interpretations, some children might grow up viewing everything about life negatively. By that time, it wouldn't be possible to retroactively rectify misconceptions they might have had. In my case, my people whom I have left behind are at peace with themselves as far as their belief system is concerned. They are fine with the way they have always viewed the world. The problem is rather mine and mine alone, being torn between two worlds. In brief, I think interpretation of religion could be—among other things—a function of time, place, and culture, but I may be wrong.

Below are some superstitions that guided our lives, growing up. They might make little sense to many people, but they did play a role in educating and entertaining children, as well as giving interpretation to unexplained phenomena, particularly when science did not play much role in people's daily lives. The goal was to make children observe these rules, despite being ridiculous, so that, in the process, they might stay out of trouble and wouldn't hurt themselves.

If a child swallowed lemon seeds, he risked a lemon tree growing out of his belly, making it impossible for him to walk up straight. He would always be lying flat on his back, considering the fact that trees grow up vertically, and the village children would come and throw sticks at his belly-tree to drop off the lemon fruit.

It was considered a bad sign for a donkey to, habitually, stick out its tongue. That might lead to the demise of one of the couples who owned it. The owners would sell it off at a heartbeat, but, of course, without revealing to the buyer the true reason for the sale.

It was, again, considered a bad sign for children to grind their teeth while asleep. This was also thought to result in the death of one of the parents. To prevent that, dirt would be poured in their mouths. It couldn't have been crueler. I also witnessed two forms of punishment administered on two children at different occasions. Their crime was wetting their beds. It was so cruel that I don't think it is appropriate to talk about it here.

It was believed that whistling discomforted the spirits and awakened the djinns. Definitely none of us wanted to pay a price for angering the spirits. Kanab's mother was known around the region for going crazy whenever she heard someone whistling. Children went by her farm and whistled, purposely, to drive her out of her mind.

Frankincense burning would chase evil spirits form homes. It was widely believed, and still the case today, that some people possess the ability to cause harm to others by merely looking at them, their family members, or valuable properties, such as cars, homes, and jewelries. They were locally known to have "hot eyes". Frankincense smoke would help mitigate the damage that could be caused by such evil eyes. This tradition could have trickled down from ancient Egypt. The Pharaoh's sent their ships as far as Punt Land to bring back frankincense for burning inside temples. A couple, who were friends with our family, applied this tradition here in America when they purchased a new home. They made sure that the interior of the house was entirely covered in layers of smoke whenever they had visitors, just in case. Nowadays, you never know the whereabouts of hot eyes. They could be anywhere, including America. I guess this is a valuable piece of information that home and property insurance companies could use to reduce their clients' premiums. To qualify for the discount, insurance companies could ask a question to find out if potential clients are intending to burn frankincense in their new homes or not. They could also develop techniques for proving if a property damage was caused by a hot evil eye, or something else.

Donkeys were central to people's daily life because they were the primary means of transporting both people and goods. It is, therefore, understandable that people went to extreme limits to keep them healthy. It was widely believed that if a donkey drank water from an open metal container, at night when the moon was mid-sky and its image was reflected in the container, it would get sick and die. To protect it, a knife would be dropped inside the container before letting it drink. I personally dropped many knives, many times, in my gray donkey's water container. I don't know the origin of this superstition and I never asked anyone for an explanation. I simply followed "Just do it" principle. What mattered to me was my donkey's wellbeing so that my water business would not be adversely impacted. But, most importantly not to run out of drinking water at my house because, in the end, water shortage was my problem to sort out.

If a donkey stepped over a wood mortar pestle used for pounding grain, it would catch hoof disease in one of its front hooves; crippling it, hence preventing it from carrying out its donkey duties. This is also a very serious thing because a lingering donkey is of no use for riding or transporting goods. The donkey's condition could affect the entire family. I remember times when my gray donkey abruptly showed up in the front yard, looking for water to drink. If it happened that there was a pestle lying there, every one of my family members present would shout and rush toward the pestle to pull it away before the donkey stepped over it. The whole place would descend into chaos. Those who were closer to the pestle would rush to pick it up, where as those who were farther away would make a hell of a noise to chase the donkey or at least scare it into stopping in its track and not move an inch forward. The look on the donkey's face, especially its eyes, would be saying something like, "These people must be crazy, very very crazy." Every time I saw a donkey lingering in a farm here in America, I silently concluded that it must have stepped over a pestle. Then again the question begging for an answer is; How come this is happening here when there are no pestles lying around? I always wondered.

Hedgehogs had a secret that gave them extreme powers. If a heavy wooden mortar was flipped upside down and a hedgehog was kept inside it for a night, in the morning it would be gone. It would always escape, but without leaving any signs of digging or dropping the heavy mortar to its side. On the other hand, if it was dropped inside a standing mortar, it would not be able to escape. As children, we genuinely believed that hedgehogs were another wild creature owned by the spirits, so they have special powers bestowed on them, enabling them to disappear without leaving traces. I tried both experiments. Once I kept a hedgehog under the mortar. In the morning, not only it was gone, but also left no footprints around the mortar to tell me if it walked away. I concluded that its spirit masters were the ones who came to its rescue. On another occasion, when I dropped one inside a standing mortar, I found it intact in the morning. I was baffled by the paradox that in the first instance it was an act caused by the spirits, but what about the second case? The best thing was to avoid messing with hedgehogs inside mortars, period. I grew up to learn that my childhood beliefs in hedgehog super-powers was full of flaws, and I found endless interpretations to their disappearance. The problem is how to convince my people that, once again, the spirits had nothing to do with this.

It was believed that the devil resided inside black ant chambers. Stepping on an anthill would lead to undesired consequences. Could this be some tactics adopted by adults to protect children against ant attack? Do you remember Amu Ibrahim about whom I have written earlier, who suffered from Madura foot cancer, also called ant disease or *Kongoo-lah,* in Kanuri language? I was convinced that he had stepped on an anthill and the devil took care of the rest. His foot was dotted with holes that resembled the holes in anthills, hence the name ant disease. I heard that some people held magic secrets, which made their enemies sick with Madura cancer. This usually took place when there was rivalry between two men over a woman. If one of the men won the fight and the loser happened to have Madura secret, he would spell magic on the winner, rendering him ineffective as far as his relationship with the woman was concerned. The disease was believed to affect different parts of the body in the same way it affect the feet. It was also believed that people who step on the devil's house would catch Guinea-worm disease.

It was believed that valuables such as jewelry, especially gold, buried in the ground, would disappear and never to be found again, as the earth would claim it. During a recent visit to Kokoland, one of my cousins told me that his father had buried gold somewhere in the house, but he passed away without telling family members about the secret burial place. He spoke with some resignation that the buried gold would never be found again. I told him to borrow a metal detector brought in to the area by gold prospectors and look for the missing gold. I don't know if he took my advice seriously or not.

My friend Jalal's father also buried a stack of cash somewhere in the wilderness. He too died without revealing the whereabouts of the money. Similarly, my friend Yassin's father died without telling his children about his money, but in his case, they found heaps of large denominator bills in thousands of Sudanese pounds strapped to his waist. Unfortunately, that was about five years past the date declared by the government, which had recently come to power, to exchange it for a new currency, printed to replace the old one. As you can tell, people were at peace and harmony with nature. Everything goes back to earth. What safe-custody and bank deposits are we talking about?

I suppose some of the above superstitions were good for preserving the environment and maintaining biodiversity. Looking back, I guess it was a way for adults to teach children about the importance of interdependence between humans and nature. The easiest way to explain the unexplainable was to blame it on another unexplainable thing such as spirits. If my analyses were true, then we, in Kokoland, have been environmentally conscious, way ahead of the rest of the world. However, on the other hand, there were practices that were harmful to certain animals and plant species. For examples, people have no mercy on snakes and scorpions due to practical and religious reasons. We were warned against rattlesnakes, which were common to the region because they were deadly. We were told they were so fast that they could strike a running cow on all four legs, if it stepped over one. Giving the cow example was a way to paint a closer to home picture about the consequences of messing with rattlesnakes so as to keep our distance.

It was believed that hanging hyena skin on fences and gates would chase away stray dogs. I don't blame you if you think this whole thing is just messed up. How more impractical could this be? You remember the earlier story about the neighbor's dog that tried to pull the peanut sack from our hut at night when we were asleep, and we thought that a hyena was responsible for grabbing my brother Aziz? On that day, a neighbor came to our house and advised my father that all he needed was a hyena skin to hang on the gate and that would put an end to our troubles with stray dogs. Just imagine for a moment if the world followed our neighbor's advice and built hyena farms especially for marketing their skins as a dog-deterrent. The commercial would read something like, "Hyena skin, dogs be gone."

As I mentioned above, there was prejudice against everything black, be that cats, dogs, or sacrificial animals. Black roosters and black billy-goats were highly sought after by black magic practitioners. Poor everything black. One continues to wonder why there is bias against the color black.

It was considered a bad sign for wild guinea hen to fly over a village. The village residents would desert it for no reason, in no time. This is what happened to Wad Toum neighborhood in Kokoland. People believed that a flock of guinea hen flew over it because families began abandoning their homes, one after another, until the whole borough turned into ruins and nature claimed it. Was it natural events that caused ancient civilizations to collapse or that was due to flocks of guinea hen flying over? For us in Kokoland, the guinea hen theory was more appealing, since it was an idea close to home. Probably, someone remembered seeing a flock of birds flying over a neighborhood and shortly after that people deserted it. He connected the dots, and *voila.* A guinea hen theory was born. I guess this was an easier theory to grasp than trying to understand or show concern for what had happened to the lost continent of Atlantis or the Mayan Empire. It did not matter much to us, since we did not know if these empires ever existed in the first place. That was the last thing for us to worry about.

It was taboo for children to flip over food as they ate. This certainly needs some explanation. Food in Kokoland, has a different meaning than food I was introduced to at a later point in my life. To most Kokolanders, a meal meant one plate containing sorghum porridge mixed with dry okra soup. Were there exceptions to this porridge-okra diet rule? Yes, but seasonally during harvest time when there were different varieties of food. Sadly, today, forty years later, even that one dish meal is hard to come by for a vast majority of the population. There was neither such a thing as dinner tables crowded with different types of food, nor could I have imagined one. There was no electricity forty years ago and it is still the case today. Drinking water was not always available. Everything was scarce, so wasting food was not an option or a problem to worry about.

As a child, I waited impatiently for the porridge pot to come down from the three-stone fire, since the neighborhood children would already be congregating at the village playground in the moonlight. They too got impatient when I failed to show up sooner. I would be under pressure to join them because they would soon start calling names insulting those who decided to stay with their mothers rather than come out and play like men. That was why you urged your mother to give you your porridge-okra portion to gobble up and rush to the playground to show your manhood. Here comes the superstitious part about the risk of flipping porridge upside down. My mother used to tell me, "If you flip your porridge while eating, the village boys will defeat you in wrestling games." You may be wondering what is the correlation between flipping porridge and losing a wrestling match. I think, what my mother had in mind was that wrestling games were grounds for testing one another's strengths and fighting skills to create ranks and seniority among ourselves. Losing a match had dire consequences to the loser, seeing in him a weak and an easy target for the winner and other children to bully him like hell. Mothers, including mine, figured out a way to remedy this great risk of bullying. If they could relate gobbling up of food to losing a wrestling match, they might be able to convince their children to eat slowly. By eating slowly, the child would not flip the porridge. That way, he would eat more, stay healthy, and be prepared, both psychologically and strength-wise, to win wrestling matches, hence avoid being bullied.

Sometimes competition over women led to disputes, which were settled through arbitration. In other cases, young men resorted to deadly violence to square off conflicts. For better results, some people solicited the help of evil spirits to intervene and be on their side. Even though tradition and culture generally called for refraining from use of black magic, people sometimes practiced it to inflict harm on their enemies. Probably, the whole thing was nothing more than playing on people's emotions and fear of the unknown. However, holy men played their level best in supporting whomever came forward asking for help. Good holy men strictly used legitimate prayers to seek help from God to support weaker parties who might have been unjustly treated. Bad holy men resorted to black magic and sorcery to hurt their clients' enemies. In either case, the rituals involved spilling of blood. They normally asked for advance fee and sacrificial animals such as chickens, sheep, and goats, preferably in either black or white colors. A good holy man would ask for a white animal to help his client, whereas a bad holy man would ask for a black animal to carry out his magic. In extreme cases, black oxen were slaughtered to reflect the gravity of the problem that needed addressing. Some of the black magic practices involved slaughtering the animals according to certain guidelines. In other cases, the animals were buried alive, and that depended on the severity level of animosity and the nature of harm intended.

In all fairness, the use of animals for black magic rituals was not the norm. It was a tiny fraction of the overall offerings people made to God as part of religious worship, which was augmented by slaughtering animals for the purpose of feeding orphans, guests, or travelers. Spilling animal blood, coupled with prayers, could also be intended for asking God for a quick recovery of a sick family member or for success in some undeclared personal matters. However, animal sacrifice was central to all of these activities.

It was widely believed that a fear-stricken man at the verge of losing his mind could be brought to his senses by slapping him real hard on the face. Mind you, slapping a man could call for serious undesirable consequences, except in situations it was administered for treating fright cases. It was customary for people to get slapped in the event of lorries turning over due to mechanical failure or over-speeding. Because lorries were the means of transporting both humans and goods, accidents always led to fatalities as a result of people being trapped or pinned down under heavy loads of merchandise. This is coupled with lack of access to emergency service. At times, a fear-stricken accident survivor would start talking rubbish, and that was when people would volunteer to slap him, believing that, equally, shocking the man would immediately bring him back to his senses. Any delay might cause him to lose his mind permanently. For this reason, people rarely objected to the practice. It was not uncommon for a do-gooder, if you will, to go around with a hand stretched out ready to slap anyone who needed help to recover from a shock. It was invariably a judgement call. A perfectly sane person could receive a massive slap out of nowhere. However, that was never a cause for objection when an accident moment dictated that.

As I mentioned above, at times, young men, resorted to deadly violence to settle disputes over women. Do you remember the story, in chapter 8, of our young neighbor, Barood, who fled the battle ground? Barood was a timid person by nature. He was not known for riding hardships, if you will. Someone planted an idea into his mind that he should be a man and stand side by side with young fellow, Bibi, tribesmen to fight the Kanuri boys, over girls. He was told it would be an honor and a lifetime achievement if he could defend the tribe's girls, especially if he ended up dead, or got injured in the process. He enthusiastically agreed, got carried away, and showed up at the predetermined location of the fight. The two groups collided and soon there was death and serious injuries in both sides. Barood had never seen anything that horrific in his entire life. He could not take the heat of the battle. He basically underestimated the whole thing. He thought that women were worth sacrificing for, but not to the extent of paying the ultimate price, so he ran away. He lent his legs to the wind and took off running Kokoland bound. He got there in no time, but he was in bad shape, too. He could not stop on his own until a few men obstructed his way. When they asked him what was happening to him, he responded, "They are all dead, everyone is dead."

Barood was trembling with fear all over his body and having difficulty standing up. He was wearing one goat-skin shoe that was most likely made locally by my relative Heeran the shoemaker. He probably lost the other one on the way as he fled the battle zone. He might have not noticed that, or he might have felt it when it slipped off his foot, but he did not think that it was worth the risk of spending a few seconds going back a couple of yards to retrieve it, so he carried on running with one shoe. His *baft* cotton *jellabiya* was shredded to pieces from his knees downwards. He was drenched in sweat and the cloth was glued to his wet body on the back and shoulders. It was visible to everyone around that Barood was shaking because the shredded edges of his *jellabiya* were moving in all directions like leaves on a windy day. Barood's eyes were half-open, but it was unlikely that he was seeing anybody or anything, or even aware of his environment. You could sense that his brain was working faster than his mouth could cope up with what he was thinking, translate that into sentences, and spit them out. There appeared to be a jam of words in his mouth. It seemed as if the words were elbowing one another, each trying to emerge out of Barood's mouth first. No wonder when he finally spoke, everyone around exploded with laughter, for nothing he said was comprehensible. It was something like the sound of bullets bursting, in one go, out of a machine gun barrel. The only sentence that everyone could clearly hear was, "They are all dead, everyone is dead."

One man commented in a sad tone, "Today, this man must have seen all colors of death, including the red one." Another man said, "Poor guy, something must have caused his heart to drop." A third man shouted, "You are strange people. What is wrong with you? Can't you see and tell? It is *haram* for you to congregate around a man suffering from such a condition." He then looked around and saw a young boy standing by, so he called him, "Boy, run and get some drinking water from Mahdi's home."

As Barood was facing a barrage of questions about what happened to him, Hijori, the wise man, showed up and immediately started enquiring, "People, what is here?" A few men volunteered and briefed him of the situation, so he got nearer to Barood to further investigate for himself. He looked deep into Barood's eyes, which were rolling uncontrollably; a sign of a horrendous fear. Hijori had seen similar cases in the past and knew exactly what to do. He was quick to diagnose Barood's condition and prescribe a treatment right there. He blared, "Slap him, I told you slap him." In a fraction of a second, six hands simultaneously went up in the air to execute the wise man's orders. Their garments' sleeves dropped to their arm-base, revealing charms and knives they were wearing around the arms. Unlike Barood, they decided to be prepared for whenever the moment of truth about a fight was upon them. Less faithful men usually took the practical route of wearing knives, whereas others of more faith opted to relying on supernatural powers for protection, so they wore charms. In any case, both groups did their homework for times of emergency. Nobody could tell if Barood had his defense tools initially on him when he went to battle, but lost them the same way he lost one shoe as he was fleeing the battle ground. The truth of the matter was that, Barood chickened out and let down every member of the Bibi tribe, starting with his own mother.

The six or so men with their hands up in the air, ready to take full advantage of a free and consequence-less slapping session, took pity on Barood and lowered their hands in a coordinated movement. They just did not have the courage to add to the man's miseries by humiliating him even further. Hijori gave his final orders, "Then, take this man to his relatives." At that moment, more people closed in on Barood to help lead him to his house. Barood could not walk steadily, so two men shouldered him and the entire group walked off in the direction of Barood's house. After a couple of weeks, Barood disappeared from Kokoland and stayed away for over ten years. As I mentioned in chapter 8, Barood became the joke of town for betraying his friends and letting down the tribe's girls who were quick to link him to every cowardly act imaginable under the sun. He could not take it, so he, again, ran away, but this time, from Kokoland. When he returned, he was completely a different person. He had become a *sofi* dervish who cared little about life. No one could tell his exact reasons for adopting such an ideology. Nevertheless, that did not change much of whatever had been engraved on people's memories that Barood was the man who beat the wind, running.

My dear elder sister had her own way of dispelling evil spirits. She had her secrets for keeping them at bay, particularly at times of feeding her babies. People believed that food attracted evil spirits and that harm was likely to befall persons who failed to invite strangers to share their food, particularly if they happened to be hungry or wished if they could have tasted the food. Sharing food, not only dispelled evil spirits, but it was also a sign of generosity. These practices could have been adopted to promote community cohesion. Probably, over time, societies added spiritual dimensions to encourage people not to become misers.

When I first moved to Britain, I found it hard to understand the concept of "English pocket," when people, individually, paid for their food and drinks. We lived in a semi-communal life, sharing everything from food to clothes to homes. Any Kokolander would find it strange to see people eating in others' presence without inviting them to share their food. My problem was that I thought the entire world operated according to my Kokoland way of thinking. I could not have been more wrong. It was not even fair to think like that. At that time, I had not had the slightest idea about the complexity of issues pertaining to individualism, personal responsibilities, and preferences. I laid my exclamations to rest now that I fairly understand how the world works.

My elder sister was an expert in making homemade baby food. Her favorite one was boiled and filtered millet mixed with butter and milk. She fed her infants according to a strict regimen. Right before feeding the babies, she would make sure that evil spirits got their share of the food, just in case they had a desire to taste it. She fed them by holding her right hand fingers together and dipping them in the baby's food. Then she would remove and push her hand in one direction; simultaneously spreading her fingers outward, causing the liquid food on the tips of the fingers to sprinkle up in the air. She would repeat the process four times to cover the four corners of the globe. That was her way of becoming certain that she had perfectly insulated the baby and left no open space for evil spirits as well as humans to penetrate her imaginary capsule and possibly harm her infant. Her actions were equally aimed at humans, if they accidentally got in the way. If I happened to be sitting next to her, then I got my share of liquid baby food sprinkled all over my face, unless I managed to dodge her hand, just on time. That was in case I too had any desires to share her baby's food. Her actions were accompanied by series of serious prayers. She was so protective of her babies, so she left nothing for chance.

Sometimes I wondered why the spirits would leave healthier and tastier foods in the city, come to a village, and eat baby food. It did not make sense to me at all now knowing that there are more gorgeous French, Italian, and other international cuisines available to them. I grew more convinced that those spirits who travelled all the way to our village and settled for baby food, made out of boiled millet, were the biggest losers and the lousiest of all spirits.

The manner in which babies were fed was rough, considering their age. The Kanuri word for the process, literally, translates to stuffing, pumping, or filling. The baby would be stuffed with that soup so much that it left little room for breathing, let alone crying, which was the very reason for stuffing in the first place. Over eating, especially with babies, could cause disease and lead to death. Nevertheless, that was how mothers in the villages put their babies to bed and made them sleep, just like babies, so they could be free to work in the fields. Children suffered because mothers worked in the field during the day, attended to their cash crops in their backyards in the evenings, and took care of numerous household responsibilities at night.

Other village practices involved tactics adopted by parents to control disobedient sons. For example, my cousin Omran was being viewed by many family members as a lazy young man because he hated working in the field. I don't blame him at all, since I too hated working in the field. People labored for years without seeing any progress or improvement in their living standard. Despite that, they would continue doing the same thing, year after year. In fact, in most of the cases, conditions worsened over time. Omran was just a rebel who rejected the idea of living in a village. He broke traditions and travelled to the city to try something different. I also travelled away from the village and where I ended up was probably a testimony to how far away I wanted to be. I just did not think that relying on my muscle power for farming would get me anywhere. I worked for many seasons and I could not afford a bicycle. I can not complain that I left the village behind.

It was traditionally accepted for Kanuri boys to get married when they barely reached the age of majority. It was common for boys to marry at the age of sixteen and for girls to be wed at the age of fourteen. Fathers were the ones who arranged for that, so neither the groom, nor the bride had any say. After every good harvest, fathers would roam the villages investigating about potential teenage brides for their boys. In many cases, weddings took place without couples having had the chance to meet, not even a single time. Omran saw things differently, so it was natural that his attempts to break away were resisted by both his father and grandfather, in particular. His ideas amounted to disobedience and doing away with traditions that required sons to get married at a young age, continue living in the family home, and work in the family farm.

The only way to prevent Omran from running away was to keep him captive in the village by tying him to a marriage, but he managed to escape to the city for a brief period of time. He bitterly told me how his father and grandfather colluded to invite him back to the village. His father told him that his grandpa was very sick and he had better come and see him for he thought his days were numbered. Omran returned to the village the moment he got the message and went straight to see his grandpa, whom he loved dearly. He told me something strange happened when he got there. He said his grandpa, in the process of shaking his hand, slipped a silver dime into his hand. He alleged that the dime was affected by magical powers intended to strip him of his free will. The magic did work. Omran could not leave the village for a long time. Skeptics may think that there could have been other reasons for his inability to leave the village. That might be the case, but the problem was that Omran fully believed in his magic-caused inability to exercise his free will and go back to the city as he wished. Anyhow, after the passage of sometime, the magic rendered ineffective, and Omran could break free and travel back to the city, but after the damage had been done a long time ago. By that time, the dreams he had as a young man had already faded away. He told me his story with great fury.

Another family member, Shafi, went through the same experience as Omran. Shafi's mother sought help from a holy man to bring him back to the village and prevent him from returning to the city. There was the misconception among many people in rural settings that cities corrupt young men and they end up going astray. Contrary to the belief held by his mother, Shafi worked for a prominent family in the city. They were willing to help him further his education. He was doing very well. Just like in Omran's case, the magic did affect Shafi because he ended up staying in the village. Sadly, he turned into an addict, most likely from depression and the lack of anything useful to do. The magic that prevented him from going back to the city could have been nothing other than the sense of being torn between following his dreams and obeying his mother's wish. He finally decided to settle for the latter option. Such dilemma could have affected anybody living in a society that considered disobeying parents as a deadly sin.

I remember one time visiting Grandma in the village when I was in middle school. I also went to visit a childhood friend who had just gotten married. When I asked him about his wife, he responded, "My father brought her from the village of Dalaib." He was fifteen and she was thirteen or so. He, like everyone else in the village, had not had a chance to attended school, so school for his wife was unthinkable. The harsh reality for this couple was that the following rainy season the father allotted them a piece of land to farm and make a living on their own. With little preparation or training to become independent, they struggled to make ends meet. Their case applied to most newlywed young couples in the area. The young wives' problems were aggravated by the fact that they, on top of working in the farm, were expected to cook and feed their husbands as well as their in-laws. My Kanuri people call it customs, traditions, help, and respect for the in-laws, and I call it something they would definitely not appreciate hearing it coming from me, being one of them. I thought my cousin Omran's and my friend's parents should have searched for a type of magic that could help chase away every single boy from the village and allow them back only after they had learned something, mastered a trade, and improved their standard of living. There was a high chance that anywhere else, away from the village, presented an opportunity for a better future. If the boys did well, they could help the very parents who were obstructive to the idea of children moving away.

Village elders usually congregated under trees by village mosques to discuss issues and make decisions pertaining to the functioning of the community. There was hardly any discord in opinion between elders, and that consensus and harmony were the norm. Dissenters were shunned aside and considered community outlaws, and, for that reason, nobody wanted such a title. Men were in full control of everything, and women blindly followed their orders. For example, mothers rarely had a say in who their daughters should marry. The decision entirely rested with the fathers. If a father agreed to wed away his daughter to a man, that decision would be his business and the mother would have no choice, but to abide by it. Men in the village saw it a sign of weakness and lack of control if a man consulted his wife. He would be characterized as a "wife-listener." Women, lacking power, accepted such fate and refrained from challenging men's authority because any tampering with it could lead to undesired consequences ranging from divorce, to the husband taking a second, a third, or even a fourth wife. There were disastrous cases of fathers agreeing to marry their young daughters to men decades older. Some men took full advantage of these customs at the expense of the weaker party; women, due to lack of strong legal systems to hold them accountable for their actions.

"Tadaa laleo, tadaa laleo" in the Kanuri language means "Hello, boys, hello, boys." This was a song my childhood friends and I used to sing when we were at the age of five years or so. We normally sang it on the seventh day of the birth of a baby boy. It was a way to glorify the arrival of a baby boy as a new addition to a family. On that day, members of the community from all around the region would flock to the village of the newly born baby to name him. We would usually sit in the dirt, form a circle, and wait for food to arrive, which in most probability contained something special, such as barbecued goat head.

After eating our special meal, we would sing the boy-glorifying, girl-undermining, song that went like this: "Hello, boys, hello, boys, if it is a boy, softly put him on the mat, but if it is a girl, over the fence she goes." The irony was that we sang this song in the full presence and blessing of our mothers, aunts, and sisters. Not only had they just finished feeding us, but they also had been caring for us our entire lives. What were we thinking? If we sang this derogatory song in some other parts of the world, we would be whipped on our little behinds, and the least we could get away with would be something like, "You ungrateful little bastards." Unfortunately, the superiority of man was engraved in the social fabrics so much that it had become the absolute norm, to the extent that women fully believed in it, so they never challenged or questioned it. In fact, to the contrary, they promoted it.

Life was generally a struggle, but a woman in a Kanuri village took the brunt of that. A typical day during the rainy season went like this: In the morning, she would prepare tea, cook food, and take it to the farm to catch up with her husband, who would have left earlier after having his morning tea. She would work in the field with him and also take care of her infant, if she happened to be nursing. It was probable that they had other children, normally left behind in the village to look after themselves until they returned in the afternoon. To be productive, the mother would stuff the infant, as I described above, so he or she would sleep as long as possible, under the shade of a tree in the middle of the farm, as she worked. In the afternoons, after attending to the fieldwork, she would collect firewood, carry it on her head, with the baby tied to her back, and head home. At home, she would attend to the needs of the other children she had left behind, then go to work in the backyard and look after her cash crops such as okra, corn, black-eyed peas, cucumbers, and melons. At sunset, she would come back to the house to cook dinner for her kids, her husband, and her in-laws. She would go to bed with no single iota of energy left on her body. She would repeat the same scenario the following day. This would go on for the entire rainy season. There was always hope that the farm would produce enough harvest to store and use during the dry seasons, and also to sell some in the market to get cash. When crops failed, all the efforts went down the drain. Men would leave the village during the dry season, travel to the city, and work as day laborers. Women and children would stay behind to get by on bare minimum. Lack of schooling for girls did not help either. The best they could do was knitting mats out of palm leaves, all day, all summer.

The male-dominated society enacted common laws and customs according to men's whims, giving themselves wide powers. Those customs were imposed on women on the presumption that they were called for by religion; a conclusion that could not have been more further from both logic and truth. For example, it was customary for women to refrain from eating in front of their husbands. It was considered disrespectful if they did so. Women ate last after they had catered for men and children in the family, even though, most of the time, that came at the expense of their own health. This was one form of women's absolute self-denial. It is not surprising that development agencies call for supporting mothers because they do a better job looking after the well-being of the entire family.

In the evenings, women would cook food and take it to the food court, by the village mosque, when men would have just finished sunset-prayers. Upon arriving on site, they would slip off their slippers, walk a few feet to the center of the court, sit down on the ground, and place the food. Then they would get up, walk slowly backward, put on their slippers, and quietly head back to their home. Anything short of this protocol would brand the ill-fated woman disobedient and disrespectful to their majesties. Some men thought that this practice, too, came from religious teachings. Wives did not call their husbands by their names. This also showed lack of respect if they did so. They used the names of their firstborn child, be that a boy or a girl. They would say, "Father of so-and-so."

Another tradition was that women were supposed to take off their shoes, to express respect, whenever they passed by a group of men gathering in a place or sitting down under a tree. They would remove the shoes, carry them in their hands, and walk bare footed, until they got out of the men's sight, then they would drop them to the ground and wear them. They would do so even when they walked on a hot ground, which could be riddled with that nasty goat-head thorn. I must say that these were man-made Draconian rules imposed on Kokoland women, who, in most probability, thought that they were universal rules for respecting men, so they hardly questioned their validity.

People used "Korbaj rule" as a term to refer to anything unjust. The term came from the following story, which people believed to have actually taken place few centuries earlier. Korbaj was a tyrant king who ruled his kingdom with an iron fist. Through some of his crazy acts, he subjected his citizens to horrendous pain and suffering. One day, while riding along with his entourage, he passed by a hilly site. He stopped and thought for a moment, then turned to his chief of army and said, "Why there are many hills on the right side of the road and only one hill on the left?" His chief of army panicked and started trembling from fear. He resigned to the fate that the king would chop off his head for failing to respond promptly with a correct answer to the question. The king paused for a moment then gave his orders, "Dig up this lonely hill and bring it to the other side so it can be happy among its brothers and sisters." It was believed that people dug around that lonely hill for years in a futile attempt to uproot it. Many people lost their lives in the process. They continued digging until the death of the king, and then they had a break. People say there is a ditch around the hill, visible even today, centuries later. Tyrant Korbaj's story became exemplary punishment and the highest level of injustice people could possibly endure, so the proverb *Korbaj Rule* is used to describe everything unfair or unjust that one person does to another. It is true that rules imposed by society on women, such as the removal of shoes, are humiliating, but the problem today is that there are forms of tyranny, such as genocide and crimes against humanity, that are perpetrated by states against their own citizens. These crimes measure up to and go way beyond *Korbaj Rule*. Sadly, Women continue to bear the brunt of these cruel acts.

Few women did revolt against social norms that were unfair to them. The wife of a renowned member of the community proved that she was an exception to the rule and a bitter pill for her husband to swallow. She was one of few wives who rebelled against their husbands. She turned his life upside down. They used to fight a lot, and her preferred act of revenge was breaking the clay pot used for keeping the most valuable commodity; water, which took the man many hours every day to fetch. She figured out that wasting it was the ultimate pain that she could inflict upon him. Whenever they fought, the first thing they did was taking a few seconds staring at each other to assess one another's intentions, before, simultaneously, dashing for the water pot. The man would fight ferociously to protect his valuable merchandise, and the wife would exert equal effort to try to reach it, break it to pieces, and waste the water. The man would be shielding the pot with his body by wrapping his arms around it in a desperate attempt to prevent her from reaching it, but she was always able to overpower him due to her way larger physique. The clay pot was no match to her strong legs. In a single kick, she would smash it, causing the water to runoff and spread in the tiny hut's ground, soon to seep through the sandy floor in front of the man's teary eyes, leaving him bitter, depressed, and helpless. The fights lasted only a few minutes. They both did not have justifiable reasons to continue fighting after the pot was broken because the woman would have achieved her goals by demolishing the pot and the man would have run out of motivation after the water was spilled over. The man could not take it any longer, so he finally divorced her.

The husband happened to be one of my relatives, so I occasionally visited the couple in their nearby village of Kaloumi, especially during religious festivals and events. After they divorced, I used to meet the wife on market days in Kokoland. For some reason, she used to greet me with some kind of a wicked smile. I wanted to believe that she thought I was too young to remember the details of what had happened between her and her husband, but, deep down, I also thought that she smiled to amuse herself and pass me the message that she got a kick out of kicking the water pot to pieces and hurt the feelings of my uncle, real bad.

Another couple in the village, also fought a lot. The village men felt that the woman controlled the husband, so they came to his rescue. They gave him a tip to help him claim back his powers and reinstate his authority. They told him whenever she picked a fight; he should rush to the china hutch and pretend he was going to lift it high up in the air and smash it to the ground, along with its contents. They encouraged him to be brave, try the trick, and not to worry about a thing, arguing that his wife would immediately cool down and come to her senses, the moment he rushed toward the china hutch. The plan did succeed and the man was finally readmitted into the real men's club. It was a very serious thing to tamper with Kokoland women's china hutches and collection of ceramic dishes. They would do anything to protect them from destruction, including submission to husbands. This was an abusive tactic and I doubt that it truly happened. It could be a pass time story, but I guess the idiom, "A bull in a china shop" must have originated in Kokoland.

Amassing china and glassware by Kanuri women was considered a sign of wealth. They displayed them inside their bedroom huts for decoration and show off purposes. It was customary for women to use the money they made from selling cash crops to hoard cups, bowls, and plates made of aluminum, china, and glass. The success of the work they carried out in their backyards during the rainy season was reflected in the frenzy trips they made to Kokoland or to the city to buy dishes. As soon as the market started buzzing with harvest activities, mobile merchants, who were familiar with Kanuri culture, rode their donkeys into town carrying their merchandise for sale. Their colorful and beautifully displayed plates shone under the sun and were visible from far distances. Women were attracted to them, so they spent their money buying plates like there was no tomorrow. They came into town on market-day mornings carrying agricultural products on the back of donkeys and on their heads, and went back to their villages loaded with aluminum cooking pots, bowls, plates, and chinaware.

Harvest times were also happy times for Rabba Ayna, the town carpenter and his assistants. The number of hammers at work and the fast frequency of knocking on nails were an indication of urgency to fill orders for hutches and tables. Mothers gave the hutches and the plates they had horded over the years as wedding gifts to their daughters. Carpenters also proudly displayed their finished and work-in-progress hutches to attract new customers. Rabba Ayna and his team laughed more frequently; a sign of happy times. Money was not a problem. He ordered tea from Zaid, the café owner, for his clients and anybody passing in front of the workshop. When women shopped in Kokoland, atmosphere of generosity and happiness prevailed. You could sense that everywhere in town. The number of hutches in display gave an indication of the number of potential weddings that were likely to take place in the community during that particular harvest season. Rabba Ayna did take breaks to visit Burrah to pick up bottles of *aragi,* his favorite local alcohol drink, but he never missed his delivery deadlines. He was Kokoland's example for just-in-time deliveries. Rabba Ayna was a king of multi-tasking. Besides his carpenter job, he was also a source of entertainment. He, being a city boy, entertained people by singing Indian songs he had learned by going to the movies. He sang while clearly drunk, but that did not affect his work. He was always able to knock the nails right on the head.

I experienced these customs first hand, because my elder sister was addicted to hoarding dishes. Her argument to me was that by buying dishes in pieces over years she would be prepared when it was time for her daughters to get married. She told me she did not want any surprises from her husband, if she had to wait and buy everything at once. She also worried a great deal about her stance in the community in case her collection of dishes was not impressive. She did not want to risk being undermined by the community, considering the family she comes from. "What will people say about us", she told me. Whenever I expressed the view that she was just wasting her money, she always laughed and shrugged my criticism, considering it a mere harmless comment from a kid who deeply lacked knowledge about life's secrets. Plates and dishes were central to her station in life within the community. How more traditional could anyone be? I love my sister.

During weddings, the mother of the bride would display her possession of dishes in the center of the house as a show of wealth for every woman to see, admire, and hence respect her. Women competed among each other to show who owned more dishes. Rare, exotic, and more colorful items fetched more admiration. Dishes helped women gain few steps up the social strata.

Once, I told my wife about our Kanuri customs pertaining to men, in an attempt to claim some of my community given rights. She responded with a prolonged silence and her facial expressions read, "Do you want to sleep outside?" written all over. I, too, responded to her with a deafening silence, closing that chapter forever. I was dumbfounded having being caught off guard. I thought for a moment and concluded that was a risky route not worth taking. I certainly did not want to be homeless here in America, so I never brought up this subject again, ever. It was my mistake that, for a moment, I forgot I was in America, the land of the feminist movement. In the presence of my wife, not only have I been avoiding bringing up any topic about Kokoland customs pertaining to men's rights, but I also helped change the subject any time she brought it up herself.

As I have indicated in many instances above, the absence of enforceable laws protecting women's rights left them always vulnerable. With lack of education for men and women, in particular, it will be a long time before issues relating to social injustices can be addressed. However, someday, Kokoland men will tip hats to women. That time is coming, for the status quo is just unsutainable.

CHAPTER 13

Middle School: My Renaissance Era

My Middle School in Darsail; My Renaissance Era (1973 – 1976). Photo 2016.

The year 1973 was a tumultuous time for America. I learned that after reading about the Vietnam War, so I was able to connect few dots. That was also the year I transferred to middle school. Progressing from primary to middle school is a normal thing to most school kids, but in my case, it was a big deal because it meant fewer troubles for me. Hundreds of us competed for forty seats; therefore securing a seat in middle school was almost a life-and-death situation, in view of the bullying problems I faced in primary school. Recognizing that there was so much at stake, I studied hard in sixth grade, motivated by two things. The first one was to put an end to the era of teacher flogging for not doing well at tests and exams. We heard from middle school students that teachers hardly whipped them. The second reason was that I saw in middle school a stronger justification for less work in the field and less donkey responsibilities. I was able to convince my dad that middle school was a new chapter in my life involving intellectual responsibilities such as more homework as well as learning a new language; English. It was time for use of brain power to replace human muscle power. My dad agreed. I worked very hard, got good grades, and ranked twelfth in the district. It was somewhat an over kill, but I could not afford to take any chances. Darsail Middle School was a stone's throw away from my primary school, and for that reason I thought it was going to be an easy transition, but I was wrong.

As I said earlier, the transformation from primary to middle school was nothing to ride home about. However, those of us who succeeded were triumphant, as if we won a battle, but in fact, it was a battle. For a brief moment in time, the community talked about our achievement, mentioning our names in households all over the village. We saw an upward shift in our "respect-o-meter" scale and we, most importantly, became famous as far as girls were concerned. Our newly earned status called for new shoes and clothes, which parents happily provided by foregoing other priorities. To many fathers, including my own, sending a child to middle school was an uncharted territory, so we were able to package anything we wanted under the phrase, "The school said we should get it," and presented it to our fathers, who, not knowing the consequences of refusal, happily met our demands. Parents began to realize that sending us to school might translate into something good down the road, someday, so both our parents and us students guarded our newly conquered middle school territory with our teeth.

It was time for everything middle school; a uniform, a pair of shoes (proper shoes this time, and gone the days of slippers), a bed sheet, a blanket, a metal suitcase for clothes, and a tin container for storing foodstuff such as ground sesame mixed with sugar, dates, and boiled peanuts, to supplement the school food rations. What a transformation? Those were happy days for Abu Ali the village blacksmith, who worked diligently to fill orders converting empty oil tins into supply containers. My dusty and dirty feet were very lucky that not only did I get proper shoes, but also a pair of socks, yes socks, for the first time in my life. Boy, the level of joy and sophistication I felt every time I wore them was unparalleled. I reserved my socks and wore them only for special occasions. I was the first person in my family to wear socks. This is just to let you know how far I have come when a trivial thing such as wearing socks meant a big deal for me.

The beginning of the school year always coincided with Saturdays, which was also the first day of the week. So, one Friday in August 1973, we seventh, eighth, and ninth grade students flocked to the village of Darsail from all directions, depending on which village we came from. Students from out of town who lived in nearby villages carried their luggage and walked or rode donkeys to the middle school boarding house. Those of us who came from farther away villages travelled by lorries in groups, and arrived in Darsail market center. We then walked the one-mile distance between the market and the school, carrying our colorful metal cases and supply containers. We arrived at the school happy that we were going to embark on a new chapter in our young lives. A chapter that involved acquiring knowledge, which was hard to come by, considering the fact that we mostly came from remote villages that might as well be nonexistent, as far as the rest of the world was concerned. We anxiously waited for Saturday morning, our first day in middle school.

I barely adjusted to my new environment in middle school when a group of senior students, led by El Pasha, called all students for a secret meeting and told us that we were going on a strike. Those of us who were in first year did not know most of the jargons the leaders used in explaining the meaning of strike, leave aside understanding the objective of the intended action. I was so worried because I did not know what all that meant and what to expect. I had a gut feeling that it was not a good thing. Something told me that in the end, our actions would not pass unpunished. We would probably get whipped, just like in the elementary school, something I thought I had parted ways with for good. It seemed to me that I was terribly wrong about middle school. In the evening of that day, I sat with my first year peers and deliberated over the idea of going on strike, but we could not come up with a satisfactory answer to calm our fears. I went to bed and thought all night about different scenarios for what the future could be holding.

Rumors circulated the school that we were going to strike because students from Khor Taggat, one of the top high schools in the country, as well as college students in the capital Khartoum, had gone on strike, so we must follow suit, and that was it. The rumors got confirmed by the strike leaders, but they failed to tell us the reasons why we, in a middle school in the middle of nowhere, should go on a strike. The fact that my peers and I were kept in the dark could have probably been attributed to having wandered around in the school yard with cluelessness written all over our little faces for everyone to see. The leaders might have thought it ain't worth explaining to us because we won't get it, so why bother. We heard senior students talk about freedom, but had only vague idea about its meaning, so I wondered; freedom from what? It took me many years to fill in the gaps.

As I mentioned earlier, the Vietnam War was winding down in 1973. Even though it had started in 1969, news about it took until 1973 to trickle down to some of us in our towns and villages. By that time, whatever we had learned about the war was outdated as well as distorted. This is besides being an event which was of no relevance to our situation in the villages. We exercised full liberty to modify and localize the Vietnam War to address school issues, hence the strike. It is safe to say that many people did not know about the war, neither then, nor now. We truly were, and still are, at periphery of life.

In the morning Amu Idris, the school guard, rang the bell, calling us for morning assembly. We stared at him from a distance, but did not walk up to the assembly court. We could tell from his body language that he was panicking. His assistant, Makki, appeared in the scene and rang the bell again for a prolonged period, only harder and faster, indicative of sense of urgency. The principal and the teachers showed up and appeared talking to each other. The school was in strike. It was official. El Pasha told us earlier on that we should not leave the boarding quarters when we heard the bell ringing. He said if we did so we would undermine the will of the group. Responding to the bell meant one thing; abandoning group solidarity, so whoever did that would be branded as a coward and a traitor. Who could live in isolation from everybody else? It was a tough choice. I had no idea what to do. Nobody responded to the assembly bell, so the strike organizers declared it a success. I thought to myself, "What does this mean? Is it over? Shall we go to classes?"

Soon afterwards, the organizers announced that we should march into town. We were organized in two lines lead by third year students followed by second year, then first year in the tails of the lines. In each class, the tallest and the biggest students held advance positions in the lines and behind them stood students of lesser weights and shorter heights. I guess the strike organizers wanted to "shock and awe" the enemy by overwhelming it with a formidable show of middle school students marching force. Being in first year, the skinniest, and the youngest, sealed my fate of trailing the line. My last position was shared by three of my friends Sinada, Salama, and Madani, who all, equally, shared my agony about the strike. We headed toward town. I had no idea what we were going to do there, nor did members of my clique who were also as clueless as I was. Probably, there might have been strike goals and objectives, but nobody bothered to explain them to us. May be we did not matter that much. We started marching toward town, but, for reasons unknown to me, we took a detour and passed in front of the girls' primary school. I guess the leaders wanted to demonstrate to the girls that we were men enough to take on the authorities, hoping to make them (the girls) proud of us. Please bear in mind that the middle school represented the highest body of knowledge in town, so the strike organizers might have thought that we could be trusted with making the right decision about current affairs such as fighting for freedom on behalf of the community.

The strike leaders chanted slogans, and the rest of us repeated after them. My tail gating friends and I at the rear end of the lines heard vague words that made little sense. We looked into each other's eyes for answers, but none of us could console the other or come to his rescue with an explanation. We tilted and turned our heads sideways so that our ears could hear well. We hoped that the winds would carry to us audible sounds from the front of the lines, but to no avail. After the slogans were repeated several times, we thought we had heard enough and understood what had been said, so we gathered enough courage to repeat what we had heard, "Tation tation - tation tation." We grow more confident every time we shouted, "Tation tation—tation tation," louder and louder. The slogans were aired in English, and by that time we, as first-year students, had not even completed learning the English alphabets, much less understanding slogans in English and repeating them loudly during a strike for a noble cause such as seeking freedom.

There was a legitimate reason for me and my friends trailing the lines. Had we appeared in the front, shouting, "Tation tation—tation tation", we could have inflicted serious damage to our cause as well as our standing in the community, which was partly represented by the primary school girls, who could have well been our primary target for the whole strike fiasco. Then again, what difference could our slogan have made, when nobody in town had a clue about the meaning of the words we shouted, anyway? I guess the idea of passing in front of the girls' school was done with ulterior motives. As we walked, the girls ran toward us, only to be obstructed by the barbed wire fence. They stood there, rested their hands on the wires, and watched us in admiration. I wanted to convince myself that their admiration was equally distributed among us marching, from the head of the line to the tail. I was disappointed to realize that by the time we, at the end of the lines, got to where the girls were standing; they had already started walking back. They must have decided that we were less exciting to look at than the big and tall boys in the front. They left us staring at their behinds, hence depriving me and my friends the chance to look at their beautiful faces and cute smiles of admiration. I was very disappointed.

I later on found out that, "Tation tation- tation tation" meant, "No separation for one nation." We were close enough. Not bad, ha! but; wait a minute, who is calling for separation, from whom are we separating, and why? It turned out that the strike leaders had received some fuzzy news about Americans revolting against their government for fighting a war in Vietnam. By the time that information reached Darsail, it got distorted into, "No separation for one nation," which was further mutilated into, "Tation tation- tation tation." Ironically, in 2011, forty years later, the country of Sudan did split into two separate nations, North and South, after fighting a civil war that had lasted 25 years and claimed the lives of millions of Sudanese people from both sides. It seems the strike leaders were, somehow, able to foresee what was coming in few decades.

We marched on to the town clinic, where we met with Mr. Clear, the most dreaded English-language teacher, who was nicely dressed, as usual, and was on his way to school. We named him Clear because he mentioned the word "clear" in class every time he completed a sentence. He was totally shocked to see the entire middle school right in front of his face, since he had no idea what was going on. Some students, out of nowhere, started throwing rocks at Mr. Clear, while shouting, "Clear, clear." It was not a pretty sight seeing Mr. Clear, the most feared schoolteacher, fending off rocks with his arms, hiding his face, and dodging from time to time. He soon realized that it was a fruitless exercise, so he took off running in a zigzag pattern to limit the chances of being hit by rocks. He fled the scene probably thinking that the students were coming to his house, which was around the corner, to kill him or something. It was humiliating to see Mr. Clear running so fast and uncontrollably. At that moment, I came to the realization that we were officially in trouble. I thought to myself, "Only God almighty knows what disaster will come upon us. What have we done? God help us." What we did was a crime of an epic proportion, which was unprecedented in the school's history. After all, was it freedom or Mr. Clear that we were after?

We roamed the streets of Darsail until the strike leaders felt satisfied that our action had become a common knowledge all over town. Besides; it was getting hotter and we were getting thirsty and hungry, so we headed back to school. Once we were there, the leaders told us to go straight to our residents and should not wander, under any circumstance, out of our rooms or get anywhere near the schoolyard. While we were doing our strike work, the school principal and his team of dedicated teachers were also doing their part. The principal sent a message to the city advising the district superintendent of the strike taking place at our school.

That night; I went to bed overwhelmed by the burden of what the following day had in store for us. I was mostly worried about the punishment that could come in the form of flogging, which everyone of us dreaded, I must admit. I was also worried that the principal would give an order to shut down the school and dispatch us to our villages. I wondered if he would summon our fathers to attest that we would never commit such an act in the future, before we could be allowed back in school. I was not too concerned about being punished by my dad, for that was unlikely. I was rather concerned that the incident would play into the hands of school-haters within the Kanuri community. I feared that they would argue to proof their point of view to my father that school was a bad idea because it spoiled children. Many community elders thought that my dad had committed a mistake by sending me to school in the first place. They might tell him that the strike was an opportunity for him to correct his mistake by pulling me out of school. Even though the strike was a matter between my dad and me, any fellow tribesman could intervene, adopt the issue as his own, and volunteer to give my dad free advice about proper ways of reining children, and that keeping me out of school would be the best thing he could do. Many people regarded school as a challenge to their authority, believing that it disrupted community order. They would use undermining tactics to portray school kids as ungrateful, saying things like, "At school you are eating, you are drinking, so what are you missing? You are unthankful. You are just like fish, whenever over-fed; it commits silly acts like jumping out of water. You children of today are just like that." In fact, these aren't mere thoughts. I had heard words to this effect directed to me many times.

In the morning, we woke up to the sound of a vehicle entering the schoolyard. Soon the exhaust fumes hit my nose. It was gas and not the familiar smell emitted by diesel lorries. Gas in the air meant that a senior government official was in the vicinity. I did not even bother to walk outside the room to verify. Another district-wide feared person, the renowned school superintendent Mr. Allobah, and his assistants were at my school, in flesh and blood. They drove into town in two Toyota Land Cruiser vehicles, 1970 models, synonymous with authority and power of government officials who drove them. Mr. Allobah was known throughout the district for being a strict superintendent who did not stand any nonsense or shortcomings from teachers and principals alike, leave alone middle school kids, so everyone feared him. The decisive moment of truth was upon us. All morning long, we observed activities taking place in and around the school administration area. Around late afternoon, we were all summoned for a meeting with Mr. Allobah and his team. We timidly gathered in the shade of the seventh grade class and we all jockeyed for positions in the rear. Mr. Allobah was sitting on a chair behind a table. He was centering a row of twelve people comprised of school district officials from the city, the school principal, and the teachers. Every one of us wanted to be in a place that guaranteed avoidance of eye contact with anybody, especially the superintendent and, even, the clean-shaved, nicely dressed, "teeth-less" city officials, who were hardly a threat under normal circumstances. Usually, school officials from the city were too benign, so we did not fear them a bit. However, riding to town with the superintendent and sitting by his side called for as much precautionary measures as possible. That day was a totally different ball game all together because they could "bite". Avoiding eye contact by all means was the least that we could do. They all posed a great threat, no exceptions whatsoever. We backed as far as we could from them only to be obstructed by the class wall, which left us no room to go any further. We were gem packed and it was unfortunate for some kids that there was nowhere to go but to stand and confront authority, face-to-face. Every open inch of standing ground, away from the officials, was a prime real estate, which was squeezed out and used.

We perspired, breathed fast, and impatiently waited for the questioning protocol to begin. We had never experienced anything like that before. Mr. Allobah spoke first by saying, "It has reached my ears that you are in a strike and have demands to be met. Can anyone tell me about those demands?" The moment he completed his sentence was a perfect time to avoid eye contact with him. Our eyes raced to look downward at the ground. We kept them glued to the ground, but we were actually looking at nothing. Every few seconds, we forced our heads to embark on a treacherous journey to slowly look up so our eyes could steal a split-second glance at the line of officials sitting down, before dropping them down and continue staring at the ground. We wanted to be sure that we were not under the surveillance of their hawkish eyes. Nobody spoke as we aimlessly looked at the ground and counted the seconds, which passed very slowly. Speaking was suicidal and no one dared to do that.

Mr. Allobah spoke again: "How come you all went on strike and now you don't want to tell me why you did so? We left our responsibilities behind and drove all the way here to listen to you, but you are refusing to talk to us. Do you really think this is a joke?" Again, silence was the master of the general mood. Then, he slowly lifted his head up and surveyed the front line. Those of us who were short and were standing in the back could easily avoid eye contact with him, but not those in the front line. Mr. Allobah's eyes stopped at Hassoon. We all breathed a sigh of relief that a victim had been identified and singled out. Directing his question to Hassoon, he asked, "Why did you go on strike?" Jumping upward from shock, Hassoon gasped for air in a manner that had probably caused damage to his lungs' airways. Hassoon could not spell out one single word. He started sweating and trembling. He was in a real shock, but Mr. Allobah would not let go of him. He repeated the same question to Hassoon, "Why did you go on strike? For the rest of us, that meant surviving two questions out of many more Mr. Allobah was going to ask. Even though we had no idea what the man's next move was going to be, we all, except for Hassoon, felt that surviving two questions out of an unknown number of questions was not a bad outcome. Finally, Hassoon responded, but he had grave difficulty speaking. In a hoarse voice, he said, "We want ironing machines." Mr. Allobah responded, "I did not hear what you just said. Could you repeat that again? What did you say you want? What is your name?" Hassoon spoke again, "My name is Hassoon. Ironing machines, we want ironing machines." After giving that answer, Hassoon became totally preoccupied by the thoughts and prospects of being seriously punished as a result of the superintendent knowing him personally by his name. His brain completely froze and he couldn't have been able to respond with anything comprehensible after that, had Mr. Allobah came back with a follow up question. Mr. Allobah said, "Hang on. Am I hearing you right? What have ironing machines got to do with your strike? Are you all crazy?" He then looked at another student and asked the same question. He got the same answer given to him by Hassoon. He asked a third student, but this time the answer he got was, "We want ironing boards." He asked him again, "Ironing machines or ironing boards?" The boy responded, "Ironing machine, ironing boards," hoping that one of the two answers would click and be satisfactory to Mr. Allobah, as if saying "Take whichever answer you please and drop the other one." By answering that way he hoped that he would enhance his chances of being let off the hook. While waiting for Mr. Allobah's next move, he silently prayed for that dream to materialize.

I thought to myself, "Lord, have mercy and bring peace upon us all." We were in a dire situation and our credibility was terribly harmed. That was no time for flip-flopping from one demand to another. Then again, the damage might have already been done that Mr. Allobah did not believe what we were telling him was the truth, anyway. The strike had put us in a hole, and being inconsistent in our demands meant we were digging ourselves deeper, but definitely not to find gold. That was not a day for ironing boards. It was a day for ironing machines only. If we could survive by getting away with the ironing machines' argument, then we would not mind spreading our wet clothes on the dirt to iron them. There was no need for ironing boards. What we needed at that moment was consistency of demands. Ironing boards could wait for the next strike, which I was not planning to take part in, come what might. I made up my mind right then and there. These were thoughts that were going through my mind for the few seconds intervals that had lapsed between Mr. Allobah's questions.

By looking around, I could tell that no one was happy about the inconsistency of demands. Immediately after the third boy answered differently, another boy standing by his side elbowed him to back track and give Mr. Allobah the original answer, "ironing machines." We all got relieved when he did so. Not only did he answer the question, he overkilled it by saying, "Ironing machines," twice. With such emphasis, he wanted to be sure that the second unfavorable answer he had given earlier to Mr. Allobah would completely be erased from the man's memory so we would not suffer from lack of credibility with our demands. I was baffled by the idea of ironing machines and ironing boards suddenly becoming the core of our strike demands. I had no idea where that came from. I was pretty sure that our slogans did not go beyond, "No separation for one nation," or, if you like, "Tation-tation tation-tation." We were very desperate, scared, and sad.

I thought to myself, "It is safer to show unity by sticking to one single goal rather than straying away, for, in that, the enemy will find our weakness and easily defeat us." Somehow, we all shared the same thoughts. After that, every other student Mr. Allobah asked settled for "ironing machines." I guess that was because the rest of us also helped with serious "prayers for consistency." We nodded our heads whenever the correct answer was aired, indicating solidarity and knowledge of what we were doing, saying, and demanding. What we really wanted was to get over with the terrible predicament we put ourselves into. Mr. Allobah whispered in the principal's ear and looked back in our direction. Now what?

He spoke again, "You all are hiding the truth from me. I am fully aware of the severity of the plot you were knitting. You want to topple the government, don't you? The slogans you shouted out clearly demonstrated your intentions. Let us face it." When he said that, the whole sky crumbled onto me. God forbids. I thought to myself, "Toppling the government? Is that what we did? We are dead. The government always kills people. It is a great pity that we are going to die at such young ages. Only three years ago, I heard adults talking about army officers who attempted to topple the government and they failed. The sitting president, General Numairi, prevailed and he executed them all. We are going to face the same fate, no doubt about that."

Allobah continued, "I drove into town along with a garrison of soldiers in two army Majiruses [a German-made army truck synonymous with power and force, known for inflicting fear on people, causing fatal accidents all the time due to the reckless manner in which soldiers drove them]." He said, "I left them behind in the dry streambed [a mile or so away from school], ready to deploy at a moment's notice." Murmur prevailed, and body movements engulfed the whole area. "Now tell me the truth," he said. "Is it true that you were plotting to topple the government?" Before he even finished his question, we were ready to give our definitive answers in the negative, both vocally and through body language. Some boys said no, others shook their heads sideways, and yet others, with their index fingers pointing upward, prepared themselves to swear by the name of God almighty, if need be, that plotting to topple the government was never the intention, whatsoever. The upward pointing of the finger was a gesture, signaling the number one, to imply swearing by the name of Allah– The One and Only God, that the person was telling the truth and nothing but the truth. What we meant to say was that we were rejecting the strike in unequivocal terms. It was a life-and-death situation.

Mr. Allobah spoke again. He said, "I want those of you who want to topple the government to step to this side, with his index finger pointing to the right, and those of you who don't have an issue with the government to move to the left" Without the slightest hesitation, we all started moving to one side. By doing so, we laid our fate in the hands of Mr. Allobah. Our facial expressions and the way we rushed made our fears visible to the officials. It was time for reverse psychology. While each one of us was trying to figure out if he was in the right camp, the non-government-toppling camp, or not, we heard Mr. Allobah say, "Now I understand that you all want to topple the government." When he said that, the place became chaotic as we moved in opposite directions, bumping into each other, trying to figure out where we should be standing. Finally, we all flocked to one side. In all fairness, three of the strike organizers were the last to join us. That was probably their way of face-saving.

Allobah spoke for the last time, "Are you all sure that you have no plans to topple the government?" We all thought it was time to be vocal. We collectively and loudly responded, "Not at all." He turned to the principal, whispered something in his ears, got up, and left, followed by his entourage of restful city officials. He left us wondering and could not tell what he was exactly going to do next.

Mr. Allobah drove away in his convoy of two land cruisers, purportedly on his way back to the dry streambed where the army garrison lay down waiting for his orders to attack. Neither did I see him again, nor was I interested in doing that, or finding out about the garrison plot of his. I doubt it if there was any army. I also doubt it if the school principal had told him that we were plotting to overthrow the government. It was a genius idea of a highest standard that Mr. Allobah had carefully knitted to inflict fear in our unexperienced souls, for the rest of our lives. He was absolutely successful in doing so. We melted down in front of him like butter on fire. He burdened the principal and the teachers with the administrative task of handling our hapless strike. What a waste of time?.

The school administration decided that we should all get punished for our illegal action. Five lashes for third-and second-year students, and three lashes for first-year. I thought that was a blessing, since the school would not be closed and our fathers would not be summoned to school to sign documents committing us to be on our best of behavior for the rest of our time at the school. I thought to myself, "Superb. Three lashes? That ain't punishment. I could handle that any time." Considering the worse that I was expecting, I felt as if I won a prize for taking part in that strike.

We all lined up to receive our rations of lashes. When it was my turn, the teacher pointed to me with the whip in his hand to keep on moving. He thought it was not even worth wasting his energy to give me those three lashes. It was obvious to him that I was clueless, totally unaware of my environment, and had no grasp of what was happening. Do you know how humiliating that was? The teacher's action deprived me of the opportunity for claiming some heroism and bragging rights for having taken part in the strike, accepted the consequences, and paid for that, like a man, in three lashes. I could have used that to gain recognition and admiration from future students. Anytime my friends spoke about their flogging ordeal, I worried that they would remember that I was not even punished. I would keep quiet, eager for the conversation to change course. We rarely brought up the strike subject amongst ourselves for the entire three years my first year friends and I had spent at Darsail middle school. It was as if we all wanted those horrible memories to fade away into oblivion. I still wonder where did the slogan, "No separation for one nation" come from. Shady or half knowledge is extremely dangerous.

Middle school was a transformational era, as far as I was concerned. Books were a valuable commodity, being the main source of information, which I soaked up any time I laid my hands on one. The fact that I started learning English did enhance my transformation process because a door to other cultures and literature slung wide open. We had no electricity, television, or movie theaters in town, so every gap in knowledge or understanding of issues was left for books and our imaginations to fill. I liked that because I had the option to read books of my choice and there was no limit to what I could imagine. One problem I had was that I did not have control over the input I received from the radio. The country's news agency was not a newsmaker. It was rather a news broadcaster. It relayed to us foreign news originated by agencies such as the BBC, Reuters, etc. There was little coverage for regional or local issues. Sometimes I found the whole thing to be very confusing.

I learned about the Bandong (Indonesia) conference of the non-alliance group. I learned about the Khmer Rouge and the atrocities they had committed in Vietnam. I learned about work carried out by the United Nations and its Austrian secretary general, Mr. Kurt Valdheim. I learned about African freedom fighters such as Ebil Muzorewa, Joshua Nkomo, Robert Mugabe, and Nelson Mandela. These are some of the few political issues broadcast regularly on the radio around that time.

It was not just me who was confused by such type of news. One of my relatives named Gasim also had similar experience. I admired his dedication to seeking out help to understand what was going on around the world. He lived in a nearby village, but owned a canteen in Kokoland. Every market day he rode his donkey to town to open his canteen, which was absolutely empty of groceries or anything for sale. Despite that, he never missed market days. He came to town primarily to socialize with fellow Kanuri market goers. He was always interested in current affairs, even though he had little use for it or any idea what it all meant, due to the fact that he did not read or write Arabic, the official news language, or speak it well. Whenever I returned to Kokoland during school breaks, we met and compared notes on current affairs. He, understandably, lacked grasp of the ideas and the issues he raised, but he always wanted to know. He was one of the few relatives who were supportive of Kanuri children attending school.

The trail to Uncle Gasim's village passed in front of my house. On market days, on his way back to his village, he would invariably find me sitting in the shade of the fence listening to my Philips transistor radio. He would always stop so we could talk about news and important events. I think his donkey also noticed that pattern because it used to slow down as soon as it got closer to where I was sitting. After greeting, Uncle Gasim would randomly pull a topic off the top of his hat, just to start the conversation. He would then retreat, stay calm, and listen to me filling in the gaps. He might start asking me if I heard about the news pertaining to the meeting held by the Sudanese Socialist Union in Khartoum, or if there was any BBC news on the speech delivered by the United Nation's Secretary General Mr. Kurt Waldheim. I think he was fascinated by the UN Secretary's strange name. I knew he could not pronounce the name because he used a technique of jumbling up a statement which might include the word secretary. That was enough clues to pave the way for me to come to his rescue by confidently completing the name, hence putting my years of schooling to good use. What the Secretary General said, why, and to whom he spoke was immaterial. Uncle Gasim was always pleased with my performance. Whether I was right or wrong in my analysis was of no significance to him, besides, it was all news for him. Just listening to me articulating my middle-school-level thoughts was quite satisfactory for him. I look back and wonder why we discussed those issues in Kokoland in the first place, for nothing was of any relevance to our reality then. How ironic?

Uncle Gasim's donkey would stand calmly with its eyes closed in near-hibernation mode. After sometime, it would start moving its back legs forward and backward, interchangeably, in an effort to relieve one leg to rest, while leaving Uncle Gasim and his shopping load for the other leg to, partly, carry. It would soon start fanning its tail from one side to the other to chase away flies and signal to Uncle Gasim that it was time to get going. By that time, Uncle Gasim would have been satisfied that I had done justice to his queries. He would bid me farewell, then slightly rock the donkey with his heels, hinting to it that it was time to hit the road. We would repeat the same scenario the following market day until I informed him about the day I was planning to leave and go back to school. I wanted to give him a heads up so he would not be surprised if he passed by my house and found out I was not there waiting for our weekly session in politics and contemporary affairs.

While I was in Britain, my father relayed to me the news of Uncle Gasim's passing away. He got sick and travelled to the city for treatment. He received prescription drugs to use over a timespan. Because neither did he understand the doctor's instructions, nor could he read what was written on the medicine container, he over consumed the medicine and died from drug overdose. In 1986, news about the past of Uncle Gasim's favorite UN Secretary General came to light, revealing his involvement with the Nazis. After his tenure at the United Nations, Mr. Waldheim went on to become Austria's Prime Minister. Had Mr. Gasim lived long enough, I could have reached out and explained to him that the Secretary General was party to committing horrible acts that resulted in the death of millions of people. I have no idea if he would understand the full gravity of the holocaust and the concentration camps. The one question I am sure he would have raised would be; why would any human being commit such an act on another fellow human being?

Before I even partially recovered from Mr. Allobah the superintendent's false accusations that we plotted to topple the central government of General Numeiri, words spread in school that General Numeiri, the country's president himself, was visiting our school town, Darsail. "Now what is this? Why is he coming here? I think we are getting tangled up into something far much bigger than we could bear. Why on earth does the president of the country want to visit this dusty village?" These were some thoughts that went through my mind when I heard the news.

General Numeiri came to power about four years earlier, in 1969, in a military coup d'état. It was widely believed that the officers who took part in the coup had socialist affiliations. He initially pursued socialist and Pan-Arabist policies, but quickly changed course and turned against his partners. That triggered resentment from a group of army officers who plotted in 1971 to topple his government. The coup failed, so he executed many of the officers who took part in it.

Before the 1969 coup, there were few parties dominating the country's political arena. The Mahdist party was headed by the great-grandson of El Mahdi, the founder of the Mahdist movement of the 1880s, which fought against British rule in Sudan. It happened that Darsail, my school town, was a main hub for supporters of this party. The famous battlefield of Sheekan, fought in the 1880s between the Mahdi forces and the Anglo-Egyptian army, led by Colonel William Hicks (also Known as Hicks Pasha), took place a few kilometers from town.

Since that time, the region remained a Mahdist-party strong hold. It was common knowledge that people did not support General Numeiri's regime. The history of the region, the coup attempt of 1971, and our middle school strike that was branded by the superintendent, Mr. Allobah, as a plot to topple the government, all connected the dots. It became clear to us why the country's president was planning to visit our school town. We thought he was going to show his opponents who was in control, and might also teach them a lesson or two for not supporting his government. As far as our strike was concerned, I found it too horrifying to contemplate the consequences, vis-à-vis what the president had in mind for us, if it was true that he was coming into town because we revolted to topple him. After all, we should blame no one for putting ourselves under the government's radar.

Army logistics showed up at our school to set up base in preparation for the president's arrival. The visit was real. Not only was the president coming into town, he was going to stay at our school. All of my fears were legitimized by the sequence of events culminating in the president showing up in a convoy of army helicopters. The community leaders had made all necessary preparations for celebrations reserved only for people of presidential statue. That day, different tribes performed their respective folklore dances, while knights on horsebacks raced and put a spectacular show. From the way he was received, one could conclude that not everybody was against his government, and that he had many supporters. In the afternoon, our school principal, Mr. Haroun, called us to line up in front of the school gate to greet the president and his entourage on their way over to the school's dining room for lunch. Our principal proudly strode in front of his presidential guests and led them through the school gate as we happily lined up at attention, all wearing our school uniforms of beige shirts and khaki shorts. Standing in full view with our unmistakably noticeable ashy and skinny legs, it appeared as if we were primarily there to take part in a national contest for the ashiest and skinniest legs, rather than to receive the country's president. Nevertheless, we were clearly enjoying the fact that we were in the middle of a historic event in the making. At that point, I realized that we did not seem to be in trouble. Everything looked fine and there was nothing to worry about. I enjoyed the sight of photographers jumping in front of the president and his officials, every few seconds, to take pictures with their big and bulky cameras that produced noisy sounds and spectacularly bright flashlight of no parallel, except in lightning. My sense of ease evaporated for good when the president's bodyguards caught my attention. They were moving and acting strangely. I never met such weird, strong, and tough looking people. They appeared different from the healthy, soft-skinned, harmless, and unintimidating city officials who accompanied Mr. Allobah the superintendent.

I'm confident that my photo image by the side of the president on that date is stored somewhere in the government's archives. Once, I found myself gazing at a photo of President Bill Clinton shaking hands with President J. F. Kennedy. I kept on thinking if there is a positive correlation between being in a photo with a president and later on becoming a president yourself. I wondered what my chances were, and then I slapped my face to wake up from my daydreams.

The president got in his helicopter and left without an incident. People were surprised that he left town without delivering a speech. It was unusual for him to do so. "Why bother visiting a place if he has no intention of talking to the people?", we exclaimed. Rumors spread in school that the president became furious when the presidential reception organizers of the visit, led by Chief Mukhtar, one of the village dignitaries and a well-known Mahdist party supporter, delivered the president a gift comprising of a spear and a Tribulus Terrestris (goathead thorn) made out of iron. Both of these objects were used as weapons during the Sheekan War of the 1880s. Colonel Hicks Pasha scattered goathead metal thorns over the battlefield to cripple the Mahdists' army horses, whereas the Mahdists used spears in the same battle. Some interpreted the gifts as a reminder to the president that, even though he had bombed and killed many Mahdist party supporters in Abba Island, few years earlier, they remain loyal to the Mahdi, come what might. Had Chief Mukhtar and his team gone overboard and offered the General a third gift in the form of *Jibbah Ansariyah* (a type of dress originally worn by the Mahdist Dervishes during battles), our fate could have been sealed. The General could have ordered his air force to bomb our dusty town of Darsail, the same way he bombed Abba Island. Thank God, our punishment was limited to not having the luxury of listening to the president reading a letter, promising to transform our school town into heaven in a blink of the eye, but, of course, without anything happening in a zillion years.

The following incident took place a few years before the president's visit to our middle school. It is related to the incident at Abba

Island I just mentioned in the above paragraph. My dad and I were sitting in front of our shop when a man approached us. He was carrying a spear that was comfortably resting on his shoulder. He was holding it with one hand and a stick with the other. He was also wearing a knife under his sleeve on the arm holding the spear. On the other arm, he was wearing a number of leather-covered charms held together by a thin leather thread. He firmly tied a long white turban around his waist. The two ends of the turban were loosely dangling down a foot or so, touching his knees. There were four large charms knitted on a leather robe hanging diagonally on his chest. I could tell from the way he was dressed that he was a man ready for battle. He was equipped with both physical and spiritual tools he needed for survival on the battlefield. He was someone I could facially recognize, but I did not know his name. He lived in the village of Jadeed, about three miles or so to the south of Kokoland. Upon reaching where we were sitting, he lowered the spear to the ground, piercing it with its sharp tip, as he greeted my dad by calmly calling his name, "Wad al Sharif [son of Sharif] Salaam. Are you alright?" My dad responded by saying, "Alaikum Assalam. Welcome Haj Ghalib." He asked him to come forward and followed that by saying, "I hope nothing is wrong?" By that time, I had already removed myself from the wooden bed my dad and I were sitting on, providing room for the man to sit by my dad's side.

Around that time, there was constant news broadcasting on General Numeiri's army and air force attacking Abba Island, the main base for the Mahdist party followers, located a few hundred kilometers away from Kokoland. The grandson of the Mahdi was said to have fled the area. From my dad's and Haj Ghalib's low tone conversation, I could gather that Haj Ghalib, being a devout Mahdist, was on his way to Abba Island to aid his leader, the grandson of the Mahdi. He equipped himself with everything he needed for battle, or so he thought.

My dad, being a Kokoland resident, had a better chance of knowing what was going on, relative to people living in surrounding villages. In life, everything is relative. He told Ghalib that, according to the news, the Mahdist leader and a few of his followers were captured by the army near the eastern border of the country and were all killed. "It is over," he told him. I was listening attentively to get some idea about what was really happening and how was this man going to fight the government's army with a spear, the same way as in the battles of the 1880s. Haj Ghalib started sobbing as soon as my father finished talking. I could not believe what I was hearing, so I swiftly looked in his direction. I saw him covering his face with both hands and sobbing. I had rarely seen men cry, unless it was a matter of great concern. This looked like one. Haj Ghalib's crying image vividly stuck in my mind for all these years.

In the morning, Haj Ghalib travelled to the city to board a train to Abba Island, his final destination. I did not know if he made it or not, but I heard stories about people dressed up for battle, the same way as Haj Ghalib, being stopped and detained at military posts erected near entrances into the city. They were ordered to return to their villages. I have not heard any news about Haj Ghalib after that day. Many people around Kokoland felt obliged to come to the aid of their leader. Even though the Mahdist movement was crushed by the British in the battle of Omdurman some seventy years earlier, people remained loyal to the movement.

Somehow, many Mahdists did not believe the government's version of the news about the death of their leader who fled Abba Island. A year from Haj Ghalib's incident, my dad travelled to Mecca for pilgrimage. Upon his return, people came over to our house to congratulate him on successfully completing his Haj mission. Some people quietly inquired if he had encountered their leader because it was rumored that some pilgrims claimed to have seen him in Mecca. To their disappointment, my dad told them that he did not meet him, and that the story of his survival was totally untrue, but no one seemed to believe him. Haj Ghalip was definitely among those who remained unconvinced.

As you can tell, things had not changed much around Kokoland. People did not have full concept of government. Preparing for battle by putting up a gear suitable for the eighteen eighties to fight the government in the nineteen seventies was suicidal. In fact, war records show that the Mahdi army was decimated in the battle of

Omdurman, as Mr. Winston Churchill, the former British prime minister, wrote about in his war reports. The Mahdists' spears and arrows were a no match to the British armaments, which included Bazooka Cannons, used in war for the first time ever. The result was so devastating to the Mahdists, causing an outcry from members of the British House of Parliament about the overuse of force involving machine guns, considering what happened an immoral act.

My troubles with General Numeiri never seemed to end. He declared that the nations of Fallata, about whom I have written above, don't belong in Sudan. He decided that they must be shipped back to their respective ancestral homes in West Africa, be that the country of Chad, Nigeria, Cameroon, Niger, Mali, Senegal, or wherever. As I have written earlier, tribes whose ancestors have migrated to Sudan from West Africa were called Fallata. They are primarily comprised of three tribes, the Hausa, the Fulani, and the Kanuri (Borno), my own tribe. That declaration had a disastrous effect on my life as a child, being a minority in Kokoland and an absolute minority at school. I was one of five Kanuri students, and the most senior. As a result, I took the brunt of troubles that we faced. My problem, I was never the timid type of person who shied away from speaking up whenever wronged or undermined.

Students at school happily talked about the prospect of dispatching me to West Africa, a place even my grandfather did not know much about, leave alone me. I had no idea how to deal with this "immigration" issue. I became so vulnerable and my pride was scarred due to the deep sense of rejection. I lived horrible times and was immensely troubled by the situation, not knowing what would happen to me and my family. That was a matter for adults to handle, but I was away at school and my dad was not available to me so I could reach out to him for consolation. I could not tell what were his thoughts on the whole matter. The issue became the talk of the town and students, who constantly brought it up to my attention. The conversations with them varied according to their characters and tribal backgrounds. For example, boys who belonged to the Bibi tribe, which I have written about earlier, were crueler. Very few students shared my agony. Sympathy was a scarce commodity and hard to come by at my middle school.

Some boys told offensive and mocking jokes, while others used words invented in an imaginary language depicting the way Kanuri people, supposedly, spoke, and yet others took the moment as a valuable opportunity to tell me what they had heard at home. They would say things like, "You have taken the land and controlled everything. You must give it back. We need you out of here so we could rest for good." Not only was I worried, but I was also sad, very sad for being rejected in such a humiliating way by people whom I considered as my classmates, friends, buddies, and, in fact, more than that; family, since we all lived in boarding school away from home. The bitter feelings of alienation was awful. So far, forty years have passed, but I still remember those horrible times, vividly. The irony is that both my father and my grandfather were born in the villages of Goni-rih and Um-Garoon, less than three miles from Kokoland. Despite that, we were viewed as aliens to the land and must be repatriated to where we supposedly had come from.

The Bakhit brothers, Bashar and Hargan, lived at the southern edge of Kokoland. For many rainy seasons, my dad dispatched me to their home to ask them if they could come and work at our farm as day laborers, and most of the time they agreed. In fact, I rode my gray donkey alongside them to and from the farm. I enjoyed listening to their stories about wrestling and bravery. Over the years I developed a special respect for them. My dad paid them generously for their service and he, at times, gave them sugar, tea, and coffee for free from the shop when money was harder to come by, especially around the end of the dry season. He also sold them merchandise on credit to pay back after they had harvested and sold their crops.

We were shocked that both of them expressed joy about the prospect of my dad being sent away to West Africa. One night while we were preparing to close the shop, they showed up to buy some groceries. One of them mockingly said, "Wad Al Sharif [son of Sharif]," and, as he was raising a stick he was holding in his hand and pointing to the fabrics on the shelves, he continued, "Are you going to leave all this behind?" My dad did not respond, so the other brother said, "No way he can carry all this merchandise with him." Then my dad told them that they should feel free to own the shop and run it when we were gone. They left; we closed the shop and walked home. None of us said a word to the other. I could tell that my dad was hurt, deeply hurt. I also felt betrayed by the two brothers. I had limited understanding for what was going on, so I waited, but without knowing what was really going to happen. I felt powerless, but never reached out and sought help from my dad for fear of worrying him even more, if he learned that I was preoccupied by the prospect of being chased away from the only place that we had known.

News circulated amongst the community that the Fallata in big cities had gone on strike. Strike again? This word brought chills to my spine every time it was mentioned. I concluded that getting shipped out of the country was a matter of time, since the government would view the strike as a challenge to its authority. That was a far more serious crime than challenging the authority of a middle school principal. Luckily, the strike succeeded because manual labor involving loading and unloading of goods in most parts of the country was handled by the Fallata. Unfortunately, making a living by carrying heavy stuff on ones back is an unsustainable job, but that was the kind of work available to them, considering their lack of education. The country came to a halt, particularly when porters at the main port (Port Sudan) refused to unload ships anchored there. The strike caused the government to back down from its decision to repatriate the Fallata. The issue subsided and eventually died down, leaving unimaginable damage to relationships between the Fallata and the communities they lived in.

The fact is that, today, there are millions of Sudanese of West African backgrounds. It is believed that the Hausa tribe is the third-largest tribe in Sudan, after the Dinka and the Nuba Mountain tribes. Now, with the separation of South Sudan, they probably rank the second-largest tribe in Sudan. Despite these realities, there exists a huge misconception about the country's identity. I think the failure to accept and embrace diversity in Sudan was a factor in the ongoing conflicts in many parts of the country. Alienation of any group from mainstream society can be damaging to the social fabric of a nation by adversely impacting its performance in many fields.

As I have indicated earlier, the Fallata worked mainly in the field of agriculture, kept a low profile, and avoided anything that exposed them. That was the case, especially in rural settings. Those who had access to education got a break and were able to improve their economic conditions, and hence transform their social lives. Sadly, many people in this group preferred to hide their background information, probably thinking that it was too much of a burden to carry around such an identity. Due to social stigma, they abandoned their real tribes altogether and adopted new ones. The problem was that they lived dichotomous double lives by being neither here nor there. Many People could assume a new identity, plant themselves in a new community, and live happily, until it was time for social events such as marriage of a son or a daughter, when relatives from both sides met to take part in the event. The two groups would naturally inquire about each other's backgrounds and that was the time when the jigsaw puzzle was completed. At times, unravelling of hidden facts did result in wedding cancellation. Some people had great pride in their tribal affiliations, heritage, and culture. They would go to great lengths to keep that alive in their families, even if that meant last minute annulment of marrying into tribes they did not approve of.

The government's Fallata repatriation decision, above, created an environment which encouraged some people to take advantage of the situation. Our neighbor, Siraj, colluded with his friends to take over the shop my dad was renting, putting an end to our only source of livelihood and seriously affecting our living condition. I wrote about this incident in the chapter titled, "My Father".

The fact remains that there are hundreds of different tribes in Sudan, but only a few of them claim to have legitimacy, bragging rights, and (false) originality, if you will. Affiliation to any one of these tribes made all the difference between having a decent job, access to power, and a fair share of the economic pie, on one hand, and being unemployed or living in a refugee camp in South Sudan, Dar Fur, or the Nuba Mountains, on the other hand. I must admit that the Fallata aren't the only group of people that are treated disadvantageously under the successive regimes.

Sadly, corruption, tribalism, and discriminatory practices took deep root in government, unfortunately, under the banner of religion. A senior government official recently declared in a public speech he was giving that the Hausa aren't Sudanese. He paid little attention to the ramifications of his statement, which led to rioting and civil commotions in couple of cities, where a few people died. It is as if history repeating itself. In fact, over the years, thousands of Sudanese Fallata abandoned the country altogether and took residence overseas. While in the diaspora, many kept to themselves, shying away from maintaining any form of contacts, and ultimately severing links with home. This is a great loss to everybody. I must also admit that the country's troubles not only impacted the Fallata, but millions of Sudanese from all parts of the country. They either migrated, or became refugees due to wars, economic hardship, and lack of freedom.

Today, institutional powers in Sudan are being eroded due to the way the country was ruled over the past five decades, especially the last thirty years. The corrupt and nepotistic nature of the government led to inefficiency in all aspects of life, and the country is gradually coming to a halt. Therefore, belonging to one of the few ruling tribes no longer guarantees lasting access to power, considering the dwindling opportunities and inefficient use of resources.

Generally speaking, I enjoyed my three years of middle school, apart from the above unpleasant experiences I had gone through. There weren't major issues other than our boarding room being struck by lightning, one time. Luckily, we were in class at that time, except for few students who decided to skip classes. The roof collapsed and two students (Radhi and Suleiman) got away with broken legs when cement blocks fell on them.

Toward the end of my middle school term, I felt more and more confident about myself. I began to use my newly-acquired knowledge to free my mind of fallacies, misconceptions, and misinformation that I believed them to be facts, during my childhood in Kokoland and my primary school years in Darsail. I started questioning what some kids in my primary school had told me many times that God had created the Fallata way after he had finished creating flies, as an indication of their unimportance. I no longer believed that my Kanuri people could turn into hyenas at night or suck out people's guts using black magic. Unlike my time in primary school, I suffered less beating from fights I did not initiate. I had lesser frequency of bandages around my legs because I learned how to take better care of myself as I took bath more often and visited the clinic whenever I injured myself while playing soccer. There was a relative improvement in quality and style of my clothing. They looked more appealing to the eye, if compared to the sharp and irregular pants, shorts, and shirt colors from hell that I used to wear earlier on when I was in primary school. My taste for fashion improved dramatically. Miracles do happen sometimes.

By the time I was in middle school, I already had an opportunity to visit the city and see electric light for the first time. That was a big deal to me. Metaphorically speaking, I got the eye of my mind lit, so I was able to see how city people lived and functioned. I was able to maintain my class rank among the top five students, and that gained me recognition from my classmates. As I indicated earlier, on the last day of school in Darsail primary, we lined up in the school yard to receive our final results. The principal and teachers called our names according to our class ranks, first calling students with the highest grade totals and ending with those with the lowest. Everybody in the entire school saw and heard everyone's results. To many, the whole exercise was humiliating beyond imagination. This was one of the reasons I worked hard to avoid embarrassment, besides I was motivated by other factors such as progressing to a new environment with less conflicts, fights, and beatings. Working hard became part of my system and I continued that in middle school. I enjoyed the fact that I did well in class and was able to beat my competitors, though not physically.

In middle school I started to get more confident about school in general, but most importantly, I received less criticism from the community for the simple fact that I was attending school. I also got more respect because I was viewed as a model, if you will, for a well-behaved kid. The refusal of some Kanuri parents to send their children to school stemmed from their belief that schools would turn them into disrespectful and disobedient sons and daughters. They believed that they would develop snobbish mannerisms once they could read, write, and speak the country's official language; Arabic. Parents also feared that schools would teach children to smoke, drink, commit sins, and hence become bad Muslims. Some people argued that once a Kanuri kid got educated, he would abandon his ancestral heritage and stop speaking the Kanuri language. In fact I speak the Kanuri language as fluent as anyone still living in Kokoland. They could not have been more wrong. Nevertheless, unlike many people, I am lucky that I am under no duress to abandon my Kanuri language and heritage for the sake of gaining recognition from any mainstream culture, whatsoever. I don't think that maintaining one's heritage and gaining recognition from others are two mutually exclusive things. I strongly believe that the beauty of life is in its diversity, for it is that what makes us all unique in our own ways.

In middle school, I came to the realization that most of what Habib, the master bully at Darsail primary school, had told us was nothing, but misinformation mixed with pure fantasies. He told us that the nuclear bomb was the size of a grain of pearl millet. I stopped believing that because I had the opportunity to read about and see images of nuclear bombs and mushroom clouds in a magazine cover. I also listened to the news about nuclear tests being carried out in the Pacific Ocean by nuclear powers such as America, Russia, and France. Middle school was time to remove all the nonsense that had polluted my mind in primary school. It was time for trusting what I hear, but after full verification. In fact it was time for true liberation of the mind. Middle school was my Renaissance Era.

CHAPTER 14

High School: A Threat to Village Status Quo

My transition to high school in 1976 was problematic in the sense that it brought new challenges to the already complicated relationship I had with my community. As I indicated earlier, the mere transition from primary school to middle school was a big deal; therefore, moving to high school deserved all the fuss that you can imagine. I took the high school exams with no guarantees that I would progress to the next level due to the high competition for limited number of seats available.

Khor Taggat was the premiere high school in our province and also one of three top schools in the country. Those of us who earned a seat in this school thought that we had conquered the world. We could not have been more wrong. With due respect, no one should claim academic invincibility for merely attending high school, but, as I have written on a few occasions, everything in life is relative. I was dealing with many layers of misconceptions, which I can only attribute to knowledge-scarcity at that time; a situation that made the few who had access to it to believe that they were chosen or something. Exposure to different living environments is important for appreciating other's view point. Lack of such exposure was my biggest problem, so I was laboring under the heavy shortsightedness of, "This is it." Then again, "This is it" could be a blessing, even though in disguise. I did not know that some things even existed, and for that reason I did not miss a lot. However, I was faced with big dilemma later on in my life when I had the opportunity to see and compare between both sides of the coin; Kokoland and the rest of the world

There was a strong dichotomy between my realities in Kokoland and the material I learned in high school. Books continued to be my main source of information. Through them, I could draw mental pictures about some of the things that were happening around the world, even though much of that did not make sense to me. I was left with many gaps to fill; something that I found quiet confusing.

There were different student associations available for membership, based on individual preferences. Most of them were academic, focusing on science, social sciences, arts, music, poetry, and culture. There were also associations for those interested in politics. The school was a battleground for recruiting young cadres to join political parties later on, when they went to college or transitioned into working life. Students were recruited and flooded with information, which was incompatible with their realities on the ground. I was not clued about certain jargons that some students repeated, such as communism, pluritaria, bourgeoisie, and dialectical. I doubt it if they understood the full extent of the words' meanings. I revisited them later on in life and also learned new ones such as perestroika and glasnost; concepts that were mainly associated with Mr. Mikhail Gorbachev, the former Soviet Union statesman. There were legitimate questions that passed through my mind. Who in Kokoland needed perestroika and glasnost? Besides; perestroika and glasnost from what? Do you remember how unprepared I was for our hapless middle school strike when we called for, "No separation for one nation?" I was equally unprepared for high school "perestrika and glasnost." On the other hand, I must admit that those high school organizations did play a role in expanding my horizon and desire for acquiring knowledge.

One student, named Abdeen, fascinated the entire school with his mastery of such terms, which he used in general conversations to support his argument. He would lecture us about classless, moneyless, and stateless social order, structured around common ownership, when we could be discussing how to cut down grass around our boarding house to prevent mosquito breeding so we could get a break from malaria attacks. Our immediate need would be to clear the area from goathead plant. Abdeen could not have been more pretentious and elitist; practicing both at the wrong time and place, just for the sake of it. In spite of that, I admired his patience and willingness to attentively listen to others' opposing views. Some people were admired for the simple fact that they could put together complex phrases, which may translate to a whole lot of nothing in real life. It is absolutely fine to exercise such fantasies at high school, but when fantasies, coupled with political party affiliation, becomes a visa toward holding senior posts in governments, then we have a serious problem on our hands. This must be true elitism, I guess. In fact, today, many of the country's leaders belong to that 1970s' generation of high school students. They had enlisted under some party banner, went on to join the work force, and finally implemented an ideological manifesto as a foundation for governing the nation, with the view toward a, supposedly, prosperous future. Forty years later, the outcome of those policies proved to be disastrous for the country, as the entire world can attest to that.

In high school, I seriously believed that I had too much knowledge under my belt. I must admit that I, like many of my friends, had also suffered from the plight of elitism, relative to my environment. I thought I could speak with confidence to the community about the round shape of the planet earth. My confidence stemmed from reading about Christopher Columbus. I read some pieces about space exploration and the fact that America had placed a man on the moon. I learned about gravity laws and concluded that the "eureka" principle was a piece of cake; a knowledge that was augmented by the fact that the name of my class was Galileo; named after Galileo Galilei. That was too much load of knowledge for one person. It could last me many lives over. I thought such talent would go to waste if I kept it to myself, so I decided, with absolute confidence, to share some of it with my community back in Kokoland. Was I asking for trouble? You bet. On another note, you must agree with me that I had come a long way in my understanding of what was going on around me, particularly if you look at times when I mixed between

Neil Armstrong and Yuri Gagarin. Then again, why would anyone living in Kokoland need to know who the two men were?

The problem was that our high school level of pretentious elitism was viewed by many people in Kokoland as a threat to the status quo. We wrongly assumed that people were no match to our mastery of knowledge and outlook on life. We threatened them with our attitude, and they, naturally, resented that conduct, only fiercely. Due to absence of common ground for a civil dialogue, simple disagreements were invariably addressed through fights. Actually, there was a hidden war going on between us, high school students, and adults in Kokoland. Our efforts to introduce new ideas to help improve lives in the community were mostly torpedoed down or undermined, to say the least. The problem was that we foolishly played the, "We know it better" role, which left people no choice, but to resist our arrogance. Personally, it took me many years of schooling and life experience to grasp and appreciate concepts such as team work, involvement, collaboration, participation, respect, and understanding other people's view point.

My high school friend Jabra talked elaborately to people about Pan-Africanism when they hardly knew anything about their own country of residence, therefore knowing anything about the African continent was a stretch. Explaining the meaning of pan could have been a night mare, so pan-Africanism was certainly out of the question. To begin with, I doubt that my friend Jabra fully understood what that meant, anyway. May be we should not have complained about being smacked on the face whenever people felt that it was the best way to make us understand.

My other friend, Jalha, who went on to become a renowned Sudanese lawyer, often went back to visit Kokoland during college breaks. He frequently visited the borough of Keekah to have a local drink with people he had nothing much in common, anymore. When they got drunk, he gave them lectures on English law, making references to *the Magna Carta* and principles such as *ratio decidendi and obiter dicta*, and they, in turn, reciprocated by telling him about the best hunting grounds for fat and juicy squirrels. Of course, what mattered was that they had a drink and a nice talk, but how relevant was that to one another was less important. As you can tell, Kokoland was at a crossroads and a melting pot for different branches of knowledge, stretching from best techniques for hunting squirrels, all the way to laws enacted by the House of Parliament in Great Britain. Sadly, my friend Jalha died prematurely in an accident. Somebody pushed him into a stream, and he drowned. He was the prosecution lawyer handling a murder case in the city, and it was believed that the individuals accused of the murder were the ones who drowned him.

The general view held by adults about us, high school students, could be summarized in the following statement, "Children of today care about nothing but play, talk nonsense, and disrespect their elders. They have no manners at all. They are good for nothing. Absolutely nothing." I guess they were wrong. During school breaks, we organized community workshops to share our freshly acquired knowledge from school. In one of such meetings, I enthusiastically spoke about my favorite piece of information; "America's moon landing." My speech made many people furious, worried, and uncomfortable, at a minimum level. They thought it was blasphemous to even contemplate such an idea. They had no terms of reference for things like that, so they resorted to threats to get at me for offending them. In fact everything that was beyond the grasp of people was considered holy and should not be tampered with. For example, lunar and solar eclipses were phenomena that people responded to by sacrificing thank offerings to God. One man commented by saying, "Landing on the moon? What landing on the moon are you talking about? You people better not do such things. My fear is that one day you, with your *shalaga* [uninvited interference], will end up poking the eye of something that has been sleeping for a long, long time. You will end up waking that thing and, at that time, nobody will have the chance to escape to safety. My advice to you is to go and get something else that is more useful to do. That will be better for all of us." He addressed us as if it was we who had landed on the moon and ran the risk of stirring up trouble. The lunar landing remains disputed even today. We were truly out of touch with reality in Kokoland.

We also spoke about WWII. We told people that more than fifty million souls were lost during the war. Once again, this story did not go down very well. People expressed disgust that was visible on their faces and through their body language, but there were limited arguments from the crowd, compared to the moon story. They might not have had any comprehension of the number fifty million. One man told me that the British authorities came by his village some time ago (most probably around WWII) and ordered every man to work for free. He said they were told to clear a nearby trail from shrubs and trees, widen it, and make it navigable for the British army heading to the Abyssinian (Ethiopian) war front. He told me he was not happy about not being rewarded for his efforts. I guess that was the extent of his understanding of WWII events and how it affected him and people in nearby villages. In any case, I did not know why he complained to me, so he left me wondering.

Community elders perceived us high school students as antiauthority. The two police officers were the highest authority in town. Once, I came home on a school break and found one of my relatives, Haj Yarwa, who lived in a nearby village, at our house. A neighbor accused one of his sons of stealing a gram, or so, of gold. I accompanied him to the local police station where his son was being held in custody. The station was comprised of three rooms; an office, a court room, and a prison cell. We found Sergeant Gassas beating up the boy to extract a confession. He did not need any written laws to follow. He carried out his policing duties according to his whims. Some Kokoland residents also showed up at the station at the same time we arrived there. They heard the news, so they went inquiring to find out if the boy had confessed. That was none of their business, but what else could they do in Kokoland? The boy was already being condemned by Gassas, so everyone else went by his verdict. No one dared to challenge his authority. The boy's father and I approached Sergeant Gassas and I asked him if he was beating the boy because he had confessed of stealing the gold. My question did not go down well at all with him. He responded angrily by shaking his right hand's index finger and getting it closer to my face, as if he was intending to poke me in the eye, forcing me to tilt my head backwards. He said, "You shut up or I will lock you up with him. I don't want any *falfasa* with you. [The word *falfasa* means philosophy, but localized, as the sound suggests]. This high school thing is messing up your heads." Obviously, Sergeant Gassas had already formulated a negative view about me and other high school students. All it took was a simple question to trigger that wave of anger. He did not like the idea that I had accompanied the boy's father and spoken on his behalf. To Gassas, I had overstepped my boundaries and challenged his absolute authority, so he had to tell me off with unequivocal firmness by threatening to jail me, if need be. We withdrew from the scene, went back home, and told my dad about what had happened. My dad left to see Sergeant Gassas, who complained to him about how disrespectful I was. My dad told him, "You know how children behave nowadays." That statement worked like magic in appeasing the sergeant who sensed that my dad was in his camp. It was enough to bring closure to the case. My dad secured the release of the boy after the sergeant satisfied himself that the boy was not party to the disappearance of the gold. Haj Yarwa, filled with anger, sadness, and helplessness, accompanied his son and went back to his village. There could have been many scenarios for the disappearance of that gram of gold. The old lady could have hid it and forgot where she hid it. She could have buried it somewhere inside her hut and the earth claimed it, as it was always believed when it came to precious metals buried in the ground. There was the possibility that a house mouse could have dragged it to its burrow in a corner of the hut.

Five years after the incident with Sergeant Gassas, I returned to Kokoland from the city and went to visit my aunts and uncles in a nearby village. A man came by the village and said to my uncles, "The government man is no more, they said." He was a holy man and a leader in the community, so he conveyed the message by giving hints only, leaving us to look elsewhere for clarifications about what had really happened. Such people did not want their names to be associated with gossips and tell-tales, which were considered great sins. Nobody urged him to expand on his statement. In fact, what he meant to say was that someone killed Sergeant Gassas, the police officer. We waited until another person came from Kokoland and confirmed what the holy man had told us earlier. He said that Gassas was stabbed to death, the night before. The Sergeant passed by Kokoland's main playground and found a few young men there, including Mudawi and Bilal. He got into an argument with them, and Mudawi stabbed him in the heart and killed him, instantly. There was an ongoing animosity between Gassas and Mudawi over a girl. Gassas, being a police officer who held all powers imaginable, wanted things his way. Everything he did was under the law, only that laws of his own creation. He was not used to being challenged until that fatal night.

The news about the death of Sergeant Gassas, being a government man, had to be relayed to the authorities in the city. His body also needed to be transported there. The incident took place during the middle of the week, so there were no means of transportation to the city, until Friday. An owner of a horse-drawn cart, used for moving agricultural goods, was called to Kokoland to transport Gassas's body to the village of *Safarog* (boomerang), a few miles away, where a main road to the city passed by. The irony was that Gassas's body and Mudawi, the young man who committed the crime, were carried on the same cart, side by side, one sitting upright and the other stretched and covered with a white sheet. They got to the village and waited until sunset before a truck showed up and took them to the city. There was another twist to this incident. The village of Safarog happened to be the same village of my relative, Haj Yarwa, whose son was beaten up by Gassas about five years earlier. People believed that Gassas's body lying there all day in the open by the roadside, a matter of a stone's throw away from Haj Yarwa's house, was a message from God answering his prayers about the injustice his son had endured at the hands of Gassas. Also the fact that his body was not buried for two days was another sign of a bad last chapter in the Sergeant's life. Many people held the view that he was a very abusive man and they felt relieved that he was gone. They thought he lived and died horribly.

Mudawi, somehow, avoided the death sentence. He spent some time in jail and got released. Believing that he had paid for the crime he had committed, he returned to live in Kokoland. Someone tipped him that the authorities in the city were looking to re-arrest him because they reopened his case. Mudawi was a cop killer who miraculously skipped the death penalty. Having his case reopened meant one and only one thing; he would be hung as soon as the authorities laid hand on him. Double jeopardy was not unheard of in Kokoland. Mudawi disappeared and no one saw him again or heard of his whereabouts.

Airing an opinion such as the comments I made about the beating of the boy to confess were always viewed by those associated with the government as interference with their jobs. That might have been the case, but, even for us in Kokoland, witnessing that level of abuse was a difficult thing to be silent about. I think any reasonable person would express discontent. Speaking up against injustice is not something that one always calculates its consequences. Upon graduating from college a few years later, I got a job in the city and had to look for private accommodation away from campus. I put up with a group of people from my district. One person in the group, named Sanjak, worked for the secret police. That was during the ruling period of General Numeiri, the country's president who came to visit our middle school a few years earlier. One night, Sanjak played a cassette, which contained insults and mocking of the president. After listening, I commented, "How come you are a secret police and you let us listen to material that is insulting to the president? His immediate response was, "Ya, you shut up or I turn it in and tell that it is you who own it." What was I thinking? How much more naive could anyone be?

Violent incidents in and around Kokoland were rare, but bloody in the event they took place. The community was divided between farmers and animal herders. Conflict between the two groups erupted over grazing rights. There used to be an unwritten code that governed the relationship between them. The code implied that farmers would allow animals to graze on crop residues in the fields, after the harvest, on condition that animal owners would prevent their herds from breaking into farms to graze, as long as they were not declared open. These rules became obsolete due to environmental factors such as desertification. Over time and due to lesser grazing areas, more and more incidents of animal owners, out of desperation, intentionally allowing their herds graze crop fields. Fighting broke out when farmers resisted or attempted to drive the animals to the authorities in town to keep in a fenced-up area, especially built for this purpose, until the farm loss was evaluated. The animal owner would go and release his animals, leaving few of them behind to be sold to compensate the farmer. The community depended primarily on local arbitration to solve problems. The central government was not always available to intervene. Its role was mostly limited to tax collection or, if you will, taxation without representation.

President Numeiri (again) decided to conduct military maneuvers (exercises) in the forest of Sheekan, a few kilometers from Kokoland. Sheekan forest, as previously described, was the same location where the Mahdi and the Anglo-Egyptian armies fought the battle of Sheekan, some ninety years earlier. The government did not conduct any orientation or campaign before the event to familiarize the local population with what maneuvers meant or entailed so they and their animals could stay away. "The government decides and people abide." That was the government's modus operandi.

A local sheikh, named Abu Kalam, claimed that the spot where the maneuvers were taking place as his ancestral land. There were no documents to support his claim and it was basically land ownership by laying hands. The sheikh used his powers of sheikhdom to allot pieces of land on the edges of the forest to the locals to farm. A portion of the harvest was given to him as *futra*, which was some form of sharecropping. He made a living off the land without lifting a finger. Local farmers resented that and felt bitter about being exploited.

As you can imagine, sheikh Abu Kalam had many enemies, considering the fact that most people were farmers. Someone went and reported to him the news about the presence of thousands of soldiers not too far from the village. The sheikh, being the land owner by default, decided that it was unbecoming for any entity to conduct activities in the area without his consent or permission, or so he thought. Accompanied by few of his aides, he rode his donkey and, together, they headed to the forest where the national army was conducting the exercises. What really happened when they got there was anyone's guess. The story circulated around the region was that the sheikh, upon reaching the place, asked to speak to someone, so he was directed to a tent. He got there, greeted everyone, and asked to talk to the person in charge. A man in uniform stepped forward and asked him if he could be of any help. Sheikh Abu Kalam told him that the land belonged to him. He had inherited it from his ancestors and, as such, the national army had no business conducting any activity on it, so they must leave. The officer looked puzzled, thought for a moment, and told Sheikh Abu Kalam to wait for a minute. He went inside the tent, came out with a piece of paper, and handed it to the sheikh. He pointed to another tent and told him to go and hand the note to anybody there, and the sheikh did exactly as he was told. He handed the note to an officer, who spent few seconds reading it. He then told Abu Kalam to dismount his donkey. The sheikh would soon find out about the content of the note and if his claim to the forest of Sheekan was appreciated by the national army establishment or not. The officer ordered two of his soldiers to pin the sheikh down and a third one to flog him ten lashes. They released him after that, leaving him in total shock from what he had experienced. His companions were also horrified to see their leader being handled in such a humiliating manner. He was ordered to leave the place immediately and never come back. Sheikh Abu Kalam went to give orders or negotiate with General Numeiri's army, at minimum. Instead, he encountered something else that was not in his wildest of dreams. The story spread like wildfire in the community. People were excited about the lesson taught to the sheikh that there existed a more powerful authority than his. He was no longer that invincible man. The incident, on one hand, exposed the man's weakness, but, most importantly, on the other hand, it emboldened the people after realizing that there was a new kid in the block. Not only Sheikh Abu Kalam became fully aware of how much damage the national army people could do to his reputation, but he also became certain that his invincibility, as far as the local people were concerned, had dissipated forever. From that incident onward, he became subdued and carefully calculative of his future moves. It was very possible that sharecropping farmers gave him lesser quantities, or nothing at all of *futra* portion of their harvest, without the sheikh daring to take any action against them. I think the story could partly be true, but I doubt it if the sheikh was pinned down to the ground and was lashed the same way we were being lashed in my primary school in Darsail. He could have been rouged up a little bit. The story might have contained some exaggeration, dramatization, and a wishful thinking from the many farmers who held grudges against Sheikh Abu Kalam. Most probably, people spiced it up to blow it out of proportion, before passing it on.

This incident was indicative of the the place's remoteness from authorities in the center. Many people had little understanding for limits of their power and where that should stop. Sheikh Abu Kalam's case was not different from Haj Ghalib's, who wanted to travel to Abba Island to support his leader in the fight against General Numeiri's army. The problem was that the central government, also, did not think it was obliged to take into consideration local norms that governed communities. Lashing a local chief would certainly not help keep law and order in the area. It would diminish his authority and create a power vacuum. The government was too far away to enforce local laws.

In another incident, a local judge sentenced a farmer to three-month imprisonment as punishment for a crime he had committed. The farmer stood there, thought for a moment, and then said to the judge, "Only one month, imprisonment." The judge, with a puzzled expression on his face, inquired, "Why one month?" The farmer responded, "Because the rainy season will soon be upon us, so if I go to prison for three month I will not be able to peal enough peanuts in time for the planting season." Obviously, this man did not fully understand the concept of punishment. Even though ignorance of the law is no excuse, I wonder if there should have been some leeway for people like this farmer.

I think, girls are the best part of high school life. Despite my lousy sense of fashion that I have described above, Kokoland girls sang songs of praise and poems about me. The only reason for this wrong conclusion could have been their equally low standard for good fashion. I just could not stop believing the good things they said about me. There was one particular song about my green and white striped shirt. That was the fashion of the time, and I was the first person to introduce it to Kokoland. I remember wearing that shirt most of the time to take full advantage of all the attention that I could harness from girls. My peers were envious and unhappy about that. Fame came with a price that usually involved fights, which I did not shy away from whenever they were brought upon me. Girls are worth fighting for, anytime.

Handkerchiefs, embroidered with silk and hearts with arrows piercing through them, neatly stitched on the corners, were easy to come my way. They were given to me as gifts. That was a sign of love without limits. I was famous; you know. My situation was not different from artists who come up with a single album that propels them to the limelight of fame. Before that light fades away, they will try to take advantage of the opportunity by branching out into everything marketable under the sun. I could have invented myself a product line in Kokoland had it not been for my limited exposure; besides, who would buy them, anyway?

I folded my handkerchief in a triangular shape and put it in the front pocket of my shirt, making sure that the heart shape was always visible for everyone to see. I frequently pulled it out of my pocket, purportedly to wipe my face, but I overdid that, of course. My intention was to expose the heart and keep it at eye level of the person whom I wanted to impress or score points against so he could clearly observe and take notice. Those were usually my top competitors. That way, none of my teenage peers could doubt the appreciation I received from girls. By implication, and also through my conduct, I was able to silently declare to my peers that I was in love and that the handkerchief, with a heart on it, was a testimonial gift given to me by a girl.

During school breaks, my friend Kabsoon and I anxiously waited for the sunset so we could meet to exchange notes about girls. We would sit in the moonlight and talk about our day's imaginary adventures with them. Kokoland was a tiny village where everyone's move was fully exposed. It was also a very conservative society, so talking to girls was not easy. We saw girls from time to time when we gathered at parties, and that was usually during the harvest season when most marriages took place. Nevertheless, Kabsoon and I talked about them when we both knew damn well that we were lying to one another. We would spend the day attending to our shops, but at night we took turns to tell each other stories. The truth of the matter was that those were, by all accounts, imaginary stories about imaginary girls. They were nothing more than embellished fake fantasies of high magnitude.

As I mentioned previously, I shared my newly acquired high school knowledge with my community. Some people appreciated that and finally approved the school path I had taken, while others did not and continued to antagonize me. The latter group was frustrated because they could do nothing about it. Once, I told my favorite story about the global shape of the earth to a group of my dad's friends. I said, "Because the earth is so round, I can literally walk in the direction of Halfa (a village three miles west of Kokoland) and, if I keep on walking, after some time, I will be right back here, exactly where I began my journey." Magic, huh? I told them, "On my way I will pass by Chad and Nigeria (westward country names they were familiar with), pass the sea of darkness, cross America, and pass another bigger sea of darkness. God willing, if I am alive, I will continue walking and after years I will come back right here, but from the side of Alloubah (a village to the eastern side of Kokoland)." I continued, "Similarly, if I start walking toward Alloubah in the east, I will pass the Salty Sea (the Red Sea), Saudi Arabia, India, and a so big body of water (the Pacific Ocean) that takes planes many hours to cross. Then I will pass America again, Nigeria, and Chad, but this time from the western sides of these countries, and end up right here entering Kokoland from the western, Halfa, side."

When I finished talking, some people shook their heads in fascination and murmured religious words such as God is great. Some kept quiet and had nothing to say. A few of them expressed anger and the rest looked puzzled. One man named Abu Mala, known for his rejection of everything not supernatural, reacted differently to my story. He got up abruptly, picked his pair of goat-skin shoes stitched by Liman the local shoemaker, banged them against each other to shake off some wet mud hanging on the bottom, before dropping them on the ground to wear them. He got disgusted with my blasphemous speech, so he decided to leave the place. While doing that, he muttered something like, "When one of you talks, he better talk sense or else shut up. The earth is round he said, what nonsense." He angrily stormed out of the straw shade and hurriedly walked away.

I used the same analogy to explain the variation in prayer times between Kokoland and Khartoum, the capital city. I told them that because of the global nature of the earth, there were different time zones at different places and that was why the radio always announced to the public to observe such differences between regions. I stopped short of telling them that the sun is stationary and that our earth is the one that revolves around itself and the sun. How could anyone dispute a given fact such as the sun rising up from the east and setting down in the west? Tampering with settled facts about the sun would be too much of thinking out of the box, and I could have alienated the moderates and, certainly, the extremes. My very belief in God could be questioned. Who knows. I could have risked being beaten up to bring me back to my senses.

In another incident, I remember making few of my dad's friends uncomfortable when I told them that cutting down trees would reduce the amount of rainfall and the farmlands would turn into a desert. They rejected my argument by asking me the question, "Fine, then how do you expect us to farm and feed our families without cutting down trees?" Nobody believed or accepted my school-based theories even though there was tangible evidence for people to see. Every few years, farmers would abandon their lands due to fall in crop yield. They would pick up a new area, clear the trees, and farm for a few years, only to repeat the same process after that. In a matter of a few decades, the entire region was turned into a desert.

My dad's face lit up with pride whenever I told people these types of stories, for he also had his own motives. Such talks elevated his status in the community and he could indirectly prove his point about sending his children to school, even though against the advise of many members of our own family and the Kanuri community, at large.

Writing letters on behalf of people also gave my dad great satisfaction. Our shop was a magnet to Kanuri community members who came to shop for groceries and, sometimes, seek my help with writing letters for them. Every market day (Fridays and Mondays), a few people came by and asked me to write down some secret messages to send away to relatives somewhere in the country. There was no mail service in Kokoland, so these letters were mainly hand-delivered. The person seeking my help and I would sit in a corner of the shop, away from everyone, in observance of secrecy and confidentiality. He would then tell me his stories and problems, which could range from a simple greeting message to more serious matters relating to marriage, sickness, disputes, money, or any other social issues. He would speak to me in Kanuri language and I would listen attentively until my brain could cram no more. I would hint to him to stop, and then we would both, simultaneously, turn our eyes to the paper in front of me. I would embark on writing what he had just told me. At the same time, he would be closely and quietly following with his eyes the trail of writing left by the pen in my hand, moving his head from right to left, in absolute synchronization, as I poured down the message on the sheet of paper. After exhausting what was in my mind, I would look up at him, signaling that I was ready for another round of listening comprehension in Kanuri language. We would repeat the process many times, depending on the severity of the issues, until I finished writing everything he had to say. After that, I would read over each paragraph written in Arabic and conduct an instantaneous translation back into Kanuri language to get his confirmation and be sure that I had captured what he wanted to communicate. Remember that people spoke to me in Kanuri language, whereas I wrote the letters in Arabic. They did understand little Arabic, but not to the extent of expressing themselves, so I was very careful with my translation and transformation of their thoughts between the two languages. As I wrote the letters, I also bore in mind the language skills of the recipients at the other end. They could be illiterates as well, and might need assistance from someone else to read and translate for them.

There was a huge risk of messages getting lost in translation. Mischaracterization of words could have grave consequences as was the case in the following instance. A man received a letter, but because he could not read, he sought help from someone whose reading skills and understanding of the language were limited, even though he would not admit it. He sort of read the letter and translated it to mean, "Someone dear to the receiver of the letter had died." The sentence supposed to read, "We are all fine and happy." You can only imagine the ramification of such wrong conclusion, therefore I took these factors into account when I wrote the letters. I tried my level best to use simple words for the recipients and their interpreters to understand correctly.

After reading over the letters, people would usually express their satisfaction with the service I had rendered by smiling and looking in my dad's direction. He would be busy serving customers, but he always stopped and asked them if I had captured their thoughts and committed them to paper. They invariably gave him positive feedback and he reciprocated with a wide smile, implying his approval that all was in order. My dad and I shared the credit for providing service to the community, which appreciated both of us. That was just and fair, since the letter writing skills I had gained from school was a fruit of my dad's decision to send me to school, in the first place.

People talked about the letters that I had written for them at social gatherings, so more people showed up at our shop to seek help. I did feel overwhelmed at times. In one instance, I tried to find an excuse for not writing a letter by telling one man that I left my pen at home. I wanted to have some time for myself to wander in the market, since it was a market day with lots of activities going on. My dad scolded me by telling me that the writing skills I had was a gift from God that I must share with others any time they asked for help. That statement registered well in my mind; besides, I did not want the good letter writing reputation that I had built over time to be tainted by some foolish act of my own making. Letter writing had certainly enhanced my special place among the Kanuri community in the villages.

A few of my high school friends and I came up with the idea of running a program titled "Rural Community Development." We geared up our development efforts toward reducing illiteracy among adults, primarily focusing on women who never had the chance to learn. We also wanted to organize plays and theatrical activities in an attempt to help the community to do away with negative practices. Choosing the venue for our school-break activities was a no-brainer. There were two venues to choose from, the boys' school and the girls' school, so it was a very easy decision for any high school kid to make. Besides; women of different age groups would feel more comfortable coming to the girls' school.

People in Kokoland generally appreciated our efforts. However, some saw that as a challenge to the status quo and an effort to change their way of life. They also saw in us rebels who were trying to expose children, especially girls, to new ideas and turn them against their parents. The first thing we did was to convince the community to change Kokoland's indecent name and choose a more respectable one. As I have described in the first chapter, we failed miserably in our many different attempts to do that. In fact, I recently went back to Kokoland, after thirty years, and found the same old ugly name still in use.

Around the same time we were organizing community development programs, the government was also encouraging citizens to take membership in the official government party. Its representatives in Kokoland used religion to silence voices expressing different viewpoints, branding them as dissidents and enemies of the state. That has always been the government's approach to discredit the several military coups d'etats carried out against it. It's readily available message for radio broadcast was, "The coup executors are communist perpetrators." That was enough propaganda to turn the public against organizers of coups. People were suspicious of the word communism, even though they had little knowledge of what it stood for, so religion was conveniently used by governments to convince everybody that communism was a bad thing for their belief system. The fact of the matter was that local government representatives used religion for their own personal benefits by undermining any efforts seen as likely to upset Kokoland's social and teeny economic status quo that was based on a few goats, cows, and seasonal self-subsistent agricultural products, which they fully controlled.

Our community gatherings were very messy. We usually informed people about the meeting agendas and topics for discussion, ahead of time, but they shunned them aside and each speaker talked about his personal concerns and what he deemed more important. Abood was one man notoriously known for bringing irrelevant topics to meetings. On one occasion, we met to discuss how to organize a competition to celebrate Independence Day. Abood raised his hand and asked for a chance to speak, and everyone murmured, "Here we go again." He stood up and spoke in an angry tone of voice, "Last year you told us you landed a man on the moon. That was a lie. Now you are here again putting your hands in your pockets ready to tell us another lie. I don't have time for your nonsense." According to Kokoland's behavioral code, putting hands in the pocket was a sign of arrogance, the kind of which usually reserved for those who wore pants and shirts, unlike the rest of the population who mostly wore a local garment called *Jallabiya*. Pants were associated with sophistication and elitism, so people were always suspicious of the motives of those who wore them.

Breathing rapidly and fuming with anger for no particular reason whatsoever, Abood decided to abandon the meeting, while making a hand gesture to everyone to follow him out of the meeting venue. He thought that people were just wasting their time by sitting and listening to us. To his disappointment, nobody left the meeting. People laughed as he walked away, which made him even more furious. He muttered some cussing words as he disappeared as fast as he could, as if he had a more important engagement to attend. A few hours later, we found him sleeping under the neem tree, in front of the flour mill, by the side of his friend, Abu Ali, Kokoland's blacksmith. So much for, "I don't have time for your nonsense." Abu Ali sat under that tree and received village women who brought damaged aluminum cooking pots to be fixed. That was Abood's favorite pastime location.

There weren't many artisans in Kokoland. Teerab was another blacksmith who lived in a nearby village, but he sadly committed suicide for an unknown reason. Suicide incidents were very rare. The only other incident that I knew of, while growing up, was about a young girl who was forced against her will to marry a man her father's age. She burnt herself to death.

The flour mill in Kokoland was, and it is still today, the only fabricated object operated mechanically. It was the main place for action, as men and women from Kokloland and the villages around brought grains for grinding. The mill was also a parking place for lorries that came from the city. People gathered around them to greet passengers and listen to news from the city.

One of my relatives, named Heeran, was a shoemaker. He stitched cow-leather shoes under a shade in his house in a nearby village. On market days, he would come to Kokoland and display his merchandise for sale in front of Guaiz's shop, and then sit and stitch more shoes. He basically had a monopoly over the market, until Chinese-made plastic shoes flooded Kokoland. He could not compete anymore, so he decided to do something else. He got himself involved in politics. Heeran, even though illiterate, was instinctively outspoken, ambitious, and had possessed leadership qualities. Being a Kanuri, he spoke the language very well, but not the official language, Arabic, which was used in his new political career. Ironically, people in the village nominated him as their spokesperson to represent them in meetings with government officials. He regularly visited the city to participate in party conferences. I had no idea what he learned from those conferences, or what messages he relayed to the community, upon his return. In the Kanuri language, there were no slogans such as anti-imperialism, anti-capitalism, dictatorship, backwardness, etc.; terms used by government officials to undermine their opponents. Heeran lacked political vocabulary and skills in both languages, so, I think, he did a magnificent job confusing people beyond imagination.

I listened to him in a couple of occasions while trying his level best to articulate issues such as voting rights. People sat down and attentively listened to his speech with great admiration for the simple fact that he could stand and talk in front of them. When he had done talking, people gave him a prolonged round of applause. What he did was he basically jumbled up few words he thought he had mastered, but neither did he understand their true meanings, nor could he explain why he was using them. Middle and high school kids joked about his speeches, but he did not mind that. From a shoe maker to a renowned politician over night! It was all worth it. He presented his findings to people who grabbed it and ran away with it, each person reaching his own conclusion about the, supposedly, an important political message on voting rights. Does Heeran seem like some politicians who will say anything to get elected? You bet. Heeran was not harmful, at all. He simply enjoyed the attention he was getting from everyone, so he did whatever it took to stay under the limelight for as long as he could.

One man, named Saleh, was envious of Heeran's newly adopted profession in politics because that gave him an opportunity to mingle and rub shoulders with government officials in the city, despite knowing little about what he was doing. Saleh was of the opinion that Heeran was too ambitions and was operating out of his station in life, so he decided to remind him of who he was and his, not so distant, past. He insinuated to Heeran, but in an advising tone, that he would be better off if he went back to his original trade of shoe making. Heeran told him off that he was not honest in his advice and what he did was none of his business.

Another man named Haj Mardi also got involved in politics. He religiously followed one political party. The military-civilian cycle brought election campaigns to Kokoland and its vicinities every time a military government was toppled and elections were organized to form a civilian government. Around election times, healthy looking candidates from the city would show up in Kokoland and enjoy days of festivities, when many oxen and sheep were undeservedly slaughtered in their honor. Taking full advantage of Kokoland's region-wise renowned generosity, they would consume a lot of quality barbequed meat. After that, they would tell people how to vote, who to vote for, get elected, and disappear. They would never show their smooth faces again, until the next round of coup and elections. In fact, people did not mind that much, especially when they had successful harvest seasons, and would need little help from the government. Many people did not have respect for democratically elected civilian governments, anyway. They held the general view that they were weak and incapable of doing a good governing job. People firmly believed that those in military uniforms have the right and the ability to govern better.

Not so many people understood how democracy functioned. They replaced the principles that they were ignorant of with their own rules. In the case of Haj Mardi, he took his understanding of democracy and his affiliation to his political party to a whole new level. He and his brother-in-law supported different candidates from two opposing parties. He wanted his brother-in-law to vote for his, same, candidate. The man refused and the dispute escalated to a point whereby Haj Mardi gave him an ultimatum to choose one of two options; vote for his candidate or divorce his sister. In some places, marriage lives of sisters and wives could simply be forsaken and become democracy casualties. It is safe to assume that democracy cannot be planted, be that in Kokoland or Iraq. It needs to evolve from within, and that will take time, I think, but I may be wrong.

While people relied mainly on locally produced agricultural goods for their diet, they bought other stuff like sugar, tea, coffee, and oil that came from the city. There was always a shortage of these complementary food items. Sugar was the most demanded, and, understandably, the scarcest commodity. The government had to introduce a rationing system whereby each district received a certain weekly quota, collected from the city for distribution to people at a reasonably low price. Contracts were awarded to certain individuals to receive sugar, tea, coffee, and oil quotas. The process provided fertile ground for corruption and favoritism, involving the sale of these scarce commodities in the black market. In many cases, contractors did not deliver the weekly rations. They simply told people that they did not receive any quotas for reasons such as delays in deliveries. Village people had no means of verifying the accuracy of such excuses. The quotas were mainly being received and sold in the city, in the black market, to wholesale merchants, who, in turn, sold them to retailers, who finally sold them to individuals, at more than double the government's stated price. People were desperate for the commodity, but some shop keepers preferred to hide it and sell it only to those who could afford it, willing to pay black market price, and keep quiet about it. Few shop owners enriched themselves from these corrupt practices, and that caused a lot of tension between them and the community.

High school students were branded by shop owners as troublemakers because they challenged them and, at times, took them to the local court to be fined for hiding sugar. Jundi was one of those troublemakers. In one instance, he wanted to confirm the accuracy of a statement made by one particular shop owner that he did not have any sugar for sale. He hid himself in a corner and sent his little sister with some money to find out. The shop owner told the little girl that he did not have any sugar to sell. The girl went back and told her brother Jundi. They waited until someone else walked into the shop and bought sugar. The customer, on his way out of the shop, met Jundi and told him he paid black market price. Jundi confronted the shop owner, and that led to a big row. The matter got referred to the local court, which wanted to imprison the shop owner, but arbitrators intervened, so he was let off the hook after paying a heavy fine.

Because of sugar's importance, politicians sometimes used it to sweeten the false commitments they gave to people, to get their votes. They would promise remote communities that they would build schools, hospitals, and roads to connect them with markets in cities. They would tell them that the government would contribute a certain percentage of the promised projects' budget, provided that the communities agree to raise the remaining balance. Poor village people would believe anything the government told them. They would happily agree to forego part of their sugar quotas, for collection and sale in the black market, with the view to raising enough money to execute the projects. They would be donating for years, but, in the end, nothing happened. The money would be used for buying expensive four-wheel-drive cars, for party officials, and military equipment.

CHAPTER 15

My Father (1927–2009)

I dedicate this book to my father. He was my only backup and source of security while growing up. I had a special relationship with him. Had it not been for him, I would not have made it beyond Kokand, so travelling the world and settling in America would have certainly been out of my reach. I am indebted to him, and I miss him greatly. My father was the youngest child among his siblings and he was the only child from his mother. His father died in 1945, at the age of 101, when he was eighteen years old. His mother died six month later. His half brothers and sisters were not helpful, so he was on his own at times when he needed help most. He lived a brutal life growing up because he did not have close family members, until we, his children, reached ages we could be supportive of him. He did not receive any formal education, but, in his childhood, he attended Quranic school to learn the principles of the Islamic faith.

My dad once told me that, during the British rule, a building contractor came to Kokoland to construct a marketplace. He looked for people who could haul water from nearby ponds for use in the buildings. My dad and his friends came forward with their donkeys and water containers, made from leather, to show that they were ready and had all the tools needed for getting the job done. The contractor asked if any one of them had been to school. None of them did, except one person, named Jadalla, who had completed first grade. Because he was the highest-educated person in the group, he received preferential treatment. The contractor appointed him in a supervisory position, gave him a chair, a table, a notebook, a pencil, and a place under a tree shade. He asked him to keep daily records of deliveries made by each person. My dad told me that it took him two hours to complete one delivery. He said, "Once I emptied my container, Jadalla, who would be sitting on a chair, looked at me, then looked at his notebook, and drew a line; 1." By the end of the day, Jadalla would hand over the notebook to the contractor, who would sum up the numbers, page by page, to get how many deliveries each person made. My dad, while telling me this story, used his index finger to draw a line in the dirt to explain the simplicity with which Jadalla carried out his job. He also hinted to me that Jadalla did not know that the lines he was making in the notebook, for every delivery, represented the number one. This was how he resented Jadalla. According to him, luck played a big role in the senior supervisory position Jadalla held, despite his meager education, which did not expand beyond first grade.

As you can tell, my dad did not accept the fact that he labored for two hours, got bossed around, and received less payment than someone whose job was limited to drawing lines on a notebook. Beside the high pay, Jadalla enjoyed other amenities, including sitting on a chair under the shade of a tree. Jadalla's fate was sealed. He no longer belonged to the common class. His first-grade education elevated his status in the community.

That incident was a turning point in my dad's life. It became a motivating factor for him in everything he did afterward. He led a different life than many of his contemporaries. As for Jadalla, he progressed to become a prominent figure in Kokoland. Those days, the British mayoral form of local government was in place, until President Jaafar Nimeiri abolished it in 1969. He replaced it with a new system made of five community leaders working as a panel of local judges. The court assembled every Saturday and each panelist presided over the court for one month, then got replaced by another judge. Jadalla went on to become one of these high-profile judges. That was attributed to the miracle of first grade education.

Getting married was not an easy thing for my father, being an orphan. Two holy men tribe-elders, Haj Hamza and Gony Al Waly, took him under their wings and spoke to the girl's father on his behalf. The girl's father, Merchant Aziz, was the richest man in the region. Such a bold move was bound to bring about resentment from young men who might also have interest in marrying the girl, especially if they happened to have the backing of rich parents. Even though my dad was not rich and did not have the support of parents, he was lucky to get the approval of Merchant Aziz to marry his daughter. Family members told me that on the wedding day, two people resorted to black magic to prevent the marriage from taking place. He did go through with the wedding, but what happened few years down the road was blamed on a delayed effect of black magic. His wife, after having three children; my two elder half-sisters and my elder half-brother Aziz, who was named after his grandfather, lost her sanity and never recovered from that until her death in 2009, forty days after my father's death. I heard people say that black magic also caused my brother Aziz's mental illness, which I discussed earlier.

Another relative, Uncle Mahjoob, was also married to Merchant Aziz's daughter. He and my dad were considered the two men of wisdom within the Kanuri community. Marrying up might have been a factor in helping my father carve himself a role in the community, but he certainly had inherent leadership traits. He refused to live a village life that was based entirely on conventional farming, and for that reason he took residence in Kokoland, but that came at a price of living away from his community. We were the only Kanuri family there, and hence were a minority in every sense of the word. As discussed earlier, that situation turned my life into a constant nightmare.

My father was among the first few shop owners in town. He was the first to get a passport, first to board a plane and travel overseas, but most important, he was among the first to send his children to school. That decision most probably came as the result of his experience with Jadalla, the building contractor's foreman. He always provided advice to the community on issues pertaining to disputes over land and family feuds. He advised those who needed legal assistance by directing them to the right law offices in the city. He was an activist in his own right. I remember, during the time when General Numeiri ordered the expulsion of people of West African origins, he visited Kanuri villages around Kokoland and explained to them the situation. Many Kanuri young men worked as porters loading and unloading lorries with sorghum produced in the area. Their service was vital to shipping the product to cities, so truck owners drove by the villages and looked for them. My dad told them to refuse to provide their service, if the authorities decided to go ahead with the expulsion order.

I remember my dad talking about discrimination and racism in the General's decision to expel people whose ancestors were born, lived, and died in the area. That was at a point in time when I did not know much about these two terms. He explained discrimination by giving an example of one particular Greek merchant who relocated to the area and enjoyed a preferential treatment from the local authorities. He argued that newcomers enjoyed more rights than he did. He told people it was a form of racism to treat the *Fallata* differently when records show that their ancestors lived in the area for centuries.

At the time when most members of the community shied away from speaking out about being subjected to injustice and preferred to keep a low profile, my father did not. The problem was that some members of his own community undermined his efforts. They thought he was just wasting his time and that he was better off keeping quiet so as not to draw attention to himself. Some people told him that we, his sons, being Kanuri, stood low chance of progressing at school. They believed that school authorities would sell our grades to non-Kanuri children. On the other hand, the non-Kanuri community leaders considered his stances as antiauthority and too ambitious, considering his Kanuri background. They constantly plotted against him. He refused to be in a village setting because he rejected the share crop concept, which involved renting a plot of land to farm and sharing the harvest with the landowner, so he chose to move to Kokoland and open a shop. The business furnished the family a fairly comfortable living, and for that reason he was envied by both the Kanuri and non-Kanuri communities.

My father was a farmer turned merchant. The mercantile and farming models he had adopted were not always successful. As far as bookkeeping is concerned, he commonly relied on mental account of unit costs of merchandises, until I got involved and started keeping simple records when I was in sixth or seventh grade. I would calculate and give him unit costs of grocery items (weighed in pounds and kilos) and fabrics (measured in yards and meters). Antoine Harbi was one of my dad's wholesale suppliers from the city. He was notoriously known for inflating the cost of fabrics he sold. Antoine was a standard for so much dishonesty that one local Kokoland merchant, named Ali Safi, also known for cheating his clients, was named after him.

Antoine had market monopoly over some commonly used fabrics, so retailers had little choice, but to buy from him. Upon my return home on school breaks, I would find piles of invoices set aside for me to go through and review to spot inaccuracies that had crept in, with Antoine's full blessing. Ironically, I rarely found mistakes that were favorable to my dad. I sorted out and gave him the wrong invoices to take back to the city to present to Mr. Antoine to claim the differences, which he always paid. He never expressed any sense of guilt or embarrassment, nor did he apologize for his actions. It was as if business as usual. He joked and talked his way out of it. Despite that, many merchants continued to buy from him, arguing that his prices were less expensive, relative to other wholesalers. That was a sign of village collective behavior, if I may say so. Once one person took a certain action, the rest followed, regardless of whether such action was appropriate to their specific case or not.

Growing up, I was constantly worried about tomorrow. There were three things that used to cause me a great sense of insecurity. The first one was draught, which, obviously, translated into bad harvest, considering the fact that we relied on rain-fed irrigation. The second one was the sight of empty shelves in our shop. The stock of merchandise in the shop depended on good harvests, and hence the importance of abundant rainfall. Many a time, it did not rain enough, so we ended up losing everything. The sight of dark clouds in the direction of our farm used to give me hope. Any raindrop inched us closer to a successful harvest, which meant maintaining shop shelves packed with merchandise; an image that I found to be very pleasing. The third sense of insecurity stemmed from worrying about the well-being of my dad. Everything depended on him, since I did not have any backup or support from anyone else, whatsoever. He was the ultimate guarantor of my survival.

Kokoland shop owners who focused only on their business by staying away from farming, always did better than those who got involved in both activities. It took time for my dad to harvest, sell the produce, and buy merchandise for the shop. By that time, half of the shopping season would be over. He would have missed most of the wedding season when people spent money like there was no tomorrow. After that, sales plummeted due to lack of liquidity, and that was the time my dad raised cash from the sale of his harvest and bought merchandise for the shop, when it was already too late. On the other hand, at the time he liquidated the shop, bought seeds, and prepared for the rainy season, other shop owners stayed put. They sold their merchandize at prices higher than average. Also, at that time of the year, people had limited cash, so they bought groceries on credit at higher prices. They hoped for successful harvests to make enough money, pay off their outstanding debts, and, still, have money left to marry off their daughters, help pay for their sons to get married, or get another wife for themselves. Many times these dreams were put off until the next successful harvest, which, for many people, never materialized.

My dad also allowed his clients to borrow to get by, until the harvest season. We maintained records of debtors, but he rarely followed up in a systematic way to ask for repayment. Some people fully honored their obligations, voluntarily, but many made only partial payments, or never paid at all. I remember one time when we lost the debtors' notebook to termites. My dad kept it between a wooden beam and heaps of straw that covered the roof of the shade in front of the hut. In fact, we coexisted in full harmony with moths, wasps, termites, ants, and other creatures, which all built neighborhoods in the straw shade. I guess the termites found it more convenient to feed their babies from the close-by paper starch and save their energy for harsher times. They just did what was logical. The disappearance of the notebook came in handy for some borrowers. Once they discovered that we could not produce records of how much they owed, they took advantage of the situation by avoiding shopping from us altogether.

To maximize our chances for having a successful harvest, we planted millets and sesame seeds ahead of the rainy season. When it rained, only a fraction of what we had buried emerged from the ground. Our pre-rainy season efforts represented a gift from heaven to birds, rats, and squirrels, which, by that time, would be desperate for food because of the long dry season. They would dig out most of the seeds before they had a chance for rain, germination, and emergence as plants. When the planting season arrived, my father would have already liquidated the shop to use the proceeds for hiring day laborers to help with farming, all the way from planting to harvesting.

The rainy season brought additional responsibility on top of what I already had. My day was divided up between working on the farm in the morning, opening the shop in the afternoon, fetching drinking water, bringing hay to the donkey, and, if time permits, playing soccer in the evening. These were my daily tasks when I was as young as ten years old. I used to go to bed very exhausted. My dad, for sure, was one of the best motivators I had ever known. He used to encourage me to perform my responsibilities to the best of my abilities. He was very successful at detecting my downtimes. He would come up with statements such as, "This year, God willing, you will get anything you want." What he meant to say was that I would get the bike I had forever been yearning for, but never got it.

I would be very exhausted by the time I returned from the farm in the afternoon. After eating lunch, I would usually drink a cup of tea, which caused me to sweat. My dad would say, "You see? All the fatigue is gone now." What he meant was that the energy that I had lost while working in the farm was replenished and that I was ready for other tasks. That was his way of motivating me into getting on with my remaining duties for the day. Once, I told my wife that my dad had some scientific knowledge about the medicinal value of black tea. She looked at me, but did not say a word.

My wife has full respect for my people in Kokoland, but sometimes she gets skeptical about their conclusions on certain issues. Her skepticism is evident in the following story. I used to watch wildlife and documentary programs, so, sometimes, I would share with her topics I found interesting. One day, I told her that regularly feeding a skinny horse is not enough to turn it into a healthy looking animal. It is important to keep a pile of hay in front of it to give it a sense of security, otherwise it will never put on weight. Ten years or so later, we revisited and discussed this scientific piece of knowledge about horses, but I also mentioned the original source of the information, which was a farmer from Kokoland. She responded with some fury because she all along thought that the information had a credible source such as the United Nations' Food and Agriculture Organization (FAO), or the National Geographic. From that moment onward, every time I tried to tell her any scientific fact, she would interrupt and ask me, "Who said it?"

The high hopes about getting a bike kept me working as hard as I could. Sadly, I never got one. In hindsight, that was a blessing in disguise. The bike could have come at the expense of my progress at school. I could have used it extensively to roam the nearby villages, attending weddings and possibly going astray. Not having a faster means of transportation meant I had to stay grounded at home and use my limited free time for reading old books and outdated magazines, which, somehow, found their way to Kokoland. I convinced myself that was a good thing to do, but deep down, I remained honest to myself as to how I really felt about the bike.

Almost everyone in and around Kokoland worked in farming. Farm sizes were few acres, and the farming practices were labor intensive shifting form of agriculture. As I have written about earlier, we used ancient human-powered farming tools. I don't know why nobody ever thought of using donkeys or oxen to plough the land when most people could afford to own them. That could have made a difference in productivity and people's standard of living. A friend of mine once told me if his great-grandfather, who had died a hundred years earlier, came back from his grave and saw the way people farmed in the 1970s, he would say, "I have not missed a thing," and return to his grave with a smile on his face. By the end of the day, the harvest, even when the rains were plenty, was, for most people, a few sacks of different crops. The revenue generated from the sale of the produce was not enough to meet the basic needs, let alone setting aside money for buying luxury items such as bikes.

In the evenings, I visited the houses of select day laborers to obtain their verbal agreement to come to our farm the following morning. Half of them would not show up, despite the assurances they would have given me the nights before. There was fierce competition for good labor. My dad's competitors, especially one man named Shamy, would appear the moment I leave the laborers' homes, offer them higher daily rates, and succeed in persuading them to abandon my verbal contracts, which were simply based on the principle of, "My word is my bond." By increasing the minimum wage rate, Shamy caused serious damage to the farming business in Kokoland. I am certain that both he and my dad were better off not farming. The labor rates were so high that both of them were financially worse off year after year, and we all could have made more money selling our labor to other farmers willing to pay my father's and Shamy's rates.

The daily rate offered, even though negligible, was not compatible with the service rendered by the laborers. It also impacted our shop business because my dad paid out in cash the same day of the service and waited for the rains to come. At the same time, what was paid was too little to make a dent in the living standards of the laborers. In fact, there were no true winners.

The mornings were extremely hectic because any time wasted came at our expense. The day laborers were supposed to show up at the farm around eight in the morning, after walking forty-five minutes or so, but in most cases they did not make it until nine. I had to get up early enough to load the donkey with the seeds, digging and grass-cutting tools, and small bowls for each planter to carry the seeds. It was very important that I filled the goatskin water container and tied it to the donkey's belly, whereas I loaded everything else on his back. That way, I could make optimum use of space and the donkey's weight-bearing capacity. I would rush to make it to the farm ahead of the laborers so they would not sit idle and wait for my arrival with the seeds and the planting tools. The whole workday lasted a mere three hours, roughly from nine to noon. Sometimes it rained, so we had to wait under a tree for it to stop before going back to work. In other occasions, due to too much rain, we would return to the village without planting a single seed. As far as the workers were concerned, they had earned their day's work and got paid for it. No wonder they prayed very hard for rain.

Every one of our helpers was a clock-watcher. Since there was no clock to watch, they resorted to closely monitoring the lengths of their shadows, which got shorter as time approached midday. That was when they would start exhibiting certain body language to express their readiness to leave the farm. The eyebrows would start forming a "V" shape; a sign of anger and discontent for feeling exploited by continuing to work one or two minutes after midday. The speed with which they planted the seeds slowed down drastically. Some would start gazing into the horizon. If all these "time is up" tactics did not convince my dad to stop for the day, someone would volunteer and say, "It is about time we went home." My dad would call it off and start walking toward the big tree in the center of the farm, followed by everyone else. There, he would pay out each worker what was supposedly a day's labor.

Buraima was a worker we sought out his help as a last resort. I think he did us more harm than good. He was the laziest of all workers and a typical clock watcher. He was also the first to bring his planting activities to a halt. He would just stop planting whenever he decided for himself that it was time to go home. I remember, in one instance, he visited the seed-sack, to fill his seed-bowl, repeatedly and more frequently than everyone else, but, at the same time, the speed with which he planted the seeds was slower than everybody else. We knew that there was a problem. Our worries were materialized one week from that incident. Persons holding hoes would dig holes about one foot apart, whereas planters like Buraima would drop three pieces of peanut seeds in each hole and cover them with dirt, using their feet. There was a high chance that at least one out of the three seeds would germinate and surface a week or so later, depending on rain. Sure enough, in a week's time, and contrary to the norm, we found out some rows had between twenty to thirty seeds competing to surface. Buraima, simply, poured the seeds in the holes instead of picking and dropping three peanuts at a time. That was his way of getting the job done as soon as possible so he could go home. His idea was if he could bury the seeds in masses, there would soon be nothing left to plant; hence, my dad would declare the day's work over due to lack of seeds, pay out a day's worth of work, and release everyone to go home.

Buraima also had other time-wasting tactics. He would take many breaks to drink water and visit the bathroom more often. He would occasionally volunteer to fetch water on behalf of the group. He would carry the empty four-gallon tin to the water pond, a half-kilometer walk, only to return with it half full. That way, he would stand a chance to pay a second visit to the pond before the end of the working day. Buraima did a lousy job.

We would leave the farm and walk back to the village when hunger was the common thing among us all. At that time, the utility we could have driven from biting into an onion might equal that we could have gotten from the best apples grown in the state of Washington. Then again, none of us had any idea how apples looked, tasted, or if they even existed, so leave aside the question about where they were grown.

The flowering of the peanut plant was one of the best times for me. It was a signal that a successful season was just around the corner. It meant it had rained amply. I also liked those times because I had a break from work. My dad and I would just roam the farm, pull out weeds here and there, and check everywhere to make sure that no animals had gotten to the farm and destroyed the plants. I used to follow my dad and literally walk into his footsteps to minimize the damage to the tiny plants from stepping on them. I enjoyed listening to his stories about the perpetual enmity between dogs and hyenas. Sometimes he would volunteer and tell me that I was closer than ever to getting my dream gift; a bike. He would say, "You wait. This year, God willing, you will get the gift you wanted most." He knew that those words energized me and made me even more committed to carrying out my duties towards home, the farm, the shop, the donkey, and fetching drinking water. A week or so would pass before I would bring up or mention anything about the bike. I figured out one week was neither too long a period that my dad would forget about his promise, nor too short to annoy him into completely changing his mind about it. One time, I told him I would rather go for a fat-wheel double-style bike than a rallying or a thin-wheel sport bike. I told him that with a fat-wheel bike I could cross the sand dunes between Kokoland and the farm in no time. That was my strategy for carving an image of a productive and a hardworking kid in my dad's mind. That was also to convince him that the bike, besides being an item for entertainment, was an instrumental tool for carrying out my duties.

It was customary among the Kanuri people to volunteer and help each other during the rainy season, especially when a community member became sick and could not attend to his farm work. This activity was known as *suruwah,* in Kanuri, or *nafeer*, in Arabic, which means collective help. The rainy season was short; therefore, any time spent away from the farm meant hardship to the family. Men from surrounding villages would carry their farming tools and flock to the sick person's farm. In a few hours, the work needed at the farm, be that planting seeds, cutting weeds, or harvesting crops, would be complete. As you might have guessed, there was no safety net such as social security or federal disaster programs in place for times of need, so the community would step in to help.

My dad spent time looking after my sick mother before she passed away. For that reason he could not work on the farm. As a token of solidarity, the community carried out a *nafeer* on our farm, which was completely overtaken by weeds. One morning, tens of men showed up to help. At the same time adults worked in the field, my brother Aziz and I, together with other young boys who accompanied their dads, went around and handed out bowls of energy drinks made from millet. Around midday, many Kanuri women, carrying food on their heads, arrived at the farm. Witnessing so many people descending on our farm to lend us a hand was the most comforting feeling, which has left a lasting impression and an image vividly carved in my mind. The job was completed in a single day. It could have taken my dad, relying on day laborers such as Buraima, an entire rainy season to accomplish half of it.

In the mornings, we would load the donkey with seeds, water, and tools, leaving room for only one person to ride; my brother Aziz or me. We would swap places so that, every day, one of us would ride to the farm and the other would walk. There wasn't much load to carry back home from the farm, in the afternoons. You would think we would happily ride home, side by side, considering the fact that we would be very tired after a day's hard labor. No, you are wrong. The saddle could only fit one person; therefore, if both of us were to ride, one of us would be sitting in the saddle and the other would be riding bareback, behind him. There was nothing more humiliating for either of us to be seen by our friends, not only riding a donkey bareback, but also sitting behind someone riding in a saddle. Naturally, it was not possible to have two saddles on one donkey. Even if that was the case, we would still argue as to who would be riding in the front saddle and who would be in the back. Our high egos and self-esteem just would not allow us to compromise. We would rather walk all the way back to the village than to be seen riding second-class seat on the back of a donkey. The donkey, understandably, welcomed the friction between my brother and me. That always worked to his advantage. Every time I saw siblings, here in America, scuffling to sit in the front car seat, I smiled to myself as I remembered my own experience. There is always something about front seats, be that on donkeys' backs or inside cars.

Twenty years after the days of sharing donkey rides, I got a job at a bank in the Middle East, which offered me first-class plane tickets as part of my employment package. Every time I took my first-class seat, I remembered the donkey-saddle situation. I thought to myself that had the company known about my background, they would have downgraded my entitlements, and I would not have minded a bit. I guess, first or economy class plane seats might not make much of a difference if your best and fastest mode of transportation, one day, happened to be a donkey.

On our way back from the farm to the village, my brother Aziz, a friend named Safi, and I, sometimes, stopped and played in the forest. We involved ourselves in activities such as cutting down tree branches to make boomerangs and hunting for squirrels by chasing them all the way to their burrows and digging them up. This was a very risky game for which, one day, we received a severe punishment from my dad. It was believed that squirrel bites caused rabies. Safi's elder brother, Hamad, paid a heavy price for messing with one. He went hunting and got bitten on the hand as he dug up a squirrel out of a hole. He became very ill. Peanut-like bubbles covered his entire body. He was sick for many years and finally succumbed to his illness.

As I mentioned above, by the time we sold the harvest and bought merchandise for the store, half of the sale season would be gone. I started noticing a yearly decline in our financial standing. Gaps started to appear on the store shelves, revealing the white wall that used to be hidden from sight; a sign of less merchandise on display. I, later on, learned that the decline was caused by the fall in the value of the Sudanese pound and its purchasing power due to inflation in prices of goods. Over time, we purchased fewer merchandise for the same units of money we generated from the harvest sale.

Annual stocktaking at our shop was a nightmare. I used to be worried to death because, by simply looking at the shelves, I could tell that they were emptier than the previous year. Things were just not good. Since there would hardly be any liquid cash in the safe, we would hope that our wealth would be stored or reflected in the physical stock of merchandise, but deep inside, both my dad and I knew beforehand the bad news. On the stocktaking day, we would both appear calm and subdued. We would go through the whole shop, first measuring the fabrics, then weighing and counting units of grocery items, before summing up the total value for both categories. In fact, by the time we had finished measuring the fabrics, I would have already had a good idea as to where we stood. The rest of the stocktaking amounted to something like finishing the job we had started, when we were both certain that would only bring more misery, once we tallied the numbers. Our business continued to go "south" until we got to a point some shelves became completely empty of any merchandise. We were at a point of no return.

A combination of factors to do with our farming practices and shop keeping model had adversely affected our business. Debtors partially paid or completely failed to pay back money they had borrowed from my dad. Termites also helped the debtors by consuming the notebook, which contained lists of names of people who bought merchandise on credit. Inflation in prices of goods made it impossible for my dad to run his business at a profit. All of these factors took a toll on the business and contributed to its decline, which also led to a decline in our living standard. Even though my dad fared better than many farmers and merchants, that did not mean a lot to me at that time. I cared about one and only one thing; a bike. The fact remains that I did not get one. My hopes evaporated as time progressed and our business further declined.

Kokoland merchants organized their shops by stocking groceries on one side, fabrics on another, and a tailor occupying the third side. There were wide doors on the fourth sides, making it possible for potential customers to have a good view of the shops' contents from a distance, and hence, increasing the chances for transforming simple curiosities into full sales. The store-fronts were used on market days as extensions for selling cooking oil, onions, and palm dates.

Successful harvest seasons, which were normally sporadic, had helped some farmers transition into businesspersons with little or no training in business, whatsoever. Our good neighbor Sarky was one of them. He once gave his son Adam money to travel to the city to shop for merchandize. The shopping list usually contained different items, for diversification's sake. At the outskirt of the city; Adam met with a merchant who had a full truckload of onions for sale. The merchant quoted him a price and managed to convince him that he stood a good chance of selling the onion for, at least, three times his cost. He told Adam there was a scarcity of onions in the market due to bad harvest, so, if he wished, he could store it for a few months and make even more profits. Adam, with his limited experience, took the bait. He paid all the money in his possession to the onion merchant and together they drove back to Kokoland to off-load the truck in front of the shop, which was next door to ours.

It turned out that half of the load was rotten. Bad smell engulfed the entire market area and beyond. The whole village talked about it. It was summer time, so it took only a few days for the rotten onions to spoil the entire stock. No wonder the merchant was in a hurry to sell off his load at a heavily discounted price. Adam did not stand a chance for retail-selling that load in time before it all went bad. It was just too much onion per every single person living in Kokoland.

The morning after the delivery of the onion load, which happened to be a market day, Adam's father, Sarky, rode his donkey into town, coming from his nearby village. From a distance, at the edge of the marketplace, he saw a high pile of gray sacks, but could not tell what it was or if it was in front of his shop, or the other three shops in the same row, including ours. He got to the pile only to realize that it was in front of his shop. He came to the realization right there and then that his son Adam had just made a life-wrecking decision. That gave him the shock of his life. One village joker spread rumors about the incident by telling that Sarky's stomach rumbled loudly and violently once it was confirmed to him that the onion belonged to him and nobody else. Sarky did not recover at all from the impact of the fiasco committed by his son. The village joker also said, from that moment onward, Sarky avoided eating any food containing onion, until his death. Adam's onion load represented a windfall gain bounty for some village animals, especially stray goats and donkeys. They ate plenty of fermented onions, got intoxicated, and behaved in a very funny way.

Ganamah was my childhood friend Omara's father. He did not own a shop in town, but he sold cooking oil and onions on market days. On one occasion, upon returning from the city, he went to his usual place of business and prepared to sell his merchandize. He emptied one sack of onions on the ground and created a half-foot-high square-elevation of dirt, on top of which he displayed the onions, in bunches of four. He then sat down on the ground and waited for customers. On the other end of the market, another retail merchant, who also happened to have returned from the city the night before, had a sack of onions missing. He desperately roamed the market looking for his merchandize. As he passed by Ganamah, he saw him attending to customers buying onions. It struck him that Ganamah, while in the city the day before, did not buy any onions. He wondered why he had a whole pile by his side.

Word spread in the market that there was a sack of onions missing. Everyone got worried and feared for the worse. The Kanuri were known for being hardworking people who lived a dignified life. As such; accusing a Kanuri man of theft was considered a very serious matter. So, the onion situation needed utmost care in handling because any false accusation could lead to an irreparable damage. A group of Kanuri elders congregated at Haj Ramadhan's shop, first, to discuss the matter, then off they went to Ganamah, whom they found sitting down on the ground, using the empty onion sack as a mat. He knew why they were visiting him, so he told them that he had nothing to do with the missing sack of onions and asked them to leave. They were about to depart when one man asked the group to wait for a minute. He bent down and picked up the gray jute sack from the ground, shook it to drop some dirt, and turned it to look at the other side. Everyone saw a name written with green ink, but it was not Ganamah's. It was the true owner's name. It was over for Ganamah. There was no place for him in Kokoland, anymore. He had to leave town, since he committed an act considered disgraceful to the Kanuri tribe. Sure enough, he vanished without a trace, leaving behind my friend Omara, who was about eight then, his mother, and siblings. Ganamah never returned to town. Kokoland's common laws dealing with disgraceful acts such as stealing were very harsh, considering the voluntary self-exile that persons like Ganamah could impose on themselves.

My friend Omara lived in the village of Manga-ri, a rural setting where he stood limited chance of attending school, especially with his father gone. He came to visit me during my recent visit to Kokoland, after forty-some years from the onion incident. We talked a lot about childhood stories. He is clearly a bright person, but, sadly, his situation did not serve him well. I noticed that he was carrying a newspaper, so I assumed that he taught himself to read on his own. I was very happy for him.

Ironically, petty thefts commanded harsher punishment than another type of theft known as *hambata*, which entails acquiring or taking properties, usually livestock, especially camels, against the owner's will, in broad daylight. It was considered an act of bravery rather than theft. The practice is slowly disappearing nowadays, but it is still being upheld in certain parts of the country, for the wealth and fame it brings to the outlaws, who were known for their generosity. They shared what they took by force with poor people, which makes me think of Robin Hood of Sherwood Forest in England. Even though violence was part of the practice, men recited poems and women sang songs that glorified the deeds of the *hambata*, making some of them knights whose fame was spoken about for generations.

CHAPTER 16

My Father: Plots and Hard Times

Living standards in Kokoland deteriorated across the board. However, my dad had the lion's share of troubles caused by ill-wishers. Our neighbor Siraj colluded with three Gadim brothers to buy the shop he had been renting from the owner for over ten years and remove him from it. A friend told him that a final sales price was agreed upon by both parties, and that it was a matter of time that the new landlords assumed ownership. My dad sought communal arbitration to resolve the dispute. He wanted to argue his case and to express the view that he had priority over any potential buyer, if the owner decided to sell the shop, because he had been a good tenant for a long time. Some people supported his bid to buy the shop, whereas others joined Siraj's camp. For some members of the Kanuri community, my dad was a leader and a valuable resource they could tap into for advice, whenever they needed help to address issues involving the authorities. A second group thought he was someone who abandoned his ancestral way of life (farming), moved to Kokoland, and chose a different path, so why bother burden themselves with his troubles. This view was also shared by some non-Kanuri people in Kokoland. They thought that my dad was truly trying to live out of his station in life. The last two groups, together, formed a formidable opposition to my dad, leaving only few people standing by his side.

In fact, shop owners and their families, in general, enjoyed decent living standards, relative to the rest of the community, so it was not surprising that they were envied by some people, at times. In my dad's case, removing him from the shop was one of the many plots knitted against him. The idea was to undermine him by, first, clipping his wings, and then pushing him over the cliff, if you will. The shop was our life vein. Cutting it would completely ruin our livelihood.

The story circulated in town was that our neighbor Siraj and his allies approached Zaidan, the shop owner, and convinced him to sell his shop. They told him he would be better off receiving a cash lump sum and did whatever he wished with it, rather than relying on a monthly rent amount, which was not enough for engaging in big projects such as buying cattle. He agreed and accepted Siraj's offer. By the time my dad found out, it was too late to do anything about it. He began shuttling between Kokoland and the city looking for a lawyer to represent him and obtain an injunction from a court to stop the sale from going through. He argued that the law entitled him to make an offer on the shop. He thought in case there were higher bids, he should either be given the option to counter-offer, or time to look for alternatives.

To my dad's bad luck, our neighbor Siraj was the merchant in charge of collecting Kokoland's sugar quotas from the city. As such, he had good connections there, and for that reason, my dad feared that Siraj might have access to lawyers who could influence the outcome of the case, if an action was raised in court. It was also unfortunate for my dad that the local judge Dallami who questioned Aseel the illegal butcher, in Chapter 4 above, was not only a friend of our neighbor Siraj, but also a business partner. He was the one who looked after the shop whenever Siraj travelled to the city for a few days to collect Kokoland's sugar quota. Therefore, it was unwise for my dad to try to seek justice by suing locally. He was convinced that judge Dallami would stand by Siraj, his employer.

During one of his visits to the city, a friend told him he could be entitled to goodwill compensation, arguing that in the event he lost the bid to buy the shop, the new owners would benefit from the customer-base he had built over the years. In the beginning, my dad was excited about the idea, but, because it was an unknown concept to the village, no one took his goodwill claims seriously, so it did not make much difference in the direction of the case.

Some village foxes, if you like, decided to look after the chicken coop. Under the mask of arbitration and good intentions, a group of known antagonists formed a team and called for a meeting to resolve the problem between my dad and his opponents; Siraj and the Gadim brothers. Two men, Abu Amna, the local mosque prayer-caller, and Hijairi, a community leader who crystallized the meaning of myopia, led the group. They all along felt ill-will towards my dad, even though for no apparent reason, so we knew very well that they were dishonest and that the arbitration attempt was nothing more than a cover-up to conceal their true intentions.

One Friday around noon, three weeks into the dispute, a hundred or so men gathered in Muaz's house to find a way to settle the disagreement. First Abu Amna, the prayer-caller, spoke and gave a pathetic summarization for the nature of the dispute. He concluded his speech by quoting a "goat" example. Abu Amna also happened to be the government's official who collected taxes levied on animals and agricultural products sold in town. Therefore, it was natural that he gave an example related to what he knew best; goats. He said, "I don't understand why Wad El Sharif [son of Shari] is making all this fuss about Zaidan's decision to sell his shop. For example, if you have a goat and you want to sell it, who am I to tell you whether to sell it to Hassan or Ali or Khamis? Am I not right? Or what do you men say?" Many people in the group, who were primarily there to knock the last nail into my dad's business coffin, responded by saying, "Yes, this is true in God's name." The next person in line was the second arbitrator, Hijairi, who stood up to pour out his wisdom on the crowd. He said, "Zaidan wants to sell his shop, and that is his right. We could not tell him not to do so. Wad El Sharif can look for a shop elsewhere to buy or rent, if he likes, or what do you think people?" The response, as expected, was "Yes, in God's name."

Some people in the crowd murmured words of disapproval in Kanuri language. The problem was that they were not confident enough to air their views openly and loudly in Arabic. Others feared retaliation from Siraj and his employee Dallami, the local judge, in case they took my dad's side. Next was my dad's turn to lay out his defense, but the verdict had already been announced by the supposedly neutral arbitrators. Few people seemed to buy into his argument. Judge Dallami concluded that the sale was legitimate, so he ordered my dad to vacate the shop in two weeks' time. In less than half an hour, it was all over for us. Everyone got up and dismissed. I had never seen my dad that angry and distressed. As for me, my hopes for a bike, be that a fat-wheel, a thin-wheel, or any bike for that matter, went down the drain for good, right there in front of my eyes. With the shop gone, I should not be worrying about bikes when I had no idea how I was going to eat in two weeks' time.

As if the sad saga of removing my dad from the shop in such a humiliating manner was not enough that it required further push involving some form of voodoo magic. The following Friday, a week after that ill-fated arbitration, I found a bunch of dry green leaves placed on one empty shelf inside our shop. Someone snuck in and deposited it there without being spotted. I drew my dad's attention to it, but he told me not to touch it, keep my distance, and stay away from it. Whoever that person was, his intention was to chase us as far away from town as possible. The magic was a strong one, for it did work, considering where and how far from Kokoland I ended up. Contrary to what the magician had intended, Northern California is, not only a good alternative, but also another blessing in disguise.

Those days were very tough on my dad. Another incident took place around the same time we lost our shop. Our only donkey got entangled in a rope and broke its front right leg at the shoulder. It could not stand up or move around to feed itself, so we collected dry hays from a nearby forest and piled it in front of it, even though it could not eat or drink much, due to the pain it was enduring. Lacking other means of transporting the hays from the forest meant I had to carry it on my head. I was twelve years old then. I could not bring home enough hay, so, one day, my dad accompanied me to the forest to help. He carried his load, I carried mine, and, together, we headed home, he was in the front and I was trailing him. The image of my dad walking with a heap of hay on top of his head filled me with great sadness. That image was a crystallization for everything going wrong in our life. I just couldn't get it out of my head. I think it will stay with me forever.

It was obvious that our living standard had deteriorated to an unsustainable level. The donkey succumbed to its wounds and died. It is worth mentioning that donkeys were indispensable, being the primary mode of transportation and carrying loads; most importantly water. For this reason, my dad had to look for another donkey. He travelled to a distant village and purchased one. He returned home and told me how lucky I was to get a strong replacement. He said, it would help me a great deal with my water business, since it could carry more gallons of water than its predecessor. That was a valuable piece of information because I could make an additional half a penny for every three-hour trip I made to the water pond. I stood a chance to make a lot of money in the long run, so I became very excited about the prospects. Unfortunately, that was a short-lived happy dream. My dad left the donkey he purchased behind with one of his cousins who promised to deliver it a week later. The man took the liberty of riding the donkey to a faraway village to attend to some personal business. On the way back, the donkey collapsed due to exhaustion and died of heat stroke. My dad's cousin proved to be too heavy for the donkey to carry all that distance during the summer heat of the day. That was a great loss. Obviously, things did not look good for us. I guess the black magic was working hard against us in all fronts. My experiences during those dark days, more or less, dictated my actions and framed my outlook toward life. Today, I still feel a sense of insecurity in my heart whenever I remember them.

After my dad lost the bid to keep the shop, a holy man advised him to go south. He told him he would make it big if he did so. To the holy man, south was certainly not Brazil or South Africa. He meant relocating from North Kordofan province to South Kordofan, to one specific place called Habila, a mere 150 kilometers or so southward. I wouldn't have let my dad move south had I known the meaning of the phrase "went south" at that time.

My dad's shop during the 1960s and 70s. It is a place that harbored so many happy and sad childhood memories for me. Photo 2016.

I returned to Kokoland some thirty years after the shop incident. I went to find out who was occupying our old shop. I met with Gadim Senior, one of the brothers who took it over, but he did not recognize me, until I told him who I was, then he started crying. He left me wondering whether he was shedding tears because he, his brothers, and their friend, the Judge, had wronged us pretty bad, a few decades earlier, or due to something else. I thought to myself, "He might as well save his tears, since he did us a great favor. May be, I should thank him for what he and his brothers did." I took a moment to survey the shop. The shelves were absolutely empty and the square wood frames neatly exhibited the white wall paint, even though that was no body's intention to keep them that way. It was a beautiful sight, but, at the same time, a dreadful one, as far as I was concerned. It evoked in me the worries I felt on stock taking days, which always meant one thing to me; crisis of epic proportions. I felt very sad because the shop embodied some of my childhood memories, both good and bad. It was clear that business continued to deteriorate over the years. Gadim Senior, sobbingly, told me he had lost his only son, Gadim Junior, in a car accident in the city. He also told me not to forget to pass by our old neighbor, Siraj, who colluded with him to take away our shop, to offer my condolences, since he too had lost his only son, Sameer. Both sons were around my age and we used to be childhood playmates.

My dad relocated his business to Habila in the Nuba Mountains in Southern Kordofan, just as the holy man had suggested. The land was fertile, and there was abundant rainfall. In the 1970s, the government distributed thousands of acres of farmland to large scale farmers to produce sesame and varieties of sorghum. One problem, visible to any observer from the get-go, was that the land was allotted, primarily, to people from outside the region. It was a recipe for a future conflict because locals openly resented the fact that there was little for them in the agricultural boom the region was witnessing. Production was abundant, but the local economy did not benefit in any way. A great deal of the harvest was smuggled westward to neighboring countries. It is not surprising that, today, forty years later, the Nuba Mountains in Southern Kordofan is one of the country's regions where war is raging. The bounty ended in a few years due to deterioration of the security situation. Initially, the instability was limited to sporadic skirmishes, which, in later years, escalated into a full-fledged armed conflict. Upon the death of one neighbor, named Wad Maki, and his son, my father decided to move away from Habila. Wad Maki and his son left the town to visit their farm, but they never returned. Their remains were found six months later.

Many people in Kokoland had little understanding of what the armed conflicts in the Nuba Mountains, Southern Sudan, the Blue Nile, and Dar Fur, were all about. The government, which was the main source of information, invariably misled them. Even though the closest fighting front was hundreds of miles south of Kokoland, many thought that it was just around the corner due to their limited knowledge of geography of the place, or geography in general. That misconception was worsened by the fact that there was a language barrier, as I have indicated in many instances throughout the book. For that reason, many people did not make sense out of the news about the conflict, and they were in the dark about what was really happening.

One of my cousins told me about an incident that took place in the village of Rushash, when people fled their homes one night. They heard a loud sound of engines roaring just south of town. It was past midnight. The first thing that came to their minds was that the Sudan People's Liberation Army (SPLA) was attacking the village, so they took off running, heading northbound. What really happened was that a vehicle broke down in the outskirt of the village. Trucks, one by one, arrived and stopped to help fix the broken vehicle. They got the job done at about past midnight, after which time every driver headed to his lorry and started the engine. The simultaneous roar of engines triggered one thought in the people's minds that the SPLA was attacking the village, so everyone took off running. My cousin thought what happened was funny, but I did not share his views.

Information is power, and that applies to Kokoland, too. It is more so when the matter involves war. It is a question of how it can successfully be used. The extent of its usage can range from the extremes of supplying arms to both warring factions, to participating in humanitarian missions, all the way to embezzling a penny from the less informed, to buy candy. Here is a story involving another cousin who took full advantage of the war and insecurity situation. She happened to be one of a few girls in the family to attend primary school. As such, she was better informed about matters involving current affairs, conflicts, and wars, than most members of the family. Please, again, be reminded that things are relative. She had fairly a good understanding of the distance that separated the village from the war front. She knew that the source of strange noises in the vicinity of the village was unlikely to be the rebels attacking. She thought that was too valuable insightful information into what could be happening, and that such knowledge shouldn't be wasted, so she figured out a way to use it to her advantage. She decided to embezzle a little candy money from her totally uninformed and very frugal grandmother, who was not in good terms with her. She found out her grandmother was terribly worried about the war. Grandma did not know what to make out of this entire war thing or its implications on her life. She was totally in the dark. My cousin thought of a devious plan to exploit the situation. She would pass in front of Grandma's hut and casually say, "The rebels are here." She noticed every time she said that, Grandma came out of her hut and stood looking puzzled and confused by what she had just heard about the rebels. She knew that the word rebels meant trouble, but she did not have enough vocabulary to ask questions about what was going on. My cousin kept playing that game repeatedly, without volunteering any additional words to explain to Grandmother what she really meant. Information is power and words cost money. Grandmother grew impatient and could not take it anymore. She was worried to death that it might be too late to flee the village in case the rebels were about to attack, unless she did something about that, and did it very soon.

One day, the moment she saw my cousin passing in front of her hut, she called her and asked, "Did you say rebels?" My cousin responded, "Yes," and kept quiet. That short answer left Grandma even more confused, since she didn't have a follow up question to ask. After some thinking, Grandma left my cousin standing there, went back inside her hut, and came out with a penny, which she handed to my cousin. She told her to go and buy herself some candy of her choice. Money talks, so Grandma would rather let the penny do the boring war talk on her behalf. She basically wanted to buy information. My cousin had her doubts about such a sudden change of heart because she was not accustomed to seeing Grandma this generous. That doubt dissipated the following day when Grandma called her again and gave her another penny. By doing so, Grandma, was able to normalize the relationship with her granddaughter, who decided to take it upon herself to tell her everything about the war. She told her about the rebel's whereabouts, of which she herself knew absolutely nothing, of course. She thought that as long as Grandma was willing to pay for her peace and security, information could easily be obtained, but the degree of its accuracy was both immaterial and unguaranteed. Telling her any nonsense would just be fine. One penny a day became her daily wage for bringing Grandma fresh information from the war front. That penny secured her daily ration of candy. Whenever she needed extra money to spend, she painted a bleaker picture about the war. She told Grandma that the rebels were at the outskirts of the village. That additional information fetched an extra penny, enough money for candies and some fruit.

Sometimes my cousin gave Grandma partially comforting information to keep her in suspense. That way she could always stay relevant and not risk losing her candy benefits. She would say something like, "The rebels went back to their village, but they said they will return." The rebels' village could be a matter of a few miles from Grandma's village or in a place as far as Timbuktu. It did not matter, so long as they went back to their village. That also meant the rebels were at a farther point from Grandma's village than a few days earlier, and that was good news, at least for the time being, since they would not pose an immediate threat to her. Grandma gave my cousin the penny without questioning the inconsistency in the story. Why didn't the rebels attack the village if they were in the outskirts? Why did they go away? What was the purpose of getting nearer to the village in the first place? But, the two most important questions were; why Granma's village and what was there to attack? In fact, nothing mattered much as long as the rebels were gone.

Also, by changing the information she relayed to Grandma, my cousin wanted to guarantee a steady flow of candy money. This way, she would regularly collect one penny a day, but occasionally, two pennies. She figured out that if she claimed a high reward every day, Grandma might grow concerned about rapidly losing her money. She might be forced to choose between staying uninformed about the rebels' whereabouts and live with the consequences, but keep her money, or lose everything for the sake of peace of mind. Another factor she took into consideration was that a high daily reward for both candy and fruits could deplete Grandma's savings and very soon nothing would be left anymore for either one. The safeguard for a continuous payment was the above statement, "But they said they will be back," which implied that Grandma should continue to feel insecure, since the rebel promised to return.

The relationship between my cousin and her grandmother turned from hostility into a mutually beneficial one. Grandma designed mats from palm leaves, which she sold in the village. To cement the newly developed trust between them, Grandma gave my cousin the mats to deliver to customers and return with the sale proceeds. She paid her a penny for doing so. The clients also paid her an additional penny as a small token of their appreciation for the home delivery. She lived a comfortable life and never craved for candies. Ironically, it took a war to secure a daily ration of candies.

Another friend of mine used similar embezzlement tactics to milk money from his mother. He found out frogs scared her to death, so he decided to take full advantage of her fears, the same way my cousin, above, did. Whenever he had craving for candy, he would use a frog to get it. First, he would politely ask his mother for a penny, but he knew well in advance that she would say "No;" an answer that would usually be sitting on the tip of her tongue, ready to come out at a moment's notice, even before he finished the question. She would not only tell him she did not have a penny to give, but also he was good for nothing other than wasting money. He would then quietly leave the scene, walk and kneel by the water pot, dig up a frog from under the pot, and carry it back to where he left his mother standing. He would drop the frog right in front of her by her feet, but without saying a single word. His mother would freak out, run inside the hut, emerge with a penny in her hand, and drop it on the floor, by the side of the frog, also without saying a single word. This was what amounted to a, both implied and by conduct, binding contract between him and his mother. The contract stipulated that my friend would get the reward money, on condition that he would remove and dispose of the object causing the threat. He would bend and pick up the penny and the frog, glance up at his mother's frightened face, and silently walk away, wearing a mischievous half-smile. First, he would get rid of the frog as part of the deal. He would bury it under the same water pot so he could easily dig it out again at another time, when necessity arose. Next, he would go and shop for his candy. Even though his mother knew exactly where he buried the frog, she would not dare risk removing and disposing of it for good. She thought frogs were too scary to deal with.

During the rainy season, frogs were readily available. They were well-fed, since there were plenty of insects around. Somehow, they hardly moved when my friend dropped them in front of his mother. I guess, because their bellies were full and the weather was cool, they stayed calm and nonchalant, if you will, posing no immediate threat. Nevertheless, she happily paid him the penny. The dry season in summer was a different case. The reward was higher. Frogs, being dug from beneath the water pot out of their hibernation, exhibited jitters and irritation for being waken up from a supposedly long and uninterrupted six-month sleep. Also, the exposure to the dry summer heat did not help improve their moods. As much as it was bad luck to the frog, summer presented an opportunity to my friend. The frog would start jumping around as soon as he dropped it on the hot ground, further intimidating his mother. That threat doubled her fears, so it fetched many reward pennies. Getting rid of the frog would be the only thing in her mind at that time. Summer was good for business, but certainly not from the frog's viewpoint. I am sure my friend's mother must have complained to his father for both scaring and embezzling her. He must have had his fair share of punishment, but he might have thought that it all worth it. Candy was a valuable and scarcer commodity than flogging, which was readily available in the village, any time you asked for it.

A college roommate once told me of another bizarre technique he and other children in the village used to steal chicken from an elderly woman who raised them for sale in the market. She kept a close eye on her flock of chickens and was quick to get out of her hut to investigate, whenever the noises they made alarmed her of an imminent danger. She feared elements from the neighborhood, such as dogs, but she mostly feared the neighborhood children. Whenever they craved for chicken meat, they would try to sneak in to steal a rooster to barbecue in the forest, but the woman would always thwart their efforts. She would sense their presence and immediately come out and chase them away. Finally, the children came up with a plan. They would roam the village to find out which house had a visitor or guest in any given day. There was a high chance that day the host would have killed a chicken for his guest. They would get hold of the discarded chicken guts from the house, give it a good cleaning, and use it as bait to steal chicken from the elderly woman. First, they would gather outside the woman's fence. Then one of them would poke a small hole in the fence and, while keeping a grip on one end of the gut, he would put the other end through the hole until it appeared on the inside of the fence. After that, they would all sit quietly and wait. A rooster and its harem might probably be cooling off under the shade of the fence. Upon spotting the gut, the rooster, being the most senior, would rush to claim it, thinking that it was a worm that had strayed out of the fence. It would start swallowing, and the boy, holding on to the other end of the gut, would slowly release it little by little until the rooster had swallowed half a foot or so. He would then start blowing air from his mouth into the gut, pumping up the rooster with air. It would soon faint due to breathing difficulties. At that moment, the children would dispatch one of them rushing to the other side of the fence. He would snatch the rooster, which could barely move or make any sound, and throw it over the fence to his friends who would grab and subdue it to prevent it from making any distress calls, just in case.

The boy would slowly leave the woman's house without alerting her to his presence. He and his friends would take off to the forest, carrying the rooster and laughing all the way. They would build a campfire, barbecue the rooster, and have good time. No one would suspect them of any wrongdoing when they returned to the village. They would see the elderly woman wandering around in the neighborhood, looking for her missing rooster. She would suspect that the children might have something to do with it, but she would not have the courage to ask them, for fear of stirring trouble with their parents. It was a very serious offense to accuse children of theft. Such accusations would badly reflect on the parents' stance in the village, and that was something not taken lightly. The children took full advantage of the village norm and went on to repeat their ingenious technique whenever barbecued meat craving dictated. I guess they did have the brains, but there was no proper setup to channel them in the right direction. They also had effective survival skill, even though it was illegally used.

I have an aunt who was scared to death from chameleons. During the rainy season, she would avoid walking near trees, shrubs, or anything green. She would also abandon using any trail for good, if she, once, encountered a chameleon there. She just could neither understand, nor make sense of the fact that such a tiny creature could voluntarily change its colors as and when it wished. She thought if a chameleon, unlike any other creature she knew, could do that, it might as well possess other undiscovered magical powers, be that turning into a snake, a black cat, or a genie. The best thing for her was to avoid chameleons at all cost. Her vulnerability to the creature made her an ideal candidate for embezzlement of candy-money, but I never felt the urge to threaten her with one because she was generous with her pennies. She was known for distributing money to children, especially during religious holidays; besides, I had enough candy at my disposal, since I owned a candy business.

My father relocated back to Kokoland due to the war in Southern Kordofan. He left behind a number of debtors who owed him money, but without telling me exactly how much. Three of those debtors were of particular interest to him. I knew it was serious money when he told me to travel back to Habila to ask them for repayment, considering the high travelling cost I would incur. I left to Habila with little knowledge about debt collection or bounty hunting, if you will. My first client was Sibair who worked as a guard for one of the large-scale sorghum farms in Habila. Farm guarding job was very lucrative, especially for corrupt guards. It was a common knowledge that they siphoned off truckloads of sorghum from farms, sold them secretly, and funneled the proceeds to their personal accounts. The harvesting machines worked day and night in remote locations and the farm owners were not there all the time to supervise the operations. They fully relied on the guards, some of whom were not trustworthy.

One such example was a guard I knew, named Ahmaru. He lived an extravagant life not compatible with the job of farm guarding. He regularly invited merchants and government officials to attend on-farm feasts held on their honor. He spent lavishly, but, obviously, using money that was not his own. In one farming season,

I went to Habila during school break to farm a piece of land that we owned. My dad was in Kokoland at that time. I was able to secure the rental of a tractor, but finding diesel proved to be a challenge. A friend of Ahmaru, the farm guard, heard about my situation, so he came forward to tell me that was a simple matter. Expressing a fake anger, he blamed me for not reaching out for his help, when everyone in town knew he had enough fuel in storage. I, being so naive, fell for the trick and ordered around a hundred gallons of diesel. We agreed on price, which was surprisingly lower than the prevailing market price. That left me believing that the man was genuinely out to help. I paid him in advance, in view of my desperate situation trying not to miss the farming season. Around sunset; he drove a truck to my dad's place of business and we began offloading the fuel. Amidst of the action, someone approached and asked me to stop. When I inquired about who he was and the reason for asking me to stop, he responded by telling me that the fuel was stolen. It turned out that he was a farm owner and the fuel was from his farm stock and it was sold illegally. He found out about missing barrels of diesel and followed the trail after receiving a tip from a whistle blower. He caught me red-handed. When I told him I bought it from the fellow up in the truck handing me down the fuel, the man denied selling me anything and that he was just helping me off-load the fuel. I landed myself in big trouble. People gathered around the truck and I heard one man say, "If you receive stolen goods, you and the thief will have the same prison sentence." Another man spoke from a distance and said something to the effect that the new judge in town had been giving longer prison sentences for cases of similar nature. I thought to myself, "God forbid." Thanks to Uncle Heeran for intervening and convincing the man that I was tricked into buying the fuel, and that I was there just for a couple of weeks, after which I would go back to school. Uncle Heeran was an influential figure within the Habila community. Finally, the man relented and let go of me. He agreed to do so, but only after scolding me and making me commit to never buy stolen goods. He acted like a judge, and I obediently nodded my head, indicating to him that I was concurring with every single word that came out of his mouth. I desperately wanted the nightmare to come to an end. A few days later, I dropped everything I was doing and disappeared from Habila.

I walked four hours to get to the farm guarded by Sibair, one of my dad's debtors I was primarily visiting in Habila to collect money from. Sibair was an exception to the rule of guarding farms. I have known him to be honest and did not seem to be stealing money from his employer. He was surprised that I showed up unannounced. I told him that I was dispatched by my father to seek payment from him. He asked me when I was planning to go back. I told him, in the morning and as soon as he paid me the money, so he said okay. That night, he killed a chicken in my honor. In the morning, after drinking tea, I told him that I had better get going before it got hot, and demanded that he pay me. He said, "I want you to carry this message to your father." I impatiently said, "What message? He said, "When you get there, tell him that I said I don't have the money." We stood there awkwardly staring at each other for some time, without saying a word, then I decided to hit the road empty-handed. He kept looking at me as I walked away, probably singing to himself, "Hit the road, Jack, don't come back no more," before disappearing inside his hut.

The second debtor was my dad's good friend, Tobain, who lived in a foothill village, south of Habila town. I asked someone about the distance to the village and he told me it was a short one. I took his word for it without asking him for further clarification. I walked for four hours to get to the village. I suffered from dehydration as I did not carry any water with me; besides, it was summer. For some reason; it was not customary for people to carry drinking water when travelling between villages, even though there were incidents of people who got lost in the forest and died of thirst, as in Bulama's case. His body was recovered after many months.

I reached the village and went straight to Tobain's house, only to be told by his daughter Hadia that he had travelled to Dilling town. Again, I left my second debtor empty handed. The one thing that I learned from walking to Tobain's village was that one should never guess distances to mountains by simply looking at them. Mountains are huge, so they give false sense of closeness. If you are heading for a mountain that is blue in color, you should never take a step without adequate preparation, especially if you are walking. The blue color of a mountain is indicative of its far distance. Unless you can see the trees and shrubs on a mountain with your naked eyes, you should not risk walking. I learned that the hard way. I have never been so exhausted and thirsty.

The third debtor resided in the village of Daju. I decided to get there early in the morning to enhance my chances of finding him before he left to his farm. I found him sitting with other village elders, and as soon as he saw me, he sprang up to his feet and greeted me warmly. He knew why I was there, but expressing some fake surprise about my unannounced appearance, he told me how coincidental that I showed up when, in fact, he was planning to visit my father the very next day, and that he was so glad to see me. That was a lie. He invited me for tea and kept talking. It was obvious to me that talking continuously was tactics he used to keep me silent, so I would not elaborate any further on the debt issue in front of the other village elders and embarrass him. He showed unexplained excitement and kept me preoccupied with drinking tea. He topped my cup as soon as I put it down, while exhibiting extreme generosity by insisting that I drank more. Was this man hiding something? You bet he was. He continued to do all the talking and I kept quiet, refraining from interrupting his speech. It was considered disrespectful for young men to interrupt elders as they spoke. The man took full advantage of this common custom.

I finally had a chance to speak. I quietly told him that my dad sent me to seek repayment. Wearing a big smile, he told me that there was absolutely no problem, but first I had to finish drinking my tea. Upon doing so, we both got up, and then he told me he wanted to see me off, as customs dictated that hosts accompanied their travelling guests and walked with them for some reasonable distance out of the village before telling them good bye, and then return to their homes. He was also implying that he was going to take care of the debt. The village of Daju is about twenty kilometers from Kokoland. Together, we walked for fifteen minutes or so. At that juncture, I think, he satisfied himself that I was at about a point of no return.

He abruptly stopped walking, looked me in the eye, and said, "Now it is better for me to go back." I said, "Okay, but the money?" He responded, "Tell your father that times are tough," and he started walking back to his village. He left me standing there, furious at the manner in which he tricked me. The entire nicety that he had exhibited at the village, miraculously evaporated and he became a different person in seconds. He left me standing there, without even saying, "Have a safe trip." I walked for four hours to get to Kokoland, yet empty handed for the third time. The three debtors were unmotivated to pay back their debts. I never found out how much they owed us. Our situation was tantamount to a business owner who closed down his shop, relocated to another state, and then tried to recover money from people he had left behind. My dad stood zero chance of getting paid. We did not have concepts such as collection agencies, as you might have rightly guessed. Collection agencies are not bad, sometimes.

My dad told me a story about an abnormal phenomena that took place in Kokoland during a busy Friday market in 1956. He said, as people were going about their business buying and selling goods, they saw a long white line crossing the sky over their heads. Everyone dropped whatever they were doing and took off running toward their respective villages. Rumors spread all over town like wildfire that the world was coming to an end. People hurriedly gathered around holy men to hear their explanation of the phenomenon. The learned men's official verdict confirmed everyone's fears that judgment day was upon them at hand. They told people that the white line was caused by the Antichrist who appeared and cracked the sky into two halves. That was it, and it was all over. The holy men suggested that people ordered their wives to pound on millet and make *bolloh* pudding to give as offerings to God. It would be even better if they spilled blood; an advice happily embraced by many. Poor sheep and goats were randomly grabbed and slaughtered. That was no day for price haggling, which, under normal circumstances, took all day to settle. Extraordinary measures were needed for extraordinary times. Spilling sacrificial blood was an act compatible with the gravity of the occasion. Nobody hesitated in doing so. The world was ending.

In fact, the white line dividing the sky into two halves turned out to be an airplane smoke-trail. That was the first time such types of planes appeared in the skies over that part of the world, so nobody had ever seen anything like that. People resorted to religion to seek interpretation for unexplainable phenomena; therefore, it was logical to conclude that what they saw has something to do with the end of the world. It was holly men's role to step in and put whatever they had learned over the years to good use, but giving opinion about a broken sky was way beyond their scope of knowledge. They usually had ready answers to every type of question, so it was not surprising that they came up with the verdict, "The world is coming to an end." "We don't know the answer" was never an option. It would have been nice if somebody warned my father and his people of what was coming. At least the Mayans of Central America forewarned us by telling the exact day for the end of the world; hence giving us enough time to prepare. Luckily, their math turned out to be wrong and we are still here. Someone owed my father and his fellow village people in and around Kokoland a big apology. Who invented jet aircrafts and flew one over Kokoland on that memorable Friday in 1956? Whichever entity responsible for that incident, must honor its obligations, come forward, and offer the people of Kokoland a sincere apology, I think.

One of my dad's friends, also a distant cousin, was a man named Zari. He was a celebrity among the Kanuri and other communities in and around Kokoland because he was among the first and few people to own a lorry. As a child, I had the privilege of getting to ride the lorry, sit in the driver's seat, and play. This is something that must not be underestimated, for very few kids had access to such special rights, considering the limited number of lorries. He used to bring me a lot of gifts from the city. He was the one who gave me the tastiest bread I ever had, when I was about five years old. We were living in a farm village and we did not have a bakery there, so bread was an absolute delicacy to have. Things taste different when you are hungry; believe me. Uncle Zari, on his way from his village to Kokoland, used to pass by a water pond and shoot doves. He gave me some of it. Overall, I enjoyed the fact that I had an association with someone who owned a lorry and a shotgun; a rare combination that propelled their owners to fame among members of the community.

Upon the death of my mother, my father got remarried. My stepmother had a brother, Musa, who lived and worked in the city. It happened that he also owned a lorry. My association with celebrities was further strengthened, or so I thought. My father, in good faith, advised Uncle Musa that there was an opportunity for him to serve the route that connected Kokoland and the city. There was a shortage of lorries to carry people and produce form Kokoland into the city and to bring merchandise into Kokoland. My dad's view was that there exists enough room for both; his cousin and his brother-in-law. He was wrong. Uncle Musa, being the new kid in the block, started attracting the community's attention. Uncle Musa also took away passengers and contracts for transportation of goods from Uncle Zari. The celebrity status uncle Zari had been enjoying for decades, was slowly getting eroded, and he resented that so much. In the beginning, my dad played a neutral role by keeping quiet and staying out of the conflict. He thought that soon the dust would settle, the jealousy and the rivalry would disappear, and everything would revert to normalcy. He was wrong. The intolerance to each other turned into a full-blown war. The dispute between the two became the talk of the community. My dad found himself in a difficult situation. He tried to arbitrate a couple of times between them in an endeavor to settle the disagreement amicably and within family boundaries. He miserably failed, in spite of his serious attempts to tackle the problem.

Lorries were the means of transporting humans, agricultural goods, merchandise, and small animals such as goats, sheep, and chickens, all at the same time.

The dispute between the two celebrities got out of control. At one time, they met at a spot between Kokoland and the city, known for its sticky mud, especially after heavy rains. Drivers worried about getting stuck there. The city-bound lorry was loaded with harvest and people, whereas the Kokoland-bound one was carrying merchandize from the city. Customs and common traffic laws dictated that city-bound lorries got out of the trail and gave the right-of-way to approaching vehicles, unless they were carrying heavier loads. It had rained heavily that day, so there was a good chance that leaving the trail would result in the lorry getting stuck in the mud, and that might require off-loading the entire merchandise before pulling it out. Neither of the drivers was willing to give way. That was not a day for observing common laws about rights of way. Uncle Musa who happened to be city-bound refused to leave the trail, arguing that his load was heavier and he would certainly be stuck in the mud. He also feared that people might question his driving skills if his lorry got stuck, and that might cause him to lose the fight against Uncle Zari. He did not want to jeopardize the reputation he had built over the years for being fearless, when it came to venturing into tough terrains with his British-made Austin lorry. Uncle Musa just could not contemplate the image of his truck being roped-up and pulled out of mud. He did not want sympathy from people for owning a truck so week that it could not release its wheels on its own from the grip of mud. He would rather be the subject of applause and admiration from them after victoriously crossing treacherous rivers. He dreaded the prospect of receiving a severe blow to his ego, hurting it for the rest of time.

The two men faced down one another, each determined to come out victorious. The lorries were a few feet apart, also literally facing each other, as if standing in solidarity with their respective owners. The stand-off went on for over an hour. During that time, the poor passengers tried helplessly to intervene and solve the problem peacefully. Some nearby villagers sensed the problem, so they flocked to the conflict zone to investigate. Soon, an arbitration industry evolved around the area. Good wishers shuttled between the two camps, when each driver held on to his ground and refused to budge. Finally, Uncle Musa agreed to give way, claiming he wanted to do that only to show respect for all the men who had intervened to settle the dispute, and that his decision was by no means an act of surrender. Deep down, everyone believed Uncle Musa gave way in an attempt to hold the upper hand or the high moral ground, if you will, even though many people felt that he was violating the customary laws, which were observed for a long time.

Uncle Musa always bragged about his driving and unparalleled navigational skills under harsh conditions, and his expertise with automobiles. One evening, a crowd gathered around our house to hear him talk about his brave adventures and the risks he had taken to get delivery jobs done. Someone brought up the incident with Uncle Zari when they refused to give way to one another. He told us that Zari did not know a thing about automobiles. To show Uncle Zari's level of ignorance about trucks, he held his right hand thumb and index finger together, squeezed them hard, and said, "Zari doesn't know even this much. He continued bragging, "What does Zari know? If I want, I could do something to this lorry [pointing to his vehicle parked nearby] and make it run nonstop." He said that in a matter-of-fact way, then took a moment of silence to survey the crowd's clueless faces to reap looks of admiration for his secret automobile knowledge. You could tell that his statement baffled us all because you could see it in our eyes that we were all releasing the reins of imagination to roam free and look for an answer to the question, "What could Uncle Musa do to his vehicle that makes it run nonstop?" In my case, the only thing that I could think of was driving his truck without brakes. "Uncle Musa is a genius man," I thought to myself. I have been looking around, but I still could not find a car company that was able to come up with a technology to match my uncle's. It is rather unfortunate that the car industry is going through such turbulent times. Uncle Musa and his secret could have been a great help in rescuing the industry, if it isn't for his old age and related health problems. I wonder what he meant and what he could have done.

Whenever Uncle Musa came to the village, we gathered around him, gave audience, and listened to some unverifiable stories. Because he lived in the city, he could speak Arabic better than most Kanuri people in Kokoland could. However, he occasionally injected words in his sentences, which were not part of the Arabic language. They were of his own creation, but they went by unchallenged. His assistant Tayeb, also from the city, could detect some of those strange words, but would not dare to say anything. He reused them mockingly in the absence of Uncle Musa and we laughed a lot. We never took Uncle Musa seriously.

The death of my mother was a great loss to the family. My dad was overwhelmed by grieve and sadness. I was aware of the situation, but he did not think that I had full grasp of what had happened because of my young age. He used to sit alone in silence for hours without saying a single word. His condition affected my activities and brought them to a halt. I used to sit down and observe him from a distance, but without letting him know that I was watching. I would not leave him in that state to go and play or do anything. I would wait until he recovered from those sad moments. He would usually get up and walk away, pick up something to do, or call my name to get him drinking water. That gave me some sense of relief and normalcy. After that, I would get up and wander away to catch up with a soccer game or look for my friend Tiffah to go bird trapping. I vividly remember one of these sadness attacks when he quietly sat on the bed at his usual spot. This time, I chose to sit a few feet away from him, on the concrete at the edge of the shop verandah. We did not talk to each other for the entire time, but, every now and then, I would catch a glimpse of his sad face. I remember telling myself that I would grow up and, one day, make him a proud father. I wanted him to forget all the pains he had endured in his life. That image stuck in my mind and was instrumental in whatever help I extended to him. I am very lucky that he lived long enough so I could reward him with a few surprises.

My father was the one who told me where planes came from. "America," was his answer whenever I spotted one flying over Kokoland and asked him about its origins. In fact, I am always fascinated with airplanes and flying. As I mentioned above, I promised myself to make him happy as much as I could, so, on one occasion, I surprised him by booking him a ticket to travel by air for the first time. That was quiet something for both of us. I did a similar thing by arranging for him to fly overseas to visit me. He bragged a lot to his friends about these two experiences. I am grateful for having had the opportunity to help, even though what I had done was negligible, if compared with all the help and support I received from him.

An ancient castle in the country of Oman.

I took a job in the Middle East, so he flew in to visit me and my family. Upon arrival at the airport, the immigration officer enquired about the reason he was visiting, then granted him the entry visa and welcomed him into the country. Instead of leaving, my father reached for his pocket and handed the officer my business card, asking him if he knew me. The officer looked at the card and told him that he did.

My father told me about the airport incident, expressing his happiness that the immigration officer and many senior government officials, including the country's rulers, knew me personally. I took the opportunity to clear the misunderstanding he had. I told him that the immigration officer did not know me in person, but he did recognize my employer. My dad did not seem to like my explanation that I was not as famous a person as he had hoped.

My dad and one of his cousins, named Uncle Mahjoob, had a funny friendship. They were married to sisters who were the daughters of Merchant Aziz, about whom I have written earlier. They used to tease one another a lot, each trying to gain the upper hand by showing how exposed he was to worlds outside of Kokoland. Whereas my dad claimed leadership role and expertise in dealing with the authorities, Uncle Mahjoob exhibited panache and sophisticated attitude, which, in all fairness, was true in the manner he carried himself and lived his life. I remember, during the dispute over the shop, my dad went to the city to seek help from a lawyer. Upon his return to Kokoland, Uncle Mahjoob asked him if his trip was successful. My dad told him it was and that the lawyer had asked him to claim goodwill from the shop owner, if he insisted on selling it to someone else. The problem was that goodwill was a word unfamiliar to my dad, so he did not pronounce it correctly. He basically butchered it; providing Uncle Mahjoob ample ammunition to use for entertaining himself by asking my dad, every now and then, to say goodwill so he could laugh. He would say, "Sharif, my dear brother, could you please tell me, one more time, what the lawyer told you?" They both used to laugh a lot.

Uncle Mahjoob held the view that some people did not meet his expectations with respect to etiquettes, attitudes, and good behavior. He got annoyed when people did not adhere to certain code of standards and good demeanor. I guess, he was in the wrong place, for the village people had no way of knowing much about etiquettes. He confided to my dad how much he was annoyed by some individuals' conducts. My dad, equipped with this knowledge, occasionally used it to get back at Uncle Mahjoob to score points for himself as well. Once, he jokingly told me that Uncle Mahjoob had two guest rooms in his house; first and second class rooms. One room was properly furnished and always well looked after. He kept it locked at all times, opening it only for special guests or occasions. The other room was accessible to anybody in the house and it was hardly furnished. My dad told me that when guests visited Uncle Mahjoob, he received them at the gate and quickly decided which room was appropriate for them. He would politely lead the sophisticated guests to the clean and elegantly furnished room, whereas he led those who did not meet the first-class standard to the commoners' living room. My dad, with a little bit of dramatization, told me that the community found out about the secrets of the two rooms, so when people visited Uncle Mahjoob, they would stop at the gate and wait to see to which room he was leading them. If he pointed to the first class room, they would step forward, but if he took them in the direction of the useless inferior room, they would turn around and leave. So, whenever Uncle

Mahjoob had visitors, my dad would jokingly ask him, "Today I heard that you had a few guests. I am just wondering to which room did you take them." Uncle Mahjoob would find himself speechless and they would both burst into an uncontrollable laughter.

Uncle Mahjoob earned a living by trading in mercury when no one had the slightest idea what it was. He guarded his secret with his teeth. He used to travel overseas and return with bottles of the chemical. He would then go around visiting cities to distribute his merchandise to goldsmiths for use in their jewelry business. Nobody knew anything about his movements, since he did not say where he was going or coming from. He led a very comfortable life, if compared to the rest of the Kanuri community who mostly worked as farmers. Uncle Mahjoob made enough money from his trade, moved to the city, and bought a house in an affluent neighborhood, commensurate with his financial standing, as well as his aspiration for high-class city life. In fact, he adjusted very well to his new lifestyle; something unattainable to most of his Kanuri people he had left behind in Kokoland.

When it was time for Uncle Mahjoob's daughter to get married, the community decided to show solidarity with their fellow Kanuri man. On the wedding day, men, women, and children rode a lorry, brought along with them their gifts (chicken, potbelly goats, sheep, millet, etc.), and travelled to the city to visit Uncle Mahjoob in his new residence, and spend a few days to attend the wedding. This was also to congratulate him for buying a house in the city. A lorry packed with village people showed up in front of Uncle Mahjoob's house, unannounced. The tragedy was that those people also brought along with them Mairami, the sharp-tongued *griot*.

Griots are African historians, storytellers, praise-singers, poets, and musicians. This form of art was culturally recognized among the Kanuri of Sudan, even though a dying one due to being cut off from its roots in West Africa. The culture of griots goes back to the Kanem-Bornu Empire, which peaked in the sixteenth century. Griots had a special place in the emperor's court. They went around praising rulers, nobilities, and speaking about generosity, bravery, and generally promoting characters of such natures. They continued to play that role way after the collapse of the empire, especially maintaining the praising and storytelling part, even though in smaller scales. Griots roamed the villages to attend gatherings such as weddings and naming of babies on the seventh day of birth, the same way as local barbers (wanzaams), whom I have written about in previous chapters. Mairami, the sharp-tongued, was one of few griots left. He earned his living by attending and telling stories at Kanuri events. He generously praised those who paid him lavishly by speaking loudly about their noble, brave, and rich ancestral heritage, while exercising liberty by adding, from his imagination, fabricated stories that could fetch him additional money. On the other hand, he brutally assassinated the characters of those who failed to meet his pay expectations, calling them all sorts of names and attributing to them every negative personality traits that you can imagine. That is why I gave him the title: Mairami, the sharp-tongued griot. What mattered to him was using any means necessary to make money. As far as he was concerned, there was a thin and a blurred line that stood between truth and lies, and that only money could separate them and set them apart. People went to great length to appease him and money was never an issue when he was present, for the damage he could inflict on a person could never be overturned. Character assassination was neither reversible, nor reparable, and one thing was for sure: no one wanted that.

I gave you this background about Mairami so you know he had no place in Uncle Mahjoob's affluent city neighborhood, especially during his daughter's wedding. *Griotting* was a deeply rooted tradition in the Kanuri tribal culture and was kept within the community. Very few people in the country knew of its existence, and city people were the last to know.

Mairami and his cultural baggage, on one hand, and Uncle Mahjoob and his city life and guests of honor coming to attend his daughter's wedding, on the other hand, were two mutually exclusive groups. They just could not mix. So, Mairami, feeling out of place and out of touch with his surroundings, looked very subdued. He picked a remote spot and sat down quietly observing the city people. He was just not used to the sight of clean, healthy looking, and worry free city people, who laughed a lot for no apparent or convincing reason.

One member of the village delegation said to Mairami, "Hey, Mairami, at every village event, you deafened our ears with your loud voice like a he-goat mating call. You behaved and carried yourself as if you were the only man around and no man was a match to you. You praised people who paid and raised hell for those who did not. Now you are sitting timidly like a mew. What happened to you today?" Everyone laughed and looked in Mairami's direction to see how he was going to react. Mairami felt humiliated. He thought for a minute, evaluating his options. He was in an unfamiliar territory, so business was certainly not as usual, but if he shied away from doing what he normally did, then that would be his last day to earn easy money through praising, intimidation, or defamation. He would not be able to justify his action to the people in the village, if he kept quiet in the city. On the other hand, if he got up and started *griotting*, he would risk getting chased away because none of Uncle Mahjoob's guests from the city would understand or appreciate what he would be doing or saying. His predicament was that Uncle Mahjoob might choose to side with his city guests. Mairami bought more time to think as everybody else impatiently waited for a response from him, then made up his mind. He suddenly blared, "Somebody else, but not me. I will never be quiet." He sprang to his feet and started yelling his *griotting* act in Kanuri language, a secret Uncle Mahjoob never wanted to reveal to his newly adopted society of city elites. He portrayed the image of a rich man from one of the country's most popular tribes. Mairami's action would flush him out, tarnish his image, and life would never be the same again. Seconds earlier, everything was calm and tranquil, and city panache was felt in the air everywhere, then, all of a sudden, words from an untrained crude vocal sound, spoken in an indigenous language that was closer to yelling than singing, filled the airwaves. You have to understand that the ears of city people were more accustomed to hearing voices singing alongside orchestra that produced beautiful, harmonious, and soothing music, than anything like Mairami's voice. So, it was not surprising that Uncle Mahjoob's city dignitaries and guests attending the wedding dropped whatever city conversations they were having and prepared to take off running.

Man has two options; fight or flight. There was a big difference between men from Kokoland and men from the city. Heroism and bravery were the norm for Kokoland men. For them, fleeing a scene for whatever reason amounted to total betrayal and dishonoring of family and tribal values, for the rest of time. On the other hand, men from the city, whenever confronted with a fight or flight situation, were quick to choose the easiest latter option. They were of the opinion that absolute bravery was nothing short of absolute foolishness. Their modes operandi was; first run, and then investigate. Fearing the consequences of family or tribal disownment was the least of their worries. No wonder they were about to flee the scene. City dwellers are rational thinkers. Ironically, Mairami's *griotting* was considered a form of art to some people, whereas it represented an imminent danger to others.

It took people a few more seconds to absorb the shock and identify the source of the strange yelling. In my case, it took me few decades to get to a point where I could understand and appreciate why the men from the city wanted to run away upon hearing Mairami's voice. I accompanied my ten and twelve year old boys to a mall in Houston, Texas, to do some shopping. They were goofing around and would not listen to me when I asked them to stop, so the villager in me kicked in and I, kind of, raised my voice. My twelve year old son got closer and spoke to me in a hushed tone, saying, "Dad, don't yell in a different language. It scares other people." He reminded me of Mairami the griot in the city. I thought for a moment and said to myself, "My boy is right."

Mairami's voice hit Uncle Mahjoob's ears like a haunting sound in a nightmarish dream, causing him to spring to his feet the same way Mairami did. They both sprang to their feet to damage control. Mairami; desperate to safeguard his source of livelihood and Uncle Mahjoob; frantic to protect his reputation. Uncle Mahjoob wanted to get to Mairami before he had said much, but in the eyes of the city people, the damage to his reputation has already been done. Mairami spoke in a language unknown to them, so the few words he had shouted were more than enough to tarnish uncle Mahjoob's panache, style, and image for good. He also feared that Mairami would turn against him and start assassinating his character, using the Kanuri language which was understood by everyone who had come from the village. There was the risk that the story about smearing Uncle Mahjoob's name would be carried back to the village and told to every person left behind. If that happened, Uncle Mahjoob would lose at both ends; the city and the village. All of these considerations went through his mind in a matter of seconds, and that made it crucial for him to get to Mairami before it was too late to safe anything.

Uncle Mahjoob sprang to his feet, left his shoes behind, and rushed toward Mairami. It must be a matter of great urgency and grave consequences that leads a man to leave his shoes behind and run barefooted. He reached Mairami and started begging him to stop, but Mairami would not, so he decided to appease him. Uncle Mahjoob reached for his pocket, took out a large bunch of money, and shoved it in Mairami's hand. Mairami had a quick glance at the money in his hand while he was still *griotting* loudly. Upon noticing the bunch of large bills, his voice got subdued and he literally dropped himself down to the ground, ending Uncle Mahjoob's embarrassing moments. Witnesses said Mairami did not decide to sit down voluntarily. They said he had a mild heart attack, knocking him out of control. He was shocked to see someone give him all that money in one go. Another joker suggested that what happened to Mairami was not a heart attack. It was rather his legs buckling on him for holding all that money, so he came crumbling down to the ground. People thought Mairami never held that much money in his life, and that tells you the seriousness of the matter as far as Uncle Mahjoob was concerned. Mairami was a great embarrassment to him.

Uncle Mahjoob's original plan was to have two events, one for his special guests from the city, and another for his Kanuri village people. He thought that way he would give each group their freedom, especially the people from the village, so they could do their wedding ceremony traditions and rituals. His Kanuri people did not see it that way. They felt it was their duty to show up without invitation and that there was no need for giving Uncle Mahjoob advance notice, since they considered the wedding as their daughter's and the event belonged to the community, in the first place.

My dad was so amused by this incident between Mairami and Uncle Mahjoob. He always brought it up whenever he felt like teasing Uncle Mahjoob. They enjoyed one another's company and laughed a lot at each other's mishaps. I loved listening to their stories. Both my dad and Uncle Mahjoob passed away seven years ago. They died only a few months apart. God bless their souls.

Coming to terms with one's identity is central to any form of progress a person or a community aspires for. Uncle Mahjoob's case was a classic example of the kind of dilemma people face. They go to a great extent to gain recognition, only to be failed by someone like Mairami, who, with their actions, would remind them of their true identity and, hence, prevent them from assuming a new mainstream identity that falsely represents the social strata they are aspiring to join and be part of. The irony is that the mainstream culture itself is fake because most people adopt it at the expense of their original cultures. In the process, many people don't fit in either cultures. People cannot actualize their potential, if they are in doubt about their identity. The first step toward happiness and prosperity is the love of oneself because if you hate yourself, you should not expect love from others. If your community embarrasses you, you will be on your own. In my opinion, the continuous crisis we are experiencing in the country today (for those of you who follow Sudanese affairs) is partly rooted in identity problems. The solution begins with coming to terms with who we are.

I met Mairami for the first time in 1980 at a family gathering organized in honor of a cousin who had returned on a vacation from one of the Arabian Gulf oil rich countries where he had been working for many years. My cousin's return called for celebration and the killing of sheep. Community members were invited to the feast and Mairami was among the first people to show up. He was not the kind of a person who wasted time waiting for an invitation, bearing in mind the fact that the feast was organized for a man returning from an oil rich country, so money was never an issue. That certainly justified Mairami in raising his expectations. He convinced himself that his reward would be enough to last him an entire year, so he could take a break from work, if he so wished. He was wrong. My cousin did not rise to that level of expectations. That led to a hostile response from Mairami, the sort that was dreaded by Uncle Mahjoob, above. He butchered my cousin's character. People enjoyed the lies he carefully knitted to portray my cousin as someone who was not worthy of his time. He told him that no woman in her right mind would agree to marry him because she would starve to death. Mairami was very unhappy about the gift money he had received. People laughed so hard.

A different griot, Gamboor, came to visit me when I recently returned from America. Gamboor also did not hesitate to fabricate stories of his making. He showed up at events and entertained people by telling them egregious lies, which he absolutely believed. I was away for over twenty years, so I had no idea who he was and what he did. Someone poked him to tell me his story. The first thing he said was that he was friends with Omer Bashir, the current sitting president. I was obviously shocked to hear that because what he said absolutely did not make any sense, but nobody intervened to make any clarification or shed light on who this person was. He continued telling me how he became friends with the president. He said their friendship goes back to earlier times when the president was an army general deployed at the war front in South Sudan. There he planned for the quo that brought him to power in 1989. Gamboor continued to tell me that when it was time to execute the plan, the president, still an army general, decided to drive to the Capital. He said the president passed by his house, spent the night there, and continued his journey the following morning. He told me that he executed the quo in few days after reaching Khartoum. Gamboor was hinting to me that Omer Bashir finalized the plan for the quo in his house. He left me wondering why would an army general who was about to take over and rule the entire country spend the night in this man's one room mud house in the poorest neighborhood in the outskirt of the city. Why would he drive one thousand kilometers to get to Khartoum, when he had planes under his command. He swore to me that's what had happened, then everyone started laughing. They later on told me that the whole thing was in Gamboor's head and nobody believed it except him. That was how Gamboor made his living. People found him entertaining, so they encouraged him to tell them more about his imaginary adventures, and he continued to lie generously. He enjoyed the tips he received from people, but most importantly, the fact that he was the center of attention. Fully remembering what had happened between Mairami and Uncle Mahjoob, I was so generous to Gamboor that not only did he refrain from tarnishing my image, but he also praised my dad and his ancestors about whom he knew nothing. He left the house very happy and that what mattered to both of us.

My dad told me about a story that took place when he was a young man. The British Rulers of the day installed some form of a public administration, based on dividing the country into regions run by tribal mayors. They empowered the mayors to rule their respective regions according to local norms, customs, religion, and culture. Each mayor's individual character also played a role in how they ruled. Serious crimes such as murder cases were transferred to proper courts to handle in cities, unless parties involved opted to settle them locally by agreeing to some form of blood compensation known as *diya*. Some mayors exhibited great wisdom and kindness in carrying out their responsibilities and were renowned for that all over the region, yet others were tyrannical and equally renowned for their cruelty, brutality, and injustices. They punished those who resented or challenged their authority through antagonism, levying of excessive fines, deprivation of rights, wrongful conviction, and imprisonment. Therefore, any attempts to file an appeal at a higher district authority was a suicidal act. Few people dared to take such actions. Besides; many people did not know that such an option even existed.

My father, to his bad luck, grew up in a region run by a tyrant mayor. For example, one of the things the mayor did was that he commanded his subjects to go and serve gratuitously at his farm during the rainy season for at least one day. As I wrote earlier, It was a common practice that in the event of death or sickness of a community member during the rainy season, the whole community volunteered and flocked to the deceased's or sick man's farm to plant seeds, weed out grass, harvest crops, or carry out any type of farm work needed. Even though there was no urgency in the case of the mayor, he demanded that people, involuntarily, went to serve at his farm.

On the day he scheduled for such service, the mayor would dispatch his guards to block the village's exits to prevent people from leaving to their farms. The guards would tell every man to change course and head to the mayor's farm. Most people obeyed the orders and did exactly what they were told. Rebels like my dad did not follow such exploitive rules. He told me that, in one instance, the mayor announced a day for the public to attend to his farm. That day, he left the house before sunrise, hoping to get out of the village ahead of the guards, but to his bad luck, he found them waiting there. They ordered him to go back and head to the mayor's farm. My dad refused and continued his journey to his farm, but, in the end, he paid dearly for his action. The mayor levied a heavy fine on him for disobeying his orders. My dad told me that was the beginning of a long period of antagonism from the mayor. He said that he lost every case that was brought in front of the mayor, to which he was a party, no matter what. For example, he was targeted, singled out, and fined for selling merchandise out of his shop to the public at prices deemed by the mayor as unofficial and were not set by the government. In fact, there was no such thing as government prices. Besides; some of the mayor's shopkeeper friends were untouched, even though they also sold their merchandize at prices equal to my dad's. How much my dad paid for the merchandise was immaterial. You remember the dispute over the shop between my dad and the Gadim brothers that I wrote about earlier? Many of the arbitrators who intervened to settle the dispute were aides of the mayor. I was not surprised at all that my dad lost the bid to buy the shop.

Growing up, I have witnessed few incidents of injustice and ill-treatment, which happened to other people. One such incident took place in 1974 when I was in first year of middle school. It was during the Eid festival, which was held after Ramadan when people had just ended a month of fasting. Most of us children who attended school elsewhere were home for the holidays. One late afternoon, as we were gathered in the center of the marketplace, a man named

Wady showed up in front of the local judge's house, which was a stone's throw away from the marketplace. The judge, Jadalla, about whom I have written earlier, happened to be the same person who recorded the number of water deliveries my dad made per day, few decades earlier. As you can tell, Judge Jadalla's first grade education had propelled him into fame and prominence. As I mentioned before, the government of General Numeiri abolished the mayoral system of local administration. He replaced it with a system of five local judges who were appointed and given authority to settle routine disputes over land, marriage, family feuds, inheritance, etc. They judged by rotation so that each judge ruled for one month at a time. It was Jadalla's turn to rule and that was why Wady showed up at his house to report an incident. Wady lived in a hut by himself on the western edge of Kokoland and he was rarely seen in the village. He spent most of his time in the forest, hunting squirrels, rabbits, wildcats, or any creature he could find. We were surprised to see him in town in front of the judge's house. He was accompanied by Aseel, the guard, carrying his World War II rifle. We joked about Aseel's rifle that it was inoperable and good for nothing beyond a decorative object. Aseel was in his khaki uniform of T-shirt and shorts. He had a khaki-colored puttee, tightly and spirally wound around his legs, covering the area from the ankle to the knee. He was also wearing his World War II British army metal helmet, it too, covered in khaki color. Seeing him in that uniform was a declaration to the public that he was in full gear, ready for battle.

We got curious, so we congregated at the judge's house to find out what was happening. Aseel and Wady emerged from inside the house and went away in the direction of Wady's house. Half an hour or so passed before they returned, but this time they were accompanied by two nicely dressed men walking in front of them. From their looks, we could tell that they were from South Sudan. Judge Jadalla emerged from his house and joined them. By that time, a big crowd had gathered around the judge, Aseel, Wady, and the two men. We kept quiet so Aseel would not chase us away. Wady spoke first. He said to the judge, "I found these two gentlemen in Kaltham's house drinking *mareesa* (local alcohol), and from their looks, I think they are thieves." As simple as that. Then, the judge asked Aseel if the men had any belongings. He told him they did, so he ordered him to go and get them. Aseel quickly left and returned with two suitcases. The judge told him to open them, so he did. Both suitcases contained new and neatly ironed shirts, pants, and pairs of shiny shoes, as well as other items we did not recognize. Judge Jadalla appeared to agree with Wady's assessment that the two men were thieves, so he ordered Aseel to tie them up. Yes, tie them up.

Aseel started to execute the orders, but the two men resisted, and it turned into a bloody fight. Aseel hit the men on different parts of their bodies with his old rifle butt. Nevertheless, he could not subdue them until three adults from the crowd volunteered to help him pin them down to the ground and tie them up. They lay on the ground, with their hands tied to their backs, bleeding from their mouths and noses. It started getting dark, so Aseel ordered us to disperse. We left the scene without knowing what plan Judge Jadalla had for them. I heard some people say that the two men were travelling by train on their way to Wau, a city in South Sudan. They got stranded at the train station a few miles from Kokoland because the railroad, further up, had been swept away by heavy rains. They had to wait until it was fixed, so they walked to Kokoland to look for food. They appeared educated and could be civil service employees, or returning from overseas, on their way home. That was their only crime. Wady, probably, had never seen anyone so nicely dressed in his entire life. He just assumed that they were thieves. Sadly, Jadalla the judge also adopted Wady's conclusion. The two men were probably released overnight, but nobody knew for sure what happened to them or where they went.

In most of the cases, local administration judges were chosen in accordance with tribal considerations, which, sometimes, resulted in the selection of judges who lacked wisdom needed for carrying out judicial responsibilities. Decisions could be made arbitrarily, autocratically, or on personal whims, and no one dared to challenge them or file for appeal, for fear of retribution. On the other hand, there were judges who, despite their limited or complete lack of education, were exemplary in righteousness, kindness, and wisdom. Therefore, it is prudent and fair to say that judge Jadalla's unjust ruling was not the norm. However, this is by no means an underestimation of the terrible treatment the two men had suffered.

It is one thing for a local administration judge to, sporadically, hand down cruel judgments, and another entirely different thing for a country's government to avail resources at its disposal and unleash its military might to fight its own citizens, under the banner of holy war (jihad). The events of the contemporary history of Sudan were an outcome of accumulation of decades of injustice. Millions of Sudanese lost their lives in the North-South war that lasted twenty-three years. In the end, South Sudan decided to secede and part ways with the North. Today, the civil war is still going strong in three fronts in the country. Obviously, the seeds for these wars were planted way back and the successive rulers of the country miserably failed in building a nation ruled on the basis of equality and citizenship. As a result of laboring for decades under injustice and alienation, many citizens resorted to picking up arms to fight for their rights. It will take drastic measures to prevent other parts of the country from following the secession path taken by South Sudan.

One day, I met a fellow Kokoland man in the capital city where I was attending college. In the course of our conversation, he casually mentioned the death of Judge Jadalla, which was news to me, so I exclaimed, "Is he dead?" His response was, "Ya, where have you been? Let me tell you. He was gone, gone a long time ago. By now, he had enough of death." He said that as he looked at the ground and shook his head. He was replaying images of injustices he had personally endured at the hands of Judge Jadalla. He looked at me and, with great sadness, said, "I lost every single case that I took to Judge Jadalla. He always judged in my opponents' favor." The man looked distraught, but, at the same time, relieved that judge Jadalla was no more because God had taken him away.

Below, are two incidents involving my friend Bijawi and me, but, first, I need to give you some background to the story. As I stated earlier, lacking the support of an elder brother or children from my tribe at school to create a pact, was a big problem for me. At the same time, that very reality turned out to be a blessing because I had to look up to no one, but myself. I navigated my way on my own and learned from my mistakes and experiences. I thank my dad for many things, but especially for teaching me how to become self-reliant. It is a concept he had instilled in me through repeatedly emphasizing its importance for my future.

Bijawi was a high school colleague and a friend who was also two years senior to me. Over the summer school breaks, we met at the village playground in the afternoons and played soccer with other boys. In the evenings, Bijawi and I met again either at my house or his to eat dinner. My stepmother, occasionally, prepared for us light meals such as rice pudding with milk, donuts and tea, or spaghetti with butter and honey. These were special treatments for special persons. My dad and my stepmother had respect for Bijawi's father, who was a holy man and the local leader of the Sofi sect of Islam, which my dad had been following. On Friday evenings, my dad would go to perform Sofi prayers with Bijawi's dad at their house. That was why Bijawi and his family had a special place in our household. Both my stepmother and my dad were comfortable seeing him and me hanging out together. They expected nothing bad from my association with the son of a holy man. That way, I would stay out of troubles and avoid bad influences that could lead to smoking cigarettes, drinking local alcohol, or hanging out with school dropouts.

After eating dinner, Bijawi and I would talk at length about girls. We frequently talked about two sisters, but the girls had no knowledge of our interests or fascination with them. One night he told me that he wanted to talk to the younger sister and that I should settle for the elder one; a recommendation that I rejected outright and bluntly, revealing to him that my interest lay on the younger one. I argued that was unbecoming because he was two years senior to me, so, ideally, he should settle for the elder girl and I take the younger one. You can tell how limited our knowledge of girlish matters then; otherwise why fight over two girls who did not know that we even existed. We made up our minds and thought that was all it took. That was the last straw which broke the camel's back; as far as the friendship between Bijawi and I was concerned. We dissolved it at once that very night and stopped meeting one another. He went to college in the capital and, after graduation, he migrated to one of the rich Arabian Gulf States, so we never saw each other again.

Here is the second incident involving my friend Bijawi and me. While in college, another friend of mine enrolled in a correspondence course at a school in Britain. He told me that upon completion of the program, he would receive a certificate, which would help him a lot when it was time to look for jobs after graduation from college. My friend happened to have an elder brother working in the Arabian Gulf, who arranged to pay the $30 course fees on his behalf. I wanted to do the same, but I neither had the $30, nor a brother overseas. I decided to turn to somebody for help, then I remembered my friend Bijawi. I was so happy that I, too, could enhance my English language skills, as well as my chances of landing a good job after graduation. I wrote Bijawi a letter asking him to lend me $30. I explained to him what I needed it for, promising to return it as soon as I graduated and got a job. I mailed the letter and waited impatiently. Few weeks passed, then I received a response from him in the mail. I was so happy to get it. That day, after classes, I went to the hostel, sat down on my bed, and prepared myself for good news. I thought I was seconds away from pulling out; either a check for $30, or its equivalent in local currency, and both methods of payment were totally acceptable to me. I remember, my face was glowing with excitement and expectation. Upon opening the envelope, I noticed something strange. Inside, I found another smaller envelope that looked familiar. I pulled it out very quickly and looked at it. I was surprised to realize that it was my own handwriting on the outside. For few seconds I stared at both envelopes, one in each hand, trying to make sense of what was going on. I looked inside the large envelope and pulled out a folded piece of paper, unfolded it, and started reading. I was shocked. It was the same letter I had mailed to Bijawi a few weeks earlier. Then, it hit me. He got my letter, read it, put it in an envelope, and mailed it back to me, without adding a word, not even "Hi." I got Bijaw's message. He was retaliating for what had transpired between us about the two sisters a few years earlier. He was punishing me for rejecting his offer to accept the elder sister so he could get the younger one. I sat on my bed for a long time gazing at nothing. My throat burned as if I was swallowing fire, but I refused to let my eyes get teary. I remember biting my lower lip until it bled. It was humiliating. Nevertheless, I thank Bijawi for not helping me because what he did turned out to be the greatest help as well as the best gift that I ever received from any human being. That was the first and the last time I asked anybody for a personal financial favor, ever. I set out to build a name for myself relying on my own efforts. I have been doing that for over thirty years, and I am not done yet. In fact, I don't hold any grudges against Bijawi. A little dose of humiliation can be a healthy thing, I guess. I also think that dark moments in our lives can shape us in many positive ways, and that darkness, itself, can be a blessing and a motivational push-factor that helps us seek light. I think Bijawi's incident ignited something in my soul. Somehow, I developed the habit of trying my level best to do what I can, anytime a family member or a close friend reaches out for help. Has Bijawi a role in all this? May be, but I don't know for sure. I don't mean to suggest that I respond positively to every person asking me for a favor, but I make sure that they don't regret asking, in case I fall short of their expectations. Like many people, I get a great deal of satisfaction in extending a helping hand whenever possible. Thank you, Bijawi.

There was not much to do in smaller settings such as the one in Kokoland, my primary school town, and the towns where I attended middle and high schools. I got very excited when it was time to go to college in the capital city. I was wrong about the city because it posed its own challenges. It required that I carried myself in a certain way to gain acceptance from college girls. Social order demanded that I adopted the behavior of city dwellers, appeared and sounded sophisticated when communicating with others, and, most importantly, refrained from speaking in my crude and unpolished Kokoland way. The capital city also demanded that I acted cool, a term that I learned its connotations and magnitude here in America, some twenty years later. Looking cool in the city called for wearing imported white and blue American jeans, corduroy pants, and designer shirts, items for which I neither had the resources to finance or knowledge of where to find them, nor the physique to look good in them. Hardly any of the city boutiques that sold imported fancy clothes had my size. I was very skinny and had long arms and legs. I was an outlier by all measures. The shops made no money catering to the needs of outliers, so the sizes available were mostly average. I thought to myself, "Without some form of divine intervention, my efforts to assimilate and gain social recognition in the city will be doomed to failure. I was wrong about my friend Bijawi, affluent college girls, and big city life." Neverthelees, I grew more confident about the direction I wanted to take in life. I thought that travelling overseas might be the answer, but I knew deep down in me that if I was having trouble securing $30 correspondence course fees, then for sure travelling overseas would be one big hurdle to overcome. Miraculously, my dreams materialized and I was able to travel abroad and discover the world, as shown in the next chapter.

I would like to end this chapter, which I have dedicated to my father, with a few things that I had observed him do while growing up. Performing acts of kindness and generosity for as long as I had known him typified his high character. I have learned many great lessons from him and here are special things about him that I would like to share with you. Sudanese people are generous by nature. Despite the economic hardships the country is experiencing nowadays, people still share the little that they have with family members and strangers (guests), alike. I have personally experienced this in my own house. My father was of the view that guests came to our house for a reason and that God chose to put us on their path. They came along with their blessings. He told us that we did not know which guest brought us good fortune and that we were special and lucky to have them. He was very firm and never compromised when it came to taking care of guests. His words were orders, which I did not like at the time because they loaded me with additional tasks that upset my plans for doing my own things such as playing soccer. It did not matter even when I had important matches to play. I had given up my bed and slept on the floor many times, especially when guests arrived from the city in my uncle's truck and had to spend the night at our house.

Kokoland is known all over the region for being a hub for the Kanuri people who lived in many villages all around it. During the harvest season, holy men and people with disabilities came from many parts of the country and went roaming around in nearby villages for a couple of weeks to collect *zakat* on agricultural products. *Zakat* is an obligatory payment made annually under Islamic law on certain kinds of property and used for charitable and religious purposes. They would return to town on market days loaded with cash and agricultural goods. From there, they would catch lorries and travel back to their respective cities and villages, until the next harvest season. Some of these people took a different approach in asking for help, which may look strange to some of you. They would usually come to town on Thursdays and spend the night at our house to be ready for the big market day on Friday. This group, unlike the others, did not go and roam the villages. They used to sit down in a quiet corner of the market place and loudly announce their demands, be that money, clothing, agricultural produce, or a combination of all. People congregated around them, listened carefully, and left to get them what they had exactly sked for. A few men would go around in the market to spread the word about these people's demands, which were met individually or collectively. Surprisingly, this group would refuse to accept nothing short or more of what they had exactly asked for. This was a well-established and a culturally accepted form of asking or giving, depending on how you look at it. It also showed the high level of solidarity between members of the Kanuri community, for I don't remember these people ever going away with their demands unmet. For some reason unknown to me, my father paid a great deal of attention to this group of people asking for a specific donation amount. In few instances, I had seen him listening attentively to them dictating what they wanted. He would hurriedly leave and come back with money and fabrics, and hand it over to them.

Some of the guests were vision impaired. It was my job to lead them to their first destination, then hand them to a man at a house on the edge of the village. I would leave and run back to Kokoland to catch a few minutes of a soccer game before sunset. The man in the village knew exactly what to do. He would lead them to the guest house and the village community would cater for their needs for the entire duration of their stay. After that, they would move on to another village, taking with them the cash *zakat* they had collected from the village, but leaving behind any in-kind donations. They would make arrangements with someone in the village to carry and bring them to Kokoland on a predetermined market day in few weeks' time. That would be the day they had planned to return to their usual places of residence. The same way I led them to the first village, someone else would lead them to the second village to collect more donations, and so on. On the day they had scheduled to return home, a person from the last village they had visited would lead them back to Kokoland. Also on that day, people would deliver the in-kind donations they had left behind at different villages to Kokoland and give it to them. They would happily load their stuff up on trucks and head to their destinations, until the following harvest season, when the same process was repeated.

Our farm was another place that reflected my dad's kindness. It was forbidden for us to harm any living creature there, unless they posed a real danger to us. The farm was truly a bio diverse plant and animal kingdom. There were thousands of living creatures such as ants, spiders, grass hoppers, geckos, snakes, squirrels, rats, rabbits, all kinds of birds, just to name a few. In fact it was a beautiful sight to see birds constantly flying in to pick sorghum, sesame, pearl millet seeds, or catch insects, and flying back to their nests in the baobab tree in the center of the farm, or trees in the nearby forests. Even though squirrels and rats were known for destroying recently planted seeds, my dad used to scold us for digging up their burrows. He told us they were like us humans, simply doing their best to take care of their offsprings.

He also warned us against scaring off the migratory birds, especially the gooses, which returned every year to build nests in the baobab tree. He told us that they were special guests. He also told us to avoid stepping on tiny creatures such as lady bugs and beetles, as much as possible. He always used to remind us to be careful with the hoes and grass cutting tools, not to injure or kill bush creatures like geckoes. He strongly believed it was an honor that God created humankind to be his *khalifa* (deputy) on earth, and that what we did impacted everything else. Besides; he thought that making the farm a source of food that sustained life, was a kind thing to do. He believed that the help we extended to animals would return to us in some form or another, be that good health or safeguard from hazards of life.

From time to time, my dad would tell me to take dinner to Koko in the market center. Koko was the man after whom I named my village Kokoland, to replace its ugly original name. He was mentally incapacitated and totally unaware of his environment. He lived in a deserted part of the market, inside a dilapidated shop, filled with pieces of clothes he had horded over the years. It was usually after dark when I took dinner to him, so a torch (flash light) and a heavy stick were important tools for the trip. Once I got to Koko's place of residence, I would call him, "Wald-Abba," meaning son of my father. He would respond with a, "Hmmmm." I would then approach and hand him the food, sit a few yards away, and wait for him to finish eating. Koko neither knew who I was, nor did he care. I would collect the empty container and head back home. My dad would ask me, "Did you find him?" I would respond, "Yes," and that was all he needed to know. Every now and then, my dad would ask me to carry out similar tasks for different people, some of whom lived out of Kokoland, in nearby villages. They were appreciative of the food, cloth, or money that I used to take to them. My dad's face lit up with joy whenever I went back home and told him I had successfully completed a delivery.

It was a routine thing that whenever I returned to Kokoland on a school break, my dad arranged for and invited the neighbors to our house for a big meal. He usually bought a ram and called Tiris, Kokoland's only hearing-impaired man, to slaughter it and prepare the meat for cooking. Tiris happily helped himself with as much meat as he wanted, plus the skin, the stomach, the head, and the shanks. After all, the whole thing was about feeding people and giving. For that reason Tiris's discretion was never questioned. I miss my dad dearly. He was a very unique, special, and a kind person. God bless him.

CHAPTER 17

Overseas Adventures: Great Britain and Beyond.

Central London and the famous red London bus.

I helped create a branch for AIESEC organization in Khartoum Polytechnic, in 1981. AIESEC is French abbreviation for the International Association for Students of Economics and Commerce, headquartered in Copenhagen, Denmark. In December of that same year, I travelled to Accra, Ghana, to participate in an AIESEC students' presidential conference held in the University of Legon. That was my first flight experience. It was also my first time travelling abroad, at a point in time my understanding of everything overseas was minimal. The problem was that I had no idea how to even get to my destination. The flight route to Accra was a multi-stop one, which meant I had to change planes and take connecting flights. Not knowing what to do, I missed my Lagos Accra flight and had to wait until the following morning. I asked a taxi driver to take me to a hotel. After a long drive we reached the, supposedly, hotel destination. It was a slum city made of shacks and cartoons. The place looked like it had nothing to do with anything lawful or legal. The driver got off and went inside one of the shacks. I could hear him talking to some people. After few moments, two men poked their heads out of the shack, looked at me, and went back inside. Then the driver emerged and said, "Here." I said, "No. take me back to the airport." I somehow had a bad feeling about the whole thing. He stood there for several moments in silence, staring at me, then got in the car and drove me back to the airport. I was clueless about his reasons or intentions behind taking me to a shanty town. Could he have mistaken the place for a decent hotel? Looking back; I am glad that I made the decision to leave. I would not have liked the outcome, had I stayed until sunset. I spent that night at Murtala Airport in Lagos and in the morning I caught a flight to Accra.

The conference was a three-day event, but I was stranded for over a month. Jerry Raulings, the former Ghanaian president, executed his second coup d'état and toppled the government of Haley Liman. It was a bloody coup, which warranted the closure of the borders and the cancelation of flights, both local and international. I certainly did not understand the gravity of the coup situation I found myself in. Luckily, I had a few dollars in hand at a time the Ghanaian economy was in shambles and the currency was very weak, relative to the dollar. I managed to comfortably survive the ordeal, taking full advantage of the favorable black market exchange rate, offered by female currency traders of Makola Market in down town Accra.

I tried to leave Ghana by road through the Ghana-Togo Aflauo border, but I could not. Finally, flight operations resumed, so I was able to fly back to Khartoum via Lagos and Kano, in Nigeria. While standing in line to pass immigration and security checkpoints in Kano airport, a man (a Sudanese looking, from the way he was dressed) approached and asked me about my flight source and target destination. I happily, but, of course, naively told him everything about me in just a few minutes. He said, "Since you are a student, the immigration officers will not check your briefcase, so could you please also carry this one and give it to me inside the plane?" Without the slightest hesitation, I said, "Okay, no problem." He handed me the brown Samsonite case he was carrying and disappeared. Holding two Samsonite cases, one in each hand, I stood in line to clear customs and immigration. Mind you, up to that moment, I did not have the slightest idea, neither about the man, nor the contents of the case. Yes, you heard me right, no idea whatsoever. The seriousness of the situation stemmed from the fact that Nigeria, at that time, was applying restrictions on the smuggling of foreign currency out of the country by levying a heavy penalty on anyone involved in such an illegal activity. It is needless to say that smuggling drugs was a far more serious crime, in case I happened to be carrying some.

I approached the immigration officer with both cases, while wearing a big smile that wrote "clueless" all over my face. I placed the cases on the floor and handed him my passport. He looked at me for a second, stamped it, and handed it back to me. Without saying a word, he gestured for me to move forward. I bent down, grabbed the cases, and walked past him to board the plane. After a few minutes, the briefcase owner came on board, so I handed it to him. He thanked me for helping him and sat down a few seats away from me. The plane was half empty, and there were vacant seats between us, so he initiated a conversation. He told me about his hotel business in Cameroon and that he was on his way to visit home, Sudan. Out of curiosity, I asked him about the contents of the briefcase. He told me it contained $50,000. He opened the case, revealing stacks of dollar bills. I said okay, and that was the end of the conversation. We landed in Khartoum and parted our ways. I had no grasp of the gravity of what I had done until a few years later, after I travelled to Britain and settled there for some time.

Once again, I found myself making preparations to travel overseas, but further away this time. I did very well in college and landed me a full graduate school scholarship in Great Britain. What did my friend Bijawi know about my future? He would soon find out that I neither needed the $30 loan from him, nor the correspondence course certificate from the school in Britain. I would soon be there in Britain, in person. I thought I had learned a few things from my first trip overseas, so I prepared myself, in case I faced similar situations in London. Great Britain turned out to be a different ball game altogether. Nothing prepared me for the culture shock. I landed in London Heathrow Airport one Sunday evening, in October, 1986. Frankly and honestly speaking, I had no plan in place when I boarded the London bound plane in Khartoum. First, I landed there, and then I started figuring out what to do. I did not know where I was going to spend my first night in London. A friend and I took a taxi to a hotel in the city center. We approached the front desk and spoke in an English language that was certainly not commonly used for asking about hotel room vacancies. Somehow, we managed to secure a room that night and, in the morning, we hired a taxi to take us to the embassy of Sudan. The driver dropped us by the side of one wide street, pointed to the embassy building across, and drove off, after we paid him. He left us, assuming that we would use the tunnel to cross to the other side. He was absolutely wrong. We had neither crossed walking an underground tunnel before, nor had we ever seen one in our entire twenty some years of lives. We resorted to the best way we had always known for crossing streets back home, which was charging at the street and forcing the oncoming motorists to slow down to allow you cross. I hope I am not offending my fellow Sudanese, for that is certainly not my intention. At least, that was how I personally dealt with road crossing back home. My friend and I planned to wait for traffic to lighten up a little bit, then attack the motor way. We held our dusty, torn-up, and out-of-fashion suitcases containing a few pants and shirts from the sixties' styles, and stood ready to charge at the road at the appropriate time.

My friend decided that it was time to attack the four-lane road, so he took off without warning, leaving me behind. After crossing the first two lanes, he realized that he would not make it all the way to the other end, safely. The cars were rushing toward him, so he decided to backtrack, only to realize that they were approaching the road section he had crossed a few seconds earlier, even faster than he thought. He sped up, and also got help from the car drivers in the front of the line, who slammed on their brakes, saving my friend's life. He miraculously got to where I was standing, defying death by a split second. He was sweating and breathing so fast. I could have clearly heard his heart beats, if it wasn't for the cars' noise. In less than one single day in London, his dreams, his family's, and the dreams of the whole nation, which sent him to Britain for graduate studies, almost ended. After the near-death experience, we concluded that there must be a better way for crossing London streets. Sure enough, we didn't see anybody crossing the road the way we did. We discovered the tunnel crossing and safely made it to the embassy. My friend and I never talked about that horrible incident. We buried it deep inside our minds and hoped never to remember it ever again.

Even though it was the mid-eighties, I roamed the streets of London with pants, shirts, platform shoes, hairstyle, and everything else that was synonymous with the 1960s. No one could have mistaken me for anything other than a young man from a gone era. Unlike Kokoland, London was full of mirrors. I could easily see my image and the way I looked, many times a day. Although I no longer needed to wait for the rainy season so I could see my full body reflection in still waters from ponds, I continued with my outdated looks for some time before I made full sense of my surroundings.

I fully blame the British Embassy in Khartoum for entertaining the idea of granting me a visa without any proper orientation. To me, coming from Kokoland, London was a dream city. It was surreal in every sense of the word. I was truly overwhelmed by the experience of being in London for the first time. The transition was both a quantitative and a qualitative one. Prior to arriving in London, I mostly saw the world through a black-and-white television screen. That exposure to TV was also limited to watching programs broadcast sporadically and for few hours of the day, electricity permitted. What I saw on TV was left to the whims of the authorities. Half of the airtime was allotted to news about the sitting ruler of the country and his engagements. Limited time was assigned to local news and nothing was left for other things. The public had little idea about what was going on around the world.

I hardly had enough time to know my surrounding environment in London, when I came down with malaria. I brought the malaria virus along with me after visiting one particular village, a month or so before arriving in London, to say good-bye to some dear family members. The night I spent in that village was the most horrible night of my life. I have never been exposed to that many mosquito bites. It was a matter of time that I caught malaria. The health authorities in London, rightfully, quarantined me in a hospital for few days before releasing me to join the public. That was the last malaria attack I had for the thirty years I have been living in the West. I used to get malaria attacks at least once a year, usually during the rainy season. Every time I got an attack, I came back from the brink of death, for as long as I can remember.

After a few weeks of my arrival in in London, big brother Ayoub, one of my fellow Sudanese roommates, came back from school one evening and told us he had found a shop, which sold inexpensive quality pants. He meticulously drew a map to show me how to get there. It was important that I did not lose my way back to the house in the Northern London neighborhood of Finsbury Park. I went to bed that night determined to show up at the shop first thing in the morning to buy me new pants, so I could diversify away from my old and dirt-stained pants. In the morning, I found my way to the shop, got what I wanted, and returned home safe and sound, carrying my valuable shopping items. The first person I met in the apartment was Ayoub. I told him that I went to the shop and I was lucky to find the pants still on sale, so I got me two pairs. He said, "I hope you did not get the burgundy color." I replied in the affirmative. I told him that I also bought me a pair of boots, a heavy-duty pair probably made from camel skin. I reached for the bags and showed him my merchandise. He stood there dumbfounded. He could not say a word. Now looking back, I must admit that the colors of my pants and boots were ugly, very ugly. I later on found out that my boots were the types used for mountain climbing or coal mining. Unfortunately, I did not see that until my ego was irreparably damaged a few weeks later. To me, shoes remained as protectors of my feet from getting pierced by sharp objects, especially thorns. I did not know that there was a fashion dimension added to the formula of wearing different shoes for different occasions. In London, I was knocked off my feet and all the fashion expertise that I thought I had harnessed over many years in Kokoland were rendered irrelevant.

My first Christmas in London was two month after arriving there. Hatim, Othman, and Yassin, were fellow citizens studying in a college in the city of Hull, northeast of London. They invited us (my two roommates and I) to travel to Hull and spend Christmas and year-end with them. We happily accepted the invitation and headed to Hull on Christmas Eve. It was a wonderful time of the year and people looked very happy, but my happiness exceeded everyone else's, since that was my first time to experience such an event. While in Hull, Othman, our host, introduced me to James Bond movies and I had an incredibly valuable opportunity to sift through his music cassettes and listen to many English groups for the first time. Back home, I had limited access to Western music that was mostly played in the evenings, when, for few hours of the week, stations such as Voice of America, the BBC, and Mont Carlo broadcast songs played by bands I hardly knew anything about.

After sun set on new year's eve, 1986, Yassin suggested that we go to a disco hall to celebrate and spend some happy moments experiencing the year end count down. I said great. When it was time to leave, I dashed to the room to get dressed. I was the first one to be waiting in the living room. Hatim walked into the room and upon his eyes falling on my pants and shoes, his legs kept coming forward while the upper part of his body leaning backward. He nearly fell flat on his back. Yes, I was wearing my burgundy-colored pants and my ugly camel-skin boots. Next, Othman, our host, walked in and immediately started laughing hysterically. Fathi, my roommate, walked into a tense room and sensed something was going on. He stared at my pants and boots, and half-smiled, but sarcastically. Yassin looked extremely worried. The expression on his face showed that there was no way in hell he would go out to the disco with me as part of the group, while dressed like that. Yassin was a "wannabe elite." He was new to Britain, so he had not had enough time to fully grasp aspects of socialization and adherence to British norms, but he was doing well, if compared with the rest of the group, minus myself. My presence at the disco hall by Yassin's side would reduce to zero his chances of mingling with beautiful English girls from Hull at midnight. It is needless to say that a random kiss from a stranger at midnight would be out of the question because we would not make it even past the entrance of the disco hall, as long as I was part of the group. Yassin was never proud of associating with me, being a new arriver to London. I was a downgrader to his reputation, he thought. As you can tell, nobody was sympathetic to my plight.

While standing attention in my boots, the group conferred for a minute and aired the view that my boots must not come to the disco, or we all risked expulsion. The problem was that I did not have second pairs of pants and shoes, more suitable for disco, so Othman and Ayoub let me borrow a pair each. After that, we all silently set off and headed to the disco. I was trailing the group. My pride was seriously hurt. Do you know how humiliating it is for people to take pity on you to the extent that they offer you things like shoes and pants for a disco? Where would you get the courage to talk to a girl while wearing borrowed shoes and pants? It is even more painful, if you are a proud person holding yourself in high regard. Let me put it this way: any form or shape of pitying is not good. That was the price I paid for being unfamiliar with the meaning of dress code. I was under the misconception that one chooses to wear what he deems fit and the rest of the world abides by his decision.

From the get-go, you could tell that I was a misfit. As soon as I passed the doors and entered the disco hall, I started looking swiftly in all directions. I certainly caught people's attention, but I did not realize that until later on. That was my first visit to any disco pub in my entire life, be that in Great Britain or elsewhere. There I was wearing a hairstyle definitely incompatible with the twenty-some-aged men at the disco. My body language was threatening and, on top of that, I constantly wore a wide smile for no apparent reason.

I was just not cool at all. I wanted to know about everything going on, so I turned my head to the left, to the right, leaned to the sides, looked backward, and occasionally stretched my neck so I could see beyond the persons standing in front of me. I pretty much scared the hell out of everybody around me. I did all that without fully being aware of my environment. I only gained my senses when I had an eye contact with someone. I would wear even a wider and weirder smile that was certainly unjustified, considering the fact that I would be smiling at a total stranger. I would soon go back to my old mission of further exploring the hall. I realized that I was standing in a circular space surrounded by people some six feet away from me. As for the rest of the disco hall, there was no space to drop a needle. Word had probably spread around the hall among the disco goers warning one another to keep their distance away from me. I just could not find good justification for the vacancy of such a valuable real estate around me.

A minute or so before midnight, people started counting, and I did figure out why they were doing that. At midnight, the lights went dim, so I immediately concluded that was caused by some power failure, similar to the one that I used to experience, regularly, back home. I had no idea that lights could be dimmed. As far as I knew, power was either on or out. I embraced myself for departure because such power failures, sometimes, took days to restore. Then I realized a slow music, different from the earlier fast beats, was being played, and people started to pair up and get closer and closer to one another. Then I noticed every man and woman couple kissing each other. My jaws fell and I felt numb. I stood there registering and processing the event in my mind as fast as I could, thinking to myself that what I was witnessing was a rare event such as an asteroid hitting the planet Earth or something. I asked myself, "Do people kiss in public?" I slowly started filling the gaps in my understanding of what was going on. No wonder why my friends were nowhere to be seen. They must have concluded that there was no likelihood of getting kissed, if they remained standing near me, so they decided to keep their distance, or, let me put it this way; hide from me. I didn't think I missed a thing because I didn't have any expectations for a kiss from a stranger, anyway. Besides; I didn't look cool enough to deserve one. Furthermore, the speed with which I was looking in all directions, to capture every moment, would have scared and turned off any woman from the city of Hull or elsewhere, however desperate for a random kiss she might have been. Therefore, the dimming of the light did not bring me any luck, nor was I expecting one. I was not surprised anyways because the whole year-end protocol was an uncharted territory for me. You just don't miss what you don't know, do you?

It was only after the lights were put back on, I was able to figure out what had really transpired during those few minutes. Some got carried away and did not bother much about protocols, so they continued kissing after the full light was back. That filled in the gaps in my mind. The music stopped and I woke up from my daydream to find myself carrying a big smile and also talking to myself. I was immersed in all sorts of thoughts, but the silence that followed the music abruptly ending forced me to regain my senses. To me, the whole scene was surreal and a eureka-moment. I finally concluded that it was a once in a year night for distributing free kisses left, right, and center. The only requirement was a person's proximity to the opposite sex. I was standing in an island of my own, so I did not qualify even for that basic requirement. I thought to myself; never mind. Maybe next year-end, who knows? As you can tell, I was fascinated by an event as trivial as going to the disco. Imagine, what else could have fascinated me? Almost everything not found in Kokoland, and that meant everything, period. I suffered from a severe cultural shock in Britain.

We got back home way after midnight. I lay in bed awake going over what I had experienced that evening. I gazed at the dark room ceiling and thought of the following expressions:

> In the recent past, I heard people tell me how great and more I was, but not here, not anymore. I was told I dressed well, but here I turned out to be a hapless geek.

> My dear boots, I really wanted to complain, but there is no one here willing to listen or feel mine or your pain.
> My experience in Hull is nothing short of hell on earth, maybe beyond hell.
> I wanted to sell and get out of here hoping no one would ever tell.
> Happy shoes worn on feet dancing to the disco rhythms and to the beat.
> The owls and the night creatures all are awake and the disco lights shone and did not blink a bit.
> My dear boots, you were absent and nowhere to be seen. You were tugged under the bed. You were left in the dark. You were very unhappy, and you were fast asleep. I feel for you. You were very unhappy, and you were fast asleep.

This was my experience of that infamous night of December 31, 1986.

Here are more embarrassing incidents that I had initially experienced in Great Britain. I will also tell you who was primarily to blame. One day at school back in London, I bought a small carton pack of orange juice, which I had never tried before. I carried it to a table in the cafeteria and sat down to drink it. There was another student sitting opposite to me. He recorded every action that took place over the next few minutes. I sat scratching the box for some time, trying to open the package, but to no avail. The student simply sat and watched the drama unfold, but without saying a word. I just could not tear open the carton with my fingers, so I lifted it up to my mouth to use my teeth. Tragically, that exercise resulted in spilling the yellow drink on my white shirt. At that moment, the student quietly got up and left. Amidst my embarrassment and confusion, I saw a plastic straw attached to the side of the box. Upon thoroughly examining the box, I found a tiny round silver mark, which I poked with the straw, and then I said, "Aha." Unfortunately, that *aha* moment came too late and after an immense damage has already been done.

This is one of two things. It was either that the orange juice company did a lousy job by marketing an improperly packaged product, or it was I who failed to handle a drink that was primarily packaged for school children. I guess, age doesn't always translate into experience.

One Sunday, I decided to go to the Hyde Park Speakers' Corner in London. I walked around sampling the speeches until I passed by one speaker who drew my attention, so I stopped there to listen more. When he finished talking, I casually passed a comment that could easily qualify to be one of the most politically incorrect statements, as I have learned sometime later. What I said drew the attention of an Englishman who happened to be standing a few feet away from me, so we got engaged in a discussion that was more of an argument than anything else. It turned out I was talking about a topic I had barely grasped, leave a side passing judgement with absolute confidence. The whole thing was disastrous, considering my heavy accent, limited English vocabulary, and, over and above that, my shallow understanding of the subject in question. I was overdressed for the wrong occasion and spoke with an unjustified overconfidence. Obviously, the Englishman was not impressed. Besides; what was I thinking when I tried to impress an English man in his own country, only a few yards from the Queen's palace? I wished if there was any way I could take back those words. What did I know about the British monarchy? I was very wrong. The British Embassy in Khartoum granted me a visa with no questions asked, and that, too, was wrong. I wish if they had told me that London is different from Kokoland and gave me some advice, especially telling me that Kokoland is not the absolute truth. That encounter taught me the importance of knowing when to be silent; a lesson that I closely guard and continue to cherish.

Here is another incident that took place a few month after arriving in London. One evening, as I was returning from school, I passed by a row of shops not far from my neighborhood. One particular shop caught my attention. Through the shop's glass windows, I could see a line of suits, covered in transparent plastic, hanging on a long metal rail. I decided to check it out. I strode inside the shop and saw a middle-aged English woman standing at the shop counter.

I passed her without saying a word and went straight to where the suits were hanging. I started lifting the plastic cover to check the sale price, while rubbing the cloth fabric between my fingers to feel and examine for texture quality of the suits. For a moment, I wondered why the woman did not come forward to help me with the sale, and then she spoke, "Not for sale," she said. Puzzled by her short sentence, I looked in her direction to inquire further. Upon making eye contact, she said, "Yes, not for sale." At that moment, I became certain that I had ventured into a hostile territory by mistake and must get out quickly. I thought the sales woman was just in a bad mood and uninterested in selling the merchandise. I hurriedly departed the shop, leaving the weird woman staring at my back. For a few days, I avoided passing in front of that shop on my way returning from school in the evenings. I walked the other side of the street so that the woman would not see and recognize me. Whenever I got parallel to the shop, I quickly glanced in that direction, hoping to get some clue to help me resolve the "not for sale" paradox. I was dying inside to find out the truth about the weird English woman and her shop.

One evening, I noticed the presence of two well-dressed men at the shop's door. One of them was holding, with one hand, a bundle of cloth pressed up to his chest, while keeping the door open with the other hand for the second man to come out. The man exiting the shop was carrying a bunch of suits, on hangers, wrapped in plastics. I stopped and watched so I could figure out what was going on, then came my *aha* moment. I had so many *aha* moments in London. It was a dry cleaning shop. God have mercy. To send a person from Kokoland to London without telling him the difference between items for sale and suits for dry cleaning was an unforgivable mistake. You tell me if that wasn't the British Embassy's fault.

I played the earlier scenario of my encounter with the dry-cleaning woman in my mind so I could fill in the gaps. The woman stood frozen behind the counter, thinking to herself, "Is this an armed robbery unfolding right here in front of my eyes or what?" After saying, "Yes, not for sale," her facial expressions revealed words that read something like, "Oh dear, I wonder where these bloody useless people, who can not even differentiate between sale and laundry items, come from. England is no more." I concluded why she did not volunteer to say anything beyond "not for sale" to explain further. She must have thought that it was a hopeless case not worth any further explanation. She figured she'd better keep her blood pressure down.

From that moment onward, I paid more attention to my surroundings so I was less embarrassed. I avoided taking decisions or making any move without proper assessment. Is this common sense? Yes, but it did not apply to me. In London, I had to learn everything retroactively. I tapped on my shoulder when I discovered, on my own, a grocery store section, especially designated for pet food and supplies. I knew my people in Kokoland would think I had lost my mind if I told them that cats and dogs have their own shelves packed with delicious foods, just like humans.

I kept the dry cleaning secret deep inside me for over twenty years before I told anybody. One day, a friend living in Davis, California, invited the Sudanese community members in greater Sacramento area to his house for a meal. I arrived at the house a little late and found a man kneeling on the floor and going through the shoes piled in front of the door. When he saw me, assuming that I was the owner of the house, he said, while pointing to some four or five pairs of shoes that he had sorted out and piled together separately, "How much are these?" Smiling slightly, I spontaneously responded, "Not for sale." He got up, excused himself, and left. Obviously, he was unaware of the practice that, in some cultures, people leave their shoes at the entrance before walking inside a house. Contrary to what the unlucky man thought, the pile of shoes was not for garage sale.

Unlike the English woman at the dry cleaning store in London, I, being a new migrant to America, could not say to the man, "Oh dear, these bloody useless people. I wonder where they come from. They can not even differentiate between visitors' shoes and garage sale." Nevertheless, I felt good about myself. The man relieved me from the dry cleaning embarrassment that I had shouldered for many years. The two incidents cancelled one another.

In London, I wanted to learn to swim, retroactively, at a point in time I was 26 years old grown man. I went and sat on a bench by a swimming pool and watched people swim. I had no idea that my presence would make them extremely uncomfortable. Strangers don't simply walk into a swimming pool, sit down on a bench while fully clothed, and watch people swimming, especially when they aren't the designated lifeguards on duty. People just don't do that. I certainly blame the British Embassy in Khartoum for granting me entrance visa to Britain when I was that crude. Some orientation about social and anti-social behavior could have saved me a great deal of embarrassment. Advanced learning about swimming pool protocols should have been one of the advices that could have been given to me. A simple message like, "Here is your visa young Kokoland man, go to London, but don't do anything without asking somebody, especially if it is your first time," could have alerted me to so many mishaps. The truth of the matter was that I landed in London without knowing much and every step I took led me to an uncharted territory. It was hard.

After spending some time, carefully, observing people as they swam, I convinced myself that I, too, could do it, and decided to be practical, so I enrolled in swimming classes. On the first day of class, I showed up at the pool site and met with the instructor who, based on my lack of any swimming experience, made me wear two inflated orange balloons around my arms to prevent me from drowning. Can you imagine? When I descended into the pool, the water was around my waist. The image of a twenty-six-year-old, six feet three inches tall man, standing in four-foot-deep water, and wearing inflators wrapped around his arms, was an unconventional one, not seen often. I stood there towering over the other swimmers who kept looking up and staring at my face. They appeared confused and probably asking themselves, "What is this man doing here?" It was an ugly scene, I must admit.

London was an ideal place for character transformation as far as some of my friends were concerned. They dropped everything that was a relic of a bygone era by, metaphorically speaking, throwing away the village hat and putting on a fancy London hat. They basically transitioned and adapted well to their new environment. As such, there existed a remarkable gap between those who have been around for some time and somewhat clued up on culture and socially acceptable behavior, and more recent arrivals to London like me, who were, by most accounts, unpolished folks, if you will. Understandably, these two identities did not socially see eye to eye, and that reality created rivalry between the two groups.

One of our colleagues, Husham, belonged to the more clued up group. He was an elitist who justifiably detested the idea of mingling with us commoners. He saw in us villagers who undermined his social standing and eroded his concerted efforts to propel himself to the top of London's social strata. The dilemma he had was, on one hand, he thought that any social interaction with us would tarnish and obliterate the sophisticated and fancy image he had tirelessly built over the span of two years he had been in London, ahead of our arrival. On the other hand, he saw in us a valuable opportunity for him to shine in the eyes of his elite friends, who would compare and contrast between our two characters and see a clear difference. His social achievements could not be measured without such comparison, so we played an important benchmark or yard-stick role, if you like. Damned if he socialized with us and damned if he did not. For that reason, we disagreed and argued our differences a lot. Husham, constantly tried to highlight our cluelessness by shedding light on his own high level of exposure, but we completely rejected the idea and refused to be his subordinates. It was a clash of civilization. Sadly, sometimes it takes a war to make peace.

Hisham wanted to play a leadership role, which demanded full respect from people like me. He wanted to be our only reference source on subjects pertaining to England's cultural norms, values, and socially acceptable behaviors. He told us some strange stories, which we did not have the means of verifying if they were true or not. He spoke at length about his meetings with Sir Edward Heath, the former British Prime Minister; Margaret Thatcher, another former British prime minister; Sir Neil Kinnock, the former head of the British Labor Party; and so on. By giving scary talks about his associations with these British dignitaries, he wanted to plant fear into our village-minds and make us believe in and accept his invincibility, and also to leave us wondering what else he was capable of doing. That was Basically Husham's strategy for placing himself in a different social class. However, moving from nothing to the top of the British political pyramid, in one single leap, within a matter of two years, was a bitter pill to swallow, even for someone as crude as me. Deep down, I desperately wanted an answer to the question: What all these British prime ministers and party leaders had in common with a graduate student from a village in Sudan, to the extent that they granted him audience? Didn't they have more urgent commitments to address? I think the whole thing existed only in Husham's mind. I ultimately resorted to believing that, "Pigs do fly." Husham got away with murder, easily.

As you can tell, we were no match for Husham in regard to establishing close and personal ties with public figures, celebrities, and coping with popular television shows. The little English that I spoke was straight from grammar and literature books. I found it to be different from English used in conversation in everyday life. Understanding what TV programs were all about was a big challenge for me. I had no idea what famous talk show celebrities, like Terry Wogan and Gilroy, talked about. I hated comedy shows, particularly in Husham's presence. He laughed pretentiously, hinting to us his full understanding of the jokes' punch lines and the hidden references therein. I would be sitting there with little clue about what was going on and most jokes went straight over my head. I resented that feeling so much, especially when I remembered the high rank I enjoyed among my contemporaries back home. In the open, I accepted my new reality that London was a different planet, altogether, but, in secret, I took it as a challenge and prepared for war.

Husham occasionally proved to be too much for us, particularly when he pinned us to a corner during arguments pertaining to current affairs. We used to fight back to show him that we also had damage-inflicting bows and arrows at our disposal, besides, sharp teeth for biting, as a backup. In one incident, a friend felt things have gone too far out of hand and he could not bear it anymore. He pushed back by asking Husham, "What is the use of owning a two hundred Sterling pounds' worth of a necktie from Harrods Mega Store, only to hide it in a tin case inside your straw hut, in your village of seven huts, one dong, and one donkey? At the same time, you are bedridden inside your hut, shivering from a malaria attack, and you cannot even have the treatment for it?" What my friend really wanted to do was to cram as much negative information as he possibly could in one paragraph to paint a vivid picture to remind Husham of his background and who he truly was. He told him about the reality of his village life, encompassing elements of dichotomy, deprivation, poverty, and backwardness. His goal was to humiliate and to inflict maximum damage to Husham's psyche. I think he succeeded. That statement knocked Husham off his feet. He kept quiet for some time, probably licking his wounds and trying to reconcile between his different, as well as, contradictory realties.

Husham, miraculously, built a friendship with one rich Kuwaiti royal family member in London. That man also happened to be holding a senior diplomatic position at that time. One day, he suggested that we go and visit his friend at his palace, located in one of London's fancy neighborhoods. I went along to visit this Kuwaiti diplomat, without having the tiniest idea as to why I was doing that, nor had I anything in mind to say when I got there. Sure enough, it turned out we did not have any business being there, but, to Husham, the visit presented a superb opportunity to show some level of sophistication and social skills in front of his buddy, the diplomat. The two of them basically carried out upper class fancy discussion, compatible only with people who belonged in the Queen of England's close circle. The rest of us played the attentive listening role to the best of our abilities.

Upon completing my studies in the United Kingdom, I received a job offer from a bank in the Middle East. Hisham and his wife came to visit us in our apartment in London to say good-bye. I told him about the job offer and felt, at least for once, I had scored a point against him. His response to me was, "If I want, I can talk to my buddy the Kuwaiti diplomat, and in a single day I can get a work permit or a visa to Kuwait and get to the Middle East, even before you." In an irony of life, the very next morning, Saddam Hussain invaded and took over Kuwait. He totally obliterated the country's systems and orders, an act resulting in its population, including the royal family members, fleeing the very country Husham could have relocated to in a matter of a single day. That incident brought about a big row between him and his wife who accused him of jinxing it, not only to them as a couple, but also to the entire Kuwaiti population, as well as the millions of expatriates working in Kuwait. It is common knowledge that it took an armada, put together by President Bush, to drive Saddam out of Kuwait. Hisham's "buddy," the Kuwaiti diplomat, went on to become a renowned figure in the Kuwaiti political arena, but I doubt it if they continued to be buddies anymore.

Now, the way I have described our dear friend Husham might sound, somewhat, harsh and brutal, but the truth of the matter is that it is by no means my intentions to undermine or criticize him. I must admit that Husham had a lively and joyful personality. He never meant to hurt or harm anyone of us. I hold no grudges against him whatsoever. I am by no means expressing resentment about how we as friends interacted with one another, some three decades ago. To the contrary, it was a beautiful time that we all continue to cherish a great deal to this day, after all these many years. We are in touch with one another, even though we scattered in all corners of the globe. Husham and I still remain good friends, notwithstanding the fact that I never got to build a career in diplomacy, just like his buddy the Kuwaiti diplomat.

In London, I found myself eager to explore the entire city. I used to be fascinated by all sorts of things, both natural and fabricated. I derived joy from looking at everything transformed into anything pleasing to the human eye, be that art works, architectural designs, vehicles, monuments, old bridges, gardens, roads, factories, shops, TV and radio documentary programs, sports, you name it. Why wouldn't I be so? You would accept my argument if I told you there were four types of mechanized objects in the entirety of Kokoland and its vicinity; the flour mill, lorries, sewing machines, and kerosene lanterns. That was it. In fact, many people living in Kokoland didn't miss much, but, in my case, I think I am a curious person by nature. I'm intrigued by the simplest of things.

One Monday morning in London, I met a school friend who told me he was looking forward to showing me a fascinating new invention he had found. I followed him to an office where he introduced me to a fax machine. We talked for days about the amazing things a fax machine could do. I met another friend who was also looking for me for days. He told me I would not believe what he had discovered. He took me to the computer lab and showed me a Word Perfect program. The significance of my friend's discovery stemmed from the fact that we were about to embark on our MBA dissertation projects, which involved a lot of writing, considering typewriting being the only way we could have processed word documents. You can appreciate the reason why I was fascinated by the simplest of things. A third friend waited patiently for the weekend to be over so he could tell me of what he had discovered. When we met at school on Monday, he rushed to me and said, "I was looking for you everywhere." I asked him what was going on, and he said, "Boy, you would not believe what I had found on Saturday." I impatiently urged him to tell me, so he said, "I found this butcher in Haringay [a north London borough] who sold lamb chops at a very low price. You won't believe how low his prices are." I agreed with him that was a valuable discovery, considering the limited amount of British Pound Sterling monthly stipends at our disposal. My friend, our guests, and I put on pounds of additional weight eating fried lamb chops, weekend after weekend. Being as skinny as hell, worrying about putting weight was the last of my concerns.

CHAPTER 18

America

The United States Congress

London helped shape me and my outdated Afro hairstyle, mode of dress, and Kokoland-based approach to life, into a person who could function with relative ease. I would certainly not say it trimmed me enough to fully adapt to the new and varied culture. Before I travelled to Britain, Kokoland was central to everything I knew, which was not much anyway. I thought that Londoners and the rest of the world were also subject to cultural norms that governed Kokoland, so I very much saw London through Kokoland's lens. I used to find it quite unacceptable and strange that people behaved differently. According to my way of thinking, things were either black or white. I hardly had any room for compromising or allowing space for others to think differently. I was so wrong. Over time, I was able to dig myself out of that deep hole of misconception. I think that the intolerance in the world can be attributed to many factors, certainly including short-sightedness and myopia, under which I heavily labored for the entire time I was living in Kokoland. I must admit that I have come a long way in my understanding of other people's point of view.

I landed in America swinging in all directions and ready for action. America is yet another different ball game altogether. My chaotic transition in London had helped smooth my landing in America, so I did not crash. I can not imagine what could have happened, had I flown from Kokoland to America. My first city of residence in America was San Francisco. What a fascinating city.

In America; I paid little attention to the personal baggage I brought along with me. In fact, I did not know much about the country's background or history other than, of course, what I had learned at school, which did not paint an accurate picture in my mind. I never saw myself different from anybody else and that everything was just fine. I found people very accommodating in the sense that nobody alerted me to anything that could slow me down or hold me back because of my way of doing things differently. For these reasons, I never hesitated to take decisions or felt the urge to navigate my way through more carefully. I got very excited whenever I heard statements such as, "The sky is the limit. You can make it. You can do it, if you can dream it," and so on.

It is all well and good, but what I did not know was that one cannot become an American citizen overnight. I needed to pay my dues first. In a way, looking back, I think it is a good thing I did not dwell much on my imperfections or see any aspects of me that were different from others. Had I had any advanced knowledge of American norms before my arrival here, I could have done certain things differently and most probably shied away from many of the bold steps that I had taken as soon as I arrived here in America. By the time I got fairly familiar with the system, I was already out of the woods, if you will.

Four months after arriving in America, I met a fellow citizen in Los Angeles who had been living there with his family for many years. Over time, we became family friends. I assumed that his experience in the country would matter much in helping me fast adjust to the American system. I remember one time asking him about the job market, and the response I got was somewhat strange. He told me that the only jobs available to me were either driving a taxi cab, or working as a security guard. He sounded something like, “Don’t even think of anything else.” With due respect to those who work in both fields, I did not think it was right that all new migrants should only fit into these two job categories. I told him about the skills I have, which might qualify me to get different jobs, but he responded by saying that I would be jobless for a long time, if I kept on thinking that way. I also observed that he generally had negative views about everything. To him the glass is always fully empty, if there is such a thing as that, so I slowly disengaged from his association and kept my distance. I am glad I did that. My first job was a managerial position in a renowned bank in the city of San Francisco.

The Bay Bridge and the City of San Francisco, California.

Bob Mason was a coworker who dreaded calling my name. He found it to be very difficult to pronounce. Both Bob and I were employed by the same bank in the San Francisco Bay Area. We reported to work on the same day. He introduced himself to me by saying, "Hi, I'm Bob," and I responded, "Hi, Bob, I'm Mustafa." He replied, "Hi, Gustavo." I tried correcting him by mentioning my name one more time. I waited for him to repeat it after me, but he looked at me and said nothing. For the rest of the day, even though we sat side by side in the office, I did not hear him mention my name, not even once. I knew he found it impossible to pronounce, so he avoided it all together when initiating conversations. He would start talking to me abruptly, but without making any reference to my name. One morning, a week or so later, he looked in my direction, said, "Hey," and went quiet. Figuring that he wanted to talk to me, I looked at him and waited to hear more about what he had to say. He kept on looking at me, but without saying a single word. His mouth was slightly open, and I could see his tongue moving slowly and barely, but repeatedly appearing and disappearing between his teeth. His eyes slowly closed and opened half way. His lips trembled for a fraction of a second then froze. I could tell that his brain was working like crazy to put together the word Mustafa and hand it over to his mouth to spell it out. He kept on staring at me with his bulging eyes. I feared that if I did not intervene soon, his condition might worsen and he could pass out. I am not exaggerating. In a loud voice, I said, "Mustafa." He immediately grabbed the word and joyfully said, in an even louder voice, "Mustova." He looked so relieved after that, as if resting his brain so it could recover from the fatigue caused by working so hard to come up with my correct name. I said to myself, "Close enough. Not bad. Mustova is far much better than something like Mestavo or Gestapo." I gave him few more seconds so life could creep back into his face, then we engaged in a long conversation. From that moment onwards, Mustova became my name, as far as Bob was concerned. He resigned to the fact that weird names like mine do exist on this planet, but they cause great inconvenience to people. I noticed that he called my new name only when it was absolutely necessary. He avoided wasting energy whenever possible. I was fine with that arrangement. Poor Bob. Unbeknown to me, he tortured himself for a whole week trying to say my name. I wish if I had known.

I thought of suggesting an easier name for him to use, such as Mo, but I decided against the idea. I was not too sure how I was going to feel about having a new name.

I was enthusiastic about my job, so I worked very hard, certain that I would be rewarded according to the effort I put in. Besides; I was planning to commit myself for long term. Six months into the job, the entire crew, except for the manager and I, had resigned from the bank. That was when I realized that I needed to adopt a different approach to my work. Despite the harsh working conditions, I labored for two years then decided to move on. I ventured into a truly uncharted territory by creating a business from scratch. I was amazed by the ease with which I was able to complete paperworks needed to establish an import business. I also joined the crowd and took advantage of the real estate boom in the country, particularly in California. I imported marble from overseas and distributed it retail in Sacramento as well as wholesale in the Central Valley and Los Angeles.

Even though that was my first business venture, I was able to feed my family and pay my bills. I was truly amazed by the fairness of the system here in America, especially the potential clients I visited to promote my products. I randomly picked up marble companies from the yellow pages, called and set appointments, and drove to meet them. It was a number game, so the more companies I visited the better chance I had in securing orders. I could not believe that I was given orders at all, considering my lack of any previous knowledge about granite and marble business. The system could not have been fairer. I contracted with shipping companies and freightliners that collected the marble containers from Oakland and Los Angeles ports, and delivered them at my clients' warehouses all over California. There was no advance payment for these orders. I ran my business for seven years and, luckily, I was able to collect my invoices all the time. My clients' business ethics was a source of admiration for me and, in fact, it shaped my views about many things. I did take some risk, but I am glad that nobody abused my trust and took advantage of the situation. I believe there is more good in humanity than bad.

My family members thought that I was too lenient in the way I ran my business. Once, I caught one of my employees stealing some merchandize from the store. I did not turn him in to the authorities due to circumstances surrounding his personal life, being a single father. The same employee stole for the second time, which confirmed my family members' conclusion about my management style. The employee might have reached his own conclusion, so he decided to take advantage of my stupidity. I released him from work without pressing charges against him. I have my own motivations for doing that, and I am not regretting my decision.

I survived a couple of business risks that could have landed me in serious troubles. Someone walked up to me at my business location and said he was homeless. He said he collected wooden pales and sold them to feed himself, so he wanted to know if it was okay for him to load his pickup truck with the pales in the back of the warehouse. I told him it was fine, and I asked him to wait until I had finished taking care of a customer. When I went out, I was horrified to find the man sitting on the forklift, which was heavily tilting backward and hovering over a five-foot-deep loading dock. The slightest move could have brought it crashing down. Luckily, my neighbor came rushing over with his forklift and helped lift both my forklift and the man to safety.

A few weeks later, a customer dropped a piece of marble on her foot. She said she was not hurt and left. I thought it was a matter of time before I heard from her lawyer. The problem was that I did not have business insurance coverage. I was so worried and had many sleepless nights, but, luckily, nothing happened.

Here is a funny and best-remembered incident from my time in business. One day, I went to visit a potential client at his place of business to give a presentation about a new marble product, hoping to secure a container order. He quietly listened to my presentation without any interruption. When I finished talking, he jokingly said to me, "Look man. I just can't believe every Tom, Dick, and Harry who comes and tells me he has a product that can help elongate some parts of my body, or whatever." I laughed, picked up my marble samples, and headed to another potential customer, confident that the man's rejection would only draw me closer to a successful meeting. It was both a number game and a matter of time. Overall, I was thankful for the help I received from my bankers and the Small Business Administration in facilitating my finances, operations, and payment systems. I decided to go back to school, so I liquidated the business and moved to Texas.

Image of Texas State Capirol, Austin.

Buying real estate can be tricky at times, but a strategy my wife and I had adopted, which involved buying homes in newly developed neighborhoods, did work for us a few times. We were lucky that we always had good neighbors. Choosing them carefully before moving into a neighborhood is Home-Buying 101. We were always aware of our minority status, so we avoided buying into well-established neighborhoods where we could be considered latecomers. We figured out that if we were among the first residents to move into a new neighborhood, the burden of choosing a neighbor would be shouldered by those who moved in after us. Thus, we assumed that our neighbors would always be people who were exposed to different cultures, and as such, would be more accommodating. It was more likely that they would not stereo type us before knowing who we were. In fact, we never had problems with any of our neighbors, except in one instance. I guess we were right in our conclusion. Having said that, I did not mean to be critical of anybody here because people are a product of their environment and, as such, one can expect them to think differently and reach their own conclusion about other people they don't know well. At our end, we consciously treated our neighbors with the utmost courtesy to make sure that they would not regret their decision to live by us. Things were always fine, apart from the one instance that turned out to be the exception to the rule. A neighbor did not know what to make of me being black, spoke with an accent, have a foreign name, and occasionally wore strange clothes, and, on top of that, people who looked way different visited us from time to time. His strategy for dealing with the situation was to avoid me altogether and at any cost. I did not mind that at all. I gave him his space, granting him his wish. Upon the birth of the couple's first child, my wife bought a gift and went over to their house to visit and see their newly born daughter. The rest was history. We modelled our neighborhood selection after a Sudanese proverb that says, "Pick your neighbor before your home." We kind of modified it to read, "Be there first and let the neighbors come afterwards and choose to live by you." This model has always worked for us.

Despite my thirty-years long journey from Kokoland to America, my family members, especially my elder son, held the view that my village-type conduct stayed with me all the time and did not fade away at all, as it should have been the case. They jokingly told me that my unchanged behavior was the cause of my failure to assimilate into American culture. They could be right. One of the challenges I faced as a parent here in America was not knowing how to handle my sons' school matters. That was, yet, another uncharted territory for me, especially after he joined his high school's track and field team, and I had to attend school meets. Here are a few comments from him, some of which might appear as stepping way out of line, but I would like to state that he and I are very proud of each other. He truly appreciates the troubles I had gone through to give him a good life here in America. He fully recognizes that. Some of his dark humor may sound to you somewhat disrespectful, but I take it lightly because I know he means no harm.

One day, I went to a stadium in Sacramento, California, to watch him participate in a track and field triple-jump event. I sat close to the sand pitch to cheer him up. When it was his turn to jump, I started cheering, but I guess, in my own Kokoland way, which was certainly not in harmony with the way the stadium fans cheered. The flagman who was standing a few yards from me heard my loud yell, so he turned around to investigate the source of the strange voice. After my son successfully completed his jump, the flagman walked to me and said, "Where are you from?" I replied, "From Africa," and I continued, "And that boy who has just won is my son." He stared at me for a few seconds and said, "No wonder why he won. You guys run after your food." He turned around and walked away. He left me wondering and not really knowing if his comments were an insult or a compliment. For some time, I hoped he meant well that we ate fresh and organic wild animal meat that we chased and caught with our own bare hands, and that was the reason he thought it was not surprising that my son, always eating organic and healthy food, won the competition. However, deep down, I had my doubts. When I told my son the story, he commented, "You might as well wake up to your senses and accept that the image of you carrying spears and chasing after a gazelle, while bare-footed, is more realistic than that of a university professor you are trying to portray. If I were you, I will just take the man's words as compliments and move on."

As I mentioned in the introduction, my son went on to win the California championship, which landed him a scholarship at Texas A&M University, where he and his track and field team won the national championship for the first time in the university's history. They went on to win the championship for three consecutive years. That achievement landed the team an invitation from the White House to meet with President Obama. The visit to the White House culminated in a six-month internship for my son at the White House. This is why we, as a family, are very appreciative and thankful to have such opportunities. Years later, I visited Sudan and told some of my extended family members that my son had been to the White House and had a chance to meet with the American President. They did not show any enthusiasm toward what I said, so I further explained to them that the White House is where the American Presidents lives. After a moment's silence, one man commented, "This is a strange matter. Who in his right mind goes around looking for trouble?" Those of you who are closely following the situation in Sudan will see this man's wisdom.

My son won his high school's homecoming king contest. When he told me about it, I responded, "Great," but without fully understanding what that entailed. To me, anything that has something to do with kings must be a good thing. Franklyn High School in Elk Grove, California, voted for my son and crowned him the homecoming king for the academic year 2006. On the night of the parade and crowning, I went to the stadium to attend. It was such a big deal, which I had totally underestimated to the extent that I did not even bring a camera to document the event. That was how little knowledge I had about winning a homecoming contest. America was truly an uncharted territory for me.

On another occasion, I went to his school to attend his graduation party. One of his friends spotted me, then ran to him and told him, "Your African dad is here." That was the time I realized that it would take a few generations before I could be considered a true American. Is that even possible in my case? "Your dad is here" could have sufficed, but throwing "African" in between the words was an intentional act to remind me of who I really am, just in case I forgot. The boy sounded as if my son had other dads of different origins.

I brought to America some of my foreign eating habits and food preferences. I thought that was a natural thing to do, but my son disagreed. He thought that one of my favorite soups tasted like wood chips and that I should stop eating it, relax, and worry about nothing, since I am here in America. He seriously believed that I needed some medical attention. He alluded to the idea that sticking to eating my indigenous and unfamiliar types of food was a medical condition that might have been caused by food scarcity that I had suffered from while living at the boarding school in Darsail primary school from hell; something I have written about previously. He thought the fact that I was eating one type of food day in and day out led to the development of this lasting phobia about eating a wide variety of healthy foods. My son was the one who did not know what eating healthy meant. Serious. Besides; he is not a doctor. Nowadays, he understands the nutritional value of what I ate, I think.

I once decided to take a life insurance policy with my bank. I accepted the premium rate offered to me, but also agreed to give blood tests before the bank could draft the policy. However, after the test results, the bank changed my rates and charged me a higher premium than originally offered. I complained to the bank that it negated on the original agreement. I also discussed the matter with my son. His response was, "Dude, what do you expect? You just finished eating a whole goat, so half of your blood is cholesterol, and you think you aren't a risk hazard to the bank's business? What are you thinking?" What happened was that the blood test coincided with a three-day religious festival during which we consumed a lot of meat. I guess my son was right.

One Thursday in 2004, I joined a group of deal seekers and camped all night in front of a Best Buy store in Elk Grove, California, to look for some items in the morning of that year's Black Friday. I brought along my blanket for reasons of practicality and preparation for all winter contingencies. In the morning, we stampeded the store. What do you think that made me stand out? You guessed it; my blanket. One of my son's friends happened to be a Best Buy employee who knew me, but I did not. He immediately called my son and told him that he saw me in the store wrapped in a blanket. I left the store after failing to secure the merchandise for which I had camped all night. My son took the information from his friend and dramatized it, as usual. He said that when I failed to find what I went to shop for, I urged his friend to go to the storage place in the back and see if he could find the item hidden somewhere. He told me he fully understood the reason why I behaved in that way because I was used to black market practice of hiding stuff, and that was how we did business where I had come from. He thought I had confused black market with Black Friday because of the word black in both sentences, thinking that they carry the same meaning, but I could not reconcile or solve the paradox of black market goods being sold at very high prices, whereas Black Friday goods being traded at way too discounted prices. He also added that even though people were rushing to get deals, they were intrigued by my appearance so much that they thought it was worth taking a few moments to figure out what was going on with me in a blanket; fully aware that those valuable moments could cost them dearly. He also said that I, with my bald-shaved head, wrapped in a blanket, looked like an African warrior, sans a spear. Probably realizing what he was telling me could be too much to bear, he tried to soften the blows by saying that there was nothing wrong with being an African warrior, only that my appearance did not sit well with the idea of being inside a Best Buy store in Laguna West, California, as early as 6:00 a.m. around Christmastime. He said those who stopped to look at me were trying to see if I was carrying a spear or not, and that could have made the difference between continuing their journey to look for deals or dashing out of Best Buy. He claimed that his friend, while still hiding in the back, told him, "Dude I am scared to go out there in the store. I don't know what your dad could be hiding under the blanket. I wonder if he is carrying under his arm a pet mongoose or one of them vicious, all teeth, and ready to bite African creatures. I don't want to be bitten." He said his friend decided to wait in the storage room long enough for me to grow impatient, give up, and leave the store. I did not believe him.

My son finally concluded he would perfectly be fine if I go and practice my tribalism back in my country. Every time I heard sentences such as "back in your country," all of my hopes for full assimilation into American life got dashed. After that, I would work even harder to regain my confidence so I could get accepted, only to be disappointed by a fresh rejection. It seems like there is no hope. It cannot get more black humor than this, but that is okay. It is not as disrespectful as it may appear to some of you. My son made it up for me in many other ways, so I am fine with that. I love my boy. He is my best friend, I guess.

The fact that there are domestic machines operating in my house at any given time bothered me a lot. The sound of an engine or a device spinning and accelerating faster and faster to get a particular job done caused me great anxiety. I kept this secret for myself until my wife and son found out. For a long time, I thought they did not know. The sudden spinning sounds of the washing machine and the dishwasher disrupted whatever work I would be doing. My body reaction had the words, "What is that," written all over my face. These machines start spinning slowly and keep on ramping up speed. I used to get the feeling that if they continued spinning faster and faster, it would only be a matter of time before they blew up. It is just logical. I used to count the seconds for them to slow down. The test conducted by pilots ramping up the engines, one at a time, in preparation for takeoff, too, bothered me a great deal. I only relaxed after the engines slowed down. In fact, I am less worried about flying than ground operations.

My son rationalized my phobia and attributed it to the fact that such machine sounds were not part of my daily life growing up. He is right. In fact, there were no machines in my household. Remember, we did not have electricity or running water in the village, not even today. Getting exposed to so much technology, simultaneously, was overwhelming, and that was something I could not handle well. I avoided them as much as I could, using them only when I ran out of options. During my wife's absence, I would wash the dishes the old-fashioned way, but, so far, she isn't aware of this fact.

My son also rationalized my purported lack of fondness for pets as something attributed to fear that I had developed at an early age. He told me that he was not surprised because my experience with animals was limited to two types. The first type consisted of lions, hyenas, tigers, etc., which looked at humans as a source of food. The second type were dogs, snakes, rams, etc., which resorted to biting and battering as means of surviving long enough to multiply and preserve their species so they would not be extinct. He diagnosed my condition and presented his findings to the rest of the family as facts and conclusive evidence. Below are more examples of random incidents that I have experienced while living here in America.

One day, I took my family on a road trip from San Francisco to Los Angeles. I stopped at the city of Santa Barbra for sightseeing. I parked at a restaurant by the beach. As soon as the car came to a halt, a man approached me and said, "You won't get it if you don't have hundred bucks." I was puzzled, and none of us in the car could make sense of that statement. When he got closer, I said, "I'm afraid you certainly must have mistaken me for a different individual." His response was, "You say what?" He also added a seven letter word, ending with an "-ing," placing it between the words "you" and "say."

We looked into each other's eyes for a moment, then he backtracked a few steps and took off running. I realized that I was talking to someone who was selling something he was not supposed to. I was surprised that both my son and my wife knew who he was, even before he said a word. They were angry that I spoke to him. My son expressed the view that I don't pay attention to my surroundings. I agree with him. The first thing that came to my mind when I saw the man approaching the car was that he needed help. I believe that most people think like that. I guess it takes some skills and training to be able to make calculated moves all the time. I was the wrong person in the wrong place. This is how people sometimes get caught up in the middle of troublesome situations.

I was entering my boys' (second and fourth graders) bedroom to tell them an African bedtime story when I overheard them talking about the requirements for running for the Office of the President of the United States. Upon seeing me, they both started consoling me

Annual rodeo spring festival at my boys' primary school in College Station, Texas.

by expressing their sorrow that I didn't qualify for running for the President's Office because of my birth place. I gathered they learned that at school since it was presidential election times. They have no idea that was the least of my worries. I am grateful and content that I don't have to leave the house every morning, carrying a bow and a quiver filled with arrows, and heading to the forest to hunt so I could feed them.

My wife regularly watched Oprah Winfrey, Dr. Oz, and Dr. Phil Shows, so she is well clued up on many things about daily life in America. She is transformed into a very knowledgeable person, I must admit. The Shows also did a wonderful job in equipping her with every word starting with an "en"; encourage, enable, enrich, enthusiasm, entitlement, empowerment, etc. She became at ease dealing with American pop culture. Unlike her, I found myself struggling to catch up. I still could not put my finger on what the word etiquette really means because there is one for everything, and I could hardly distinguish between them or use them appropriately for different situations. When she tried to add new nutritional terms such as calories and metabolism to my health vocabulary to help me monitor my eating habits, the outcome was disastrous. I found out that absorbing these new ideas required paying painstaking attention to details and adherence to a strict daily regimen. I needed to read about nutritional facts and figure out how many calories I should consume per any given day, and stick to that. I was challenged by my inability to provide a space in my brain to process these new health jargons that are important for a healthy life, if I aspire for one, but I could'nt do that all the time. For example, exercising regularly to burn fat is good for the body. However, in Kokoland, people believed that wasting away valuable energy is imprudent. It should rather be stored for rainy days. I could not reconcile the opposing views of these two different schools of thought. I also find myself struggling to cope with the idea of adhering to strict domestic rules such as refraining from napping on the couch and washing my dishes immediately after eating, but I think I am getting there.

The Talk Shows posed a great challenge for me, but, in a serious note, they have done a marvelous job in empowering people, especially women, all over the globe, so hats off to Talk-Show Gurus; Oprah Winfrey, Dr. Phil, and Dr. Oz.

A few weeks after our arrival here in America, we received a lucrative offer for a lifetime vacation somewhere in the Caribbean. It was for free; the offer stated. We could not believe our luck. One Saturday, my wife, our son, and I dressed up and headed to the conference address in San Mateo, California, to claim our free gift. It turned out to be a time-share promotion. It goes without saying how we, with our jumbled-up English and foreign accent, got brutally harassed into buying time-shares in a place I could not even identify on the map. I have yet to experience such an aggressive marketing tactics. To me, and to many Kokolanders, these people must be from the djinn's race or super magicians, at least, because the way they charmed us all at the conference into cheering and shouting, for no apparent reason, was unbelievable. They were able to strip us of our free wills. I wonder how anyone in our situation, being new migrants who had been here in America for three weeks only, could afford to sign on and commit to travel on vacation every three months. I found out later on that they adopted intimidation techniques to the fullest to corner us into accepting deals far beyond our stations in life. Very few of the attendees needed or afforded these vacation deals. I noticed the sales associates acted like detectives in the way they used some tactics, which shifted from super niceties when you agreed to bite the bait, to downright hostility and intimidation, if you turned out to be one of the few who knew what they wanted and asked too many questions. They perfected the good cop bad cop game. I guess it was second nature to them.

Figuring out our lack of familiarity with our environment, being new migrants, they took us to a secluded room and showed us a lush green tropical paradise with beaches, streams, and palm trees everywhere. The room temperature was perfect. They placed a glass jug filled with iced water. Crystal-colored tiny beads of water started to form in the exterior of the glass, an image I never saw throughout my time in Kokoland where nobody had the opportunity to drink water that cold, since we did not have electricity and, obviously, no refrigerators. These people must have known my weakness. They must have had some idea about Kokoland and its hot and dusty weather during the dry season, so putting me in a cool room and showing me a video about a Hawaiian or a Caribbean paradise would do the trick. I smiled throughout the film, and by the time the show ended, they had records of our names, address, social security numbers, credit cards number, expiration dates, the three-digit security code on the back of the card, and, most important, my signature, in bold, on the contract. My fate was sealed. They must have hypnotized me into signing, for I don't remember doing that. When I got home that day, I played the film in my head, only to discover that every "yes" answer I gave to all the leading questions should have been "no." None of the scenarios they had laid down, which enticed me into giving positive responses, applied to us. There was not a single reason why I should have been there in the first place, much less committing to buying a time-share in a Caribbean or a Hawaiian island. So far, we have been living here in America for the past twenty years, and we are still taking care of priorities other than vacationing in Hawaii. The deal was sealed, and I was on the hook for over two years making monthly payments without receiving any service for it, until I finally settled my debt. Breaking the contract was not an option, for it was too risky. I did not want to have trouble with the law due to failing to meet my financial obligations, so I quietly endured the pain and honored my part of the deal. I always wondered how and where they so quickly obtained our information.

A few years later, I received a letter in the mail and upon opening it, I found a pair of car keys and an invitation to visit a Lake Tahoe Casino and try my luck. If I could use the keys and have access to a car placed on display at the casino, I would win it. I said, "Again? Over my dead body." I flipped over the page and, with great difficulty, read the fine prints. The odds of winning the car were one in a few millions. Lake Tahoe is one of my favorite camping places, so I visited it regularly, but I avoided visiting the casinos for fear of being trapped into signing one of those contracts from hell.

Strange mail always found its way to my mailbox. I used to get tons of mail promotions from insurance companies. Those included property insurance, life policies, auto insurance, flood insurance, security alarms, home contents' insurance from theft, insurance for kitchen equipment, identity theft insurance, travel cancellation insurance, and many other offers. My philosophy was that insurance never hurts and it can only help protect against unforeseen events, so I enrolled in many of these offers, certain that they would bring me comfort and peace of mind. However, I lost sleep juggling my finances to figure out a way to meet my premium obligations. At the end of the day, it defeated the very purpose for which I got them in the first place; peace of mind. It took me some time to understand that not every mail offer is favorable to me and that I should sift through them to identify what I really needed. I reached this conclusion after closely examining my risk tolerance, being a man from Kokoland. When the majority of my people still live on one dollar a day, I should not be worried about the fridge breaking down or getting sick from drinking tap water in America. I no longer bother myself too much with scare-tactics such as, "Just imagine what will happen to your family if you are involved in an accident and you are dismembered." Nowadays, I have figured out how the system works, so I don't pay too much attention to gruesome scenarios, even though the risk is always there, of course.

I was also new to concepts such as Ponzi schemes and telemarketing. Telemarketers inundate homes with calls offering products and services, especially around dinnertime when they expected family members to be present. That was the case until things got out of control, and that led to the introduction of new legislation limiting such uninvited intrusions. One evening, I received a call at home and responded to it. From the get-go, I could tell it was a telemarketer calling to offer me some supposedly valuable service. The male voice on the other end introduced himself and requested to talk to the head of the household, so I said, "This is he." He then started reading from a page. From what I gathered, he was making a case for protection against identity theft. He eloquently stated his reasons for enrolling in his program. I listened attentively because he was able to hold me captive by painting scary scenarios for the consequences of someone assuming my identity. When he finished reading from his page, confident that I had taken the bait, he calmly asked me if I was interested in signing on. I responded with a yes answer, agreeing to join his company. Then he asked me about my name and I told him, Abba Gony Mustafa. He immediately said, "Never mind, don't worry," and disconnected the line, leaving me puzzled about what had just transpired between us. I thought about this tele-encounter for some time without finding a sensible reason for the man's behavior. I finally talked to a friend about it and, after thinking for a moment, he said to me, "Don't worry, no one in his rightful mind would assume your name, Abba Gony, especially after 9/11." I took his answer with mixed feelings, especially considering the tragic nature of the incident on that infamous day.

I think I have been confusing many people in America with my name and accent, on one hand, and my cowboy boot and hat, on the other hand. In fact, I can easily mingle and perform well in any crowd as long as I stay quiet. The moment I speak, my world comes crumbling down and my accent's share value falls to pennies' worth in a split second. At times, my skin color gives me away. I was approached a few times by some weird looking people in down town Los Angeles, asking me if I wanted to sell my driver's license. It was surprising to me how bold those criminals were, considering the confidence with which they approached me. I have never been so insulted. I wish if they had an idea about the principles that guide my life. It seems buying licenses from people who looked just like me was a lucrative business. I am equally baffled by the prospect of a person resorting to selling something as personal as his own identity for as little as ten bucks. I wish I have an answer.

A group of business owners from Roseville, California, including myself, flew to New Orleans, Louisiana, to attend a trade show. In the evening, we gathered at a restaurant in the famous Bourbon Street for dinner. We got seated and we ordered crocodile meat to try for the first time. Another group of diners, also from out of town, sat around the table next to us. One of the men decided to engage our table in a conversation, so he asked us, "Hey, guys, where are you from?" Before the man could finish his question, I volunteered and, with great confidence, aired my answer, "California, from California," I said. One of my colleagues, Keith, immediately burst into an uncontrollable laughter. He laughed so hard that he, with his mouth full of crocodile meat, choked pretty bad. I got the message he was sending. He meant to say I was not a Californian, yet. To be honest, I should not blame the man because the way I pronounced California has no resemblance. In fact, Arnold Schwarzenegger did a way better job saying it. However, I had mixed feelings toward Keith about the fact that he was laughing at me, but at the same time, gasping for air, after choking. From that moment onward, I decided to slow down when I responded to questions about my origin, which I got asked whenever I talked to someone for the first time. I had no idea how much alien I was until I saw that man laughing. That day, I became certain that we migrants must pay both taxes and accent dues before we could claim the full right of affiliation to America. In fact, I don't have a problem with that at all. Keith's ancestors moved to California during the gold rush some 150 years ago. From the way he laughed, I think, he wanted to make sure that I, too, had waited 150 years before I could give such a confident answer about my belonging to the Golden State. That incident was the straw that broke the camel's back. I surrendered the idea of considering California as home to my boys to claim. On the bright side, my embarrassment helped me develop the habit of carefully weighing situations before giving any answers.

While living in Texas and attending school at Texas A&M University, I bought a hat, boots, and twisted my tongue to fit in. I'd gone country, but that did not always work well for me, either. I confidently strode the Houston Galleria with my big cowboy hat and boots, but it did not take Texans long before they could remove my mask. As I have written above, the one question people asked me most of the time is, "Where are you from?" Ideally and without hesitation, my answer should be something like "I'm from the Panhandle, San Antonio, Amarillo, etc." That was never the case because I never had a ready answer. I always found myself in a dilemma. If I said I am from Kokoland, then I would have a lot of explanation to do. On the other hand, I was afraid I would get Keith's response, if I said I was a Houstonian or from Austin. Over time, I learned to give the right answers. I would carefully assess the situation with the person asking the question and accordingly determine what answer to give him or her. I would use "ummmm" to buy time. If my wife and son happened to be present, they would volunteer and answer on my behalf. While I am doing my "ummmming," one of them would jump in and say, "He is an African," hence demolishing to rubbles, in seconds, the image I painstakingly built over years as someone who had fully assimilated in the American society. I wish if they were generous enough to add the word "American" after, "He is an African." They hardly allowed me any breathing space to enjoy my newly acquired American citizenship. The worst thing is when this type of humor comes from your own family members. By the way, in a serious note, there is nothing wrong with Africa or being an African. Besides; I do not have any problem with people asking me where I come from. They don't know that I get the same question asked all the time. It is also well intentioned. What I am writing about here is the constant self-explaining that I do. I don't mind, but I think it is somewhat identity threatening.

My family members and I drove to Houston around Christmas holidays to visit the Galleria. I was waiting for my wife and kids outside a store when two young ladies cheerfully approached and asked if they could show me something interesting. I agreed, so they led me to a nearby booth where they had on display some beauty products. They asked me if it was okay to clean one of my fingernails. I hesitated for a moment, being an African who never experienced such a thing before. What do they mean by cleaning my nail? I reluctantly agreed. They cleaned my left hand's pinky nail with some stuff, then they asked me to flip over my hand so they could see all the nails at once, both clean and dirty, if you will. Once I did that, they were both flabbergasted by what they saw and loudly said, "Wow." I looked at them and also said, "Wow?" They realized that my "wow," in comparison to theirs, was somewhat subdued. In fact, I was "wowing" for their overreaction. Frankly, I did not see much difference. Sensing my lack of enthusiasm, they simultaneously concluded that it would not be worth it to invest one additional second. They both let go of my African hand, silently turned around, and went in two different directions to attract a "more wowable" person. Now, the problem is that if you, like me, have come from Kokoland, it is not only going to be difficult to get you motivated, but you will also be a demotivator. Polished nails have never featured in my list of priorities, nor will that ever be the case, not even if I am given a second life, I think. Unfortunately, people like me aren't good for beauty business. In my case, as I have written earlier about my childhood, being ashy was the norm, so things like polished nails are exceptions that would not stand in the face of grand schemes of things. I worried that my response might have caused those two young ladies to quit their jobs due to depression. If they spoke about their experience to friends in similar businesses, the ripple effect could be devastating.

I guess, the whole thing rests on disposable income. How much difference I see between my nails to the extent that I spend money polishing them depends on both the size of my bank account and list of priorities. Then again, I take that back because I am wrong. People do pursue happiness in many different ways, including the payment of loads of money for polishing their fingernails, and that is only fair. I feel bad that I failed to show some consideration to the young ladies, regardless of having bought their services or not. I am learning to be more mindful of other people's views, preferences, and take on life.

Shopping malls are also a fertile ground for marketing pyramid schemes. Upon arriving here in America, I used to carry one standard smile all the time, regardless of the circumstance. That has occasionally landed me in trouble. It took me some time to realize that it is fine not to smile frequently. Showing all of your teeth only to say hi to a stranger is unnecessary. Smiling for something you thought is a joke when the situation warranted showing of sympathy could lead to disastrous results. This is common sense, yet it is difficult for some of us to grasp, due to cultural differences.

Widely smiling for someone who approaches you in a mall may entangle you in a huge cobweb, if you aren't careful. I was once sitting on a bench inside a mall in Sacramento when a couple, who seemed to be a husband and a wife, got closer to where I was sitting and stopped. They both glanced at me and nodded their heads. I responded in kind, but I also, generously, added a big bonus-smile. They exchanged a few words and agreed that the man waited, whereas the wife, supposedly, walked away to shop for some items. The man, exhibiting signs of fatigue, decided to take a seat by my side, and that was his entry into my world. He took a deep breath and, while slightly shaking his head, he said, "Women and shopping." He then stretched his hand to greet me. "I am Joe," he said. I reciprocated in kind by telling him my name and that I was also waiting for my wife. He started talking about how much he hated shopping and asked me if I also did. I agreed with him, so we became buddies, who had a common interest, in a span of thirty seconds. After five minutes of meeting, he had already broken the ice and had cracked a joke or two.

As we waited, he gave me a lecture about the reckless way people shopped and spent their hard-earned dollars, making other people rich. Once he was certain that I agreed with his assumptions, he launched his coffee business idea, which he guaranteed that it would make me millions in no time, if I agreed to join him immediately. The idea, as you may already know, was that I would buy coffee from my own business, and every time I did that a percentage of my purchase would come back to me. If I sold coffee to other people, I would also get a cut. The same way if they made a sale. I would continue to accumulate dollars from everyone down the line selling coffee. I would soon have a pyramid of dollars stacked in my bank account. As the man lectured, I stared at a Starbucks Café across from the mall and engaged myself in mental calculations to estimate the number of cafés in California and neighboring States, all the way to Starbucks' headquarters in Seattle, Washington. Mind you, that was around the time Starbucks was opening stores in about every street corner in the country, followed by McDonald's, which, too, started to offer coffee to its customers. Add to that, I am not a coffee drinker, and I did not know many friends in America who could buy enough coffee from me to make it worthwhile for my business. My enterprise had been doomed to failure even before it started. I questioned myself, "What business have I in this coffee business?"

Even though the idea was too good to be true, it was also too good to pass. It is hard to forego an offer to become a millionaire doing something as simple as selling coffee. I signed on and shuttled the thirty-mile journey between my house in Sacramento and the couple's house in Stockton for a while attending some useless coffee meetings, until I came to my senses. One late afternoon, I left home to attend a meeting the couple had arranged for potential coffee millionaires. I drove halfway to Stockton then, all of a sudden, something reminded me of the outrageous time-share experience. I took the next exit and returned to my base. That was the end of the road to my coffee business startup that never was. What was I thinking? There is nothing like a day job.

My trouble is that I am forgetful. I could never master the art of having my guard up all the time. I was approached by shady business owners in many different ways. It is hard to fend them off. I am amazed by their ability to sustain themselves selling fuzzy and, at times, dishonest ideas. I guess the answer lies within the people targeted for such businesses. I remember once, a magazine salesman in London did his level best to convince me that, if I subscribed to his magazine, I could play a weekly soccer game and win millions of pounds sterling. The way the man picked me from the crowd is still a mystery to me. He reached into his bag, took out a magazine, and started talking about a life-changing opportunity, if I am interested in listening. He continued before I could respond and read the benefits I stand to gain from subscribing to the weekly magazine. He flipped a few pages and showed me numerous special deals. He stopped at one particular page and showed me a picture of soccer players in a pitch and a soccer ball above their heads. He told me I could play that game and make tons of money. He said one of the players had kicked the ball with his head, and that, if I could pinpoint the spot where the ball had dropped, I could be the winner. Just imagine! He made it sound so attractive that I might not have to do a thing for the rest of my life, if I win of course. I excused myself and left. I was so furious that he singled me out from the hundreds of people in the crowd and chased me down to tell me this stupid idea. The irony of his very presence at that spot was indicative of success with his business targeting seemingly clueless people.

CHAPTER 19

Back to Kokoland after Thirty Years

I returned to Kokoland after thirty years of absence. I found it dustier, drier, depressed, ailing, poorer, and sadder. There were many people walking aimlessly around in the market because there was nothing much to do. The old marketplace was dilapidated, and many of the brick shops were replaced by tiny shops built with tin. I found very few of the shop owners I knew. The rest of them were either dead, too old to work, or bankrupt. The farmers' market has shrunk, and I saw little activity buying and selling agricultural products. A few hungry goats and sheep for sale stood huddling together with their heads lowered down to avoid the midday sun-heat. A couple of lorries from the 1950s and '60s parked waiting for passengers who were unlikely to ride them into the city. You could tell they were on the last leg of

Khartoum; the capital city of Sudan. Photo 2011.

their life cycle and would soon be history. Minivans and tiny Korean cars have taken over the transportation business to and from the city. The space where market goers used to keep hundreds of donkeys was empty, except for few. Naturally, the donkey-grooming business was gone, and the big tree under which Ammu Barakat groomed donkeys was no longer there. The woods around Kokoland were all gone, and many of the giant landmark baobab trees had crumbled, including the one, named after Hajjah Maseera, where the zombie had beaten up our neighbor Saleh. The water ponds, which were scattered around the village, were no longer there. The trees that used to circle the ponds were either cut down, or had died of thirst. Many of the villages that were hidden from sight by dense forests could clearly be seen from Kokoland. The desert has claimed the land.

As far as people were concerned, I found those who were still alive to be the same people I had left behind more than three decades earlier. They were kind, decent, loving, and respectful, despite the hardships of life they had been enduring, which was clearly visible on their faces. Many people did not recognize me, so I had to remind them. Some people tried to test me to find out if I still remembered them or not. They were surprised that not only did I know who they were, but I also reminded them of certain incidents that had taken

Return to Kokoland. Photo 2016.

place a long time ago, and they were party to those incidents. They found that quite amazing. People were generally happy to see me, and they were appreciative of the fact that I inquired about their whereabouts and went to visit them in their villages. The general misconception is that once young men leave the villages to big cities, get educated, travel abroad, and make some money, their character changes and they become snobbish. People expected that type of behavior from me, but they were surprised that I proved them wrong all the time. I must admit, I have encountered a few people who did not appreciate the attention I was receiving from the community, but I was ultimately able to win their friendship. This is something you can read about in the few encounters below.

My absence from Sudan for a long time was a nightmare for my dad and other family members. It also presented a fertile ground for some ill-wishers who spread rumors that the government was looking for me because of my political stance and that was the reason I stayed away for all these many years. They were enthused by the thought that the government would arrest me the moment I set foot in the country, and that my family would never see me again. It was surprising to many and disappointing to some that I showed up without an incident. People descended to our house and congratulated my dad for my safe arrival. Women cried and repeatedly said, "Blessed that he has assembled;" a form of greeting usually reserved for people returning from a prolonged absence. They expressed sorrow and took pity on me for wasting away my valuable youth years. Those sympathetic views left me wondering. I kept asking myself if I truly missed a lot during my absence. As the women cried that I safely returned, I thought about the new life I have built for my family in America. I reached to a friend in London and expressed to him my dilemma. His response was that if his great-grandfather, who has been dead for over a century, came back to life and found out that people are still using Stone Age agricultural tools to farm, he would return to his grave after commenting, "Forget it. I have not missed a thing." That gave me some comfort and assurance.

Initially, the idea I had in mind was to travel overseas, get good education, accumulate work experience, and return home to try and help people by sharing what I have learned over the years. Ironically, many people saw my prolonged absence as a waste of twenty valuable years. I remember a friend telling me how his grandma fiercely opposed to the idea of him travelling overseas to study. She told him, "Why do you have to go all that far when you can stay here and study your grandpa's many books?" Of course, this is regardless of subjects, contents, number, and age of those books. She was most probably talking about a couple of a century old theology books. Would I have been better off if I had stayed behind and studied my grandpa's books? The fact remains that there is no primary school in my grandpa's village, even today.

To some of my contemporaries, whom I had left behind, I am one selfish person who abandoned his people and chose to live overseas, at a time when his presence was most needed. In some respects, I was wrong in assuming that I could leave home for such a long time, go back, and try to start from where I had left off. The reality was that we all went in different directions and received different inputs that shaped our characters, thinking, and outlook on life. Some people thought I returned with my Western values to impose upon them. That cannot be further from the truth and, or, my intentions.

I found that the rules of the game had changed. New community leaders have emerged and, by hook or by crook, held positions, which they guarded with their teeth. In fact, a few of them did not hide their hostility toward me. I once attended a family gathering that was composed of mostly younger people. I aired the view that we needed to organize to help with community development work. That idea did not go down well. One man told me, "You go away for all these years and come back only to tell us what to do. Who do you think you are?" He is a senior government official and a devoted party member, therefore his comments were not surprising to me.

The military government's manifesto, declared on day one of taking over power in the country, was to completely transform the Sudanese society. They did just that for the last thirty years. Today, the disastrous result of such haphazard work has caused a mess that the entire world can attest to. People like myself returning from America did not help much in furthering that goal because the manifesto was enacted in the first place to fight the West, and everything Western, led by America, the very country I have adopted as my new home. This is no news because those of you who have been following Sudan's political affairs understand that such stance was reflected, all along, in the government's policies since it took over power three decades ago.

Many of us Africans in the diaspora may have good intentions toward our respective countries and regions, but, in many instances, we were viewed as a threat and a challenge to status quo. This is especially the case with countries ruled by military dictators, or let us say; most of Africa. We don't have a choice, but to get involved to bring about positive change because it defeats the purpose if we are to stay at bay or become passive observers when we return home, for fear of stepping on people's toes, if you will.

In my case, the new community leaders repeatedly tested me to see if they could score few points for themselves through using simple undermining tactics. It was important for them to prove to as many people as they could that they, unlike me, hold the moral high ground by having sacrificed everything to remain close to the community in times of dire need for help. Anything that could legitimize their position so they stand well in the eyes of the community was good, even if that was at my expense, and I did not mind. There were many benefits gained from being community leaders, especially those who worked for the government.

As you can gather from the following couple of incidents, people, at the local level, may not have full understanding of what is going on around the world. The problem is that, for decades, the government has been bombarding them with so much negative input, turning them into angry people for no apparent reason. That was the government's way to manipulate, control, and keep people distracted from main issues.

During a Kokoland gathering, I met a man whom I had not known before. People told me he moved to the village and took residence some ten years earlier, and that he worked for the government as a health inspector. As soon as I greeted him, he started talking about current events, then foreign affairs. After that, he delved into talking about his association with government dignitaries in the capital, Khartoum. He told me about his achievements and the appreciation he has been receiving from the community for his work. As he spoke, I thought to myself it is great that he was able to achieve all of the above while living in Kokoland. Basically, in a matter of few minutes, he gave me all the warnings that was necessary to avoid messing or playing games with him, or else I would get burned for trying. He was telling me that he was a local community force to be reckoned with.

I carefully listened without interrupting his speech. I knew I was the primary target audience for all of this drama. He stopped talking when he had exhausted everything in his reservoir of wisdom and knowledge. I looked at him and posed the question, "Do you know that I'm the Prince of Wales?" He kept quiet and waited for me to fill in the gaps in this Prince of Wales conundrum, so I continued explaining to him how the Queen of England gave me that prestigious title. He listened attentively to my story, but I could see that he was thinking sporadically in many fronts trying to figure out whether I was telling the truth or not. He also wanted to prevent the lecture he had given in front of the community from being overshadowed by some nonsense talk from me. He was unsure if I believed everything he said or not. First, he looked confused, but then, wearing a beaming smile on his face, he looked at me and said, "No way, you are lying. Swear by the name of Allah that you are not." I said, "Yes, of course I was lying. I wasn't telling you the truth." He looked at me, and we both burst out laughing. Then I asked him, "Were you telling me the truth?" Again, he looked at me, for a second, and we started laughing one more time, only uncontrollably, paying little attention to our surroundings. In the process, we wiped out tears and blew our noses in the open air, causing all the hostility to melt away. He knew I did not believe in everything he said and that he had exaggerated on some of the things he told me. We both got up, and off we walked to Zaid's café to drink tea. With my false Queen of England story, I managed not only to neutralize him, but also make a friend out of him. He felt comfortable that I was neither there to pose a threat to his status, nor interested in becoming a community leader. What mattered was that we became friends. Our loud laughter raised the curiosity of some market goers who came forward to investigate. Upon finding out what had transpired between the community leader and I, we all started laughing afresh. After that, someone brought up a different subject about one reckless cattle herder who intentionally let his herds into a farm, destroying the crops. We sent the story of the Prince of Wales to the back burner as more pressing issues took over.

The problem, as I have mentioned earlier, was that most people have no term of reference for what was really happening around the world. For that reason, they were easily manipulated and misled. Tribal conflicts could erupt for the simplest reasons of misinformation and misstatements. Before you knew it, you have tribal armies fighting one another, but oblivious to why they were fighting in the first place. The government was always quick to blame every problem under that country's sky on secret foreign hands, and people mostly believed that.

In Kokoland, access to technology can propel a person up to a new level in the social strata. Cellular phones, being a new phenomenon, are doing miracles. People believe that it is the best thing that ever happened to them. In the absence of TV service in the area, Cellular phones filled in the vacuum by satisfying people's hunger for information and staying connected. Owning one became a matter of necessity, especially for young people, even when they can not afford them or the airtime charges. An incident took place when I went to visit a relative whom I have not seen in decades. As we sat and conversed about general issues, another distant relative walked in. I did not recognize him, for he was young when I left the country. He exhibited an unfriendly body language, which I could tell from the way he greeted me. We sat down and we all kept quiet for some time, then my phone rang. I took it out of my pocket and responded to the caller. I finished the call and was about to put it back in my front pocket when the man, while stretching out his hand, asked to have a look at it, so I handed it over to him. He flipped it over, carefully looked at the back, and sarcastically commented, "Why do you have this old-fashioned brick-like phone?" As he handed it back to me, he looked around and surveyed everyone's faces to see their reactions. The gist of what he was actually trying to convey was that I have nothing much to show for, despite my many years overseas. In all probabilities, someone could have relayed to him that I returned from America empty-handed. That meant he was better off that he, unlike me, stayed in Kokoland and didn't waste so many valuable years in America. As such, he has little to worry about. I knew that the whole thing boiled down to satisfying his ego, but he chose to use undermining tactics to get there. I did not mind that at all, considering the fact that I was just visiting for few days, so why make enemies, unnecessarily?

When it was my turn to speak, I said, "I left my other phone back in America because it will not work here. I brought this one, especially made for this region. It is doing the job and that's what matters. I said, "Some of the phones here aren't always good quality, especially the ones made in China." After a few moments of awkward silence, I abruptly said, "Can I see your phone?" He reluctantly reached into his pocket and handed me his phone. I looked at it and said, "You see, it was made in China." He was not comfortable when some people smiled at my comments. I tried to dial a number, but he quickly asked me to give it back to him, so I did. He probably did not have enough credit. At that point, I felt we had a tie result, so I kept quiet after that. Enough embarrassment, and I knew that was about as much as he could take. Things could get out of hand, if I continued. After that, I changed the subject by asking him about his wife, children, and life in general. I asked to show him that I was fine with what had just happened between the two of us. Feeling special, he responded with a big smile and said, "Leave all this talk aside and tell us about America." By that time, we were already cool buddies, but only after I had shown him that I, too, could inflict serious damage on him. I made sure he would never try to undermine me again in any social gathering to claim some status at my expense.

I said, "What do you want to know about America?" He took a few seconds thinking about a question. I also started thinking about giving him an answer that he could relate to, then I saw a smoke billowing from a distance, so I asked him, "What is that smoke?" He said, "A farmer burning some dry bushes in preparation for the rainy season." Then I told him, "In America, for example, if you want to burn bushes in your farm, you have to listen to the news to find out if burning is allowed on that day or not, or you call to find out from government officials monitoring air quality." He said, "La ilaaha illa Allah," meaning "There is no god but God." This is a religious verse recited when a person is in utter disbelief. I said, "What is the problem?" He said, "You mean you people have a say in God's air or what?" I said, "But God's air is for everyone to share." He said, "Your talk is not straight at all." I said, "What do you mean? If the air is already polluted by heat and dust, monitoring it is not a bad thing so that government officials could warn people to take precautionary measures to stay healthy."

My relative who was sitting and quietly listening to our conversation appeared, somewhat, agitated by my response, which turned out to be a complete fiasco, as I learned later. The more I argued my case to get out of trouble, the more in trouble I found myself. He leaned forward and said to me in a loud voice, "What does the government has to do with dust in the air? God is the one who sends air to blow dust. Another thing. Who is going to be sickened by dust anyway?" I said, "If the climate is hot and dusty, and, on top of that, people burn trees and dry leaves, the situation can only get worse and that may cause sickness, or even death, especially in the cases of people who are, for example, asthmatic."

At this point, both men wanted to respond, but my relative was first to speak. He said, "If someone dies, that means he has exhausted the days God has given him on earth." Then I said, "Inhaling the smoke from his neighboring farmer could be the reason for his death." I said that while intentionally avoiding the use of the word premature before the word death. There isn't such a thing called premature death. Death occurs only when a person runs out of time on earth. To say or believe in anything short of that was suicidal, so why bother say it when I was already in trouble and desperately trying to dig my way out of it. The other man said, "First, you ask God for forgiveness because your faith is very weak. How can you blame someone's death on another person who is simply cleaning up his farm? How can he cause bad weather?" At this juncture, I knew my "smoke pollution" analogy did not go down very well, and that I was losing the fight. I was usually mindful about refraining from indulging myself in such types of open ended conversations that could compromise my position, the longer I continue to talk. Somehow, that precautionary measure slipped my mind that day and I found myself in trouble up to my neck.

Soon, more people would join us and, in most probability, be in the two men's camp. It was time that I carefully navigated my way out of the spider web in which I had self-entangled. Any further deliberation on this subject, to try to win the argument, could only increase the chance of getting me branded a communist and a faithless person. I realized that I was not lucky in my choice of the subject about weather conditions. Obviously, the two men were keeping track of everything I have been saying and they were definitely going to share that with the community, after adding some drama from their own imaginations. The discussions would be unfavorable to me, and I would not be around to defend myself, so I decided to look for a safe exit to cut down on my losses. A phone rang, and I said, "Great." The man quickly reached for it and started talking. From his loud voice, I could tell that he was talking to someone far about some deal for selling goats, so he shouted to make sure the person on the other end understood the seriousness of the matter and heard him clearly. When he finished talking, I saw a window of opportunity to change the subject. I said, "Could you come with me to greet Yaqoob, the tailor?" Yagoob was an old friend I had not seen in decades. We all got up and went to Yagoob's shop. We found him stitching some garments. He greeted me with the question, "Who are you?" written all over his face. One of the men reminded him of who I am, so he greeted me afresh, only enthusiastically. We sat down to drink tea and talk about a new topic dictated by a different environment; Yagoob's tailoring shop. We sent the controversial weather subject to the back burner, the same way we did with my Prince of Wales story, above, and that was the safest thing to do. I was certain that they would visit these conversations after I was gone. Only God knows what conclusions they had reached.

Similar to owning a cellular phone; acquiring computer skills could also enhance a person's social standing. Remember that all these technologies are new to people, so it is understandable that they influenced their behaviors. My father-in-law, who was a school superintendent, told me about a new computer they had purchased to automate their records. They identified one secretary to be in charge of the process. He jokingly told me that, with her new position, she even changed the way she walked. He said, "She beamed with confidence and strode with her head held up high. Whenever she passed by, people moved aside to give her way." He told me, "Whoever had the opportunity to marry this woman would have married up." The irony is that she didn't get enough training to put the computer to good use. She took the title of Computer Woman and made a living out of it, but without doing anything with the computer, which sat in the office and collected dust.

I went to inspect a piece of property I owned in the outskirts of the capital. From there I went to visit a friend who happened to be living nearby. He suggested that I accompany him to visit a group of his friends who were meeting for a wedding event at a close-by house. I reluctantly agreed because I did not know who those people were, since I was out of the country for such a long time. Once we got closer to the house, it became clear to me that I had committed a blunder. I saw military jeeps and people in both army uniforms and plain clothes. I walked inside the sitting room, greeted everyone, and quietly took a seat with the intention of keeping a low profile. A few minutes later, a man in civilian clothes demanded that my friend introduced me to the crowd. He commanded him to do so in a tone that gave away his high military rank.

My friend obliged and started talking, "This is my friend Abba Gony who lives in America, but he is visiting." He continued, "He has been away for over twenty years and . . ." At that moment, I intervened by hinting to him that I would like to take over, and that there was no need for him to say anything more. I did not want him to volunteer any more information. The damage has already been done by divulging the fact that I lived in America, which could mean that I was anything, but an advocate for the government's policies. It was highly unlikely that I supported the war campaign against its own people in South Sudan. I could tell from the men's facial expressions that they had already concluded that I belonged to the opposition camp, overseas.

As the men stared at me, I thought to myself, "I am in the country at the wrong time and now I am really at both wrong time and place. I am in the country at a time when it is under American sanctions. America has recently bombed a factory in the outskirts of the capital, suspecting that it produced chemical weapons. Osama Bin Laden was granted a safe haven in the country before leaving to Afghanistan. The war between the North and the South is raging. The government-controlled media had successfully brained-washed the population into believing that the government's mishaps were entirely caused by America's animosity toward the people of Sudan. The government's massive mobilization efforts led hundreds of thousands of men to join the army and different militia groups, presumably, to fight the infidels, led by America."

The sense I got from people was that the Americans were all lined up to invade Sudan, when, in fact, half of them might be unaware of the existence of a country named Sudan. Against the above backdrop, I found myself in an awkward situation sitting face-to-face with army generals whose sole responsibility was to transform the above misconceptions into realities, come what may. I thought for a moment, "I must get out of here with minimum damage, so I have to be very careful with whatever I say."

I surveyed the crowd of thirty or so dignitaries and found that most of them were looking in my direction, cornering me for some explanation about my identity and what I had to say. Some faces gave me daring looks, whereas others wore grim expressions. Some half-smiled, and a few men stared at me with blank faces. I knew in advance that my comments would trigger responses from them. I also knew for sure that some would try to undermine me, especially if I spoke favorably about America. That was a battleground, though of a different kind. I must respond, but without disrespecting anyone of them. After all, it was an opportunity, presented to me in disguise, to speak to them about the things that I believe in and stand for, but without allowing them the opportunity to degrade me, in case they disagreed with my take on issues that I raised. All of these thoughts and scenarios crossed my mind in a few seconds.

I said, "In all fairness, America is a land of laws from which we the Sudanese and many other nations could learn a lot. In America, all people are equal under the law. It has a functioning constitutional democracy that has been in place for over two hundred years. Countries like Sudan, which have not yet drafted a lasting constitution of their own, could examine the American constitution to see if they can adopt some of its articles. It will be nice if we can agree on a way to run the country, but without being at war with ourselves." I said that while impliedly referring to the war raging between the north and the south at that very moment. I kept quiet for a few seconds, then continued, "The good thing about America is that a simple person like me, coming from a humble background, can live there and receive full rights, just like any other American citizen. In case of disputes, the law treats the opposing parties equally, even if that involves the President of the United States." By mentioning that, I had hoped to highlight the pending indictment of the country's president by the International Criminal Court for committing genocide and crimes against humanity in Dar Fur.

Finally, I said, "Please don't get me wrong because America, like anywhere else on the planet, is neither a perfect place, nor God's heaven on earth. It is run by people who, sometimes, make mistakes. The good thing is that America is governed by a constitution, laws, systems, and guidelines, which are constantly amended, modified, and improved upon. We could do the same here. I think the whole thing boils down to justice and equality for all people, and the protection of civil, political, economic, social, and cultural rights, be that here in this country, in America, or anywhere else on the planet." I stopped talking at this juncture. I took a quick glance at my friend whom I had on the edge of his seat, throughout my speech, fearing that I would say something clumsy or stupid in front of the generals and make him regret the fact that he took me over there. I found him somewhat relieved, so I knew I was not offensive or disrespectful to anyone. People started exchanging views and I sensed the person sitting next to me trying to engage me in a one-on-one conversation, but he got distracted by the arrival of the host who welcomed and invited everyone for lunch. The lunch break provided me a valuable opportunity to excuse myself, leave, and avoid the open-ended session, which was certainly going to take place after lunch, had I stayed. I left the house without angering anybody and subjecting myself to the risk of going to jail or some security personnel obstructing my departure at the airport.

The hostility and grudges people generally held against America baffled me. I carefully examined the political environment and reached some conclusion. Many people did not have good grasp of what America stands for. To them, their understanding of it was mostly represented in whatever negative image depicted by the central government. The country, in general, and the marginalized regions, in particular, had limited exposure to the outside world, which was further undermined by the high illiteracy rates. The media was fully controlled by the government, and television service was limited to areas that had electricity. The media broadcast the government's official line about the causes of the economic crisis facing the country, and the public had little chance of knowing the truth. To the government, foreign hands were the ones responsible for all of its problems and that nothing could be attributed to corruption, mismanagement, and the deterioration in all aspects of life that had engulfed the country due to some disastrous policies.

Against this background came the revolution in communication brought about by the introduction of cell phones, the Internet, and satellite channels. All of these events coincided with the attack on America on September 11, followed by the American invasion of Iraq. Many people were introduced to America and the world through satellite channels covering the Iraq war. They received their first dose from media images portraying America as an invader with the goal of destroying the region's Islamic heritage. That came in handy to dictators, all around the region, who diligently marketed to their subjects the idea that America was the one causing problems in their countries. Few people understood the truth about America, but many of them got carried away with the general mood of hatred to America. This is also to bear in mind that many of the newly mushroomed international television channels had their own agendas of undermining America, even though they, falsely, claimed absolute professionalism in their coverage of events. It takes some reading between the lines to understand their true intentions. As far as the average person is concerned, whatever news they received from those channels was the eye of the truth, and no questions asked.

I found myself talking to people who had already formed a very negative view about America, that it was anti-Islam, invades other countries, and bombs people. I tried to argue that America is not planet perfect and that it is a place populated by human beings. As such, it has its share of worldly problems, but it is a wonderful place of many good things, and that the rest of the world can learn a lot from it; hence avoid reinventing the wheel. I felt obliged to counter argue and draw people's attention to the fact that what they saw and heard was not the whole truth. I also felt that I would be contradicting myself if I kept silent. America is my new home. I should defend it and the least that I could do is to speak up my mind and tell what I think is right. I must admit that I was somewhat discouraged because my voice was drowned by skepticism and ignorance about what was really going on. I could not do a dent in people's misconception about America, for the damage done from misinformation was immense.

While I was visiting Kokoland, a friend told me that he heard some news about a plane crash in the eastern part of the country. According to the government's official line, the American embargo on plane parts was the cause of the crash. That was the news broadcast by the government's media to the public. Upon further looking into the matter, I found out that the State Department refuted the government's claim by stating that plane parts were not included in the list of sanctions levied on the country. That clarification came after the damage was done. Besides; hardly anyone knew about it. I reached out to my friend and told him what I have found out. His response to me was that I was defending my new country because I lived there and I did not want to jeopardize my interests. He said I should come to my senses, admit, and accept the injustices America was carrying out. I was disappointed because the few people I talked to did not buy my version of the story about the plane parts. It was amazing how the media could control people's frame of mind, especially when they could not read between the lines. They would just believe anything they were told. The outcome was disastrous.

I saw a slight shift in the younger generation's take on prevailing issues. Due to exposure to information that they could obtain via cell phones and the Internet, they started questioning the false promises the government had been making, but without showing any tangible results for it. They also started doubting the blame game the government had been playing. Such an awakening came at an excessively late time, but the good thing is that it is a trend moving in the right direction.

I wanted to share my experience in the West with the people, but there was too much negativity toward everything foreign. They made up their minds and did all the talking, most of the time. They were very sure about themselves and their stances, so they did not feel the need or the urge to listen to my side of the story. Very few people expressed interest in what I had to say. I wanted to tell them about Big Ben, the British House of Parliament, British Rails, Greenwich Mean Time, etc. I also wanted to talk to them about the American legal system, women's rights, the American constitution, the Civil War, New York skyscrapers, the Statute of Liberty, the Great Lakes, the Mississippi River, Bill Clinton, and Barack Obama (the first black President and what that means to the African American community, bearing in mind their struggle for civil rights). I wanted to tell them about California freeways, the San Francisco Bay Bridge, the Golden Gate Bridge, Texas cowboys, the corn and wheat fields of the Midwest, snow, and how snowflakes rained down. I wanted to tell them about hurricanes, tornadoes, Native Americans, the slave trade, the civil rights movement, the White House, the Congress, Disney World, and many other things. Above all, I wanted to tell them about President J. F. Kennedy as the man who had the vision for sending an American to the moon; a dream that had materialized in July 1969 when Neil Armstrong became the first man to step onto the lunar surface.

Do you remember how we in Kokoland mistook Elvis Presley for Yuri Gagarin; a story I have written about in chapter 6 above? Do you also remember how we lost the fight about the man on the moon when a few "enlightened" first-year middle school students and I first brought the news to the village in the early 1970s to share with the community? Again, do you recall how people became furious and thought it was blasphemous to contemplate such an idea? For those reasons, I wanted to make sure that when I returned to Kokoland, I had all the facts I needed to win the "man on the moon" case. I was ready to get back at those who humiliated me and thought that I was insane for believing in such an oblivion. I went to great lengths to equip myself with facts, thinking that I would do a better job explaining myself this time around, forty years later.

While in America, I satisfied my curiosity and went on a fact-finding mission. I read extensively about Kennedy Space Center and the Cape Canaveral launching site in Florida. I visited NASA's Christopher C. Kraft Jr. Mission Control Center (MCC-H); the facility at the Lyndon B. Johnson Space Center in Houston, Texas. I took photos as evidence to support my argument when I met people in Kokoland to show them launching-platforms for moon-bound rockets and spacewalking images. My goal was to share some facts and in the process, I might help correct the negative view about what was considered the lie of the century; in other words, man landing on the moon. I was so disappointed about people's lack of enthusiasm for listening to my stories, considering them out of touch with daily realities of life. I should not blame them for being interested in nothing other than securing meals to their families, probably one meal a day, one day at a time. Forty years later, living conditions have definitely worsened in Kokoland.

A space rocket at Johnson Space Center Rocket Park, Houston, Texas

A friend reminded me of a Sudanese proverb which originated in the Mahdist Revolt that was pursued by the colonial war of the late nineteenth century. It was believed that the British army was invading the country and was about to attack. As a matter of urgency, the Mahdi, the revolt leader, dispatched a messenger to the Hijil tribe, which resided alongside the White Nile, south of the capital, to garner support for his army. The tribesmen refused to enlist and they asked the messenger to return to where he had come from. They told him, "Tell the Mahdi we have an upcoming donkey race, so we cannot fight. Sorry." Their donkey race was more important to them than protecting the country from an imminent British invasion. The story became a proverb used whenever a person foregoes a matter of great urgency for a trivial one. My friend simply wanted to tell me that my priorities were mixed up. At the time people were fighting to secure one meal a day, I was concerned about convincing them that humans have landed on the moon. "Get a life," he said. He was right, but can you also see how frustrating it is to hear people tell you that the whole thing about man landing on the moon was a hoax and that planet Earth is not even round?

As you can see, I did not stand a chance because the timing of my visit to the country was wrong and everything else was against me. I returned with my thoughts intact. I also left behind my people certainly not missing a thing about my untold stories. How could they miss what they did not know about, in the first place? I felt defeated, I must admit.

I would like to move on to a different set of Kokoland memories. I have learned that kindness, however minimal, could leave a lasting impression on a person. Uncle Noah was a man whose generosity is something that I can attest to, from a personal experience. He lived in the village of Goat-Head, few miles south of Kokoland. He owned a camel and earned his living by transporting agricultural goods. During the rainy season, he also transported merchandise to villages that were cut off from Kokoland by two violent streams that prevented lorry drivers from crossing.

There is one thing about Uncle Noah that I continue to remember from my primary school days. Whenever he saw me in Kokoland, he called and handed me a *tariffa,* (a half a penny), for no reason, and walked away without saying a word. I had no idea why he did that, especially that we were not relatives. That tariffa was enough to buy me a handful of roasted peanuts from a woman named Hajjah Simsim. She was a sharp contrast to Uncle Noah. She and generosity walked in parallel lines. She happily took my money, but did not honor her part of the deal with honesty. She was so miser that she just could not give me half a penny's worth of roasted peanuts. She used one of those tiny tomato-paste empty cans for measurement. She cheated on the quantity of peanuts and gave me about half of it. She knocked the bottom of the can inward, reducing its carrying capacity by half. You would see the can placed on top of the palm-leaf plate containing the peanuts for sale. It would appear full of peanuts, but actually half full. I would approach and ask her, "Hajjah Simsim, how much is your peanuts?" She would respond, "*Tariffa* a can." I would already be holding the coin in my hand. The moment I handed it over to her, she would happily grab it from my hand and hide it under a piece of cloth in front of her. She would then, in an act of unparalleled, but actually fake, generosity, submerge the can deep into the plate to scoop as much peanuts as possible. That was her way of convincing me that she was happy to give me my money's worth of peanuts, and much more, and that she spared no room in the can to carry, not even one, additional peanut piece. She would do that while carefully covering the bottom of the can to prevent me from noticing the inward indentation, and hence discovering her trick. She would then pull out her hand, but continue to cover the can bottom, while leaving the top for me to see that it was full up to its neck. She would flip it on my stretched out tiny hands, which I would be holding tight together, just in case there was too much peanuts for one hand. Sometimes, I let her pour the peanuts in the front pocket of my extra-large *baft* cotton T-shirt. Immediately after that, she would quickly refill the can and place it on top of the plate as before. She would do that at the speed of light, when, in fact, there was no justification for such a rush. Hajjah Simsim never suspected that I had full knowledge of her malpractices and cheating on the quantity of peanuts she sold to me and my friends. I would walk away and leave her thinking that she was fast on her way to fame and richness with her big sale of half a penny.

At other times, Hajjah Simsim would justify to herself that peanut prices and roasting costs of labor and material, such as sand, had gone up. To avoid losing money, she would go an extra mile in her cheating practices. She would flip the can upside down and use the indented bottom-side to sell her peanuts. That would save her a few peanuts per sale and, in the long run, her bottom line profatibility would positively be impacted. I knew she did that because the tiny writing on the red can would appear upside down. She would be fooling people into believing that they were getting a can's full of peanuts. There would be even fewer peanuts on the indented bottom of the can, but most people did not know or bother to find out why their purchase is so little. She did not think that I noticed, or probably did not know that the writing on the can was upside down.

It is amazing to what extreme limits some people go to get rich. Thinking that cheating me out of half a penny could get Hajjah Simsim somewhere was a nonstarter. One would imagine that she could have died from depression had she figured out the number of light years that could take her to amass a worthwhile fortune, but life certainly functions in a strange way. Then again, I resign to the fact that human kind is the same everywhere. Examples of cheating on transaction costs could range from a meager half a penny's worth of peanuts, to multi-billion dollar ones involving things such as diesel emissions tests and scandals implicating car companies. Do you sometimes wonder why you buy a food or drink item and find that three quarters of the package is air? I guess Hajjah Simsim's type of people is not limited to Kokoland.

In sharp contrast to Noah, Jabbar, who also lived in Noah's village of Goat-Head, was one of the few unkind people that I ever met. One time, a first-grader from the boarding school went to greet him. Jabbar, sarcastically, said to the boy, "It is a *Tariffa* [half a penny] that you are after, aren't you?" Jabbar's mean-spirited behavior was very uncommon. In fact, adults who heard his comments blamed him for his cruelty. For many years, I remembered this man's meanness every time I spotted him in town. The child was not there to ask him for anything, nor was he going around begging people. Nobody, including children, begged for food or money, even when they were in need. People on their own reached out and helped those in need, without being asked. It was a weekend; a Friday, and that child was simply walking around in the market. He genuinely greeted Jabbar without expecting to get anything from him, in return.

I went back to Kokoland and was very eager to meet a few people who had played a positive role in my life. I made a list and went round looking for them. I wanted to thank them for their kindness and also to hand them some money as a token of appreciation. Uncle Noah, as you might have guessed, was among the first people I searched for. I wanted to ask him a few questions about the half-a-penny he used to give me. Sadly, I found out that he had passed away a few years earlier. He died while performing an act of generosity, which was probably the only thing he knew all his life. Whenever people found themselves stranded and could not cross the two streams by his village, they reached out to him for help, and he never hesitated in doing so. He was an excellent swimmer. One time, a man named Al Har sought his help, but, that day, one of the streams was exceptionally violent. Uncle Noah carried Al Har on his back and swam toward the other side of the stream, but the current was too strong for him. He was dragged and entangled in some tree roots, which caused him to drown. Al Har managed to grab a tree branch and hold on to it until people from the village came and rescued him. That was how Uncle Noah died. I wish I had the chance to meet him. People branded Al Har as, "The man who killed Noah." It was not Al Har's fault, but this just shows you how much people missed Uncle Noah. It is clear that helping others was something that ran in his veins. God bless him.

Incidentally, Al Har also happened to be an unkind person, just like Jabbar. His house was on the way to the market center, so I passed by it every day. He had a sister who was mentally incapacitated. Her name was Little Horns, indicative of the way she wore her hair above her forehead, resembling two little horns. No one knew her real name. Despite her disability, Al Har used to make her look after the cows. He used to beat her for making mistakes while taking the cows to a nearby forest to graze, or failing to hoard them inside the fence, in the evenings, when she returned home. He had no regards for her disabilities. The sad image of Little Horns walking barefooted year round is unforgettable.

I don't mean to give the impression that there was too much cruelty in Kokoland. To the contrary, people are generally kind and generous, despite their limited means. Jabbar, Al Har, and Hajjah Simsim, the roasted-peanuts seller, were certainly an exception to the rule. Life is truly about contrasts. Uncle Noah had been practicing generosity until the last minute of his life, whereas Jabbar, Al Har, and Hajjah Simsim were a classic example of misery and meanness. I guess there is beauty in this because only through contrasts can we highlight the differences between good and bad, and that way we can appreciate the good things more.

My cousin Baqir, being a city boy, always looked down on me, coming from a village. When I transferred to high school, which was in the outskirt of the city, I took advantage of the weekends and visited my elder sister in the city. I also went to the movies and had a chance to eat some sweets, as Baqir put it. On weekends and long holidays, hundreds of us flocked to the city in school buses and caused food shortages to its residents like Baqir. Once, he suggested to me that I should give him advance warning whenever we decided to invade the city so he could take precautionary measures and stock up on sweets and milk before our arrival. He told me that we, mostly being villagers, overconsumed these two items, believing that they were delicacies. He told me that we did not differentiate between main course and deserts, and that we ate sweets and drank milk as our main course. He also told me that another reason for my visits to the city was to enjoy myself looking at colorful neon lightbulbs. I must admit that I used to get fascinated by that, especially green neon lights. Who would not be excited about seeing electricity in action for the first time? Baqir was right as far as light is concerned and, in that regard, I was a true villager in every sense of the word.

Upon returning from America, I met Baqir and reminded him of all the jokes and pranks he used against me back in the days. It was my time to get at him and do some leg-pulling. My problem is I never forget. I told him that I lived in the same city (Sacramento) as President Ronald Reagan. I slightly twisted the facts because President

Reagan lived in Sacramento only during his term as California State Governor. I also told him that Clint Eastwood, Charles Bronson, and Sidney Poitier, all of whom were Baqir's movie heroes, lived in my neighborhood. This is obviously not true. I went as far as telling him that they all greeted me every morning on the way to their studios and occasionally asked me, "Abba, would you like to join us for coffee?" I told him that I sometimes agreed and at other times declined their offers because of my busy schedule. Please pay attention to the way these internationally renowned movie stars addressed me by my nickname and the fact that I occasionally declined their coffee invitations. It meant that I had joined his heroes' club and became friends with them to the degree that we informally dealt with one another. This was an exercise to show how an important person I had become. In a score-based game, you want to secure the maximum points against your opponent. I stood a good chance of getting away with murder, since Baqir had no way of verifying my allegations. President Reagan once said, "Trust but verify." Baqir could neither trust what I told him, nor could he verify it, and, above all, he could do nothing about that. Frankly, I got a kick out of his facial expressions as he listened to my false stories. "Fantastic," I said to myself. It took me over thirty years from being a country bumpkin, as far as Baqir is concerned, to moving to California and becoming a buddy of Clint Eastwood and his circles of close friends. Dreaming is free, and Baqir had no say in that. Not bad, ha!

Baqir used to depict himself in an image of a movie goer who was well informed on every biographical fact about his movie heroes, and I believed him. I got the sense that Sidney Poitier was his next door neighbor. He used to talk to me about Charles Bronson, his favorite movie star, as if he knew him personally. He used to address him by his first name, Chalres, and at times he referred to him as, "The Red Indian," meaning, "The Native American," to be accurate, giving me the impression that the man was as close to him as an uncle who lived with him in the same household, or something similar in nature. Baqir was terribly hurt when I said to him: "By the way, Charles Bronson is not a Red Indian as you have been claiming. He was born to Lithuanian parents who were migrants to America."

Baqir was dumbfounded. From his looks I could tell that he was asking himself, "What else does this man know." My assertion about Charles Bronson shook Baqir's confidence in himself to the core and brought his movie empire down crumbling when he realized that I was beating him at the very game he had known best.

As you might have gathered by now, going to movies was a big thing in Baqir's life and the lives of people like me who got into them, inadvertently. I was about ten years old when one of my aunts told me a bizarre story, which I vividly remember to this day. It was about a place she named the Sons of Dogs Land, or Dogland, if you will. She told me dogs and nothing else inhabited that land. She said dogs ran their daily affairs just like us humans. She elaborated on the living conditions at Dogland, but I think it is inappropriate to include what she told me here in this book. From the way she spoke to me, she sounded so sure about her story, but she left me both worried and wondering, "How come?" I found the whole thing to be so bizarre and senseless, so I wrestled to reconcile it with realities at hand. Certain that there was no such a thing as Dogland, I, upon returning to Kokoland, went to see her and ask her a few questions about the story. I reminded her of what she had told me almost forty years earlier and, to my surprise, she remembered everything she had said, so I asked her about the source of her story. It turned out that she was talking about a movie her son had watched in the city. He came home and told her about something he himself had hardly grasped, after adding scenarios of his own. Lacking understanding of movie concepts, coupled with language barriers, most of what he told her got lost in translation. On her side, she also added her own imaginations, produced a fantasy, and presented it to me as facts, when I was about ten years old. At that time, I had never been to the city or a movie theater, even though the city is a mere twenty-five miles or so from Kokoland. My aunt and I were both unaware of our environment and utterly confused.

The first few times I went to the movie theater, I did not understand the concept behind movies, nor was I sure if the images were from heaven or earth. I could not differentiate between fact and fiction. I thought all the killings were for real. I was captivated by the colors and the sceneries shown in tobacco commercials. I was so fascinated with that. I was also fascinated with the rugged looking Western style cowboys' way of dressing, especially the boots and the hats. When I came to America decades later, I searched for them everywhere, but could not find them, until I moved to Texas. I found that they were actually *grown* there. Texas is "cowboy boot land." I bought me a boot and a hat to relive those Western movies that I watched around the seventies and the eighties, but my accent let me down badly, all the time. Texas accent is hard to copy. I fooled myself into believing that I was J. R. (Black) de Dallas, or something. I wore my big cowboy hat and boots, and went roaming Texas cities and country sites, while displaying all the confidence that you could imagine. My problem I was "all hat, no cattle," and no ranch.

My cousin Baqir used to sarcastically correct the way I pronounced the names of his Western movie heroes, especially John Wayne's, which I vocalized in a way that sounded more like John Wine. It was difficult for me to say these truly foreign names, and Bagir found that very entertaining. I did not speak English at that time, so I picked up names from here and there without knowing the correct pronunciation or how they should sound. How they were spelled was out of the question. For all the above reasons, I thought it was my turn to tease Baqir. I told him I always flew in and out of John Wayne Airport in Los Angeles, making sure that I pronounced John Wayne with a twist of my tongue to highlight my newly acquired American accent. He fell for my tricks because my accent was far from any accent American. It was rather an "American wannabe accent," but he could not tell. That was my intention, and that was the point.

Baqir lived his city boy status to the fullest. He thought he belonged to the Benson and Hedges, Special Filter, Club. He smoked no different types of cigarettes other than Benson and Hedges. He forced himself into this class even though it cost him more than half of his stipends. He made sure that he had the golden cigarette box in the front pocket of his shirt so no one could miss it and misplace him in the wrong level of sophistication, just in case. When he attended parties at nights; he removed the box and held it in his hand for the girls to see, especially when the lights were dimmed. There was a chance that they might miss it in case he left it in his pocket. Those days, there were no iPhones or androids that owners could use to impress girls. Holding a Benson and Hedges cigarette box in hand was Baqir's way of making a statement and marketing himself as a classy young man. When I reminded him of my recollections of that era, he responded, "Why do you want to take me back to those days of ignorance."

Baqir tried to share with me some of his travel adventures to equally impress me. He soon realized that they were no match to my stories from the Golden State of California, so he decided to drop the idea and change the subject, away from international issues into local ones. I silently declared victory and continued chatting. I finally revealed to him the false claims that I made and told him the truth about everything I said, and we had a good laugh.

In all fairness to Baqir, I think he was right about calling me a country bumpkin. I had no idea that there were different sets of rules to follow, one for villages and another for cities. When I passed my primary to middle school transfer exams, the reward I received from my dad was a visit to the city to see my sister and spend some time with her. One early evening, I left the house on my own and wandered off to tour the city.

I walked into one building and saw a bulletin board with pinned pieces of paper and photos all over. I stopped there and skimmed through it, but did not understand or make sense of what it was, so I continued my tour. A man in uniform (a police officer) showed up and said, "Anything you are looking for?" I said, "No," and kept on walking. He stood there, looking at me all along as I roamed the place for an additional fifteen minutes, until I satisfied myself that I had seen enough, then I left the buildings and went back home. It took me a few more years and additional visits to the city, coupled with some exposure and familiarization with my environment, before I could realize that I was touring a police station in the city, but for no justifiable reason. I was a true villager, with due respect to village people. You just don't go around touring a police station according to your whim. Do you? I think I have come a long way.

Had I not ventured out of Kokoland, I could still be laboring under the misinformation that Dogland does exist and that no man has ever set foot on the moon, and I would have no means of finding out the truth. Probably, attempting to find answers to hard riddles such as Dogland and moon landing might have triggered in me the urge to venture into the world to look for answers. Another blessing in disguise.

To many of my people, the fact that I had been away from Kokoland for so long was immaterial. They expected me to resume our interactions and debates from the exact point I left. They did not make allowance for the fact that we had been exposed to different environments, which had transformed our personalities and way of thinking into, subconsciously, adopting different lifestyles. The problem I was the one who left them for all those years, so it was easier to observe changes in my behavior than in theirs. I knew I was the outlier and, for that reason, I carefully watched the way I carried myself so as not to offend anybody. I had to watch out for simple things like eating and drinking from, or at least sampling, every plate of food or tea pot delivered by different households in the community, in my honor, regardless of how many plates and tea pots were there, and no questions asked. I had to do that because I did not want to be seen as a changed person, or, even worse, offensive to anyone, but I also knew what would happen to my stomach when I did that. No one would care less about the fact that, over the years, I got used to different types of food and eating habits. To everyone, I am the same person who used to live right there among them. I had to eat and drink whatever food they offered and deal with the consequences later on. People were very generous and hospitable. It had always been this way and nothing had changed despite the hardships they were enduring.

I visited relatives at different regions of the country and constantly had to deal with an upset stomach, which was luckily mitigated by the miraculous medicine; Pepto-Bismol. I personally think it is one of the greatest drugs ever made. I had to figure out a way to take it because it would be impolite to do that in front of my host. It would signal to him that I had my worries about eating his food. In fact, there was absolutely nothing wrong with the food quality. Every relative I visited offered me the best food I could have asked for. The problem was too much food and far too many varieties. Nothing other than Pepto-Bismol could have handled such overindulgence. I would excuse myself and go away for a few minutes to take sips of the medicine, directly from the pink bottle. This is to avoid being seen and be answerable to a barrage of questions involving why, how come, what, etc. Besides; I did not want them to conclude that America had softened my character or had my toughness compromised, for a man should not be so weak that he could only survive on medicine.

Every man in my elder sister's village came to greet me and brought along a teapot. Drinking a cup of tea from every teapot was a challenging act, I tell you. Things could get to a point that Pepto-Bismol alone would not handle the situation, but bear in mind that there were no ambulances, health clinics, pharmacies, or doctors in the area. Of course, there were no private cars to use during emergencies. It would just be you and your luck, if necessity dictated. However, there were donkeys, but God help you if you had to rely on one at times of emergency. Do you remember the story about the bowls of local medicine I have written about earlier? If I fell sick, I would be subjected to the same treatment. I would be under the mercy of volunteers who would come by and recommend taking plants and animal parts they had known for their best medicinal abilities. Refusing to take them would not be appreciated. It would show lack of trust from my side. Adverse consequences and side effects, if any, would be nobody's problem, but mine.

My dad, God bless his soul, was so eager to take me around to visit as many relatives in the area as we could. He rented a car and a driver to take us from one village to another. The driver would drop us in a village, leave us there, and return in a day or two after we had finished meeting everyone, and also had the opportunity to respond to as many invitations as we could. In the process, a few roosters, sheep, and young male billy goats became casualties. My stomach could not handle all that. My sister's village was the last stop in our round of village tour. By the time we got to her, my stomach had literally stopped functioning. I was very sick.

Upon seeing me in such a condition, my sister became so distraught. If you remember, she got a superstitious mind, especially at times of feeding her babies. She was the same person, forty years later. She quickly developed a theory about one particular village we visited. In fact, she warned my father and told him not to take me there, but he did not take her warning seriously. She always believed that there were sorcerers in that village. She immediately told my dad that they must have casted a spell of black magic on me. She disappeared for some time and returned with some roots and frankincense, which she had especially reserved for times of crisis, such as the one we were experiencing. She burned them and made me inhale the smoke. After that, I went inside the hut to take some rest. It was time to reach out for my Pepto-Bismol and drink some of it. I took twice the recommended dose and lay in bed silently listening for any signs of my stomach returning to normalcy. In the morning, my sister came to see me and found that my condition had improved. She was so relieved and happy that her black magic treatment had worked, and I was equally relieved and happy that my Pepto-Bismol's magic had also worked. We were both happy, and that what mattered. I felt there was no need for informing her of my medicine or talk about which of the two treatments worked, for fear of disappointing her unnecessarily. I let my sister take all credit. Who knows? The news about my recovery in a matter of one night might consolidate and legitimize her standing in the community for being the one person capable of curing black magic spells and more. That would not be a bad thing for the family's name and reputation.

What really happened was that, in our last stop before my sister's village, I drank milk when I should not have done that. We consumed a lot of meat during the two days we spent there. We said good-bye, got in the car, and were about to leave when someone came running to tell us that one of my dad's close friends, who was out of town, had just returned. He sent the man to tell us the news of his arrival, asking us to wait for him. He showed up and swore that we got out of the car and went to his house. Slaughtering another sheep was guaranteed. He haggled with my dad for some time until my dad finally convinced him to let us move because it would be unfair for the other people who had been informed of our arrival date. They would have already made their preparations to receive us. He reluctantly relented on condition that we waited for him until he returned from his house after a few minutes. He left and, soon, came back with a bowl of milk and handed it over to me to drink, first, being the guest of honor. I, in turn, handed it to my dad to drink first, out of respect. It was also customary to do so. My dad handed the bowl back to me, so I drank the milk. After that, my stomach completely stopped digesting, and that was the reason for my sickness, which had nothing to do with black magic, as my sister thought. I feel guilty that I did not correct the wrong idea she had about the people in the last village we visited.

A photo of me and my elder sister, Fatima, taken in 2016.

It was summer when I went to visit my sister. Except for my first night, we always slept in the front yard because it was too hot inside the hut. Sleeping in the yard is like sleeping in the street, as far as my American boys were concerned. I woke up one early morning to a déjà vu incident, which took me back some forty years. I felt something under my bed, moving from one end to the other, pushing my body upward. For a split second, I searched my mind looking for any records of what I was experiencing, and then I found one. It was something I grew up with. It was a baby goat (a kid) scratching its back. Goats figured out long time ago that they could use human weight to scratch their backs. My body weight on the saggy robes created a curve closer to the ground at my waist. The kid walked up and down under the bed, pressing its back upward against my body. That was how it scratched its back. The incident brought me back many childhood memories. I wanted the kid to continue scratching its back and mine as well because the friction it created as it walked up and down got both of our backs scratched, simultaneously. To my disappointment, my nephew woke up and chased it away. Getting a goat to scratch your back is something that doesn't happen very often.

Learning of my arrival from America, an old friend called one early evening and invited me to visit him in his village before I went back. My cell phone battery was dying and there was no electricity to charge it, so I wrote down his number on the dirt by my bedside. I planned to borrow someone else's phone in the morning to call him back in case my cell phone battery went out completely. In the morning, I looked down for the number on the dirt, but could not find it. What happened was that I wrote it down on a hedgehog trail. They used it all night, back and forth, visiting a sack of peanuts a few yards away from my bed. Hedgehogs never change their habits. I had experienced them behaving the same way during my childhood. My sister's house provided hedgehogs both protection from the elements and free peanuts, which they love eating so much. The hedgehogs, on the other hand, provided valuable services such as ridding the home of snakes and geckos. They killed snakes by grabbing them by the tail, then curling in to hide their heads, completely. The snake would desperately try to free itself by banging its body against the hedgehog's body, which, as you know, is covered with sharp spikes. That would cause the snake severe injuries, leading to its death. I guess this is one form of coexistence and interdependence between humans and wild life, or to be more accurate; between hedgehogs and humans.

I got hold of my friend's number. I borrowed a phone to call him, but there was no signal. We were in a remote area, so the signal was frequently interrupted. There was one spot in the village where I could get a better connection. It was eight feet high in a corner of a straw shade in my uncle's house, a few homes away. To make the call, I had to climb a wooden log to get my head closer to the signal spot. That was how I managed to connect with my friend. People lined up at the shade to make phone calls. My uncle jokingly told me he was thinking of charging some rent for his one-square-foot prime real estate.

One of my relatives came to visit me at my sister's house. She asked me to tell her about my new village; America. I wanted to avoid getting into an argument similar to the one I had with my other relative when I talked about the farmer's bush-burning activity to prepare for planting. So, I spent some time processing the question in my mind to give her a closer to home answer that was both simple and sensible. My niece, sensing my silence, intervened and answered on my behalf, in Kanuri language. She might have thought that it was taking me too long to respond, so she decided to step in and help. She told the woman, "By the way, my uncle came from the end of the border." From my nephew's facial expressions, I could tell that she also wanted to say to the woman, "How come you don't know?" There was no way in hell that anyone knew where was that "end of the border" place she was talking about. If you lived in Kokoland and you happened to have an uncle residing in America, in all probabilities, you would have a better-than-average vocabulary. My niece could have picked up a few words by listening to occasional phone conversations I had with my sister. All my niece needed was some words to jumble up to produce a sentence, and voilà. She was already on her way to village fame and respect. As far as she was concerned, her answer was correct, since I did not intervene to give a different one, so "end of the border" stood for the name of my village; America. The woman did not need to know more than that, and any additional clarification from my side would have complicated the matter and further confused her.

Return to grandma's and my elder sister's village. Photo 2016.

I normally avoided taking initiatives telling people about life in America. I waited for them to think and ask me questions. I thought that was a better approach because they would have time to think of what they really wanted to know. One of my relatives asked me, "Abba, do you have lousy things like the ones we have here?" I exclaimed, "Lousy things like what?" He hesitated and looked blank. Then, some noise coming from a distance drew our attention. We all looked in that direction and saw a rough-looking he-goat chasing after a female goat. The man, with a smile on his face, said, "Like that ugly he-goat." I said, "Yes, there are he-goats in America." He stared at the ground for a few seconds then said, "The other day I saw pictures of America on television in the city. I did not see any dirt at all. All I saw was very green trees and grass. Do you have sand and clay there?" I knew why he was asking this question. Being a farmer, just like everyone else in the village, he wanted to know if the land in America is good for growing peanuts. I told him that the country is so big and has different types of landscapes and climates, and that farmers can grow whatever they want. I wanted to tell him about some of the crops grown in America, but I felt that I would not be able to get my point across, since the agricultural products grown there were limited to crops like sorghum, peanuts, sesame, okra, and beans. I also wanted to tell him that the television program he saw could be talking only about forests, and that there were programs for deserts, rivers, valleys, mountains, etc., but I decided to leave that for another day. I was never satisfied with the answers I gave because I knew that they were short of filling the gaps and carving a clear image in people's minds about America. It was frustrating that I was able to share only a fraction of what I know about my new village.

As I mentioned above, when I told a group of relatives that my son had met with the American President and his wife, they gave me blank stares, with no response, as if saying, "So?" They waited for me to fill in the gaps. I could sense that they had questions about the rationale for doing something as crazy as that, so I continued talking. I had hoped they would understand that it is a rare an opportunity not easily attainable to most people. To many people in rural settings such as Kokoland, the president's office represented absolute power and authority, and that was something they must avoid at all cost. Under a dictatorship, authority, represented in a military president, a police force, and a security apparatus, collectively keep a tight control over every aspects of people's daily lives. Such type of authority lies to people, collects taxes for its own use, and promotes corruption, favoritism, and nepotism. It accepts bribe, wrongly detains, wrongly imprisons, tortures, and bombs and kills innocent people. That was the image they had in mind for authority. For that reason, meeting with the president was never viewed as an opportunity. In fact, it was considered as nothing short of a suicide, so why bother doing that? I don't blame them at all.

As I mentioned earlier, when I learned at school about the round shape of the earth, I tried to share this piece of information with my Kanuri people in Kokoland and the surrounding villages, whenever an opportunity arose. That idea did not go well with some people. One of my dad's distant cousins, a man named Mala, was notorious for not believing in anything based on science, or any idea that originated in the West, represented in everything taught at school. I am tempted to say that he did not know what the blue color on maps stood for and, in fact; he might not have known the meaning of map, but he argued like hell. Sorry, I did not mean to be so unfair to Mala. I also did not know of anyone more controlling or adamant about maintaining the status quo, at any cost. He would just not let go of the cultural norm that "elders must have the final say," come what may, even though times have changed. He considered whatever I said as nothing more than a child's talk, so he always shunned me aside. The real problem was that he found schools guilty of blasphemy for teaching certain ideas. I think the most effective way for controlling people is to accuse them of tampering with matters of divinity, so no wonder why this man used words like blasphemy to scare people off from simply contemplating thoughts that were not to his liking. The whole issue boiled down to his fear of losing his grip on a favorable status he, as a community elder, had inherited. He feared that new ideologies such as schooling would erode his powers, so he did not trust anything of school nature. He refused to send any of his dozen or so children to school. Obviously, Mala had no love for school.

My two little boys taught me a valuable lesson about the futility of my relative Mala's "elder is wiser" argument. The boys played hard most of the time, but they equally fought hard when they disagreed with one-another. Recently, I found myself struggling to come up with a convincing argument to amicably resolve a dispute that had erupted between them. I thought for a minute, then remembered something my family had taught me during my childhood, so I decided to try it. I said, "When I was growing up back in my village, younger children always respected and listened to their older brothers a—" Before I could finish my sentence, both of them interrupted and said, in one voice, "Being old doesn't mean that you are always right." They torpedoed my genius idea before it even got off the ground. I wanted to complete my sentence by saying, "And older children always took care of their younger brothers." It was obvious that, with my idea from the village, I miserably failed a simple common sense test that older is not necessarily wiser or right all the time, so I abandoned it. It was a dumb idea. Even though my arbitration attempt to mediate their dispute was somewhat favorable to the elder boy, I was surprised that they both rejected it outright. In fact, as I sat there not knowing what to do, I remembered my dad's cousin Mala and his conviction that "elders must always prevail," and I said to myself, "What was I thinking?"

To Mala, it was a given fact that the earth has cliffs where you could simply fall over, if you continued walking. It bothered him a great deal that schools disputed such a simple fact. Schools were not good, he thought. I vividly remember his words challenging my "global earth theory." He said, "Doesn't this earth have cliffs?" He said that as he stretched his upper body, slightly leaned forward, and gestured with his hands to signal tumbling down, flipping over, or falling off a cliff into a deep crater below. He did that while keeping his feet firmly anchored to the ground, as if trying to prevent his body from losing balance and falling over the imaginary cliff that was very present in his mind's eye, as he demonstrated with his upper body and hands. For additional security to keep himself firmly connected to earth, Mala kept his knees slightly bent to bring his center of gravity closer to the ground. You could also tell that he was pushing his feet very hard against the ground because sand had seeped through his toes, which were half-buried under the sand. Boy; Mala did believe in his "cliff" theory. He was angry and frustrated that I did not understand or appreciate such a simple and a universal fact of life. I was equally angry and frustrated.

Mala was an outspoken person despite his illiteracy. He was able to exercise control over many of my relatives who found in him a leader to follow. In fact, he played a big role in speaking against the idea of parents, within my extended family, sending their boys to school. As for girls, the idea of keeping them at home was a non-debatable divine doctrine, as far as he was concerned. With his actions, not only did Mala harm his own children, but also the children of other family members.

I remember numerous incidents throughout my school years when I received less than fair treatment from Mala. As I stated earlier, I was one of the very few children in the family who attended school. To him, I was an outlaw, so putting me down was his way of expressing his disapproval. I was not disrespectful to him at all, but I made sure I let him know I was not fine with the way he treated me. Looking back, I think he was jealous of the relative success my dad had, in comparison to him, and the fact that my dad openly spoke his mind and was never a follower. Mala could not always hide his intolerance to this fact, so he sometimes resorted to using phrases that carried double meanings, clearly intending to put down my dad. Sometimes, I let him know that I got the message behind some weird expressions he would throw in his speech. After that, he would keep quiet for some time, then change the subject. What a waste of energy. Sadly, a number of parents within the family followed Mala's guidance and kept their children away from schools. Today, many of those children, now adults, found themselves at a competitive disadvantage and were unemployed, or unemployable, due to illiteracy. The world has changed and they were totally unprepared for that. A few of them openly expressed to me their anger about what had happened to them.

I regularly called my dad from America to talk to him. I occasionally found his antagonistic cousin, Mala, with him, so I also talked to him. I noticed that Mala had, somehow, developed interest for one thing; time. Whenever I spoke to him, he asked me about the time in my village; California, so I would tell him. Then, he would say, "God is great. The time is so and so here." It became clear to me that he was both fascinated as well as intrigued by the ten-hour time difference between our two places. I thought to myself that some form of character transformation must have taken place in the course of my absence from the country. In one of the phone calls, I took the time to explain to him that the time difference was attributed to the round shape of the earth. We were back to the same spot talking about facts he had disputed a few decades earlier. I demonstrated to him in simple terms that the sun is stationary, at least for argument's sake. Things might get complicated and way out of control if I threw in an expanded version of facts about planetary systems and told him that the sun is not stationary in the solar system; it is orbiting around every body that is also in orbit around it. Just like all the planets, it is, being part of the Milky Way, moving around its center along with the solar system in its entirety, and that it will take it about 230 million years to complete one orbit, *bla bla bla*. Not only would Mala think I have gone crazy beyond repair, especially after hearing "the sun will take 230 million years to complete one orbit," but also be quick to accuse me of being a communist, or, even worse, reach out for the use of his formidable blasphemy and faithlessness weapons, he commonly resorted to for character assassination. For these reasons, I decided to stay anchored to earth. I simplified the matter and told him that the sun is stationary and the earth rotates around it from west to east, and that, since he lived in Sudan, which is east of where I was, he would see the sun before me. I said people living in countries to the west of Sudan, such as Chad, Nigeria, and Senegal, would see the sun after him, then and only then, morning would break here in America because it is farther west. I told him that was why he would continue to see the sun before me, every day. I knew that I was able to hold Mala captive to my theory because he did not clear his throat, not even once, as he normally did during past calls. He listened in silence throughout the call time. I also noticed he stopped bringing up the subject of time in future calls. He left me wondering what he was thinking. It is worth mentioning that people are still skeptical about these facts, five hundred years after Christopher Columbus.

When I returned to Sudan after many years, I found out that Mala's views had miraculously shifted 180 degrees. He had mastered the earth's global shape concept. He went further than that by turning around and explaining the idea to me. He kept me guessing if he did that with the intention of getting confirmation from me, impress others around, or impliedly apologize for antagonizing me and shunning my middle school views when I introduced them to him decades earlier. I heard him once explaining to people the very same issue. He talked about the difference in time zones as if he had never doubted that at all. He gave the sense that he was the source of that knowledge and sounded full of planetary wisdom. It was a good thing that he changed his mind, even though very late. I wish he had accepted the idea of schooling sooner. If it was not for his stubbornness, the lives of his children and many other children in the family could have been different today.

I confided to a relative that I was planning to buy a piece of land and build a house. He told me not to worry at all. He said I just needed to let him know whenever I am ready to do that. In the meantime, he suggested he take me to see a house his friend Maina, a property developer, had just finished building. He was going to show me a model home, if you like. I said, "Fine, let us go." He led me into a neighborhood, which greeted us with a familiar odor that I remembered from my childhood; a smell of *zibala* or donkey dung used for plastering the exterior of homes. It is prepared by collecting and mixing dung with hays, sand, water, and then leaving it for a few weeks to ferment. After that, the pile would be broken open and, again, mixed with water before using it to cover the exterior of walls and homes. We got to the model home, which was freshly painted with seaweed-green donkey dung color. That was the source of the strong odor. It was a beautiful adobe-styled mud house, if it was not for the dung. My relative stood there smiling lightly and admiring his friend's architectural creativity and finishing skills, while certain that I would have one answer for him, "Yes, I want your friend to build my home too, just like this model." I stood there looking at the house and thinking about my two-story home in Sacramento, built according to California building codes. The irony is that I belong in both worlds, at the same time. I am fine with the fact that I lived in both types of houses, the California and the donkey-dunged *zibala* types. *Zibala* plastered homes were part of my reality, and what the man did was that he connected me back with my reality. He might have done that with a view toward achieving two goals; sell me a house and remind me of where I have come from, just in case I forgot. In any case, I thank him for his help. I stood there thinking for a moment. I felt I was split between two distinct worlds and personalities that hardly have anything in common. I searched very hard to come to terms with who I am. I gathered my senses and wanted to comment on the builder's work, but I had to be extremely careful about what I should say and what I should not. I realized that my California level of expectations in life was immaterial whatsoever. As far as my relative was concerned, there is where I belong, and he did his part by showing me a house that suits me perfectly well. It is rather a painful truth to be belonging to both worlds at once, but that was nobody's problem. I can't blame anyone for my predicament, but myself for drifting away. I am the exception to the rule, as I said before. I stood there and surveyed the houses, which, all, had the same look; donkey-dung-green walls. I also started seeing images of newly built track homes and building materials lined up in my California neighborhood Home Depot and Lowe's, and said to myself, "I am neither here, nor there. What should I do now?"

Having said the above, I must state here that I did not mean to paint a seaweed-green donkey dung picture for homes all over the country. I am talking about my personal situation. The truth is that there were beautiful homes of very high standards that my relative could have taken me to view, but he did not think I belonged there.

One of my friends went back home and wanted to upgrade the family bathroom. He decided to do away with the local toilet, usually fitted at ground level, and replace it with standard Western-style toilet. He went to the market and found day laborers who agreed to do the job for him. He accompanied them home and showed them what he wanted done. They assured him that they knew exactly what to do, so he left them to get on with the job. When he returned, they told him that they had completed the job, so he went to inspect the work and pay them for their labor. He was shocked to find out that they had dug a hole the height of the new toilet, lowered it down so it was at ground level, and poured concrete on the sides to cement it to the ground. They made sure that it was leveled the same way as the old toilet they had pulled out. They basically buried it. Back to square one. As far as they were concerned, there was one and only one way for fitting toilets. They made sure that my friend remained, metaphorically and literally speaking, connected to the ground as well as to his reality, just like me. He was not allowed to even change toilets. Reality to a man is like an anchor to a ship. They both just won't let their captives break free.

On the other hand, those day laborers simply could not say, "We don't know how to do the job." They were desperate for any job that came their way. Telling the truth was the last thing to worry about. They knew that the least they could get out of the job, even if they mess it up, was a free meal, and that was not bad. In the process, they inadvertently, reminded my friend not to even try to move up to a new social class, in case he was upgrading his toilet for this reason.

Again, giving these examples is by no means an attempt to portray a primitive image of a place, undermine it, or offend its people, for I, myself, belong there too. It is rather an effort to show the disparities and contradictions some of us face. In fact our realities, represented by background, culture, heritage, traditions etc., are what make us as people. We should never shy away from, look down on, or consider them as baggage that could hamper and cripple our progress in life. They are rather the engine that propels us forward. After all, it is not a bad thing to be standing on a solid platform that we can use to take off to the sky.

CHAPTER 20

In Conclusion: There is More Good in Humanity than Bad, I have learned

In conclusion, I would like to state that my bumpy journey from Kokoland to the land of Uncle Sam was riddled with difficulties. I had no idea which direction to take, or how far I would end up. In the end, the favorable outcome that my family and I are enjoying today cannot by any means be attributed to my efforts and hard work alone. I feel grateful to the many people who extended their help along the way. During my journey, I have learned a few simple things that are nothing more than common sense, to many of you, but I would like to share them, anyway.

I travelled the world and found out it is much different from Kokoland. I have learned that some nations continue to progress while others go backward. Sadly, the standard of living in Kokoland has deteriorated over the last forty years or so. Life was rural, but today it is both rural and unsustainable. For most people there, basic living conditions have not improved. Kokoland still lacks electricity and running water. The clinic and the two primary schools for boys and girls have crumbled. There is a lot of environmental degradation all around it and the desert has crept in. Everything is disintegrating and, today, things are far worse for people than ever before. The condition of Kokoland could be applicable across the board to other places all over the country. In some way, I feel guilty and have a role to play in what had happened to my people in Kokoland. I always wondered what could have been the outcome had the millions of people who migrated from the country, including myself, stayed behind. Would things be different?

Here is a reflection of my forty-year journey. It contains thoughts that are unrelated, in some way. Unlike the rest of the book, this last chapter mostly comes in the form of statements starting with "I have learned." Each statement is independent of the next one and talks about a different thought. The transition from one statement to the other is not necessarily governed by any sequentially ordered set of related ideas, so please bear this in mind as you read.

I have learned that happiness is a relative thing. Having little knowledge about worlds outside of Kokoland was a big problem for me and many people living there. It goes without saying that a little bit of exposure could have helped everyone there a great deal. The following story about my friend Rizig confirms what I just said. Rizig's uncle migrated to one of the rich Arabian Gulf countries a few decades earlier and made a fortune. He did not have children of his own, so he returned to his village, some two miles from Kokoland, to ask his nephew Rizig and see if he could travel back with him to help with the business. Rizig agreed, said farewell to everyone in the village, and set off on a journey to a new life of fame and richness. He and his uncle travelled to the city, boarded a train, and headed to Port Sudan. There, they were supposed to board a passenger ship to carry them across the Red Sea. On the day of the journey, Rizig and his uncle hired a taxi and went to the port. Rizig, upon seeing a huge body of water (the Red Sea) for the first time in his life, appeared worried and was abnormally quiet. His uncle noticed his condition and asked him if there was anything wrong.

Rizig responded: Where is this place you are taking me to?
Uncle: On the other side of this big sea of salt water in front of you.
Rizig: How are we going to get there?
Uncle (Pointing to a steam ship anchored nearby): We are going to board that machine.

Rizig: How does that machine swim? Uncle: It has a big engine similar to that of lorries.
Rizig: How long will it take us to cross this water?
Uncle: One day and one night.
Rizig: How many men deep is this water?
Uncle: About a thousand men.

Upon hearing his uncle's last response, Rizig's heart dropped into his stomach. Realizing the minuteness of the ship's size in comparison to the huge body of water that they were about to embark on a journey across, hit Rizig hard. He fully understood the gravity of being confined to the inside of a machine that would swim for a whole day and night in one thousand-man deep water, before reaching dry land. That bothered him a lot. Rizig's profession was well-sinking. He usually measured the depth of wells by the number of man-height. The wells he sank were four to five men deep. What his uncle asked for was unbecoming. It was a no-brainer, as far as he was concerned. So, at the moment they were about to board the ship, Rizig looked at his uncle and said, "By the way, I am not going." His uncle could not believe what he just heard. He did everything in his power to persuade Rizig into changing his mind, but failed miserably. That was the farthest point Rizig could go, both in life and distance. He and his uncle parted ways, so he returned to his Kokoland village and never ventured off.

People thought that Rizig had wasted a lifetime opportunity anyone could have grabbed in a heartbeat. When they asked him why he returned, he told them his heart did not like what he saw. He said, "One of my hearts told me to go, but my other heart told me not to." Rizig had two hearts, so he decided to side with his wiser heart that warned him not to venture into crossing that bottomless body of water in a tiny steam-powered boat. He had zero regrets, since he did not know what an opportunity he had missed; besides, risk taking is not for everyone. I just cannot emphasize enough the importance of orientation. Rizig was much unprepared for this journey. He had never been out of Kokoland. The whole experience was a quantum leap into the unknown, and he did not have time to absorb its implications. We should not be surprised that people sometimes fail to take advantage of life-changing opportunities presented to them by others at no cost or effort on their side. One man used a local proverb to describe Rizig's experience. It goes, "A man God almighty has dropped, who other man can dare lift up." It is believed that Rizig's fate had been sealed by God and that human intervention would not have changed a thing. It follows that neither Rizig, nor his uncle could have done anything about it. It is no wonder that Rizig returned to his village after listening to his wiser heart, but fully believing that the decision was not of his own free will. Sometimes, we can be penny wise, but pound foolish, but what if we don't know any better? A long time ago, a wise man told me, "You don't need to set a bird trap when you have to move the birds with your hands to the side to create a room for your trap." It seems we will appreciate what life gives us more, if we play a role in charting our own courses, irrespective of what others think. It is about managing our individual lives. I have learned that success mostly comes from ideas formulated by and within oneself. Rizig's uncle though for a long time about the plan to bring Rizig over, without involving him in the decision. He then travelled to execute the plan. It shouldn't surprise us that things didn't work. I have learned that human beings are a product of their environment. Our views and ways of thinking can differ from one person to another, and there may not be one absolute answer to what makes people happy. There is room for accommodating everybody, though in different ways.

A group of people from Kokoland were talking to me about hard times they had experienced during the 1980s. The country was at the verge of a full-blown starvation, caused by severe food shortage, due to rain failure for consecutive years. One man told me that former President Ronald Reagan ordered shipments of tons of sorghum for distribution, free of charge. People named it Reagan's sorghum. They are still talking thankfully about how the shipments helped them through those dire times. The man asked me if I knew President Reagan's religion. Another man immediately intervened and responded to the question, on my behalf, making it unnecessary for me to comment. I think the response he gave was inappropriate to mention here in this book. Some people may find it offensive. The bottom line is that people truly appreciated that help they had received from America. The problem is that the average person just could not reconcile between the two opposing signals he or she had been receiving about America; a helpful America that sent aid to save people from starvation, and a different America negatively portrayed in the media. I believe that nations can live side by side in harmony, but I am also privy to the reality that politics can, at times, muddy the water for everyone.

I have learned that selflessness and self-denial could result in miracles. Mahatma Gandhi, Nelson Mandela, and Martin Luther King (in no particular order of importance) were three individuals who inspired, and continue to inspire, millions of people throughout the world. It is a question of conviction and a strong belief in causes that take consistency in approach, persistence, perseverance, endurance, and patience, to succeed. We must bow our heads for those who made the ultimate sacrifice so the rest of us could live free. We should do our parts cherishing, supporting, standing up for, and defending God-given rights, such as freedom, justice, and equality, for all.

I have learned that there are those who are advocates of chaos and anarchy. They may initially have blind followers and supporters, but they will soon find themselves standing alone, once those followers wake up to the truth. Unawareness, simply put, is bad. It can lead to disastrous consequences. A few years ago, I was watching the news about a country that has recently joined the nuclear club. It was in fierce completion with a neighbor, which already has nuclear weapons' technology. Thousands of its citizens attended street rallies and demonstrations to celebrate and to express their joy. I saw a banner that read, "We want war." It seems that some of us don't have the slightest idea about the dangers of wars, especially ones involving nuclear weapons. The world, after witnessing the horrors of genocide committed during World War II, said, "Never again." Sadly the same thing has been happening again right under the watchful eyes of the very international community that said never again, a matter of a few decades earlier. The fact remains that humanity had fought thousands of wars since the dawn of history. Is that because we are forgetful, or it always takes a war to appreciate peace? That trend doesn't seem like it is going to change in the future. I believe that evil does exist, but there is much good in humanity than bad. Good will always triumphs and prevails.

I have learned that we all can contribute to the well-being of humanity in our own different ways, capacities, and degrees. Great people (in no particular order of importance) such as Albert Einstein, Galileo Galilei, Isaac Newton, Avicenna (Ibn Sīnā), Jabir ibn Hayyan, Louis Pasteur, Alexander Fleming, Eleanor Roosevelt, Rosa Parks, Salvador Dali, Pablo Picasso, Gabriel Garcia Marquez, Bernard Shaw, Alfred Nobel, Suzanne B. Anthony, Maya Angelo, Norman Borlaug, Michael Jackson, George Stephenson, Henry Ford, Thomas Alva Edison, Amelia Earhart, Farouk El Baz, Steve Jobs, and thousands of others have made tremendous contribution to humanity. At the time some people chose to build skyscrapers and space ships, others dedicated their lives to building schools, neighborhoods, and communities. There are also those who did everything in between. Even though I don't think I have any contribution of my own, anywhere near these people, and I wish I have, I'm inspired by all of them and every person making a positive impact on other people's lives, however minimal it is, and that's all that matters. In the end, with our tiny contributions, we can, collectively, move the world forward and strive to make it a better place.

I have learned that people take their time to accommodate change and embrace new concepts. Democracy, for example, may have different meanings to different people. To one group, it means that everybody's voice counts. To another group, it means some votes don't matter and it is not worth counting. To a third group, democracy means pouring all the votes in one box, counting them, then giving the total number of votes to one candidate. To a fourth group, democracy means first getting elected to office, then totally abandoning the campaign manifesto. To a fifth group, it means an opportunity to punish those who did not vote as directed. To one Kokoland man, democracy meant ordering his brother-in-law to give his vote to the same candidate as his. When the brother-in-law refused, the man demanded him to divorce his sister. No wonder why democracy is a messy process. The question is whether nations that are new to the concept have the luxury of time to fine-tune the process and evolve, particularly in view of the challenges that face the world today. One of my friends doubts that. He thinks that some people aren't doing their part. He expressed his frustration by telling me that, even though two centuries or so have passed since George Stephenson invented the locomotive, some of us are still offering chicken to the oceans to seek protection from evil spirits, and yet complaining about the ills of colonization. My friend is resentful about the fact that Africa is trailing the rest of the world in many aspects of modern life. Other friends who are more optimistic in their outlook of life think that Africa's time is around the corner. We will see. The fact remains that there is no such a thing as quantum leap in democracy. Only times will tell.

I have learned that adverse conditions are not there to last forever. Time is a great tool for fighting them, and that patience, consistency, and hard work are keys to success. I believe that one should neither shy away from, nor underestimate the power of minimum-wage or entry-level jobs, especially when they are the only two options available. We should take them and prove that we are worth more. Earning is, anytime, better than asking others for help. Nothing is worse than asking for help when one is able and can help himself.

I have learned that I was very judgmental, being a product of my limited exposure. Growing up in a remote corner of the world could mislead a person into believing that everything revolved around him or her. I used to believe that I was right about everything. I labored under this misconception for the entire time I was living in Kokoland. When I ventured away into new worlds, it became clear how little I knew. The tiny world that I had always known came down crumbling. I had to do a lot of rethinking to conceptualize my everyday life; all over again. Naturally, I could not do justice to every misconception I had, or fix every mistake I made. It is a very frustrating feeling to realize that you were wrong about many things, even though you all along thought that you were absolutely right about them.

I have learned that we can adjust to living in parts of the world that have different cultural norms than our own. The key to succeeding in doing that falls on respecting other people's values, accommodating the different things about them, and embracing the best they can offer. In life, there are both positive and negative people. We can find the two groups in Kokoland, London, or Santiago. People are a product of their environment and we don't have to do anything to change that. It would be nice if we could stop stereotyping each other as individuals, groups, or nations. Not everyone fits the mold. Nevertheless, all humans, generally speaking, are bound by the same aspirations, which trickle down to one thing; a dignified and a decent living for them and their families.

I have learned the importance of being careful with my use of words. Some words can embody negative historical connotations as well as reminders of painful events from the past. At times, they really can be offensive. One morning, a colleague at my place of work approached and asked me for help. I went over to his station and found an agitated customer standing in the line specifically assigned for business customers. I explained to her that we segregated our clients into groups, with the view to servicing everyone expeditiously. She furiously exclaimed, "Segregated, you said?" I reluctantly said, "Yeah!" Then she said, "You are damn right, you are damn right," and hurriedly left the bank. It seemed my intervention did not help with the situation. I knew that I had offended her and hurt her feelings, in one way or another, but did not quite understand the exact reason for her reaction, and that bothered me a lot.

One afternoon, sometime after the incident, while I was withdrawing cash from an ATM, I heard a male voice behind me calling "El negro" three times. I turned around and saw a man sitting in a car looking at me. He nodded his head, signaling it was me he was calling "El negro," and then drove off. The two incidents remained present in my mind and triggered an impulse to read about African-American History. I stumbled upon an article about Jim Crow laws, which I never heard about before. That article augmented my understanding of race issues in America, but I am certainly not suggesting that black America's narrative is limited to Jim Crow laws. Of course, it goes way beyond that.

I kept wondering what sad memories could I have provoked in the lady's mind when I used the word segregated. I equally kept asking myself what quarrel a man, supposedly, of a Latino background had with me to call me El Negro. It is a strange fact of life that there are people out there who blame others for who they are. I know there is nothing I can do to change that, but I can control the words I choose to use. I must admit I was unsuccessful in my choice of the word segregated, especially coming from a black man. I have learned few things as I moved forward, even though the hard way, sometimes. It can be frustrating when you find out that you have offended people because of your ignorance. It is even more frustrating if the people you have offended think you are doing that intentionally.

I have learned that I was wrong about believing that individualism means one thing; selfishness. I grew to understand that it has other dimensions that include concepts such as self-expressions; something I knew little about before. Now, I recognize the value and importance of making decisions, based on their suitability to our individual characters, environment, beliefs, and preferences. We could uniquely be different from one another, so why insist on applying uniform rules on everyone? How simple, yet how difficult for me to understand and appreciate.

I have learned that I greatly respect those who do volunteer work to further good causes or help people in need, be that by cleaning the neighborhood streets over the weekends, mowing an elderly neighbor's lawn, volunteering at food banks, or visiting sick children at hospitals. We can deduce great lessons from such people.

I have learned that one should always be mindful of the need for adopting different rules for different situations and environments. My wife and son relentlessly tried to steer me into thinking in that way, but I would not listen, until one day I was forced to come to my senses. I used to give ride to hitchhikers because the villager in me thought that it was just not right for thousands of cars carrying one person, the driver, to pass them by, when there is enough space to cater to an entire village. It took me some time to understand that such a way of thinking is not always consistent with the way societies function outside of Kokoland.

One night, despite my family members' objection, I stopped to help a man holding an empty red jerrican. He was obviously stranded and needed a ride to the gas station, a few miles away. In the brief ride to the station, he told us about his troubles with the law and that he could not walk because of injuries he had sustained from a gunshot. Sadly, that was the last time I stopped for a stranger. I get it that I could implicate myself by doing such things. That incident opened my eyes to the risks I could face in the event of something bad happening to people while they are in my property, or under my responsibility. The problem is that I still could not come to terms with the idea of not extending help to people who need it for fear of bad consequences, so I try to help the best way I can, but more cautiously and in different ways.

I recently watched a TV report about an incident of bullying in a school bus when three boys ganged up against one boy and beat him up ferociously, as he pleaded for help. I, like many people, was appalled to see the bus driver yelling from a distance, "Stop that, stop that." That was as far as he could do to help the poor boy. The boy survived with a broken arm and some bruises. I guess the bus driver was following policies and, in the eyes of the law, he did not do anything wrong, but I wonder how people remember policies in a situation like this. It is just not right. Ironically, I saw the driver show up on a TV program. He did not have much to say to defend his actions. I thought that the incident should have been a cause for hiding his face from the public rather than showing it on TV. I wish if society could agree on ways for people to help, but without worrying about getting implicated.

I have learned that I am a technology-challenged person. I find it difficult to use gadgets due to my late arrival to the tech world. The problem is that starting all over to learn these things is not feasible. My boys (six and eight years old) had been looking for bunnies in the neighborhood park for over a year. I told them if they wanted to improve their chances of finding bunnies, they must sing one of my childhood bunny songs from Kokoland. It goes like this, "little bunny little bunny come, little bunny come over and have some milk." While keeping a steady marching beat, the boys repeated the song after me, whenever we walked the park trail. I told them that bunnies love to hear them sing it in its crudest and unpolished form; otherwise, they would not show up. That song's pentatonic sound also awakened neighbors' inquisitiveness. Certain that the sound was foreign to America, they would stretch their necks over the fences to satisfy that curiosity, every time we passed by singing. They would probably tell one another, "It is them. I told you," then go back inside. Our behavior might appear to have caused disturbance to some neighbors, but I think what my sons and I did was a positive contribution to diversity in America.

One afternoon, my eight-year-old boy came running to ask me for my iPhone, which I always kept locked to prevent them from tampering with. He said he had found a bunny and would like to video it. As soon as I pulled the phone out of my pocket, he grabbed it and took off running. I called him back to tell him that I needed to unlock it so he could use it, but he continued running. I decided to sit back and wait. I was certain that he would soon return for my password. Ten minutes or so passed before he reappeared. He was visibly excited. To my amazement, he showed me a short video and five or so images of a bunny. I was puzzled, so I asked him, "How did you do that when I did not give you my pass code?" He said, "Let me show you." It could not have been simpler. That answered many questions in my mind, which I kept a secret for some time. I found images and videos on my phone that were certainly not taken by me, but I just could not ask anybody if they did that or not, for fear of embarrassment. I kept my ignorance to myself until my boy showed me the trick. I never knew I did not need to put in the security code before I could take quick shots or videos. I always wondered how people could capture split-second images of accidents that are of rare occurrence, such as plane crashes. I was convinced that by the time I put in the code, the image would be gone, so I never tried. I truly think am one hell of a tech-unsavvy person.

I have learned that there is a limit to how far my African stories could go to help me stay relevant in the eyes of my dear boys.

I resigned to the fact that I just could not compete forever with Cartoon Network, Disney, and Nickelodeon programs such as *iCarly* and Hannah Montana (Miley Cyrus). One day, I walked into my boys' playroom very enthusiastic and ready to tell them a new African story I had just made up. They looked at me for a hundredth of a second and went back to continue watching TV, leaving me standing and staring at the back of their heads, reading something like, "Now we aren't interested in your stories about some African goats and hyenas." I went away, but I just could not let go or give up my boys to TV shows. That was when I came up with the bunny idea I wrote above. I decided to localize my story, so I told them if they went to the park and sang the bunny song, the bunnies would know that they were being loved, since they have abilities to communicate with humans, and one day they would show up. This is just to show you the extent I was willing to go to stay relevant. I was desperate for acceptance and to stay legitimate and continue to be a source of interest and inspiration for my boys. The bunny story motivated them to visit the park more often. Any time away from the TV screen works for me. Funny enough, the bunny showed up, and I was able to hang on for some time, but deep down I knew I was losing the battle, actually the war. I had to face the reality that their childhood memories are right here in California and Texas. Kokoland is not about them.

Sure enough, time passed and my fears about irrelevancy fully materialized. My middle son, now twelve years old, recently talked to me for over two minutes about a topic I just could not comprehend. My brain fired in all directions, frantically trying to find a clue about what he was telling me. I was so desperate because I knew it could be my last chance to stay relevant. It was a race against time. I asked myself if he was talking to me about his beloved Japanese Ninja character, Naruto, or one of his best football teams, or his favorite subject of astronomy. Could he be relaying to me the news about the discovery of a new star in a faraway galaxy? I had no clue whatsoever, but to buy time and to keep him engaged until I could put my fingers on the subject under discussion, I wore a fake smile to show him that I was finding his story very interesting. I kept my eyes glued to his face even though I was not seeing anything. I also kept on nodding my head, mechanically, while repeatedly saying, "Ya, ya, ya," almost every second. In the middle of all this chaos, he abruptly stopped, then I heard the word, "Dad," and silence after that. It took me a few seconds to process what was going on and to realize that he was calling me, so I said, "Hmmh." I was caught totally off guard. At that time my head was still nodding, but I was able to stop myself from saying ya, ya. He said, "You aren't getting what I am saying, are you?" I said, "But I...," and he continued, "What was I talking about? I was dumbfounded. I did not have an answer, so I kept quiet. I wanted to leave, but I did not want him to think that I was fleeing, so I remained seated. After a few minutes of awkward silence, I slowly picked up myself and disappeared in a remote corner of the house to lick my wounds. All my efforts to remain relevant were shredded down to pieces in front of my eyes. I kept on thinking if it, at all, worth fighting any longer. This is just too much for a man from Kokoland.

One night, a few weeks after the incident above and while we were sitting on the couch, my, same, boy said, "Dad," so I looked in his direction to find out. He lifted his basketball he was holding between his hands and brought it a foot or so closer to my face. I looked carefully and I saw two words; Moon, his name, on top, and GOAT, beneath it. So, I said to myself, "Aha, my boy wants me to tell him some African childhood stories about my goats." I started wearing my usual story time smile, but, half way to a full smile, I remembered the embarrassing incident from a few weeks earlier, so I said to myself, "Man, stop. Don't jump to conclusion. It is a trap." I held my right hand with my left hand as if trying to lead myself away and out of a trouble zone, to prevent another catastrophe. I sat quietly and thought for a minute, "What is the relationship between my boy's name, the word GOAT written under it, and a basketball held between two hands, at a matter of a foot away from my face?" Again, I thought for another minute or so and came up with the answer, "Nothing, absolutely nothing." I slowly got up, excused myself, and left for the privacy of the computer room to consult Google. I found the shocking answer that GOAT has a meaning other than in African goats. It is "the Greatest of All Time." The writing on the basketball supposed to read "Moon the Greatest of All Time." How could I have known? Please tell me. That incident terminated my relevance for good. It was the day relevance and I parted ways. It would be hard to keep abreast of youth culture in America, especially if you migrated when you were an adult. I came to this country in my thirties, which meant there were thirty years of things about America that I did not know. It was a struggle, but a real one.

I have learned that it is our duty as parents to step forward and be the first to talk to our children about matters of divine nature. We should not leave this job to other children to carry out on our behalf. My 12-year old son recently told me he thought that six-year old kids are slow to understand things. He used a different word to describe them, but I prefer to use slow here. He was talking about an incident that happened to him and his younger brother when they were six and four years old. He said a family friend came along with their 12-year old son to visit us at our house. While the three of them were playing together, our friends' boy mentioned God during their conversation. My six year old son looked puzzled, so the boy said, "You guys don't know God?" and my boy said, "No," then the boy responded, "Oh my God, he is around us right here, right now. God is everywhere." That was the end of the lesson about God. It left my boy so worried. He said to me, "I got so frightened that God is around me and everywhere, yet I could not see him." He told me he could not sleep that night as he kept on thinking. I told him that was what you call true fear of God. I feel I should have done a better job stepping in earlier.

I have learned that I always find it difficult to make the right decision when I am given too many choices. For example, parking is problematic for me, especially when there are too many vacant lots. My boys once asked me what ice cream flavor I wanted, and I responded, "Leave flavor aside and tell me what is ice-cream." As far as I was concerned, while growing up, abundance of choices was a phenomenon so rare that it occurred only once a year, around harvest times, if rain-permitted; besides, I did not know if ice-cream – among many other things – ever existed. For this reason and for fear of embarrassment; I avoid participating in talks involving ice-creams and the likes. I face problems at Starbucks and fast-food restaurants when ordering coffee or burgers. I am one of those customers who were always being asked to pull to the second drive-through window because of my jumbled up orders that are hard to understand. Many a time, I rehearse what I am going to order, but the moment I stand in front of the counter, my memory fails me, especially when the cashier says anything beyond "Can I help you?," even if that is a simple comment about the weather. That immediately messes my thought process and makes it impossible for me to, simultaneously, comprehend what he or she is saying and what I am going to order. I have extra pressure on me, if my boys and my wife are there. My clued-up appearance gets shattered the second the cashier speaks. My brain freezes and I will be standing there gazing at the menu board, without knowing what to say, or when to say it. That will lead my wife and my boys to conclude that I have done enough gazing, so they intervene and come to my rescue. They will order on my behalf, and that is when I breathe a sigh of relief. I happily pay for the order to feel that I am adequately shouldering my family responsibilities. I just cannot get the hang of ordering fast food. There are too many varieties to choose from. I am just not used to this.

My eight-year-old son once asked me to go and get him water so he could drink. I asked him, "Because?" He said, "Because I don't want to miss anything in this TV episode." He wanted me to get up, go to the kitchen, take an empty cup, fill it from the fridge, carry it back, and hand it over to His Excellency to drink. I, first hesitated, thought for a moment, then said to myself, "Never mind, it will take only a few seconds, just do it," so I got up and executed his instructions. He, somehow, got me thinking about the daily responsibilities I used to shoulder, especially fetching water for drinking and domestic use, when I was about ten years old. Drinking water was not always readily accessible to me, so talking about fridges, coolers, ice, and water fountains is out of the question. I vividly remember times when I had to scrape the bottom of the water pot with an aluminum cup to get a few drops of water. I would tilt the cup, slowly raise it to my eye level, and quietly hold it there. While keeping my eyes glued to the bottom of the cub, I would wait a few moments to allow the debris to settle. After that, I would slowly get the cup closer to my mouth and start sipping the few teaspoons of less harmful water, leaving my kidneys to deal with the filtering job. That was how I avoided swallowing some frog eggs or baby frogs, if you like. Drinking-water shortages was something I had routinely experienced. My world must have changed a great deal.

I have learned that it is hard to acquire certain skills retroactively. Bygones are bygones, and there is a right time for everything. For example, I just could not remember birthdays or anniversaries, including my own birthday. You can imagine the number of times I get in trouble every year. I was one of five, out of forty-five, boys who had birth certificates at the time of registration for first grade. The rest were given approximate birth dates, which was always January 1st; a date that coincides with the country's independence from Britain. Therefore, celebrating birthdays was never part of the culture. How can you celebrate your birthday if you don't know it?

I have learned that I am one of those people who enjoy seeking and acquiring knowledge, almost perpetually. I very much enjoy sitting down and listening to scholars. The good thing about knowledge is that it can hardly hurt. I dread the prospect of being uninformed and, even worse, ignorant; a combination that can hold a person captive to all things bad. Nothing good comes out of that.

I have learned that it is important to think for ourselves. We should never adopt, in absolute terms, views expressed by others, or pass judgement on anything based on someone else's take, without reaching our own conclusions. However, listening to the advice of family members and friends isn't a bad idea because, sometimes, we, on our own, may not have a clear grasp of everything. We can then sift out good advises from not so good ones to make our decisions. It is important that the final say rests in our hands. It is easier to live with the consequences when we blame no one else, but ourselves.

I have learned that people generally agree on terms such as happiness and success, but there are those who may beg to differ. One African man migrated to America, worked hard, and lived the American dream. To share his success with his people, he invited one of his uncles to visit him and spend some time away from the hardships of African village-life. The man arrived in America, but he was unimpressed with what he saw. He explored his nephew's big mansion and commented, "Son, if it isn't for death, I would say you have a beautiful house." Obviously, a mansion is no place for this man. I have every respect for his conclusion, but, in a less serious note, I think he would be a great fit for the earlier saying that goes, "A man God almighty has dropped, who other man can dare lift up."

The truth of the matter is that there are *sofis* or *zahideen* people who economize on life by paying little attention to materialistic things. They consider life on earth as nothing more than a passage to cross over to a better life after death. This is why they indulge less in luxurious life and live on bare minimum. Their argument is that we are all going to die one day, including the planet, so why forego a lasting life for an ending one? They believe that humankind should live solely for the hereafter. Of course, this is a school of thought that is different from the one followed by the average person leading a normal life.

One of my cousins adopted the hereafter principle, but his actions were contradictory to his views. He repeatedly told me that I should stop chasing life because in the end I will capture nothing of substance. It seems to him that working hard for the sake of providing a decent life for my family is not substantive enough. The irony is that he himself is laboring day and night for the same things I aspire to be. In fact, he, just like me, moved away from his village to the city in search of opportunities. His advice to me would have been more credible had he moved back to the village, and then asked me to do the same. I listened to his ill-advised story of idealism and did away with it.

I have learned that generosity, however minimal it is, can leave a lasting impression on people. Life, among other things, is about taking and giving, and that could come in the form of maintaining good relationships with people we love, positively contributing to the community we are living in and the society at large, adopting caring attitudes toward the environment, etc. Exchanging simple gifts between family members and friends can go a long way in promoting love and enriching life for everyone involved. The beauty and the blessings of life stem from obvious things such as being there for one another when necessity arises. I have also learned that true friends are very hard to come by, especially at times of need; therefore, such times could be true blessings. They are valuable opportunities for sorting out who is a genuine friend and who is not. At times of crisis, real friends will rush to your aid and stand by your side to see you through, whereas others may see in your predicament a chance to run away from you. Moments of need are decisive for lasting friendships.

I have learned that worrying about things going wrong in my life is constantly in my mind. This condition might have something to do with the sense of vulnerability that I have developed after the loss of my mother at a very early age. I have learned to come to terms with my worries and keep them under control, especially when I know they are being caused by humans. However, my worries used to rise to a new level whenever the cause is a phenomenon out of the hands of humankind. For example, I have phobia from moon eclipses because there is nothing humanly possible that anyone can do to make them go away on human's own terms. As a child, I remember waiting impatiently for eclipses to disappear. I feared them because I could not get an answer from adults if we were going to die or the world was coming to an end. My mother's body language, especially her worried face, scared me a lot. Her silence meant everything was in God's hands and there was nothing she could do to help.

I have learned that the story I heard in my childhood about the moon was untrue. I was told that the moon used to be a few feet above our heads, but, one day, a naughty woman pounding millet in her wooden mortar knocked it with her pestle and sent it away into outer space, never to return to its original place.

I have learned that I have another phobia; draught. Water, especially rain, gives me a great sense of security and that it has therapeutic effect on me. I enjoy sitting down and watching sprinklers in action. I always watch the weather channel to be informed of the water situation. I find myself monitoring the amount of rain the region is getting per season. Mind you; I am neither a rancher, nor a farmer, but shortage of rainfall still worries me. Growing up, I remember, we frequently suffered from total crop failure due to lack of rains, and that meant years of hardship.

I have learned that food can come in many different types and it may have different meanings to different people. By now, you probably have developed an idea as to what I mean by that. The period immediately after the death of my mother was very challenging as far as meals were concerned. We had no one to cook us meals. Sometimes, we bought bread from the local bakery and dipped chunks of it in a solution of sugar, water, and cooking oil, and ate it. There were no restaurants in Kokoland. Ironically and despite that, as a child, I did not see any hardship in our living condition because even such meager meal was unavailable to many people in my surroundings. Bread was considered a luxury.

I have learned that I was not always mindful of my skin color. However, I occasionally come across people who take it upon themselves to remind me of it. I can live with that, but it would be nice if we don't judge one another by the color of our skin. I don't believe this is too much to ask for. Besides; there is nothing that I can do about it.

I have learned that accepting one's identity is key to leading a happy life. Some people go to a great length to build their lives on false premise to gain some form of social recognition, only to find out that they are failing miserably. We cannot actualize our potentials, if we are in doubt about ourselves, who we really are, and where we belong. The first step toward happiness and prosperity is to love oneself, for, if we hate ourselves, love from others may not make much of a difference. If you think your community is an embarrassment to you, you will be on your own. The issue of identity is also crucial to nations. In the absence of an answer to the question of, "Who are we?" the entire nation can swing between backwardness, stagnation, and a full-fledged war with itself. Attempts to force the wrong identity on any group of people will be a short-lived affair. Things will crumble. Sudan is a living example.

I have learned that travelling and getting exposed to different people and cultures is a school on its own. The knowledge gained from that cannot be matched by anything in books. I have also learned that there are many people out there who speak a lot of wisdom; only if we are willing to listen. Sometimes, we put ourselves at a great disadvantage when we do most of the talking. It is a simple fact that the benefits of listening far outweigh that of talking. It was said a long time ago that if talking was made of silver, then it was gold that listening was made of. Simply put, there is a strong reason why we have two ears and one mouth.

I have learned that the world could have been in better shape had nations adopted an open-minded approach towards learning from one-another. I don't see why we should constantly reinvent the wheel. For example, the ideals of justice, equality, and freedom should be universally embraced. I migrated to America and found a system that is fair, accepting, and accommodating, so I was able to set goals for myself and achieve them. I greatly cherish democratic values such as individual's freedom of speech, human rights, and equality for all citizens according to the law. I am afraid; majority of us migrants cannot say that the countries we have left behind had granted us half the rights we got here in America. Here is a quote from Benjamin Franklin on freedom, security, and liberty. He said, "People willing to trade their freedom for temporary security deserves neither. Those who give up their liberty for more security neither deserve neither liberty nor security." This shows how critical are some of the things we take for granted.

I have learned that it is wrong to blame others for unfavorable outcomes before asking ourselves if we have a hand in the decisions that led to those outcomes. It is understandable that some individuals, communities, and nations find it difficult to let go of the past by attributing their present condition to some historic events such as colonization. There is certainly an argument to make here because those events could be extremely painful and unforgettable. However, there is equally a justification for learning from the past to carve out a route for a more promising future. That rather begs the question; how to move forward? It is easier said than done, I must admit.

I have learned that the fact that I did not have the physical strength to become a good wrestler wasn't a bad thing, after all. I could have settled for less in life. During the rainy season, wrestling matches were organized between the natives of Kokoland and the surrounding villages, and nomad cattle herders who seasonally migrated up north and set up camps in the area. Boys and young men who won matches were knighted and became centers of attention for the entire community, especially girls. The last wrestler standing would be carried on shoulders and taken around to tour the women and girls who would be lining up to express their admiration by showering him with precious perfumes. He would be the talk of the nation, if you like. There was enough love to last him a lifetime, if it wasn't for old age intervention pushing him to the sidelines and off the girls' radar sight. Who doesn't want fame, even if it is temporary? Many young men aspired for knighthood to receive the same special treatment. Some of my Kokoland friends who won a few matches dropped everything and lived off the temporary fame. That was their destination when, in fact, the train did not move an inch from Kokoland. Most of them woke up to the reality that Kokoland did not have much to offer. Then it was too late, for certain things could only be done at a young age. I have learned that fame is a dangerous thing because it can cause crashes even before lifting off. Being a famous wrestler in Kokoland was a nonstarter, but, like everything else, fame is a relative thing, everywhere.

I have learned that there are different talks for different people at different occasions. I look back and wonder why I overwhelmed my people in Kokoland by bringing up and discussing out of place and out of touch subjects such as landing of man on the moon and buying life insurance policies. I was self-incriminating. To some of my people, a person cannot be less faithful than losing hope in God to the extent that he ends up buying a life insurance policy to protect him against risks destined by God. They argued that it is God's responsibility to cater for the needs of a man and his dependents, in case he passes away. He is already insured, so why bother to buy a life insurance policy.

I continue to be amazed by humankind's inventions. Space exploration is one thing that has always captivated my imagination. A matter of a few miles above the earth's surface, all the buzzing and human activities on earth disappears and blends into a spectacular image of a blue planet. Humans are tiny and negligible in the large scale of the universe, but, at the same time, they are giants in their ability to invent spaceships and explore space. This is a real paradox for me.

I have learned that I am Johnny-come-lately to America, probably three hundred years late. Nevertheless, I am glad that I made it here. While in America, I have learned that it has its own rules that govern norms and effective guides for socially acceptable behavior. In America, grownups just don't go shopping while wrapped up in blankets, as I did one Black Friday in California. I thought practicality dictated the need for doing that, but I was dead wrong.

I have learned never to take anything for granted. This is common sense, but, nevertheless, I occasionally tend to forget that. I have learned that some people think they are a gift to humanity. As such, they believe in two things; receiving from others and taking credit for everything. Only if they could find out how satisfying giving can be. At that point they will realize how much they have been missing.

I have learned that I have to scale down on the village stories I tell my boys. My wife thinks they interfere with their academic performance, and I agree with her. I would tell stories about my gray donkey and hyenas at the wrong times of the day, whenever I remembered one, and that could be in the morning on my way to drop them at school. I recently learned that there is a system in place for telling stories, called "bedtime stories."

I have learned that the two words "they said" are used more frequently in societies that believe in superstitions and the supernatural. In Kokoland, stories involving magic or the supernatural always start with, "They said so and so." I'm yet to come across anyone who could confirm that he was personally a witness to such events. Things could have been different if we had electricity. With light, the appearance of imaginary night creatures such as zombies could have been rare. Lack of electric power can be a bad thing in many aspects. I think international development organizations are missing the point. I believe that there is correlation between darkness and population size. With electricity, modern means of communication such as television can help a lot in educating the public. Introducing the practice of birth control, without tampering with the ethical and moral aspects of the subject, would be much easier, I guess.

I have learned that time heals, but some memories never fade away. To me, the day my mother passed away remains an epitome of what can go wrong in one single day. I remember that afternoon, one of my relatives who came over to attend the burial saw me in the crowd and called me to take care of his donkey. Can you believe that? He told me to take it to a nearby pond to let it drink. There was no way I could have said no, so I did. I had just lost my mother for heaven's sake. She was not even buried yet. How more inconsiderate could anyone be? I don't hate, but please allow me to do so in this one instance. While I was leading the donkey to cleaner water in the center of the pond, I tripped in a hole. To my misfortune, I landed with my right knee on some broken pieces of glass and badly injured my knee in two places. Some wicked person did that to hurt people. The marks on my knee, visible even today, are a constant reminder of that infamous day. That night, my baby sister and I got hold of a jute mat and spread it on the floor, in a corner inside the hut, to sleep. She giggled as she told me how my uncle Abdu, my mom's younger brother, cried like a baby that morning. She had no grasp of the gravity of what had befallen us. Memories of that day stayed fresh in my mind and I doubt it if I will ever forget.

I have learned that I have so much affinity for the phrase "a level playing field." To me, it embodies fairness. I realize that in the absence of fairness, I will be among the first casualties, and that is why I will always fight for it, both for my own and others' sake.

I have learned that certain things just don't make any sense at all. Otherwise, how come I migrate from Kokoland to America and find Americans play a game that has the same rules of a game that I used to play in Kokoland, throughout my childhood years. I love playing and watching sports games, especially soccer. Since soccer is not widely recognized here in America, I reluctantly settled for occasionally watching basketball and football games. One day, I sat down to watch a football game and decided to pay close attention to the game rules, which I did not know much about then. I was surprised to find out that American football is nothing other than the game I used to play in Kokoland. It is called *Harrah um jari*, which translates to, "The hot game that involves running." A rougher version of the game is called *Harrah um dag*, which translates to, "The hot game that involves beating."

We usually played the game in two teams of anywhere from six to twelve boys per team. Each team would occupy one half of the playground. The two teams would agree on which team should have the first run. That team would choose *Al Arsa*, or the groom. The strongest boy, muscle boy, would be chosen from the team and assigned the job of guarding *Al Arsa.* The two of them would move back and stand behind everyone else in the team. *Al Arsa* would be hiding behind muscle boy, who would be shielding him from attacks by the opponent team trying to get to him. The rest of *Al Arsa* team members would scatter and take strategic positions to form lines of defense, in the back, and lines of attack, in the front. This was an ideal formation when we had more than ten players per team. The team members would make calculated moves to navigate their way forward to create a safe passage for *Al Arsa* and muscle boy to break through the opponent team's defense lines and safely get to *Al mees* (touch down). The opponent team members would be fighting hard to get to *Al Arsa* to prevent him from reaching *Al mees.* In the process, pairs of boys from the two teams would be colliding and wrestling one another to the ground. Whoever comes on top would stand up and declare the *death* of his opponent by shouting, "X is *dead.*" Since we played in the moonlight, we could not distinguish one another from a distance, so we mostly relied on our ears for getting the news about what was going on in the battle ground. For this reason, it was important that messages about who was *dead* and who was *alive* were aired loudly so that everyone in both teams had up-to-date information about the strength or weakness of his team. That was how we were able to constantly modify our strategies to attack or defend. The ultimate goal for the team with *Al Arsa* was to lead him safely to the predetermined spot of *Al mees,* at the other end of the playground, behind the opponent team's defense lines. The opponent team would fight ferociously to get hold of *Al Arsa* and tackle him to the ground, hence prevent the team from scoring a point. If they succeed in doing so, it would be their turn to choose a new *Al Arsa* from their team and the same battle was repeated.

One important game rule was that anyone who was wrestled to the ground and was declared *dead* must stay *dead* (down) and should not move from his spot. He is not supposed to participate in the battle for the remaining part of that segment of the game. We all self-observed this rule. The punishment for those who violated the rules by getting up and rejoining their teams was branding them as untrustworthy. Such a reputation is very costly.They might not make it through the cuts in the future, especially if many kids showed up to play. We were also mindful of the fact that we had a limited window of two weeks of moonlight, per month, to play, so nobody wanted to miss a game. For this reason, the rules were rarely violated.

Now, convince me that American football game is not closely similar to our *Harrah um jari* game I have described above. There is one and only one interpretation for this. We had regularly seen objects with blinking lights that flew over Kokoland skies at night, but we did not have a clue whatsoever as to what they were, what they were doing, where they were coming from, or where they were heading to. I know the answer now that I have been living here in America for some time. They were American spy planes. Yes, American spy planes, and don't tell me this is rubbish. The planes, with their advanced technological capabilities, were able to acquire all of our game secrets. With their infra-red spy cameras, thermal imaging, and night vision technologies, they could take videos for us while in full *Harrah um Jari* and *Harrah um dag* game actions. They were able to analyze our game rules, fully understand them, and voila. American football was born. There is no way in hell that we Kokoland boys could have stolen the game from America, so how did this happen? Coincidentally? No way. Now, don't tell me it was telepathy, or that American football was invented on November 6, 1869, way before spy planes, or perhaps things happened the same way the Mayans and the Ancient Egyptians built their pyramids at the same point in time. American football was a Kokoland invention and we must be compensated for it, period.

I have learned that bygones are often best left as bygones. When I recently returned to Kokoland, I went to visit Sabir, or Abu H.; a nickname given to him for his stylishness. Besides; Sabir was renowned for his artistic skills in creating fashionable designs he especially made for Kokoland's teenage girls. I had not seen him in over thirty years, so I assumed that I could start our conversation from where we had stopped, decades earlier. I was wrong because too much water has flown under the bridge since I saw him last time. Sabir had turned into a holy man, but no one warned me in advance of the drastic and major changes that had taken place in the man's lifestyle, so I used his old nickname to address him. I even put my hand on his shoulder as I talked, and that was a sign of a relaxed buddies' type of a relationship between the two of us, which had stayed intact despite the many years, or so I thought. I was at the verge of cracking a few out of place jokes from the past, when I received a kick on my toe from a friend who was standing next to me. He saw me putting up a wide smile in preparation for the jokes. He figured out that I was up to no good, so he decided to intervene before Rome collapsed. I looked up at him and saw a horrified face that read, "Hoy [hey you], what are you doing. Shut up, just shut up and don't say a thing." That kick drew my attention to the fact that Abu H. responded to my loud talk in a, somewhat, subdued tone, as if he was sick or something, so I waited a little longer to find out what was going on.

It could have been a disaster of epic proportions had I divulged some of the secrets I knew about Abu H. What saved me from committing more blunders was the discomfort he and everyone around showed whenever I used his nickname, Abu H. I could see the shock on their faces. I noticed that everyone treated him with utmost respect. They were quiet most of the time, carefully choosing their words, and speaking politely. I also noticed Abu H. using religious words whenever he responded, so I took further notice of the situation. Then it hit me; Abu H. had turned into a holy man. I must spontaneously adjust to that new reality. I needed to shift the conversation 180 degrees and come up with compatible religious words, so I started searching my brain to compile relevant religious sentences. I failed miserably because, at the same time I was thinking about what to say, my brain was joyfully evoking every secret about Abu H. that it had maintained in store since the 1970s. It refused to give way for a brand new Sabir, the holy man. I just could not take away his old image from my mind, even though he appeared a different person. He spoke softly, wore a different type of clothes, and put on a holy man's mask on his face. Finally, I was able to change my tone, jumble up a few religious words, and treat him the same way everybody else did. I managed to pull myself out of a very awkward situation.

Abu H.'s father was the one who used to call for prayers at Kokoland's mosque. What happened was that after his death, Abu H. stopped being Kokoland's Don Juan or Casanova and turned into a holy man. He basically inherited holiness from his father. I doubt that he went away from Kokoland and took time to study theology. Nowadays, he is the one who leads Friday prayers for the entire Kokoland region. No wonder why everyone was keen that I shut up. It is a risky thing to upset a holy man. I also think it is inappropriate to reveal hidden secrets and bring up memories of his adventures with girls when he worked as a tailor in my father's shop, many years back. Abu H.'s pre-spirituality era must be left intact because bygones are often best left as bygones.

I have learned that I do not have the slightest idea as to how the world functions. Life is full of extremities and contradictions. Nothing is absolute and things have different meanings to different people. There is no such thing as one yard-stick for measuring everything. In the end, it all depends on many variables. Nevertheless, life is also about contrasts. I guess, there is beauty in that because only through contrasts we can differentiate between people, for example, so we can appreciate some more than others. We might think high of ourselves, but the world doesn't necessarily see what we see in ourselves, nor thinks that we are what we think we are. It is fine to have high expectations for ourselves, but lowering them, especially when dealing with other people, won't hurt much. Anything coming from them, unexpectedly, is an added bonus.

I have learned that the quote, "If you do not know where you are going, any road will do," makes a perfect sense. It will help a great deal if we not only know where we are going, but also what we are going to do when we get there. I think, to many people in my village, I have gone a long way, but in the wrong direction, i.e. I didn't know where I was going, and that is fine because that decision was mine. There is room for all of us to pursue happiness in our own different ways. The fact remains that Kokoland continues to be the trustee of my childhood memories. I miss it, despite everything, but I don't regret the journey I have taken.

Finally, I would like to state that I am grateful for my family and that there is nothing more important to me in life. I would also like to state that faith plays a huge role in my life. Travelling from Kokoland to America has provided me with a valuable opportunity to see both sides of the coin, if I may say so. During my bumpy journey, I met many foresighted people who taught me a great deal about myself and life. Knowing oneself is a cornerstone of succeeding in life. I could not have gotten to this conclusion had I stayed behind in Kokoland and settled for what I knew, which wasn't much, by all accounts.

In brief, it has taken me a thirty-year journey from my humble beginnings in my dusty village of Kokoland to reach America, the land of Uncle Sam. Both Kokoland and America exist right here on planet earth, but they are two different worlds, and neither one knows much about the other. This is not totally unexpected. Few people in my village have the slightest clue about life in America. To many of them, the village might be it. I'm one of the few lucky, or unlucky ones (depending on how you want to look at it, or who you talk to) who happened to, miraculously, have the opportunity to live in both worlds. I can also speak with confidence that my level of confusion can be unparalleled, as you might have found in many instances here in this book.

Growing up, I was totally convinced that the female voices broadcasting from Radio Mont Carlo were of angels. There was no way they could have belonged to humans because I did not come across any woman in Kokoland that sounded like them. I had mistaken Elvis Presley (the King) for Yuri Gagarin (the Russian Astronaut). This is not surprising because, even today, some of my people still deny that the earth is round, so forget about orbiting the earth or putting humans on the moon. It was only in Kokoland where you could find the likes of Jalha, the renowned lawyer, and Ringham and his fellow village porters, gathered in one place (Burra's house) to drink local alcohol, *mareesa*. Jalha could be giving an elaborate lecture on English law principles of *ratio decidendi and obiter dicta*, regardless of who is listening, or understanding any of what he was saying, whereas Ringham and friends could be arguing which one is heavier to carry; a sack of gum arabic or that of sugar. A third man could be bragging about his skills in locating the best hunting grounds for juicy squirrels and fat jack rabbits. Such dialogues could be happening simultaneously inside one tiny straw hut. What more confusion could you expect?

Read this book because you will love it. It will introduce Kokoland to America and the rest of the world, and I am determined to take America and the world back to Kokoland. With the internet, mobile phones, and solar panels, there won't be a need for telephone poles and power grids. Kokolanders can quantum-leap to use the latest technologies. They will be able to see how the rest of the world is functioning, in comparison to life in Kokoland. It is guaranteed that there will initially be anger and resentment for being left out and having lived in the dark for so long. However, people can start dreaming the same way I did and, in the process, good things can happen.

I plan to use the proceeds from the sale of this book to build a state of the art and self-sustaining health and vocational center. Premature death of mothers and babies bother me a lot. I have seen this at first-hand.

An overall design for a self-sustaining health/vocational center that I am planning to build in Kokoland.

About the Author

Dr. (Abba Gony) Mustafa Sharif was a lecturer of urban planning at the College of Architecture, Texas A&M University. He enjoys writing and spends time reading journals and magazines. He likes to write about disappearing social and cultural practices. He finds the most challenging part of writing to be conveying rare cultural beliefs that are foreign to most readers. Dr. Sharif is a father of three sons (the Sharif brothers): Rumzee, Moon, and Ameenov. He has been married to his wife, Sophia, for 30 years. He has four brothers, six sisters, and many nephews and nieces, as you can imagine. In his free time, he enjoys reading, playing the violin and the guitar, riding his bike, camping, playing soccer with his boys, and travelling. In the years ahead, Dr. Sharif looks forward to writing two more books; a novel and an academic book. Dr. Sharif also looks forward to learning a foreign language, if time permits.

CPSIA information can be obtained
at www.ICGtesting.com
Printed in the USA
FFHW020019110219
50478123-55718FF